Beyond Bach

Beyond Bach

Music and Everyday Life in the Eighteenth Century

ANDREW TALLE

**UNIVERSITY OF
ILLINOIS PRESS**
Urbana, Chicago, and Springfield

Publication is supported by a grant from the AMS
75 PAYS Endowment of the American Musicological
Society, funded in part by the National Endowment
for the Humanities and the Andrew W. Mellon
Foundation.

Library of Congress Cataloging-in-Publication Data
Names: Talle, Andrew.
Title: Beyond Bach : music and everyday life in the
    eighteenth century / Andrew Talle.
Description: Urbana : University of Illinois Press, 2017. |
    Includes bibliographical references.
Identifiers: LCCN 2016041694 (print) | LCCN
    2016043348 (ebook) | ISBN 9780252040849 (cloth
    : alk. paper) | ISBN 9780252099342 (e-book) | ISBN
    9780252099342 (E-book)
Subjects: LCSH: Music—Social aspects—Germany—
    History—18th century. | Keyboard players—
    Germany—Social conditions—18th century. |
    Germany—Social life and customs—18th century.
Classification: LCC ML3917.G3 T35 2017 (print) | LCC
    ML3917.G3 (ebook) | DDC 786.0943/09032—dc23
LC record available at https://lccn.loc.gov/2016041694

For J. E.

Contents

Color plates follow page 110

Illustrations

Tables

Charts

Musical Examples

Plates [*Color*]

Acknowledgments

I am extremely grateful for all of the help I have received in researching and writing this book. First and foremost, I would like to thank the current and former scholars of the Bach Archive in Leipzig, especially Christoph Wolff, Hans-Joachim Schulze, Peter Wollny, Michael Maul, Manuel Bärwald, Andreas Glöckner, Christine Blanken, and Ulrich Leisinger. I would also like to thank that institution's past and present library staff, especially Ulla Zacharias, Viera Lippold, and Christina Funk-Kunath. I received advice and assistance from many others in Germany, particularly Birgit Busse, Martina Rebmann, Birgit Renner, and Christiane Tewinkel (Berlin); Hartmut Nickel (Braunschweig); Jürgen Samuel and Inge Streuber (Cöthen); Rainer Maaß, Günter Merle, Christina Pilz, and Silvia Uhlemann (Darmstadt); Günter Preckel (Dessau); Edgar Kutzner, Bernhard Jäger, and Gerda Lobe-Roeder (Fulda); Jürgen Neubacher (Hamburg); Detlef Döring and Rüdiger Otto (Leipzig); Helmut Klingelhöfer (Marburg); Elisabeth Höpfner, Jihoon Song, and Helmut Hentschel (Rötha); and Rashid-Sasha Pegah (Würzburg). Friends in the United States offered helpful comments on earlier drafts of this book, including Susan Baron, Linda Delibero, Hollis Robbins, Chip Wass, Mark Janello, Sharon Levy, and Gary Sampsell (Baltimore); Joshua Rifkin (Cambridge); Mark Peters (Chicago); Woody and Cynthia Andrews (Minneapolis); Steven Zohn (Philadelphia); and Margaret Guroff (Washington, D.C.). I also owe a great debt to the administrators at the Peabody Conservatory of Johns Hopkins University for granting me leave to research and write this book, and to the American Musicological Society, which supported its publication through the AMS 75 PAYS Endowment. I would also like to thank the staff at the University of Illinois Press, particularly Laurie Matheson (Champaign-Urbana), and copyeditor Julie Gay (Philo) for their patience and expertise in seeing this book into print. My greatest editorial assistance came from Stacey Richter (Tucson), who did her best to make this book into something people might actually read instead of just throwing it across the room.

I would also like to express my gratitude to my parents, Kenneth and Margaret Talle. I am very sorry that my mother did not live to see its publication. I am also immensely grateful to Ulla Lindner, my longtime neighbor and friend in Leipzig. Over many years, she collected my mail, looked after my apartment, defended me against the illegitimate claims of unscrupulous landlords and the legitimate claims of unpaid utilities providers, read library books, combed manuscripts, and did everything else she could to help. Finally, I want to thank my wife, Jungeun Elle Kim, for her love and patience. Marrying her was the best thing I ever did.

A Note on Currency

Dozens of different currencies were used in the Holy Roman Empire during J. S. Bach's lifetime. The most common large coins in Saxony and neighboring territories were *reichstaler*. It is impossible to offer accurate modern equivalents but a rough estimate would value one reichstaler at approximately US$100. Readers can get a sense for the purchasing power of a single reichstaler by bearing in mind that it could be traded for twelve beer glasses, a pair of men's shoes, or the services of a servant for an entire week.[1] One reichstaler was worth twenty-four *groschen*, one of which was worth around US$4. With a single groschen one could buy a portion of bread and butter, a couple of printed songs, or a published table of a courtly hierarchy.[2] One groschen was worth twelve *pfennige*, each one of which might correspond to around thirty-five cents. For six pfennige, one could buy rosin for a violin bow, and for three pfennige some ink for writing letters. With a single pfennig, one could purchase little more than a glass of milk.[3]

Beyond Bach

Introduction

Late in the summer of 1977, Voyager I and II were launched from Cape Canaveral, Florida, on a mission to explore hitherto unknown reaches of the galaxy. Their cargo included not only equipment for collecting and transmitting scientific data, but also golden records intended to introduce any extraterrestrial life forms they might encounter to the cultures of planet Earth. The contents of these records, chosen by committee, included a great deal of Western classical music. No composer was better represented than Johann Sebastian Bach, who had three separate tracks to his name. This was not enough for one enthusiastic scientist who famously urged the committee to ignore fears of "bragging" and simply send "Bach, all of Bach, streamed out into space, over and over again."[1]

Extracting Bach's music from its earthly surroundings had a long intellectual history by 1977. In 1802, the composer's first biographer, Johann Nikolaus Forkel, asserted that his subject was "not like a human being but like a transfigured spirit who has transcended everything mundane."[2] The conviction that Bach's music was best understood in heavenly isolation hardened over the course of the nineteenth century as the names of deceased composers came to dominate concert programs.[3] His were among the first works to be installed in what has aptly been called an imaginary museum: a collection of masterpieces united not by scoring, age, nationality, or style, but rather by the perception of timeless value.[4] By sending this repertoire out past Jupiter, Saturn, and Neptune, the National Aeronautics and Space Administration gave new, physical form to a nineteenth-century ideal: pure music, floating in a perfect vacuum.

The last several generations of scholars have made great progress in bringing Bach's music back down to Earth. Diplomatic research into paper types and handwriting characteristics has illuminated many of the mundane details of his working life. Compilation and analysis of all surviving Bach-related documents has revealed much about how he interacted with contemporaries and about how he was perceived by posterity. Investigation of the careers and music of other composers of the era has helped to situate his works within the musical landscape of their time. Studies of social, political, and institutional contexts have shed light on many of the ideological forces which influenced all who made music in eighteenth-century Germany. This extraordinary research has helped to humanize Bach; we no longer seek to honor his music through isolation but rather to understand it as the product of an extraordinary person shaped by his earthly circumstances.

And yet, the lost world that scholars have conjured is incomplete. The intense focus on famous composers—especially J. S. Bach—and the institutions with which they were associated has skewed our understanding of the era. If we are to truly know the world Bach inhabited, we need to devote far more attention to the musical lives of ordinary people. The men and women who walked the same cobblestones as J. S. Bach did not think of themselves as "J. S. Bach's contemporaries." Many who heard him lead performances of sacred cantatas every Sunday morning paid less attention to his artful fugues and chorales than they did to their children's toothaches, their uncles' drinking habits, and their neighbors' church attire. Many music lovers preferred the works of other composers. Even the few who regarded Bach's compositions as the pinnacle of artistic achievement could never have imagined that they might one day be heard all over the planet, let alone sent off into outer space in hopes of impressing aliens.

The present book explores the musical culture of Bach's Germany from the perspectives of those who lived in it. The protagonists in these pages are not famous composers but rather amateur and professional musicians, patrons, instrument builders, and audience members. They are treated here not as extras in the grand sweep of music history but rather as main characters, stars in their own private dramas. Bach himself remains on the margins of the central narrative; his presence in the chapters to follow corresponds roughly to my sense of his presence in the musical lives of his contemporaries.

Reconstructing an entire world would be unmanageable without limitations; I have elected to focus the discussion around a particular instrument—the keyboard—and its solo repertoire. This decision was taken in part because Bach himself was so closely associated with the keyboard, both as performer and composer. More important for our purposes, keyboard music played a tremendously significant role in the social life of eighteenth-century Germany. The experience of virtually every musician, from abject beginners to celebrity composers, was mediated by instruments with keys. No other category of instrument was so versatile or so emblematic of music itself.

This introduction is intended to serve as an orientation in time and place. I begin with a brief account of Bach's own life, followed by a description of the wide range of contemporary responses to his music. I conclude with a summary of previous research and an overview of the chapters to follow.

☙

Any effort at understanding the world Bach inhabited naturally begins with his own biography.[5] The last of seven children born to Johann Ambrosius and Maria Elisabeth Bach (née Lämmerhirt), Johann Sebastian first blinked the light of the world in Eisenach on March 21, 1685. Music was everywhere: his father came from a long line of professional musicians and served as leader of the local town pipers. Many of his uncles and cousins held important musical posts, and he and two of his brothers would go on to do the same. The extended family maintained close ties and gathered regularly in their native Thuringia to make music and enjoy one another's company.

Tragedy struck just before Bach's tenth birthday when both of his parents died in quick succession. The bereaved orphan was sent to live with his twenty-four-year-old brother, Johann Christoph Bach, an organist in nearby Ohrdruf. Under this brother's tutelage, he began to obsessively cultivate his innate musical talents. What was already a felicitous combination of genetic ability and environmental encouragement was fused with the desperate energy of one who had lost everything.

In 1700, at age fifteen, Bach was awarded a scholarship to attend a choir school in Lüneburg where he studied with the renowned organist Georg Böhm. Upon graduation two years later, he served briefly as a lackey at the ducal court in Weimar. His career began in earnest the following year when he accepted a position as church organist in the Thuringian town of Arnstadt. Twenty-year-old Bach chafed at the strictures imposed upon his work by his civic employers: when chastised for preluding too long, he responded cheekily by playing preludes that were ridiculously short; when granted one month of leave to work in Lübeck with Dietrich Buxtehude, he stayed for four months instead.[6] After four years in Arnstadt, he left to accept a somewhat more attractive position as organist in Mühlhausen.

While living in Mühlhausen, he married his first cousin, Maria Barbara Bach, with whom he would eventually have his first seven children.

In 1708, at age twenty-three, Bach was invited to return to the court in Weimar. Here he served as organist to the dukes of Saxe-Weimar, Wilhelm Ernst and Ernst August, performing at church services, maintaining the instrument collection, and providing music lessons to various members of the ducal family.[7] It was during this period that he composed most of his surviving works for organ. In 1713, at age twenty-eight, he was promoted to concert master, a position created specially to showcase his remarkable abilities. Bach's fame by now was spreading beyond Weimar, and in 1717 he was invited to the court of the Saxon prince-elector in Dresden to test his skills against those of a haughty French organist named Louis Marchand, who forfeited the competition by abruptly leaving town. The same year, he was offered and desperately wished to accept a position as *Kapellmeister* to Prince Leopold of Anhalt-Cöthen. His fervent desire to leave Weimar, however, irked the dukes, and he was confined to prison for an entire month for "demanding his release from service too stubbornly."[8]

Bach was eventually permitted to accept the coveted appointment in Cöthen and moved there with his family in December 1717. Surrounded by extraordinary musicians and a prince who "both loved and knew music," he believed at first that he might remain in this small town for the rest of his life. As his children showed themselves to be musically inclined, he devoted more time to codifying his pedagogical methods through collections of keyboard music such as the *Inventions and Sinfonias* (BWV 772–801), the first part of the *Well Tempered Clavier* (BWV 846–869), the *English Suites* (BWV 806–811), and the *French Suites* (BWV 812–817). It was probably also in Cöthen that Bach composed the *Sonatas and Partitas* for solo violin (BWV 1001–1006) and *Suites* for solo cello (BWV 1007–1012). The composer's personal life took a tragic turn in July 1720 when he returned from traveling with the prince to find that his wife of thirteen years had died and been buried in his absence. He remarried quickly, this time choosing as his bride a twenty-year-old court soprano named Anna Magdalena Wilcke. The sense of loss no doubt lingered, however, and he began looking for employment elsewhere.

In 1723, at age thirty-eight, Bach accepted the post of cantor at the St. Thomas School and music director for the City of Leipzig. The *Thomasschule* had a long and storied history as one of the German-speaking world's premiere institutions for training young musicians. At the beginning of his time in Leipzig, Bach invested himself heavily in the new post, composing, rehearsing, and performing a new sacred cantata nearly every week, and composing monumental settings of the *Passion* according to the gospels of

St. John (BWV 245) and St. Matthew (BWV 244). These efforts seem not to have had much impact upon his employers, whom Bach found "strange, and little interested in music."[9] He considered moving again but ultimately decided to remain in Leipzig for the rest of his life, seeking musical fulfillment beyond his official duties. He directed university students in a *Collegium Musicum* ensemble which performed at a local coffeehouse. He also prepared collections of his keyboard music for publication, including the *Keyboard Partitas* (BWV 825–830), the *Italian Concerto* (BWV 971), and the so-called *Goldberg Variations* (BWV 988).

Bach's family life was a source of both great joy and crushing sorrow. With his two wives he had a total of twenty children. High infant mortality, however, meant that only half survived their first years. The boys and girls who lived to maturity were uniquely well positioned to benefit from their father's gifts as a teacher. Four of his sons—Wilhelm Friedemann, Carl Philipp Emanuel, Johann Christoph Friedrich, and Johann Christian—went on to extraordinarily successful musical careers of their own.

Frustrated by his circumstances in Leipzig, Bach sought appreciative audiences elsewhere. Through connections in nearby Dresden, he won an appointment in 1736 as nonresident composer to Friedrich August II, prince-elector of Saxony and king of Poland. Through his second son, Carl Philipp Emanuel Bach, who served as harpsichordist at the Prussian court in Potsdam, he was invited in 1747 to perform for King Friedrich II ("The Great"). The encounter was widely reported, and Bach's improvisations on a thorny chromatic theme penned by the king himself were later published as *The Musical Offering* (BWV 1079).

Bach spent his last years engaged in large-scale projects designed to showcase the skills he had perfected over the course of his long career. He assembled the *B-minor Mass* (BWV 232) from fragments of vocal works written across three decades. With the *Art of the Fugue* (BWV 1080), he brought his extraordinary command of counterpoint to bear on a single theme, exploring it in a set of elaborate fugues and canons. As he was completing this final project, his eyes began to fail and he underwent an ill-fated medical operation. Complications from this procedure eventually led to his death, at age sixty-five, on July 28, 1750.

❧

For much of his lifetime, Bach was better known as a performer than as a composer. He was particularly famed for his extraordinary facility on instruments with keys. Already in 1712, "the famous musician, Herr Bach" was attracting students eager to hear the "incomparable things" he could play on the organ.[10] On a visit to Kassel in 1732, he is said to have "run over the pedals with such facility, as if his feet had wings, making the organ resound with such fullness that it penetrated the ears of those present like a thunderbolt."[11] In 1737 a former student wrote of Bach's keyboard playing: "I have heard this great man play on various occasions. One is amazed at his ability, and one can hardly conceive how it is possible for him to achieve such agility, with his fingers and with his feet, in the crossings, extensions, and extreme jumps that he manages, without mixing in a single wrong tone, or displacing his body by any violent movement."[12] The authors of Bach's obituary described him as "the greatest organ and keyboard player who ever lived," elaborating upon this bold assertion as follows:

> It may be the case that many famous men achieved a great deal on these instruments, but we doubt that any was so accomplished, in the hands as well as the feet, as was Bach. Anyone who had the pleasure of hearing him and comparing his playing, without prejudice, to that of others will agree that this doubt is not without foundation. And whoever examines his organ and keyboard works—which, as is widely known, he himself performed to the greatest perfection—will have no objection to the position expressed above. How strange, how new, how expressive, how beautiful were his ideas when improvising; how skillfully he executed them![13]

As a composer too, Bach's image was inextricably connected with music for solo keyboard. Whereas the cantatas and other sacred works were rarely heard because they required large venues and performing forces, his keyboard music could be performed in relatively intimate spaces by a single player. They were also free of the ideological and linguistic limitations that prevented his vocal music from traveling much beyond Protestant Germany. Bach's published keyboard works in particular enjoyed a wide distribution, sold through friends and colleagues in distant cities throughout the Holy Roman Empire.

The keyboard music Bach set down on paper generally required great technical facility, earning a forbidding reputation. To be sure, many intrepid musicians felt that the rewards were well worth the challenges. A Leipzig University rhetoric professor and amateur keyboardist named Johann Abraham Birnbaum spoke for enthusiasts in 1738 when he asserted that "there is only one Bach, and no one else comes close."[14] But a castrato singer and composer named Filippo Finazzi probably spoke for a broader swath of the population when he wrote just a few months before Bach's death: "I would be a fool to criticize this great man, but one must admit that his music is not for entertainment alone, and a listener who does not understand music thoroughly will never find pleasure in such difficult harmonies."[15] The eighteenth-century owner of a print of Bach's organ works expressed his or her views more succinctly by crossing out the composer's claim on the title page that the collection was intended "for the refreshment of the spirits" (*zur Gemüths-Ergezung*) and scrawling instead "for the enjoyment of the eyes and the injury of the ears" (*zur Augen-Ergezung und Ohren-Verletzung*).[16]

The difficulty in Bach's music stems from its extraordinary measure of counterpoint, which blurs the distinction between melody and accompaniment. The composer liked to maintain an uncomfortably high level of tension in his music and seldom offered relief in the form of boundary-defining changes in register, texture, or tone. It was for this reason that contemporaries grumbled about his works being unnecessarily difficult and better suited to pleasing eyes than ears—that is, more rewarding to analyze on the page than to hear in performance.

A related problem, from the perspective of Bach's contemporaries, was that his style was at odds with the prevailing aesthetic of his era, which celebrated lightness and ease. A majority of music lovers preferred repertoire that was more accessible—more *galant*, in the parlance of the time. The voice endemic to Bach's music—presumably a reflection of the composer's personality—speaks as if avoiding eye-contact, ruminating rather than declaiming, counseling rather than pontificating, probing rather than flattering. Though his works offer affirmation in the end, their profoundly deliberative character makes this affirmation feel hard-won.

એ·

In order to understand the tension between Bach and his contemporaries, we need to appreciate the positions of both sides. The composer's side of the relationship has been the subject of intense study for centuries. That of his contemporaries, however, has seldom been explored. With regard to Bach's keyboard music, historians have cataloged and investigated the sources, and theorists have analyzed the music, increasingly through source-based research.[17] Few, however, have devoted their attention to illuminating the contexts in which Bach's keyboard works were originally performed.

Part of the problem is that the documentary evidence is thin. Despite the existence of numerous manuscripts of Bach's music, no specific keyboard work can be persuasively connected with a specific performance during the composer's lifetime. Avoiding Bach's era, researchers interested in keyboard culture have tended to focus on the period after 1770.[18] Those who have investigated keyboard culture in earlier times have focused primarily on professional musicians, who constituted only around ten percent of the keyboard-playing world, rather than amateurs, who constituted about 90 percent. Previous researchers have also tended to speak in generalities about keyboard culture, relying overwhelmingly on scraps of information from a wide range of sources rather than deeply investigating the musical lives of specific people.[19]

The present book seeks to illuminate Bach's world by alternating between generalized discussions based on diverse sources and narrative accounts relating the experiences of particular individuals. Chapter 1 sets the stage for the remainder of the book by presenting evidence for the growing popularity of keyboard music and exploring the heated debates about repertoire. Chapter 2 sheds light on the identities of keyboard instrument customers, chiefly through the analysis of a list of persons who bought clavichords from one particular maker between 1721 and 1757. I devote special attention not only to the maker himself but also to one of his customers—a tax collector—whose instrument survives to the present day.

The subsequent four chapters are all devoted to female keyboardists. Chapter 3 investigates the musical life of one of Bach's neighbors in Leipzig, a young woman who played the keyboard and who was a close friend of the composer's wife. Chapter 4 uses the diary of a Scottish aristocrat as the basis for a discussion of how keyboard music figured in his flirtations with the daughter of Berlin's city council president. Chapter 5 analyzes the repertoire associated with female players on the basis of the remarkably well-preserved music library of two teenage countesses in Darmstadt. Chapter 6 presents a study of the ways in which keyboard playing figured in the courtship and marriage of one of the most influential academic couples of the era.

Chapters 7 and 8 explore the musical lives of male amateurs. Chapter 7 discusses the place of music in the education and leisure time of boys and men; I draw from diverse sources and conclude with brief case studies of two lawyers. Chapter 8 is a longer case study of keyboard playing in daily life based on the autobiography of a young man from Stralsund who played recreationally while studying at the university in Jena and while working as a house tutor in rural Pomerania.

The final three chapters are devoted to professional keyboardists. A pendant to chapter 2, chapter 9 is devoted to instrument construction and ownership, in this case of a church organ in the small town of Rötha. Chapter 10 presents an account of the lives and careers of musicians, with a particular focus on the diverse ways they were compensated for their work. Chapter 11 is a case study of an aspiring musician who taught at an orphanage in Cöthen before accepting a post as organist in Braunschweig. The conclusion seeks to tie together various thematic strands which emerge from the preceding chapters.

I hope with this book to offer readers not only a rich cultural context for J. S. Bach's life and music but also a sense for his contemporaries as human beings. Music provides a particularly vivid link to the past: some of the same tunes that go through our minds today went through the minds of the men, women, and children described in these pages. It has been personally rewarding for me to glimpse the vivid humanity of these people in the materials they left to posterity. I hope that the reader, too, will find points of identification with them. Ultimately, the meaning of music is not to be found among the stars and planets but rather in the relationships it creates and sustains between people, whether near or far, living or deceased.

CHAPTER I

Civilizing Instruments

The denizens of J. S. Bach's Germany wore *galant* boots, *galant* belt buckles, *galant* stockings, and *galant* velvet caps. They accessorized with *galant* embroidered handbags, *galant* silk scarves, *galant* pearl necklaces, and *galant* silver tobacco canisters.[1] Restaurateurs proudly served *galant* ragouts, *galant* fricassees, *galant* mutton chops, *galant* veal cutlets, and *galant* Westphalian hams.[2] The patronage of prostitutes was known as a *Galanterie*, and venereal disease as a *Galanterie*-illness.[3] In 1687 the philosopher Christian Thomasius ridiculed university students for applying the word *galant* to dogs, cats, slippers, tables and chairs, quills and ink, apples and pears, and "I know not what else."[4] The situation had not changed much nearly four decades later when Bach's neighbor and sometime-librettist Johann Christoph Gottsched observed that "anything one can see, hear, smell, taste, feel, sense or in any other way experience or imagine has to be described as *galant*, totally *galant*, and completely *galant*."[5]

The word in question was originally associated with the "Sun King" of France, Louis XIV.[6] In the parlance of the French court, a *galant homme* was one who had "the good fortune of possessing a penetrating intellect, an extraordinary body of knowledge, an unusual ability to understand a thing thoroughly and appraise it sharply, a perfect and unaffected politesse, and other pleasant characteristics."[7] A certain "je ne sçay qvoy" enabled him to ingratiate himself with virtually anyone.[8]

In the mouths of the German masses, however, the word *galant* was not restricted to niceties of courtly comportment. The myriad objects, activities, and behaviors to which it was applied had in common a perceived measure of luxury. The galant was most clearly defined by its opposite: the unadorned and functional. A *Galanterie-Degen* was a sword intended not for actual fighting but rather a prop best restricted to display. The patronage of prostitutes was a galanterie because it amounted to the seeking of indulgences beyond the procreative pleasures of the marital bed. An ordinary Westphalian ham had all of the features of Westphalian hamhood; its galant counterpart possessed some appeal beyond the defining basics.[9]

The craze for all things galant was motivated by the rather sudden arrival of prosperity at the end of a punishing century. Between 1618 and 1648, the Thirty Years' War had destroyed large swaths of the Holy Roman Empire. Rampaging soldiers, bubonic plague, and widespread famine had emptied the countryside and swelled the cities. Priests had been slain at their altars, noses and ears of enemy combatants had been cut off to make hatbands, corpses had been eaten by rats, and parents had been forced to lock their plague-afflicted children in barns to die.[10] Some five million people—around 20 percent of the populace—had perished.[11]

By 1700 the German population had finally returned to its pre-war size, and well-situated trade cities began to generate wealth at unprecedented levels.[12] The expanding fortunes of Leipzig, a city that features prominently in Bach's own biography, were manifest in the founding of a stock exchange in 1678,[13] a pioneering court for settling trade disputes in 1682,[14] and the increasingly regular posting of its exchange rates in major capitals of international finance.[15] Streets, bridges, and the mail system were dramatically improved over the first half of the eighteenth century, and the population nearly doubled, from 15,650 in 1697 to 29,600 in 1746.[16] New wealth led to the complete transformation of the city's architecture. By 1728 a local writer could righteously boast, "Whoever visited the world-renowned city of Leipzig [. . .] at the end of the last century, and now has occasion to visit again, will be astonished by its tremendous growth and betterment. Indeed, he will scarcely be able to imagine that a city [. . .] might change so much, and be improved in so many ways, in such a short time."[17]

As the economy recovered, members of the aristocracy—the 1 percent of the population who ruled Germany's many territories—came increasingly to rely on cultural representation, rather than violence, to manifest their power. Princes, dukes, counts, palatines, margraves, barons, lords, and imperial knights adopted the "Sun King" as their role model, patronizing hunts, dances, and operas, and building palaces, gardens, and art collections like those they had admired on grand tours to Versailles.[18] In the new age of peace and plenty, social advancement depended less on a soldier's stoic toughness and more on the galant homme's ability to endear himself to all within earshot.[19] While aristocratic women had previously "sweetened their troubled hours" by extracting medicines from plants, concocting beauty balms, crafting jewelry, or painting translucent pictures,[20] those of the galant era engaged in less pragmatic, more costly pastimes such as learning French, dancing, and making music. By 1717 a Saxon writer could only wax nostalgic for the days of *Mutter Anna*—Anna Sophie of Denmark, mother of Augustus the Strong—when even noble ladies allegedly spent their days churning butter and feeding pigs: "Nowadays the aristocratic women know nothing more of this manner, but have invented a totally new occupation for themselves. One still finds here and there a few who consider their household duties more important than wasting time with the new vain and *galant*. The rational man would ten times rather have a wife who pursues her womanly tasks diligently than one who wastes all of her time with *Galanterie*."[21]

The bourgeoisie—roughly 24 percent of the population—had long looked to the German nobility when it came to matters of taste. Flush with new prosperity, they could now replicate aristocratic living more completely. Wealthy merchants, lawyers, and bureaucrats flocked to operas, collected paintings by old masters, and built themselves urban palaces scarcely less ostentatious than those of dukes and princes. Leather tanners, blacksmiths, bakers, and butchers wore powdered wigs and hired private tutors to teach their daughters to turn pirouettes and conjugate French verbs. Galanterie even trickled down to the urban poor. In Leipzig, servant girls were known to illegally wear homemade lace, a contraband fashion item they could be forced to shred tearfully before glowering magistrates at city hall.[22] Scavenger ladies, who eked out a living selling what they could salvage from the streets, astonished onlookers by drinking coffee—the ultimate luxury beverage—"from a real brass coffee pot, in the *galant* Leipzig manner."[23]

Peasants, who constituted 75 percent of the population and resided mostly in the countryside, had limited access to the pleasures of galanterie.[24] The Thirty Years' War had roiled their social world more than most, and in the wake of so much murder, rape, and displacement, the high and low had sometimes exchanged places, with land-owning farmers becoming indentured servants and vice versa.[25] Recovery was slower than in the cities, and most peasants who lived during Bach's lifetime spent their days raising livestock and tilling soil, subject to adverse meteorological conditions, malnutrition, and early death.[26] Their most palpable contact with urban galanterie came when nattily dressed university students pranced around in their taverns, and local barons and knights rode through their fields in pursuit of stags, tearing up the crops and ruining what had cost months of backbreaking labor.

Newly affluent urbanites viewed the peasants as living relics of the disagreeable past. They wished desperately to see themselves as peaceable members of an international elite, adopting cosmopolitan fashion and speaking elegant French rather than the guttural vernacular. As part of the effort to purge their psyches of "farmer's pride," they sought by aesthetic means to distance themselves from the brute, physical world. Galant ladies wore crinoline hoop skirts, or pillowed undergarments known as "French buttocks."[27] Such devices simultaneously hid their natural curves and artificially plumped them to elephantine proportions. The severe limitations they placed on movement signaled a woman's freedom from the indignity of physical labor. The galant homme wore a powdered wig whenever in public. By replacing his natural hair with manicured white curls, he too symbolically rejected nature's crass endowment. In the extraordinarily rare event that a man removed his wig, he did so in order to underscore the power of an emotion—rage, joy, or disbelief—which had temporarily returned him to an animal state.[28]

Affluent men and women emphasized artifice in their personal comportment. Their gestures and words were often memorized verbatim from published manuals.[29] They struggled to avoid being swayed by strong emotions, cultivating instead a "spirit tempered by reason."[30] One's aim at all times was to give interlocutors an impression of easy cheer, regardless of how one actually felt. Bach's contemporaries were encouraged to calculate the strategic potential of each word as if it were a chess move, seeking to turn circumstances to their advantage without betraying the slightest hint of unseemly effort.[31]

The most popular entertainments of the era offered fantasies of human dominance over nature. Popular city festivals in Leipzig such as the "Bird Shoot" (*Vogelschießen*) and water jousting (*Fischerstechen*) celebrated the superiority of humanity through the ritual torture of animals.[32] Operas and novels presented outrageously implausible plotlines based on mistaken identity: simple changes of clothing rendered it impossible for sisters to recognize brothers and husbands to recognize wives. It was appealing to imagine that nature's strictest boundaries could be altered through modest human intervention. Literary theorists argued that art should imitate nature, but the nature they had in mind had nothing to do with the rocky outcroppings and stagnant swamps that surrounded them in the real world.[33] After traveling through a patch of rough terrain in a carriage, Johann Christoph Gottsched—one of the most prominent literary figures of Bach's time and a chief proponent of the "natural" in art—vented his frustration by writing a poem in which he argued that the mountains ought to be flattened so that they better conform to his poetic ideal.[34] Public gardens of Bach's era presented nature in the form Gottsched envisioned, sliced and diced to perfection, with rows of geometrical hedges, scrupulously pruned coffee bushes, exotic apple and pear trees, and brute beasts confined to tidy pens.[35]

When commentators of the galant era spoke of "nature," they referred not to the world as it existed but rather to the world as it had been in the Garden of Eden. Adam and Eve's fateful bite of the apple had not only condemned humans to lives of suffering but had also destroyed an immaculate physical environment. In that vanished world there had been no mountains, no lakes or oceans, no seasons, and no harsh winds, earthquakes, or other natural disasters. The earth had been egg-shaped and perfectly smooth. Animals had been tame, and human beings had lived to be nine hundred years old, drinking water instead of wine. Original sin had led God, generations later, to punish Earth's inhabitants with the Great Flood. Rising waters had destroyed this perfect world and marooned humanity on islands of detritus. Bach's contemporaries saw the mountains, valleys, and lakes that surrounded them not as welcome variations in an otherwise monotonous landscape but rather as unsightly scars on what had once been a perfect world.[36] It was humanity's obligation to somehow overcome God's displeasure, in part by cultivating fleeting glimpses of this perfect world through art.

The affluence of the galant era also promoted the pursuit of science. Nature's vicissitudes had for millennia been attributed to the capricious will of an unfathomable deity. By around the time of Bach's birth, however, evidence was mounting that Creation followed a precise mathematical logic. In his *Philosophiæ Naturalis Principia Mathematica* of 1687, Sir Isaac Newton had presented a coherent explanation for phenomena as diverse as gravity, the movement of the planets, the motions and paths of comets, and the production of tides.[37] Ample leisure time and disposable income enabled gentleman scientists to follow the latest developments from the comfort of their armchairs, advertising their intellectual curiosity and support of scientific progress by filling their living rooms with microscopes and gleaming brass air pumps. Demand for scientific knowledge grew such that, by 1700, German publishers began producing more books in the vernacular than in scholarly Latin.[38] Many of these were *Lexica*—encyclopedias devoted to a wide variety of subjects, from anatomy and botany to chemistry and surgery, which enabled lay readers to dip in and out at leisure, quickly locating the information they sought without having to familiarize themselves with mountains of background literature. At public

fairs, ordinary citizens were shocked by the raw power of electricity, be-
guiled by the sight of princes eating chickens that had been cooked with
magnifying glasses, and entertained by robots who could play the flute.[39]

Scientific advances of the galant era led to breakthroughs in philosophy.
It was around the time of Bach's birth that the theory of the universe as
a giant mechanism first gained widespread currency, primarily through
the writings of René Descartes, Thomas Hobbes, Nicolas Malebranche,
and Gottfried Wilhelm Leibniz. The materialists argued that the universe
was governed by mechanical laws of cause and effect. Uncomfortable with
the idea of a Godless existence, most writers restricted their claims to the
observable, physical world, theorizing that there was a parallel, nonphysical
world of spirits that lay beyond the boundaries of human comprehension.
In this way, they salvaged a distinction between body (physical) and mind
(metaphysical), as well as the credibility of miraculous events described
in the Bible. Only a Jewish lens maker in Amsterdam named Baruch Spinoza went further, arguing that there was absolutely no world beyond the
physical. In his deeply controversial view, the fact that some phenomena
were not subject to human observation did not exempt them from laws of
physics, which applied everywhere else. Spinoza alone recognized the most
profound consequence of the materialist project: that living creatures—
indeed, even the minds of human beings—must be governed entirely by
physical processes, subject to laws of cause and effect like everything else.
His work inspired bold thinkers to question scripture. Could Lot's wife really have been turned into a pillar of salt? Might this or that biblical miracle
have been the product of a strong wind rather than divine intervention?[40]
Books that posed such questions were burned, their authors imprisoned,
banished, or worse. But the breakdown of social and intellectual boundaries facilitated by the affluence of the galant era enabled unorthodox ideas
to proliferate.

Few of J. S. Bach's contemporaries embraced all of the cutting-edge ideas
and behaviors associated with galant modernity. Nearly everyone, however,
was forced to come to terms with the destabilization of social structures,
intellectual frameworks, and spiritual convictions that attended it. Peace
and plenty were obviously preferable to violence and poverty, but freedom
from want also raised troubling questions. Where was the boundary between pleasure and indulgence? Which native traditions should be retained
and which discarded in favor of foreign innovations? How could scientific
progress be reconciled with the doctrines of revealed religion? Germans
of Bach's era confronted these questions in their daily lives, articulating
answers in both words and actions.

꙰

Music was among the most public sites at which Bach's contemporaries negotiated the challenges of the galant era. Crucially, all music in eighteenth-century Germany was live. If ever one heard a melody floating through the air, it was because a human being was singing or playing it nearby. Music was less like reading a book or looking at a painting and more like dancing or conversation. As Johann Mattheson, the most prolific musicologist of Bach's Germany, put it in 1713, "a painting is a piece of furniture; music is an act."[41]

Listening, too, was an act. An audience member's engagement with melody and harmony found many forms in the eighteenth century, from respectful silence to convivial conversation, from mild foot tapping to boisterous dancing. In the absence of audio recording technology, listening to music was more social in nature. A listener's actions, no less than a musician's, were open to interpretation by onlookers.

Bach's contemporaries understood music as a natural phenomenon, like fire, water, or gravity. No matter how well humans learned to manage it, they could never fully comprehend or control its power. Scientists documented the effects of different musical instruments on forest and marine animals, concluding that music's most basic effects did not depend on higher cognitive faculties. Deer apparently responded best to horns and other brass instruments, while crabs preferred the sounds of flutes.[42] Such findings supported the view that in humans, too, the impact of music was first physical and only secondarily mental. The author of a Latin-language treatise from Bach's Leipzig, *Tractatus physicus de effectibus Musices in corpus Animatum* (On the Physical Effects of Music on the Living Body), argued that only after tones had stimulated the "fibers around the internal organs, vessels, and skin" could they go on to "excite the soul."[43] The visceral character of music's initial effects made it a potentially uncivilizing force. Because it could affect those incapable of higher reasoning, however, music was also viewed as a potentially powerful tool for social engineering. While "certain harmonies could awaken and foster pathological affections," others were capable of "correcting a depraved character."[44]

Galant-minded men and women signaled their distance from nature by resisting music's mysterious power to engage the body. Those who made music were encouraged to follow strict rules, such as those laid out in a French treatise on comportment translated into German by Christian Friedrich Hunold, a poet whose work Bach set to music:

> If you have a good voice, or know how to play instruments, or possess a talent for making verses, you should not deliberately reveal it to others.

Only if your skills are revealed by someone else, and if that person is of high reputation and entreats you to perform, should you acknowledge the truth, though it is best to first refuse to perform. But if the company is not satisfied with excuses, you should not delay any further, agreeing promptly to demonstrate your talents in singing, playing, or making of verses. Quick obedience liberates one from later accusations of standing on ceremony, which after the performance can lead listeners to say things like: "This is all he can do? That was not worth the trouble it took to get him to perform." You should not cough or spit too much before performing, nor tune your guitar or lute for too long. You should not indulge in practiced gestures that indicate pleasure in your own performance, or say things in the midst of the music—e.g., "That is a beautiful passage"; "Here comes an even more beautiful one"; "Notice here, how artfully the music is made," etc.—as only arrogant and misguided people do this sort of thing. You should also make sure not to perform for too long, lest the company become annoyed. It is best to leave an audience wanting more, concluding your performance before anyone is tempted to say: "That is enough." A response like this can diminish you, all the more so if you are of high status. It is likewise demeaning to talk and thereby disturb another musician while he is performing.[45]

Bach's contemporaries were discouraged from trusting intuition, which tended to lead them down the paths of overzealousness, immodesty, and arrogance. Only by relying on the advice of professionals could they assuage their fears of violating decorum. Hunold's suggestion that musicians affect an air of indifference in advertising their skills and nonchalance in displaying them aimed to bring intuition in line with the prevailing aesthetic of galant grace.

Other writers took a more aggressive approach to the same end, offering cautionary tales about behavior musicians were to strenuously avoid. Johann Mattheson, for example, asked readers rhetorically in 1739:

Can an attentive listener really be moved to pleasure when he is constantly distracted by the noise of the player beating time with his foot or arm? Or when he sees twelve violinists before him who move about as if suffering from serious illnesses? Or when keyboard players twist their mouths, wrinkle their brows up and down, and alter their faces such that they might frighten children? Or when wind-instrument players screw up their countenances and puff their cheeks out, or flutists purse their lips, so that it takes them half an hour to return their faces to their proper folds and natural color?[46]

In an age that prized artful illusion, leaving one's gestures to chance was a fundamental error. Red cheeks, gnashing teeth, and absentminded facial expressions were serious lapses in decorum that could render even the most skillful performers ridiculous.

Listeners, too, aimed for galant ease in their comportment, using music to distance themselves from the mundane world. At a private series established in Leipzig in the 1740s, audience members were welcomed into comfortable, well-appointed rooms to hear repertoire composed by "the most famous and greatest masters" in a manner deemed "as selfless as it is *galant*."[47] The performers included Bach's former students Carl Gotthelf Gerlach and Johann August Landvoigt:[48]

> The attentiveness to music, which pervades society gatherings, deserves mention here. All arts, which appeal through the beauties of harmony, and arouse various passions of the heart, require attentiveness, so that their effects are not disturbed. Only silence during musical performances can satisfy ambitious listeners. To a connoisseur whose musical ear does not wish to miss a single bowstroke from Gerlach's violin, every noise—however small it may be—is insufferable. In a masterpiece there are no tones or sounds which are unimportant, and a single measure misheard can rob us of a large part of the pleasure intended by its composer. I am so irked by people asking me questions while I am listening that I take it as if they are mocking me, and I mercilessly regard those who are inattentive to music as lacking sensitivity and taste. I could not hide the annoyance recently aroused in me by my neighbor at a concert, and I cannot forgive him even though he has praised my writing in other contexts (without knowing my identity). All of my confidence in his praise was destroyed by his having shared distracting thoughts with me while music was playing. I sat there listening as one whose entire soul had been brought into order by music, so that pleasure could find a totally open path, and crawl into every crevice of my being. A solo, which Herr Landvoigt played on the flute, put me into an enraptured state of mind, and I was ready to be completely drunken with the music, to be lost in joy, when this immodest neighbor suddenly moved and got close to my ear, putting the gentle and ingratiating tones to flight, and said to me with a serious countenance: "Have you heard that Bochetta has once again been taken, and the Turks are expected to gather together in the European provinces?" I was furious that my quiet rapture had been interrupted, and my answer probably gave him a poor impression of my knowledge of current affairs. I said to him with as much haste as possible: "No."[49]

For the noisy neighbor, music was nothing more than a pleasant background for the discussion of more substantive matters. For the galant concert goer, however, it offered an opportunity to feel the full force of physical abandon while keeping his body under control: to attain an "enraptured state of mind" in which one was "completely drunken with the music" and "lost in joy." Like the great tactician Odysseus, the galant music lover metaphorically bound himself to the mast in order to experience the sirens' thrilling songs without risking physical ruin.

In settings where dancing was permitted, galant listeners were encouraged to be particularly vigilant in checking their physical responses. As Hunold advised ballroom attendees: "It is a laughable gesture for a listener to follow the dancers' movements with his head, or when he hears violins or other instruments playing, to follow the cadence or beat time with the head, the body, or the feet."[50] If the galant homme himself danced, he did so with utmost care, restricting his bodily movements to those he had been trained to make. It was the refinement of his physical gestures that distanced him from lower social orders and, by extension, from the natural world more broadly:

> Everyone knows how the common folk in cities and villages everywhere practice a sort of dancing which consists of nothing but indiscreet jumping, unruly poses, galling holds, lewd embraces, and the like (because there is no art or regulation) and can lead to bawdy mischief. It is easy to recognize and prove the motivation that drives the heart to this sort of dancing— namely, untamed, cheeky inclinations to lustful indulgence, as if the sole purpose of dancing were to promote wild abandon and, by means of the most shameful movements, the expression of illicit desires. In contrast to this, the honorable dancing undertaken in good faith at decent weddings follows the rules of art and springs from no source other than pleasure in graceful movement, and a desire to emulate one another, and to be seen. Anyone who has witnessed French dancing must admit that it includes no infuriatingly randy poses, particularly when young people of the same gender practice together on the dance floor.[51]

Like common beasts, peasants were incapable of withstanding music's sensual power. It appealed too readily to their uncouth bodies and diminished their already weak faculties of moral judgment. Only careful training could enable polite listeners to channel music's visceral pleasures safely into mental realms.

Friction was to be expected, particularly on the frontiers of civilization, where the guiding principles of galant culture had not yet achieved wide acceptance. Consider the following scene from rural Silesia in the 1690s, as described by a visiting barber-surgeon:

> In the village of Alt-Scheiting, an apprentice brought me to a tavern where countless other artisans' boys were having a good time with dancing and music. We drank and ate in peace in a separate room. After the beer got into the heads of my companions, however, they wanted to dance too. Among the barbers' apprentices, we had one who taught dance lessons. The rest implored him to show off his skills. When he started in with his French dancing, the other artisans' apprentices at first stood still and watched in

amazement as he executed his various leaps. But it went on too long for them and someone stuck out his leg to trip our dancer's lady partner. In an instant, the shouting and brawling started, and everything was chaos and confusion. The innkeeper and his farmers managed to reestablish peace, and we were allowed to remain in the tavern because they recognized that we were good customers.[52]

The ordinary tavern clientele, momentarily distracted from their rustic dancing, watched with amazement as the barber's apprentice performed his galant leaps. Initially dazzled, they eventually rejected the implicit superiority of this interloper by shoving him over the line that separated the fashionable from the ridiculous. The resulting brawl was not merely a battle about proper behavior while listening to music. It was a proxy battle in a wider cultural war: the national was pitted against the foreign, the rural against the urban, tradition against innovation, religion against science. As was so often the case, the advantage that proved decisive in the end was economic. The Francophile dancer and his fellow barbers' apprentices were allowed to stay not because they were better dancers or better fighters but because they were better customers.

❧

Of all the musical instruments plucked, bowed, blown, and struck in Johann Sebastian Bach's Germany, the most galant were those with keys. Keyboards were distinguished by their interface. A set of black and white levers, twelve to the octave, they were elegantly arrayed like buttons, hiding the disparate frequencies they elicited. Instruments with keys had been known already in ancient Greece, and used in Roman churches as early as the seventh century.[53] But it was not until the early eighteenth century that they came to dominate both private and public music-making throughout the European continent.

The vitality of the keyboard in Bach's Germany is reflected in the wide variety of forms it assumed.[54] The undisputed king of keyboard instruments was the grand church organ. Pressing a key or a pedal caused air to be driven through myriad tubes and mechanisms and forced to exit through tuned pipes of metal or wood, emitting pitched tones of varied sonic hues. These could be altered or combined by pulling stops that surrounded the console—fifteen to seventy-five, depending on the size of the organ—which evoked the sounds of wind, string, and brass instruments. Smaller, chamber organs, roughly the size and shape of wardrobes, offered a more limited selection and a fraction of the volume. Virtually all organs required two persons for proper execution: a musician in charge of the notes and rhythms and an assistant who pumped accordion-like bellows as evenly as possible to maintain a constant pitch. As with most keyboard instruments of the era, pressure on the organ's keys had no effect on sound production: notes were either on or off.

Outside of church, the vast majority of keyboards had strings. Among the most common of these was the harpsichord, a triangular wooden box containing iron or brass strings that ran parallel to the keys. Spinets and virginals were identical except insofar as their strings were set at 45° and 90° angles to the keys, respectively. Pressing an ivory- or ebony-colored lever raised its opposite end, causing a crow's quill to pluck a corresponding string. The string's vibrations were transmitted via a bridge to a wooden soundboard. Players used multiple sets of strings and muting effects to bring textural variety to their performances. As on the organ, the force or speed with which one pressed a key had no effect on the sound drawn forth from the instrument, so minute changes in articulation or dynamic were impossible.

The clavichord was the simplest and most common type of keyboard instrument. At the tail end of each key was a wedge of brass called a tangent, which rose when the key was pressed, striking a string at a particular point along its length. Though the clavichord served as a "first grammar" for inexperienced musicians, it was also beloved by connoisseurs for its unusual subtlety. Unlike the organ and the harpsichord, the clavichord was touch sensitive and therefore afforded players a measure of control over dynamics and articulation, at least at the quiet end of the spectrum. It was even possible, by pressing into the key after the note had already sounded, to bend the pitch slightly, thereby enabling vibrato effects.

Keyboard builders constantly sought to expand beyond the tried and true. We can glean a vivid sense for the frothy spirit of experimentation from the following advertisement for a new instrument, which appeared in the Leipzig daily newspaper in 1731:

> Music lovers are advised that the organ and keyboard-maker, Wahlfriedrich Ficker in Zeitz, has invented and built a new musical instrument called the *Cymbal-Clavir*. It is in the form of a 16-foot harpsichord, and has four choirs of metal strings. It is more powerful and has greater gravitas than even the strongest harpsichord, and stays in tune as long as a good clavichord without the least adjustment. It is also easy to play, as the little hammers pluck from 2½ inches above the strings. Beyond this, the *Cymbal-Clavir* exhibits a number of innovations: 1) a pleasant dampening effect, which makes the strings sound as if they are being struck by felt-covered hammers, and 2) a stop one can pull to prevent the sounds from sustaining too long and bleeding into one another, just as fabric on the tangents of a clavichord stills the strings. This instrument, which can be purchased for a civil price,

has been praised by the famous *Pandalon*, the inventor of the *Cymbal*, and has been admired and approved by many virtuosi.[55]

The instrument advertised here was not a piano, but it represents one maker's response to the desire of players to have a keyboard that combined the power of a harpsichord, the sensitivity of a clavichord, and sounds like those of "felt-covered hammers" hitting the strings.

The earliest piano (or *fortepiano*, Italian for "loud-soft") was built around 1700 by Bartolomeo Cristofori of Padua. A complex hammer mechanism enabled touch-sensitive playing with a much wider dynamic range than any other stringed keyboard. Unlike the tangents of a clavichord, however, the hammers of Cristofori's piano were designed to rebound immediately, making it impossible for players to affect a note after the initial impact. Numerous other makers tried their hands at designing pianos, but these instruments remained expensive and rare until the second half of the century.

The will to experiment led makers in other directions as well. Some constructed keyboards that enabled players to toggle between harpsichord and organ sounds, or to use both simultaneously.[56] Others designed keyboards that could imitate the sounds of other instruments. The "cymbal d'amour," for example, was a harpsichord with extra strings that vibrated sympathetically to reinforce and echo the primary strings, as on a viola d'amore.[57] Harp-keyboards sounded and even looked like harps but were controlled with keys.[58] Lute-keyboards were harpsichords strung with gut to imitate the sounds of plucked instruments. Gamba-keyboards were outfitted with hurdy-gurdy-like wheels that brushed horsehair against the strings to evoke the sounds of bowed instruments.[59] Such inventions are best understood not as experimental keyboards but rather as experimental lutes, harps, and violas da gamba. In eighteenth-century Germany, virtually any musical instrument could be improved through the addition of a keyboard interface.

Keyboard instruments were, officially, supposed to be designed and built by highly qualified professionals who belonged to guilds, apprenticed to respected elder makers, spent their journeyman years supplementing this education with experiences in other cities, and eventually established shops of their own.[60] The most prestigious work was designing church organs, and successful builders like Gottfried Silbermann and Zacharias Hildebrandt achieved a measure of celebrity that rivaled that of the greatest musicians. Demand was high. Virtually every month of Bach's lifetime, a new church organ was completed somewhere in the German-speaking world.[61] On average they cost around 1,850 reichstaler, though the budgets for some could reach 10,000 reichstaler.[62] Such investments paid dividends not only in community pride and church attendance, but also in increased commerce and tourism.[63]

Even the most famous organ builders earned the bulk of their income from constructing harpsichords and clavichords. During the 1740s Zacharias Hildebrandt earned nearly 900 reichstaler per year from building stringed keyboards "in the evening hours," most of which he funneled back into the more prestigious but less financially stable business of constructing organs.[64] His stringed-keyboard customers in 1744–1745 included not only professional organists and cantors but also a bureaucrat, a coffeehouse proprietor, a soapmaker, an unmarried lady, and an anonymous boy—who were willing to spend between ten and fourteen reichstaler per clavichord, twenty-four reichstaler per spinet, and between one hundred and 185 reichstaler per harpsichord.[65] To offer a sense for the scale of these investments, readers should bear in mind that J. S. Bach at the peak of his career earned about 700 reichstaler per year,[66] while other successful professional musicians earned between 200 and 300.[67]

Those who could not afford the high prices of the official builders turned to unofficial channels. The guild system, designed to restrict competition, made it illegal for nonguild members to construct and sell keyboard instruments, but high demand tempted many to break the law. The primary offenders were professional organists, whose attics were filled with half-built keyboards, but the ranks of illegal keyboard builders also included violin makers, saddlers, monks, carpenters, cabinetmakers, and mechanics.[68] In 1734 the famous organ builder Tobias Gottfried Heinrich Trost complained to legal authorities that his profit margins were being reduced by the illicit keyboard-building activities of a schoolmaster and a tax collector.[69]

Customers of lesser means could also purchase used keyboard instruments at public auctions. Some of these instruments were in states of disrepair and shockingly cheap. During Bach's time in Leipzig, city authorities auctioned, for example, a "very dilapidated" chamber organ worth twenty-five reichstaler, an "old, damaged" clavichord worth just four groschen, and a "small, spoiled" harpsichord appraised at just two groschen. The least expensive instruments could be purchased at auction for half the price of a roll with salami or one-third the price of a serving of hot chocolate in a local coffeehouse.[70] Perhaps these instruments were harvested for spare parts or—as Bach's friend Jacob Adlung suggested for those worth less than sixteen groschen—burned to cook fish.[71] Demand for keyboards was obviously high enough that municipal authorities nonetheless judged it worth the state's trouble to catalog and sell instruments of even deplorable quality.

୧ୢ

Keyboards satisfied the musical, emotional, and social needs of galant era consumers like no other instrument. A good-looking clavichord, harpsichord, or chamber organ was a luxury item, and frequently among the most expensive pieces of furniture in a bourgeois home.[72] Decorated with elaborate paintings, keyboard instruments could bring splendor to a baroque sitting room even when silent. Bach's German contemporaries could easily have identified with their counterparts in London who, during the Great Fire of 1666, loaded their keyboard instruments onto barges floating in the Thames.[73]

Keyboards appealed to galant-era customers in part because of their mechanical nature. Most instruments of the age required musicians to engage physically with some sort of resonating body. Timpanists beat with wooden mallets upon leather skins stretched over brass kettles, a task some courts assigned to African musicians who, according to racist ideologies, seemed well suited to playing physically demanding instruments.[74] Trumpet players blew into metal mouthpieces, adjusting their lips to find a desired partial in the overtone series, occasionally dying of overexertion in the process.[75] Oboe players produced a single tone by pursing their lips around a pair of cane reeds, articulating with their tongues and changing pitch with their fingers. String players rubbed horsehair over woven ropes of dried sheep gut, adjusting the pitch by stopping the string along its length with the fingers. Only keyboard instruments enabled players to control sound indirectly. At the clavichord, harpsichord, or organ, one could produce a tone with a single finger by applying barely more pressure than the weight of gravity. Engineering genius brought keyboard players closest to the galant ideal of physical transcendence: simply thinking of music and hearing it resound in the air.

Keyboards had a scientific character that accorded well with the spirit of the age. The most advanced research tools—telescopes, microscopes, and air pumps—did not simply measure length, weight, or time, as had earlier scientific implements. Rather, they distorted nature by magnifying it, creating vacuums, or otherwise obscuring some aspects in order to examine others more thoroughly.[76] Keyboards offered a similar quid pro quo. Whereas players of brass, wind, string, and percussion instruments could make fine adjustments so that each note had a different character—breathy or bold, with a soft or hard attack, slightly higher or lower in pitch—keyboard players gave up much control of surface detail in order to play multiple tones at once. As J. S. Bach's second son, Carl Philipp Emanuel, observed in his treatise of 1753: "The perfection of the keyboard would be easy to prove, were this ever necessary, because it unites the characteristics of many instruments; the keyboard enables a solitary player to bring forth a complete harmony, which would otherwise require three, four, or more players, to say nothing of its other advantages."[77] By largely ceding control of articulation, dynamics, and intonation, keyboard players gained the ability to more fully explore music's more fundamental mysteries, particularly harmony and counterpoint.

The unusual degree of control keyboards offered their players gave them a central role in the pedagogy of the era. As Johann Mattheson observed in 1739:

> The keyboard is to be recommended above all other instruments and is to be daily kept at hand. It is a composer's special tool and whoever does not have, or has never had, exceptional facility at the keyboard will have trouble composing anything worthwhile. I do not mean to imply that one must draw every musical idea from the keyboard, or that composers should make use of no other instrument while writing music, but it offers a much more precise concept of harmonic structure than does the imagination alone. Although this instrument also has disadvantages, the range, order, and organization of the pitches is nowhere so explicit and visible as it is in the keys of a keyboard.[78]

Everyone—from lowly village organists teaching novices to read music to illustrious musicologists persuading their colleagues of theoretical truths—relied on the keyboard as a means of illustration. Keys enabled players of all abilities to bring the eye to bear on problems they could not solve with the ear alone.

❧

Keyboard instruments often served in accompanimental capacities. Church sanctuaries echoed with the sounds of grand organs supporting the voices of choirs, whether during Sunday morning worship services, weddings, baptisms, funerals, or civic ceremonies.[79] Bach's contemporaries used harpsichords and clavichords at home to accompany chamber music and hymn singing, from the orthodox to the sacrilegious, or even the profane.[80] Professional musicians, wealthy lawyers, merchants, and aristocrats gathered in private homes or coffeehouses to read through keyboard-based chamber music.[81] Harpsichords were used in courtly settings not only to accompany overtures, concertos, and operas, but also to complement the singing of hymns before bedtime.[82]

It was solo keyboard playing, however, that made the greatest gains during Bach's lifetime. As presented graphically in plate 1, between 1660 and 1760 the German market for printed music was completely reoriented to reflect consumer demand for solo keyboard works. The production of large-scale printed works commemorating specific weddings and funerals dropped sharply. While representing less than 1 percent of music published in German-speaking lands during the 1660s, 1670s, and 1680s, solo keyboard music accounted rather suddenly for 10 percent in the 1690s, 35 percent in the 1720s, and an astonishing 45 percent in the 1740s and 1750s.[83]

The rising demand for printed keyboard music is reflected not only in the absolute number of publications but also in who produced them. Before about 1730, composers themselves most often acted as their own publishers. They set down their works in manuscript, engraved or etched them in copper, and paid print shops to ink the plates and press them onto paper. The finished stacks of music were sold from the composers' own homes or on commission through friends and colleagues. Beginning around 1730, demand for solo keyboard repertoire had increased to the point that savvy German musician-businessmen founded successful publishing houses intended primarily to satisfy the needs of amateur keyboardists.[84] They pioneered new technologies, hired skillful engravers, and organized vast distribution networks to reach the largest possible number of consumers.[85] As can be seen in the graph presented in plate 2, collections produced by professional publishers accounted for only 20 percent of the keyboard music printed in the 1710s and 1720s, whereas by the 1730s they accounted for 50 percent, and by the 1740s an overwhelming 98 percent.

The increased commercialization of solo keyboard music production, particularly after professional publishers came to dominate the market, had a decisive impact on the character of the repertoire that was printed. The music which proved most popular with consumers consisted of short, binary dance pieces of French origin such as minuets, bourrées, and gavottes. They had in common light textures—often just two voices—and four-bar phrases from beginning to end. Not surprisingly, these works came to be known collectively as *Galanterien*.[86] The term expressed to the satisfaction of Bach's contemporaries the distinction between this repertoire and more serious music. Galanterien were musical luxury items: pleasurable but not strictly essential. While teutonic counterpoint seemed to revel in its own striving, galanterien had a light and cosmopolitan feel. As Georg Muffat wrote in 1695, the French style was characterized by its rejection of "all superfluous artifices, such as immoderate divisions as well as frequent and ill-sounding leaps" in the interest of preserving a "flowing and natural movement." He was pleased that his German compatriots were finally coming around to discover "the truth of what an extremely discerning prince once said . . . with regard to this style: namely, that what they had learned previously was more difficult than what, to charm the ear, they needed to have learned."[87]

Minuets, bourrées, gavottes, and other galanterien titillated music lovers by implying bodily engagement without stepping over the line into actual dance. Whereas functional dance music required an absolutely regular pulse, galanterien were intended merely to evoke the ballroom, with a greater degree of rhythmic freedom.[88] Rolled chords, fermatas, cadenzas, and other forms of ornamentation served not only to decorate the music but also to make sure that performances remained free from the specter of untoward physical engagement. Visual artists of the era sometimes chose to evoke the dance in their portraits of society women through the use of a prop—a drum perhaps, or wind blowing against a subject's clothing—which suggested chaste, passive movement.[89] Keyboard galanterien served a similar purpose, evoking the sexual element of dance in what was effectively an animate portrait. Players remained seated and virtuously still: only their fingers moved.

Before professional publishers overwhelmed the market around 1730, galanterien were typically buried amid more serious repertoire. Self-publishing composers sought to appeal to experienced and inexperienced musicians alike, printing works that would bring them credit with their professional colleagues while offering a few concessions to the broader public. As Johann Krieger noted in the preface to a collection of keyboard suites he published in 1697: "Where there was extra space or room I have filled it up with minuets, bourrées, and gavottes, because these days such works appeal to those who do not really understand the keyboard far more than any kind of higher music; that which sounds good to the ears is more appropriate for them than are deep-meaning works of art."[90] Professional publishers, eager to separate amateur musicians from their pocket money, knew better than to confine the most beloved music to "extra space." Beginning around 1730, they began producing collections containing exclusively galanterien. They appealed directly to amateur musicians with advertisements describing their music as "light" (*leicht*), "comfortable" (*angenehm*), "playable" (*applicable*), "in the new style" (*im neuen Gusto*), and indicating that certain collections were intended explicitly "for women" (*vors Frauenzimmer*). The style of this repertoire was nothing particularly new in 1730: easy minuets, bourrées, and gavottes were the most beloved repertoire for amateur musicians already in the last decades of the seventeenth century.

The difference was that by 1730 there were enough amateur keyboard players to make printing their favorite music commercially viable.[91]

⁊♠

The galant was no less controversial in music than it was in every other realm of life. Some professional musicians welcomed the triumph of keyboard galanterien as an opportunity for renovation of a staid musical culture. Their spokesman was the musicologist and composer Johann Mattheson, who published a book in 1713 titled *The Newly Revealed Orchestra* that promised readers a "universal and fundamental introduction as to how a galant homme can achieve a complete concept of the majestic dignity and worth of noble music, form his taste, understand the technical terminology, and skillfully discuss this excellent science."[92] True to the spirit of the age, Mattheson eschewed the complex terminology commonly found in learned treatises on music and spoke directly to the needs of amateur musicians. In his view, good music was characterized not by its complexity but by the pleasure it brought listeners. He encouraged his readers to listen for three features: "harmony, melody, and *Galanterie*," trusting their ears in judging musical quality, just as the galant homme would trust his eyes while looking in the mirror to powder his face.[93]

There were plenty of others, however, who equated the arrival of the galant era with the end of civilization. Conservative theologians attacked minuets, bourrées, and the like as "flattering" and prone to inspiring "vain ideas" in congregants.[94] Even mild toe tapping constituted a bodily response, and once the starting friction had been overcome there was no telling where its aberrant inertia might lead.[95] To praise God with such music was blasphemous, implying that the Lord Himself was galant, subject to fashion and therefore nonsubstantive. Conservative musicians did what they could to hold back the tide. In the glossary to a 1706 manual for training young organists, the Berlin music theorist Martin Heinrich Fuhrmann defined fugues and other forms of serious music without incident. When it came to galanterien, however, he balked. This was repertoire that young musicians need not and indeed should not know: "To sort out the various meanings of the words minuet, galliard, rondeau, bourrée, ballet, gavotte, branle, passepied, bontade, schnakade, mascarede and other French blossoms, and to articulate the differences between these various jugglers' tricks would take considerable thought and thereby constitute a waste of my precious time, because the facile and licentious prancing of a flighty French dancer conflicts with the principles of my religion. Enough said!"[96] Johann Heinrich Buttstedt, a conservative organist in Erfurt, recognized that the problem he and his counterpoint-loving colleagues faced was ultimately economic. He asked rhetorically, "Which musicians these days study double counterpoint and strict fugue? Very few. Why? Because they are difficult to listen to, and do not pay well. That's why musicians, instead of studying properly, make do with *Galanterien*, just as in woman's adornment, which used to consist of pearls and golden chains but these days consists of nothing but kerchiefs and lace. From the former the children could expect some inheritance, but from the latter they can expect nothing."[97] Just as a child might naively prefer a piece of lace over a pearl, the novice musician might prefer a minuet over a fugue. But with the wisdom that comes with experience, those who chose pearls (fugues) would be better off than those who chose lace (minuets). In Buttstedt's view, it was the job of conscientious musicians to uphold traditional standards of quality, nobly resisting the nefarious financial incentives to indulge in galant-era hedonism.

Mattheson responded directly to these attacks in 1717. He agreed with Buttstedt's proposed analogy between musical and nonmusical galanterien but argued that the Erfurt organist's assessment of contemporary life was fundamentally at odds with reality. Prosperity had had a salutary effect on daily life, and it could be expected to have a similar effect on music:

> Are there now no more pearls, as there were in the old days? Does one not wear entire *Garnitures en echelle*, which are widely acknowledged to be even a little more elegant than those worn in the past? Are not the necks, hands, and ears of the fairer sex resplendent with heavenly oriental pearls every day? If this is not the case in Erfurt, what can be done? And what is it that he is trying to tell us with these old golden necklaces and strings of pearls? What good can these do the children? Should they be used to buy bread or wine? Are they worth nothing to the children beyond the amount for which they can be pawned? We are really on to something here. Does it not frequently cost ten times as much to make a golden chain as the gold itself is worth? This is certainly the case with the very artificially elaborate fugues which cost so much more effort to construct than they yield pleasure. If our organist could see the aristocratic ladies of Hamburg—what am I talking about? even the bourgeois ladies—who walk around wearing ten thousand or more reichstaler worth of earrings, crosses, rings, and precious stones, would it not convince him that for the worth of such precious materials one could construct a golden chain from here to Erfurt so that the cook at every way station could have one? Did he never see a bourgeois man who cannot even be called *galant* wearing pants on which the button alone is worth ten thousand reichstaler? Such items are worth far more than the golden chains of his *Stylus ligatus*. These, and indeed much greater, are our galanterien. I believe that, in their time of need, the grandchildren will be better served

by such items than by lousy golden chains. Now applying this observation to musical galanterien, one finds these days such extraordinary jewels that when an old necklace-peddler with poor eyesight looks upon them he cannot believe that they are authentic, because he never saw gemstones that were so enormous and yet real.[98]

From Mattheson's perspective, the public's new self-confidence in setting aesthetic trends was entirely positive. Dry traditions were being weeded out and vibrant new styles being cultivated. The galanterien that so horrified conservative musicians and theologians were in fact welcome signs of life. Reflexive hostility to popular taste prevented men like Fuhrmann and Buttstedt from appreciating the excellence of the music that was being performed all around them.

Debates about the merits of musical galanterien raged throughout Bach's lifetime. All parties agreed that they offered greater immediate pleasure, but not everyone was convinced that more pleasure was a good thing. As in nonmusical realms, the central question concerned where to draw the boundary between innocent diversion and nefarious indulgence. With each musical act—whether building an instrument, buying an instrument, composing, performing, or listening—Bach's contemporaries hoped to raise themselves in the estimation of those whose opinions they valued. They told themselves stories about what their musical activities meant. In the chapters to follow, I have ventured to present some of these stories.

CHAPTER 2

The Mechanic and the Tax Collector

Sometime in 1750, a fifty-three-year-old tax collector named Johann Heinrich Heyne approached the door to Braunschweig's Marstall 12. The house had been built in the fifteenth century and was of the *Fachwerk* variety, with wooden trusses visible in the plaster walls. Next door was a metal caster, and directly across the street was the *Packhause*, where packaged products such as grains and cheese were weighed and taxed.[1]

When the door opened, Heyne came face to face with Barthold Fritz, a man exactly his age, with a Roman nose and a kindly aspect. Ushering the tax collector into his workshop, the maker described the types of clavichord he could build. These ranged from "travel clavichords, which one can take into a coach and play on one's lap while in transit," to large instruments with multiple manuals and pedals that emitted flute sounds.[2] The clavichords could be fretted—in which case two or three keys caused tangents to strike a single string at different points along its length—or unfretted, in which case each tangent was paired with a unique string.[3] Heyne informed the instrument maker that he wished to commission an unfretted clavichord with a range of five and one-third octaves. Retrieving the trusty handwritten book of sales he had kept for thirty years, Fritz recorded Heyne's order in his usual shorthand: "The Tax Collector, Mr. Heyne, in Braunschweig, large" (*Hr. Einnehmer Heyne zu Braunschweig. gr.*). Fritz then explained his strict policies on fulfilling commissions:

The majority of those who ordered instruments for themselves or on behalf of others will know that I have followed a law I set down for myself to never favor one customer over another but rather to record clavichord orders in [this] book and to build the instruments in that sequence. If ever a customer was for some reason unable to pick up the requested clavichord in the allotted time, he or she often gave me a tip, because I was hindered in such cases, at my own expense, from satisfying the needs of others, who were forced to wait.[4]

Heyne agreed to Fritz's terms and stepped out into the street with the expectation that he would return in a few months when the instrument was ready. Fritz then went back to doing whatever he had been doing before the interruption, perhaps sanding down boards of beechwood, carving mother-of-pearl inlay, or tuning a new set of shiny brass strings.

Interactions like the one reconstructed here took place every day in eighteenth-century Europe. These two men have been selected for discussion because their dealings are better documented than most. Fritz eventually published his entire ledger of more than three hundred clavichord sales. The instrument Heyne commissioned is one of only four Fritz clavichords to survive to the present.[5] This chapter uses their stories as the basis for a broader discussion of keyboard manufacture and ownership in J. S. Bach's Germany.

❧

Barthold Fritz had been born in Holle, a small town near Hildesheim in the heavily forested Ambergau region of Lower Saxony.[6] His father was a miller, and Fritz had probably learned early how long oak, beech, and pine needed to be dried in the storehouse, the unique scents that each emitted when cut, and the rates at which they wore down tools. Most sons of craftsmen followed in their fathers' footsteps, and Fritz too had been expected to take over the family mill. Some force—presumably an abiding interest in both engineering and music—had inspired him to abandon this secure path. He had decided while still in his teens to pursue his destiny as an instrument maker in Braunschweig, an eight-hour walk to the northeast.

With a population of around twenty thousand souls, Braunschweig had opened Fritz's eyes and ears to a world radically different from the rural environment in which he had been raised.[7] The city owed its prosperity to economic growth powered by bi-annual trade fairs that had been reestablished in 1681, at the dawn of the galant era. By the time of Fritz's arrival, the fairs were colossal attractions, inundating the streets with thousands of merchants and visitors every February and August. The aspiring young instrument maker had undoubtedly been dazzled by the four-story houses, the manicured parks, and the wide variety of circus-like attractions, from figures carved in wax to images projected by camera obscura, to live crocodiles, ostriches, and camels.[8]

Fritz had spent his early years in Braunschweig fulfilling commissions not only for musical instruments but for all manner of mechanical contraptions, from weaver's looms to mechanical songbirds, from horizontal windmills to clocks that indicated the hours by playing melodies on a mechanical flute. By 1720 he had achieved enough success to apply for citizenship, describing himself in official documents as a "mechanic" (*Mechanikus*). Fritz eventually developed a sterling reputation that carried his name throughout the German-speaking world and beyond. In addition to being admired for the quality of his work, he was regarded as "a very honest and virtuous man, who never raised his prices under any circumstances and sought at all times to keep his promises exactly."[9] He had married a local woman named Maria Lucie Schweder and in 1732 purchased her family's home at Marstall 12.[10]

As his reputation grew, Fritz had come to specialize in the construction and repair of keyboard instruments. Braunschweig had no instrument-makers' guild, so he faced no restrictions and little competition. He had eagerly accepted commissions to repair the bellows of local church organs and replace the warped and cracked soundboards of harpsichords and other domestic keyboards.[11] His clavichords were particularly renowned for the strength of their bass registers.[12] While in the 1720s and 1730s Fritz had built an average of just two clavichords per year, by the 1740s this figure had risen to twelve, and in the 1750s it reached twenty-one. Between 1752 and 1756, working almost entirely without assistants, he would construct up to twenty-six clavichords per year—on average, an instrument every sixteen days. He owed his success to talent and hard work, but he surely benefited from the growing demand for keyboard instruments which characterized his era. Plate 3 shows that Fritz's sales trajectory over the period from 1721 to 1757 closely parallels that of the publication of printed solo keyboard music over the same period, presented graphically in plate 1.

Around 55 percent of those who ordered clavichords from Barthold Fritz lived in Braunschweig. The remaining 45 percent resided in other German cities, the most common of which were Clausthal (7 percent), Hamburg (5 percent), Wolfenbüttel (4 percent), and Halberstadt (3 percent). Nearly all lived in Germany. Just 4 percent lived in other countries, including England, Holland, Norway, and Russia.[13]

Three-quarters of Fritz's customers purchased their instruments directly from the maker himself. The remaining 25 percent acquired them through intermediaries.[14] Fritz's most active sales agent was a certain "Herr Gräfe,

Table 1. Barthold Fritz Clavichord Customers, 1721–1757

Total	English Translation	German Title	Noble	Bourgeois
3	Advisor	*Rath*	—	3
2	Agent	*Commissarius, Factor*	—	2
1	Auditor	*Rathsauditor*	—	1
1	Bailiff	*Gerichtsvoigt*	—	1
2	Baron	*Baron*	2	—
4	Bookkeeper	*Buchhalter, Buchführer*	—	4
4	Bureaucrat	*Amtmann*	—	4
7	Businessman	*Kaufmann*	—	7
4	Canon	*Canonicus*	1	3
4	Cantor	*Cantor*	—	4
1	Chamber Advisor	*Cammerrath*	1	—
1	Chamber Agent	*Cammer-Agent*	—	1
1	Chamber Counsel	*Cammerconsulent*	—	1
1	Chamber Musician	*Cammermusicus*	—	1
1	Chamber Secretary	*Cammersecretär*	—	1
1	Chamber Servant	*Cammerdiener*	—	1
2	Chamber Valet	*Cammerjunker*	2	—
1	City Musician	*Stadtmusicus*	—	1
1	City Scribe	*Stadtschreiber*	—	1
1	City Syndicate	*Stadtsyndicus*	—	1
2	Cloister Advisor	*Klosterrath*	2	—
1	Commission Advisor	*Commißionsrath*	1	—
2	Court Advisor	*Hofrath*	2	—
2	Court Assessor	*Hofgerichts-Assessor*	—	2
1	Court Judge	*Hofrichter*	1	—
1	Court Legal Secretary	*Hofgerichtssecretarius*	—	1
2	Court Manager	*Hofmeister*	—	2
1	Court Marshall	*Hofmarschall*	1	—
1	Court Musician	*Fürstl. Capelle*	—	1
2	Dance Master	*Tanzmeister*	—	2
4	Doctor	*Doctor*	—	4
2	Government Lawyer	*Regierungsadv.*	—	2
2	Head Representative	*Hauptmann*	2	—
1	Home Secretary	*Geheimer*	1	—
1	Intendant	*Intendant*	—	1
1	Kapellmeister	*Capellmeister*	—	1
1	Kitchen Master	*Küchenmeister*	—	1
1	Land Syndicate	*Land-Syndicus*	—	1
1	Language Teacher	*Sprachmeister*	—	1
1	Lawyer	*Advocat*	—	1
1	Legal Official	*Amts Justit.*	—	1
2	Mayor	*Bürgemeister*	2	—
5	Military Ensign	*Fähndrich*	3	2
2	Military Official	*Oberster*	1	1
1	Military Lieutenant	*Lieutenant*	1	—
1	Military Major	*Maj.*	1	—
2	Mining Official	*Hüttenreuter*	—	2
1	Mining Scribe	*Bergschreiber*	—	1
1	Mining Secretary	*Bergsecretarius*	—	1
1	Nun in *Kreuzkloster*	*Madem. im Creuzkloster*	—	1

Table 1. Continued

Total	English Translation	German Title	Noble	Bourgeois
8	Organist	*Organist*	—	8
1	Painter	*Maler*	—	1
12	Pastor	*Pastor*	1	11
2	Post Official	*Postsecret.*	—	1
1	Post Manager	*Postverw.*	—	3
3	Prince	*Fürst, Prinz*	3	—
1	Princess	*Prinzeßin*	1	—
11	Pupil in Boarding School	*Schüler im Colleg. Carol.*	7	4
1	Rector	*Rector*	—	1
2	Scribe	*Schreiber, Amtschreiber*	—	2
3	Secretary	*Secretarius*	—	3
1	Servant	*Bedienter*	—	1
2	Shift Master	*Schichtmeister*	—	2
2	Student of Theology	*Candidat. Theol.*	—	2
1	Surgeon	*Leibchirurgus*	—	1
1	Tax Collector	*Einnehmer*	—	1
1	Writing Teacher	*Schreibmeister*	—	1
1	Vicar	*Vicar*	—	1
14	Woman (Unmarried)	*Madem., Fräulein*	6	8
14	Woman (Married)	*Frau*	4	10

Businessman in Hamburg" (*Hr. Kaufmann Gräfe zu Hamburg*), who sold a total of eighteen clavichords between 1732 and 1756, including nearly all of those delivered to foreign countries. The sales agents included many pastors and organists but also the occasional accountant, bureaucrat, military officer, or princess.[15]

Approximately one-quarter of Fritz's clavichord buyers came from the ranks of the aristocracy. Some were members of the high nobility—for example, Prince Karl Ludwig Wilhelm of Hessen-Homburg and Prince Friedrich August of Anhalt-Zerbst—while others were less illustrious aristocrats who served as military officers, functionaries, and ladies-in-waiting at the courts of their more powerful peers. Three-quarters of Fritz's customers belonged to the bourgeoisie, but they, too, were often employed in the courtly bureaucracy of Dukes Ferdinand Albrecht II and Karl I of Braunschweig-Wolfenbüttel.[16] Some held prestigious posts such as court assessor, chamber consultant, and chamber servant.[17] Others held more modest positions at court: accountant, postal official, surgeon, and dance master.[18]

Approximately 87 percent of Fritz's clients were male.[19] Among the remaining 13 percent were a few nuns and abbesses, but the majority were wives and daughters of local court officials.[20] Around half of the women to whom Fritz sold clavichords were unmarried and thus probably under the age of thirty. Between 1745 and 1749, Fritz sold eleven instruments to an even younger group: pupils at Braunschweig's famous boarding school, the *Collegium Carolinum*, all of whom were boys in their mid- to late teens.[21]

Few of Fritz's customers were professional musicians: organists, cantors, kapellmeisters, and chamber musicians made up only around 10 percent of his clientele. His most intense dealings with professional musicians had occurred toward the beginning of his career. The first clavichord Fritz sold was purchased in 1721 by Heinrich Lorenz Hurlebusch, organist at Braunschweig's St. Martin's Church. Fritz subsequently built instruments for Hurlebusch's sons: Barthold Georg, organist and vicar at the St. Blasius Church, and Conrad Friedrich, kapellmeister at the court of Braunschweig-Wolfenbüttel, who was later organist at the Oude Kerk in Amsterdam. Fritz's professional clients in Braunschweig also included a court bassoonist named Pollmann, the oboist and violinist Nikolaus Georg Weinholtz, Georg Heinrich Ludwig Schwanberg and his son, Johann Gottfried, who would later find success as an opera composer.[22] The most famous professional musician among Fritz's customers was Carl Heinrich Graun, kapellmeister to Prussia's King Friedrich II.

Generally speaking, amateur musicians who purchased Fritz's clavichords belonged to the wealthiest, best-educated, and most prestigious segment of the German population. They were people who worked with their minds, not with their hands. The kitchen master who purchased a clavichord from Fritz was not an ordinary cook but rather a manager responsible for preparing menus, making arrangements for deliveries, and managing underlings, including the master chefs. The customers involved in mining were managers, not laborers who actually got their hands dirty digging minerals and precious metals out of the earth. The military men who bought clavichords from Fritz were not enlisted soldiers but rather officers whose role it was to coordinate the battlefield movements of men whose lives were in far greater peril than their own. Even those who were less affluent—the schoolteachers, scribes, and organists—were involved in work that was minimally physical. Fritz's customers represented an urban elite defined not only by financial circumstances but also by educational opportunities.

Fritz seems not to have sold any instruments to members of the social class into which he himself had been born. If artisans and other members of the lower bourgeoisie—for example, tailors, bakers, leather tanners, glassblowers, blacksmiths, and day laborers—purchased new clavichords, they did so from other sources. Millers generally did not play the keyboard during their leisure hours, but there were exceptions, as revealed in a 1742 report from Mühlhausen, where Bach himself had served as organist:

In Mühlhausen there lived a miller named Ziegler who played chorales on a harpsichord in his room, and accompanied mill guests in the evening, when they sang to honor God, which was admittedly something quite beautiful. Though he understood nothing of figured bass, and could not read notation, he knew how to ornament the music well enough to arouse amazement. Such examples are found in nearly all cities. Most of them can actually read music, and when pressed can even improvise a prelude, though they understand little of figured bass, and would never dream of becoming organists, or of teaching others.[23]

Although the writer notes that "such examples are found in nearly all cities," he acknowledges that this miller was an unusual case. His musical deficiencies—particularly his inability to read music—not only prevented him from joining the ranks of professional musicians, they also distanced him from ordinary amateurs.

ह्ब

Barthold Fritz approached his work not from the perspective of a musician but rather from that of an engineer. For him, the clavichord was a machine. He struggled, however, to persuade others to adopt this perspective, admonishing absentminded musicians to attach the clavichord's strings properly when changing them, never to pull on them to change the pitch, and never to allow the instrument to sit out of tune for too long because the humidity and changes in temperature could make the strings rust to the bridges. He liked to tell keyboard owners that if laziness ever tempted them to neglect an instrument, they should think of the people living in Siberia or in America who face much greater challenges every day.[24]

Like many of his galant contemporaries, Fritz fantasized about a world in which ossified traditions were jettisoned in favor of rational innovations. Over the long hours in his workshop, he mused on the question of why the keyboard had been so inefficiently designed by its originator. Why did the accidental keys alternate groups of two and three? This arrangement forced players to learn more than a dozen different fingering patterns to play all of the major and minor scales. With a symmetrical arrangement of keys, it would be possible to play all twenty-four scales using just four different fingerings. As he once observed: "Organists and instrument makers would gladly adopt this new arrangement of the keys. But would the great keyboard players of the future accept them?"[25]

Fritz's pragmatic orientation sometimes brought him into conflict with more conservative contemporaries. In 1751, the same year Heyne ordered his clavichord, Fritz was invited to provide a clavichord for a performance by a visiting celebrity: Carl Philipp Emanuel Bach, the second son of Johann Sebastian. Fritz astonished those present by tuning all of the strings on one of his large clavichords up a quarter-tone in the span of less than thirty minutes. His secret was tuning "by mechanical means." While most tuning methods of the era depended on extensive mathematical calculations, Fritz's approach required only careful listening. C. P. E. Bach's satisfaction with the result emboldened the maker to publish an account of his innovative method under the title *Guide to Tuning Clavichords, Harpsichords, and Organs in a Mechanical Fashion, So That They May Be Played in All Keys*.[26] The book had just twenty-four pages and was entirely pragmatic in orientation, eschewing all reference to mathematical calculations in favor of practical advice, very much in the spirit of galant-era literature. C. P. E. Bach himself endorsed Fritz's innovative approach, congratulating the author in a personal letter for "having said, in just a few pages, everything that was necessary and possible to say." He added that the book would be of "incomparably greater use than the many calculations over which others have broken their heads, considering that this type of guide is for everyone, including even those who are inclined to calculate, since they too depend upon their ears as much as everyone else."[27] Some of those who preferred to calculate, however, were not so enamored. Georg Andreas Sorge, an organist in Lobenstein and author of a three-hundred-page tome on tuning by means of mathematical calculation, was positively apoplectic.[28] He wrote a lengthy and scathing critique of Fritz's method, scoffing at the idea that a keyboard could be properly tuned with "a well-trained pair of ears and a tuning hammer alone."[29] Bridling at Fritz's neglect of mathematics, he accused the author of "abject niggling, defamation, vain and empty talk, self-love, and lying" and mocked him as a mere "mechanic" who had no business pontificating about music. One impartial observer of this conflict noted critically that Sorge treated Fritz as rudely as an "organist treats his calcant," i.e., the man who pumps his bellows.[30]

Fritz was undoubtedly shaken by Sorge's emotional diatribe. It was true that he was more mechanic than musician, but he felt that practical experience should count for something too. In the second edition of his treatise, amid skepticism of his accomplishments, Fritz attempted to bolster his authority by including an appendix that provided documentation: "In response to doubts that I have actually constructed over three hundred new clavichords—an achievement any keyboard maker would be hard-pressed to attain, particularly while simultaneously repairing older clavichords and building other instruments—I can think of no better response than to publish the names of those who received the new clavichords I made."[31]

There follows a list of 322 clavichords he had built between 1721 and the first quarter of 1757, along with names and descriptive terms (most often professions) associated with their buyers.[32] It is telling that the man responsible for the mechanical method of tuning should establish his authority by mechanically reproducing his entire sales log. Fritz never engaged Sorge's critique directly; his record spoke for itself.

Fritz's humility and pragmatism are encapsulated in an emblem he attached to every instrument he built. Just to the left of the bass notes one invariably finds an oval medallion of mother-of-pearl, tortoise-shell, ivory, and ebony that depicts a hand-carved landscape scene featuring rows of fertile soil and an enormous tree in the foreground. In the center is a draw well from which a bucket is suspended. To the right of the well is a tower, a wall, and a gatehouse that presumably offer entrance to the city looming in the background (see plate 4b). In selecting this image as his signum, Fritz invited his customers to see a parallel between the draw well and the clavichord. The instrument, despite its beauty and sophistication, was ultimately a simple tool, the product not of philosophical reverie but rather of sober engineering. Like the life-sustaining water drawn from a well, the thoughts, memories, and emotions that music inspired were brought about not by magic but rather by mechanics.

This image was of such personal importance to Fritz that he had it embedded in an engraved portrait commissioned toward the end of his life (see plate 4a). Perhaps by associating himself with this image he intended to suggest that his perspective remained that of a rural outsider looking in to the city. Whether or not his choice of image was autobiographical, it was certainly philosophical. Fritz was famously unmotivated by money; he refused to raise his prices under any circumstances and at the end of his life he willed his home and 200 reichstaler to Braunschweig's *Brüdernkirche* with the specification that the money should be used to support poor congregants.[33] No less than the instruments he fashioned, the maker saw himself as a humble tool, seeking to effect miraculous changes in the lives of his fellow citizens through mundane, mechanical actions.

ও

The tax collector Johann Heinrich Heyne was typical of Fritz's customers insofar as he was a bourgeois male resident of Braunschweig who was employed by the court. He had been born in Clausthal, a mining town several days' travel to the west but had spent his career in Braunschweig's sister city, Wolfenbüttel.[34] For the previous fifteen years he had served as customs and excise-tax collector at the court of Duke Karl I. The ducal court was in the process of officially relocating from Wolfenbüttel to Braunschweig, and like many court employees, Heyne was moving in advance.[35] He and his wife, as well as their seven children, would officially become citizens of Braunschweig the following May.[36]

The post of excise tax collector was typically entrusted to employees who evinced great loyalty and personal integrity. Men in such positions were often tempted to turn a blind eye to the corruption of their underlings, to overcharge foreign merchants ignorant of local tax laws, and to skim off the top of the funds they collected.[37] Over decades, Heyne had earned the trust of the dukes of Braunschweig-Wolfenbüttel and their administrators. In 1751 he received an annual salary of 336 reichstaler, considerably more than the 250 reichstaler earned by other court bureaucrats who purchased clavichords from Barthold Fritz.[38] His instrument would serve as a testament to his worldly success. Perhaps it would even inspire his seven children to follow similarly conservative paths in life. At least one of his sons would go on to lead a long and successful career of his own in Braunschweig's courtly bureaucracy.[39]

When Fritz first unveiled the new clavichord in February of 1751, Heyne was probably struck by the beauty of its diverse materials. The trees used in its construction were felled not only in Germany but also in South America: spruce for the soundboard; pine for the case; limewood for the key panel; oak for the wrest-plank, hitchpin rail, and balance rails; beechwood for the bridges underneath the strings; and pearwood for the keys. The strings were made of brass, an alloy of zinc ore from the Harz Mountains and copper likely mined in Sweden. The sharp keys were covered with the ivory of elephants trapped in nets in Guinea or perhaps Sri Lanka. It was the tax collector's job to tax imported natural materials like these, and he knew better than most how much they were worth.

The natural products Fritz had used to craft this instrument reflected Heyne's position at the apex of a vast production chain. The physical labor required to acquire and prepare the materials was undertaken by persons in intimate contact with the raw natural world: foresters who chopped down the trees and stripped the bark, millers who sawed the wood into boards, convicts who refined the wood with rasps in their prison cells, miners and smelters who dug up and forged the metals, and hunters who hacked the tusks off of struggling elephants. Some had been paid fairly for their labor, others unfairly, some not at all. Barthold Fritz, having assembled all of the component parts into this harmonious whole, served as Heyne's interface with, and insulation from, the natural world.

Before the clavichord was delivered to his home, Heyne decided to have its lid painted by a professional artist. While most keyboard owners were happy to settle for a bit of foliage, Heyne insisted that his new clavichord be decorated with an elaborate hunting scene (see plate 5). In his choice of subject, the tax collector swore allegiance to the social hierarchy he had devoted his entire career to upholding: the hunt was a pastime which celebrated the wealth and power of the few, of those who had so much food that they could afford to make sport of acquiring more.

In the hunting scene Heyne chose, a noble stag races through a wilderness landscape pursued by a pack of bloodthirsty hounds. The lead dog leaps at the stag's throat while the others jockey for position, eager to join in the carnage. Well-dressed men and women on horseback follow at some remove from the violence they have unleashed, spectators to the stag's final moments of freedom.

At one level, the painting celebrates control. The dark fallen trees, craggy rocks, and overgrown weeds that frame the scene allude to a world outside the painting which is rife with disorder. Viewers seek clarity in the forest clearing, where they are presented with a parable of human dominance. As the wild stag is brought down, civilization triumphs over nature, order over chaos. The hunters attain victory in galant fashion, maintaining a dignified distance from the carnage: horses do the chasing, dogs do the killing. On another level, the image offers a thrilling glimpse of violent disorder. Viewers identify not only with the hunters but also with the stag. Like thousands of other hunting scenes painted, etched, and engraved in Bach's time, this one is frozen at the point of greatest tension: when the beast of venery is about to lose its life. Viewers of such images were invited to consider, from a safe distance, the inevitability of death.

Like the painting, the clavichord itself both celebrated civilization's triumph and probed its limits. The instruments built by Barthold Fritz were engineered for compliance with galant social norms. Their luxurious materials and limited power to project made it unlikely that they would ever be performed in noisy or uncouth settings. Such instruments were built to avoid inspiring listeners to tap their feet, nod their heads, or otherwise abandon corporeal discipline. At the same time, the clavichord challenged listeners to express themselves creatively and thereby to explore the mysterious power of natural forces that could never be fully subject to human control. Like the painting, the clavichord offered a fleeting respite from the disorder of the real world. Music brought all ambient sounds into its tow, presenting the sonic equivalent of a forest clearing. The instrument would fill this space with a repertoire that intoned a single, fundamental theme: Johann Heinrich Heyne is a man worthy of respect and emulation.

CHAPTER 3

A Silver Merchant's Daughter

Buried deep in a thicket of eighteenth-century legal documents at the Leipzig City Archive lies a list of expenditures made by the daughter of a silver merchant.[1] Twenty-year-old Christiane Sibÿlla Bose spent her money in 1732 on the following items:

Table 2. Christiane Sibÿlla Bose Expenditures, 1732

Month	Expenses	Reichstaler	Groschen
January	Three ells of muslin fabric	.	–18
	One pair of shoes	.	–18
	Two black-and-white scarves	.	–22
March	One pair of silk gloves	–1	–8
	One black fan	.	–11
June	Food from January through June	–50	.
October	Sixteen ells of fabric for a house dress	–1	–20
	Nine ells of ratine cloth	–1	–3
	Import tax on the above	.	–2
	One piece of canvas	–8	.
	One black nightcap	.	–19
	Five ells of ribbon	.	–15
	One pair of black-and-white shoes	–1	.
November	To Herr Görner for keyboard lessons	–2	.
	For a pair of shoes	.	–18

Table 2. Continued

Month	Expenses	Reichstaler	Groschen
December	Lining for an *Andrienne* and a *Contouche* dress	−1	−4
	Gift for a godchild's baptism	−5	−8
	Other baptism-related expenses	−1	−6
	For having a hoop skirt covered	.	−20
	Tailor's bill	−9	.
	For having nightcaps knit	−1	.
	Food from July through December	−30	.
Total		−119	.

Hundreds of years after it was prepared, this payment ledger has the character of a still-life painting. It is an assortment of relics both random and coherent, offering a glimpse of a woman's life in a long-vanished time. The eye of the music historian naturally alights upon an item in the middle of the list: two reichstaler spent on keyboard lessons with Johann Gottlieb Görner, organist at Leipzig's St. Thomas Church.[2] Fräulein Bose's lessons with Görner are documented only by this and a few similar payments; no instruments, sheet music, letters, or diaries are known to survive. The other items on her account ledger, however, offer valuable context for her music making. The present chapter uses this list and other contemporary documents to explore the lives of female keyboardists in Bach's time.

≈

Christiane Sibÿlla Bose was baptized on January 1, 1712, the third of eleven children born to Georg Heinrich Bose and his wife, Eva Sibÿlla. In 1732 she was living with her mother, siblings, and servants in the family's lavish, four-story home across from Leipzig's St. Thomas Church. Valued at 9,800 reichstaler, their residence consisted of four masonry buildings gathered around a rectangular, cobblestone courtyard. It contained nineteen heated rooms connected horizontally by hallways and vertically by staircases of stone and wood. Family members and guests rode in horse-drawn carriages through front gates of filigreed iron and disembarked on the north side under a ceiling of arched stone. The building to the east enclosed water closets and kitchens that gleamed with pewter pots and monogrammed porcelain plates from Dresden, Delft, and East India. The building to the west contained bathing facilities and living quarters.[3] The building to the south included an armory as well as the *Sommersaal*, a large room for entertaining that featured plaster moldings, four enormous mirrors, and a gallery above the ceiling from which musicians could perform. A garden at the back of the property had apple, pear, and plum trees, a gazebo, a fountain, and a little wooden house from which hens could be heard cluck-ing and ruffling their feathers.[4]

The Bose family had become wealthy at the dawn of the galant era, having obtained exclusive privileges for mining and processing silver from the prince-electors of Saxony. Their primary source of income was a manufactory outside the city walls that employed some eight hundred workers, including about 150 married women, two hundred adolescent girls, fifty adolescent boys, and 150 children. Most spent their days spinning silver into wire or braiding it into lace, a product sold largely in eastern Europe.[5] Fräulein Bose's grandfather, Georg Bose, and great-uncle, Caspar Bose, had constructed spectacular gardens that had become hallmarks of Leipzig. For the price of a small tip to the gardener, men and women could walk among sandstone sculptures, carefully pruned coffee bushes, and greenhouses full of citrus trees, which could bloom even in the dead of winter.[6]

Although Christiane Sibÿlla Bose's father had died in 1731, the investments he had made on her behalf enabled her to maintain an extraordinarily comfortable lifestyle. Her personal income in 1732 amounted to more than 6159 reichstaler, of which the 119 reichstaler she spent constituted just 2 percent. Her greatest expenditure that year was a flat payment of eighty reichstaler for food. Leipzig cookbooks of the era are filled with exotic French recipes—snails and bacon seasoned with nutmeg flowers, chicken in sour cream and lemon sauce, veal in a caper-wine broth with raisins and cardamom—but the food Fräulein Bose ate most days was probably simpler.[7] A side of beef broiled on Sunday might be served all week, flavored with horseradish or parsley and supplemented with warm cucumber soup or applesauce.[8] Medical professionals tried to persuade patients that it was "possible over time to get used to drinking water, particularly if one begins doing so at an early age,"[9] but their arguments mostly fell on deaf ears. In an age when raw sewage contaminated urban water supplies, even toddlers routinely sipped beer and wine.[10]

C. S. Bose's second-largest expense—just over thirty reichstaler—was devoted to clothing. The garments she purchased were more elegant than practical, featuring expensive and delicate materials such as muslin, flax canvas, and ratine cloth imported from France or Holland. The house dress for which she bought fabric and the black nightcap she had knit were fashion items intended to give her guests the sense that they had earned her intimacy. The *Andrienne* dress she purchased had been popularized decades earlier by a French actress; it consisted of a broad, open robe with long sleeves and elaborate cuffs.[11] The hoop skirt that buoyed it around her waist was made of whale baleen that had once filtered krill in some distant ocean.

Fräulein Bose's third largest expense—around six reichstaler—went to the family of a newborn baby. On December 28, 1732, she stood over a baptismal font in Leipzig's St. Nicholas Church while an elderly pastor splashed water over the heads of twin girls born to a local wine merchant, one of whom had been named in her honor.[12] Agreeing to serve as godmother obliged her to offer the child a measure of financial support, beginning with five reichstaler at the baptism. This cash gift was supplemented by one additional reichstaler and six groschen for various other expenses, such as wine and sweets, donations to church officials, and tips for servants and nannies. She had presumably been chosen not only because she was wealthy but also because she was charitable to those of lower standing.

Instruction at the keyboard for which Fräulein Bose spent two reichstaler is the only item on the list that suggests a leisure-time occupation. For many German women her age, including the hundreds who worked in her family's silver manufactory, such an expense would have been unthinkable. Bose's extraordinary affluence, however, rendered the money her family spent on instruments, sheet music, and lessons a pecuniary afterthought. She might well have chosen to devote herself to other galant pastimes—for example, dancing, drawing, or learning French. In 1732, however, she chose to spend her leisure hours at the keyboard.

❧

Christiane Sibÿlla Bose's interest in music was probably inspired by her contact with the Bach family. In May 1723, when she was eleven years old, Johann Sebastian Bach, with his wife and four children, had moved into the St. Thomas School, directly across from her home. J. S. Bach would serve for the next twenty-seven years as cantor of St. Thomas and music director for the city of Leipzig, leading musical performances every Sunday morning. He and his wife felt close enough to the Bose family to invite Christiane Sibÿlla to serve as godmother and lend her name at the baptisms of Christiane Dorothea Bach in 1731 and Johann Christian Bach in 1735.

Fräulein Bose enjoyed a particularly close relationship with the cantor's wife, Anna Magdalena Bach. Perhaps they met regularly to talk on the *Muhmenplatz*, a park with four benches just behind St. Thomas School that had been built expressly for use by women with children.[13] Some December in the early 1740s, Frau Bach searched for a birthday present for her younger friend and settled upon a theological volume she herself had read with profit. She dedicated the book to Fräulein Bose with the following inscription:

> Upon the birthday of the noble, highly honorable and virtue-blessed
> maiden, maiden Christiane Sibÿlla Bose, my especially highly esteemed

maiden godmother and most worthy friend of my heart, Anna Magdalena Bach wishes the best with this small though well-meaning memento.[14]

This small but well-meaning memento was a 1,284-page meditation on suffering. The author, Johann Jacob Rambach, saw the behavior of Jesus Christ as a model for coping with life's trials: "When Christ asked Peter, 'Should I not drink from the cup, which my father has given to me?' he indicated that God had chosen this suffering for him. We should bear this thought in mind, when our own flesh and blood rebels against pain. Bitter agony can be made sweet when we recognize that it has been sent to us from on high. It is a cup filled by the hand of our Father, who offers his children not poison but medicine."[15] Among the passages that perhaps resonated most with Anna Magdalena Bach and Christiane Sibÿlla Bose were those that dealt with the pain of children dying, an experience they knew all too well: "God often spares his children the suffering for which they are destined by granting them an early death, just as death spared Christ the pain of his leg being broken on the cross. Through early death, God often brings His children into safety and puts them at peace before the floodgates of His justice break open and overwhelm everything, or before the world's evil intentions for the child can be realized."[16]

Childbearing and childhood itself were fraught with danger in early eighteenth-century Germany. A Leipzig woman of Fräulein Bose's generation who became pregnant five times faced one-in-ten odds of dying in childbirth. The danger was even more acute for the children she conceived, six in ten of whom would die before reaching puberty.[17] Anna Magdalena Bach was pregnant or nursing throughout the 1720s and 1730s. By 1732, five of her nine children had already died, including the baby girl she had named after Christiane Sibÿlla Bose. The following year she would suffer the devastating loss of her five-year-old daughter, Regina Johanna Bach. Fräulein Bose had not yet had any children of her own, but she had attended the funerals of her father and two siblings. She herself would go on to have only one child, a son, who died in 1746, shortly after his birth.

ৰ

The goal Bach's society mandated for women was not to contribute to the world's knowledge, to create lasting works of art, or to make a fortune; it was rather to "redeem Eve's sin" by bearing children.[18] The central challenge of their early lives was to negotiate the transition from the homes of their fathers to the homes of their husbands. Demographers of the era maintained two separate categories for adult females: married women (*Frauen*) and unmarried women (*Wittibe*), a category that included those who had never wed and widows alike, who "at least for a while had the pleasure of being called a Frau."[19] Little girls filled their leisure hours by staging make-believe weddings or baby baptisms.[20] They sought to hear their future husbands' professions by listening to soup bubbling in the oven on Christmas Eve between 11 P.M. and midnight, or to glimpse his countenance by cracking eggs in water and examining the yolk as it dispersed. Older girls tried to divine the time of their betrothal by throwing shoes backward toward an open door: if a shoe flew out into the hallway, this was the year that someone would take them away.[21]

A common dictum of the era held that women should leave their homes just three times in their lives: to be baptized, to be married, and to be buried.[22] Another suggested that a woman without a house was like a snail without a shell.[23] Such talk was not to be taken literally: women in Leipzig frequently left their homes to attend baptisms, weddings, and funerals, to participate in public worship services, to shop, walk the linden-tree-lined path that encircled the city, or to visit relatives and friends. Yet the spirit of these expressions reflects how closely women were aligned with their dwellings: time spent outside the home was transitional. The girls deemed most attractive were those whose countenances were conspicuously untouched by the effects of the sun.[24] Bright white skin indicated that a young lady had spent her time at home, comfortable and secure under the yoke of parental authority.

Parents and educators sought to instill in girls a firm sense of personal discipline. They were sometimes reprimanded or even slapped for looking around furtively or for staring. One young lady caught playing idly got an angry look from her grandmother, who found her explanation—"I have nothing to do"—nonsensical: "What? When a girl doesn't know what to do, she should cut a hole in her apron and stitch it up again."[25] Authors of the era encouraged women to suppress their feelings: "Girls are made for living at home. Their inevitable disappointments they cannot dispel outside the house, as men do. Rather, they must bear their sorrow silently and without witness. They must press their sour moods into their hearts, and not allow them to be displayed on their faces, assiduously showing a joyful and chipper countenance."[26] Momentary losses of composure could lead to draconian physical punishments, the most common of which was the birch rod. Perhaps Fräulein Bose had experiences comparable to those of a female writer of the era, who described this particularly memorable event of her childhood:

> One evening, when my wardress was removing my clothing and bringing me to bed, she bound my nightcap onto my head so clumsily that she drove a hairpin deep into my scalp. I unwillingly let out a scream. Blood ran down onto my face and my grandmother hurried in to ask what had happened.

I quickly fell to my knees at her feet, pleaded for forgiveness, and told her that I had hit my head, worried that if I told the truth she would severely punish my beloved wardress. My grandmother smacked me roughly on the head a couple of times and told me to be more careful in the future. I felt an unspeakable relief at having managed to spare my dear wardress a beating. As my grandmother turned to leave, my aunt's daughter, who had witnessed the entire spectacle, came and informed her that both I and my wardress deserved a hearty punishment, because that which I had reported had been a lie: the carelessness of my wardress had driven a needle into my head. My grandmother furiously attacked the wardress, struck her and sent her to fetch a bundle of rods with which to cane me. The poor woman, tears of love streaming down her face, was forced to hold me down and watch as my grandmother whipped me with the rods. After this was over, I was made to watch as my wardress was pushed down and beaten twenty times. My heart compressed painfully and all of my limbs trembled, but I could not allow myself to emit a single sound lest the poor woman, now even more dear to me, have her punishment doubled. After our beatings, my wardress brought me to bed. I kissed her hands and she kissed mine. We asked one another for forgiveness and offered mutual assurances that the blows had not hurt at all. From this hour on we felt the tenderest feelings for one another, and these feelings lasted until her death about ten years ago, and even extend in my heart to the children of that dear woman.[27]

This account reflects not only the rivalries and violence of domestic life but also the warm feelings that could exist between women of the same household, even those of quite different social strata.

Fräulein Bose and her sisters were likely educated less thoroughly than their brothers. As one contributor to the Hamburg periodical *Der Patriot* lamented in 1724: "We take much less care in educating our daughters than in educating our sons, and believe this to be justified. We feel that the learned sciences are of no use to women, because—owing to natural female weaknesses—such knowledge would be misused, and for this reason we let our daughters grow up in the thickest ignorance."[28] The Bose girls were tutored on the basis of Hilmar Curas's *Introduction to Universal History in which the Most Notable Events from the Beginning of the World until the Present Day Are Presented in Question-and-Answer Format*, from which they learned that in the year 1732 the world was exactly 5,682 years old and that the most important events thus far had been the Great Flood and the birth of Christ.[29] She and her siblings were also made to read Johann Anastasius Freylinghausen's *Compendium or Brief Description of all Christian Teachings*, which emphasized the three levels (*Haupt-Stände*) on which God intended for Christian society to be structured, in descending order of importance: the church, the government, and the home.[30]

University study was restricted to men. The rare woman who persevered in academia was likened to a tourist who had arrived in a foreign country without knowing why she had traveled there.[31] Because women were forbidden from working in the professions, there seemed little point in their acquiring knowledge beyond the basics. Dorothea Christiane Erxleben (née Leporin) received in 1754 the first doctoral degree awarded to a German woman, but she herself, in a treatise advocating women's access to the university, reluctantly admitted that her contemporaries were not quite ready for true gender equality: "It is not to be denied that it would be rather difficult for a woman who pursues a university education to simultaneously run a large and complex household. But this is no reason to lose heart, because I do not suggest that every woman pursue an academic career and spend all of her time studying. I suggest, rather, that the household duties be reduced somewhat so that her intellect might be cultivated. In this way [. . .] she would merely be unlearned rather than crudely ignorant."[32]

The highest academic hurdle of most German women's lives was the test administered at around age fifteen for confirmation in the Christian church. Under the tutelage of pastors, organists, and schoolmasters, girls memorized long passages from Luther's *Kleiner Katechismus* of 1529, reprinted dozens of times in the early eighteenth century. It began:

> QUESTION: Do you believe yourself to be a sinner?
> ANSWER: Yes, I am a sinner.
> QUESTION: How do you know that?
> ANSWER: Because I know I have not obeyed the Ten Commandments.
> QUESTION: Are you sorry for having sinned?
> ANSWER: Yes, I am sorry that I have sinned against God.
> QUESTION: What have your sins earned you from God?
> ANSWER: His wrath and disgrace, an early death, and eternal damnation.[33]

Perhaps like other girls of the era, Fräulein Bose had impressed her confirmation instructor by asking questions that conveyed a deep, personal interest in sacred writ.[34] Perhaps she had demonstrated her skills by reading verses for her parents, siblings, and servants before bed.[35] Girls of the era were encouraged to remember from year to year what their pastors had said about particular passages of the Bible. Some became so steeped in the holy scriptures that Apostles appeared to them in dreams.[36]

❧

Beyond mastering household skills, exhibiting a tractable demeanor, and cultivating an unshakable fear of God, women of Christiane Sibÿlla Bose's social class made themselves attractive to potential suitors by embracing courtly galanterie. In 1711 J. S. Bach's organist colleague at the St. Thomas Church, Christian Gräbner, published a book on childrearing in which he asked rhetorically: "Where can a woman find the best opportunity to make herself *galant?*" His answer: "At court. Though I have found sinful behavior everywhere in the world, the converse is also true, and a well-furnished court can be viewed as a microcosm of the *galant* world. As it is not the custom for women to attend university, they can view the court as their academy, because it is well known that the women of the court are especially worthy of praise, having finally bid their farmers' pride *adieu.*"[37] Whether from direct observation, from books, or from secondhand reports, women learned how to walk, to properly place their silverware, and to greet persons of varied social stations with correct bows and curtsies.

Beyond appearances, women like Fräulein Bose were encouraged to "achieve greater perfection" by supplementing the basic "requirements of an honest and *galant* woman" through the pursuit of courtly leisure-time activities. Among the most popular of these were dancing and making music.[38] The study of dance was justified on the grounds that it encouraged good posture and helped young women to master the complex system of reverences for members of different social classes.[39] Fräulein Bose had probably spent many hours in her youth being herded across makeshift ballrooms by dancemasters wielding pocket violins. She would have memorized the steps of English ensemble and French couple dances such as the courante, the minuet, and the bourrée.[40] Dancing was deemed better suited to women than to men, because women were thought to have a "friendlier" disposition, but the prospect of too much friendliness on the dance floor was a perennial source of concern.[41] Some argued that dancing was nothing but an exhibition of "unspiritual, ungodly, and dangerous gestures" intended to inflame the sinful passions of participants and onlookers alike.[42] One of Fräulein Bose's neighbors in Leipzig wrote a poem envisioning Cupid, the love god, standing in the middle of a lavish ballroom, indiscriminately shooting his arrows into the dancers, with counts falling in love with tailors' daughters and noble girls giving their hearts to humble scribes.[43] Especially pious women of the era felt so torn between the pleasures of dancing and their guilt at forfeiting salvation that they executed their *pliés* and *pas de deux* with tears streaming down their cheeks.[44]

Music making was comparatively uncontroversial, having been sanctioned in the Bible by King David, who encouraged his followers to praise God with cymbals, lutes, harps, tambourines, and trumpets. Even the most conservative mainstream theologians regarded sacred music as a force for good in the world. Christian Gräbner argued that music could bring moral benefits to young ladies: "Music is worth pursuing, though only if nature has endowed the young woman with a pleasant voice, or made her skilled in the playing of instruments. Music making, particularly singing, is an excellent adornment for women, as is proved by the fact that many achieve their greatest happiness through this art. In addition, music has the excellent characteristic of being able to turn a person of raw and poor moral character toward a proper manner of living."[45]

Music's power to improve morals stemmed not only from the sacred content of the repertoire but also from the isolation it imposed. Whereas dancing was a social endeavor, one could credibly enjoy music's pleasure in solitude. A skillful solo performance served as a testament not only to talent and discipline but also to tractability. Like extremely fair skin, it indicated that a young lady had spent her leisure time indoors, sequestered from worldly temptation.[46] Keyboards and lutes were ideally suited to female performers because they were chordal instruments—that is, they were sufficient unto themselves, providing both melody and accompaniment. It is no accident that Fräulein Bose's brothers studied the flute and the violin, while she and her sisters studied the lute and keyboard.[47]

Composers and publishers encouraged the view that practicing such instruments was morally edifying for girls and women. The engraved frontispiece to Johann Kuhnau's *Musicalische Vorstellung Einiger Biblischer Historien* (Leipzig, 1700)—a collection of programmatic keyboard pieces based on Biblical narratives—depicts a young, long-haired woman in a flowing dress playing a chamber organ in a large room (see plate 6). The lady musician looks to her left toward a table bearing the *Biblia Sacræ*. Behind her is another table upon which a clavichord awaits her touch. Ornate, carved moldings and elaborate frescoes with florid borders adorn the walls, signaling her family's prosperity. The emptiness of the high-ceilinged room emphasizes the player's solitude and serves as a visual analogue for her copious leisure time. Her pose suggests enthusiastic engagement: she is so engrossed in this musical rendition of biblical narratives that she ignores the viewer entirely. A male relative—presumably one of the men whose worldly success furnished her with wealth and leisure time—looks down from a portrait above the door, mutely watching over her as she practices. She appears to be thoroughly at peace with this arrangement, unperturbed by the benign gaze of parental authority. The image seems to suggest that for the price of this published collection (thirty-two groschen), parents might not only fill their homes with music but also purchase tractability from their daughters.[48]

The notion that the keyboard could serve as a means of keeping girls at home is invoked more explicitly in a song from the bestselling collection of Fräulein Bose's Leipzig: Johann Sigismund Scholze's *Sperontes' Singende Muse an der Pleiße* (1736–1745). The poetic speaker is an unmarried woman who simultaneously sings and accompanies herself at the keyboard:

Shall I name my favorite treasure,
That which brings me greatest pleasure?
Surely it's the work of art,
Which best satisfies my heart.
My *clavier*
Brings my ear
Joy from which I will not part.

Joking, laughing, dancing, card games,
Are the things which often lay claims
On the free time of my kind,
But to them I pay no mind.
When I hear,
My *clavier*,
Joy in solitude I'll find.

Often in the mirror glancing,
Daily going out and dancing,
That is what some like to do,
Fashion they will e'er pursue.
I'll stay near
My *clavier*
And such drollery eschew.

Visit gardens! Go out walking!
Ride in coaches! Spend time talking!
Take his hand! Give him a kiss!
These are things I'll gladly miss.
Let me hear,
My *clavier*,
For a few more hours of bliss.

How your tedium now waxes,
Feeding indolence and laxness!
As the tangents strike each string
I can never fail to sing.
It is clear,
My *clavier*
Ever will amusement bring.

Daily chores sap all my power,
Though it's late I've still an hour,
What can then my heart delight?

> What can put my cares to flight?
> Let me hear,
> My *clavier,*
> Play a song to say good night.[49]

Unwholesome pastimes such as playing cards, chasing fashion, or kissing men in the park are presented as afflictions the keyboard can cure. Music provided relief from the stresses of life, and yet the asocial nature of practicing ensured virtuous isolation. Three of the song's five stanzas end with lines emphasizing solitude: "only to pass the time alone" (*Nur zum Zeitvertreib allein*), "sit for several hours" (*Manches Stündchen sitzen kann*) and "remain in quiet privacy" (*Und verbleib' in stiller Ruh'*). The melody of the song itself has a lilting naïveté that underscores the calculated innocence of the text. In this fantasy, the clavier plays the role that will eventually be adopted by the speaker's husband: it satisfies her heart, comforts her, entertains her, encourages her to remain at home, and wishes her a good night.

The image of the musical instrument as surrogate husband is evoked explicitly in a drama published in 1747 in Leipzig by Christian Fürchtegott Gellert. The main character is a young princess named Lucinde who finds herself at the mercy of competing desires. At the outset, she is completely innocent and knows nothing of the opposite sex, having spent her early life at the keyboard. But after a man sees her sleeping and falls deeply in love, he employs an elderly female magician to help him win her heart. Lucinde delivers a soliloquy that exposes the tension between her long-held emotional attachment to her keyboard and the desires kindled within her by this mysterious suitor:

> What feelings do I feel!
> Thoughts that heat my blood.
> As much as reason tries to fight them off,
> So much more does my heart protect them.
> How? A male person . . . A man!
> A man! Who . . . What is it that I saw?
> My whole heart begins to feel.
> I want to play a piece on the *clavier*
> To drive away my displeasure.

> (She goes toward the harpsichord, but stops and turns around.)

> But now it occurs to me:
> I should have gone with that magical lady;
> She was spying on me before; I should have spied on her.
> That way we could have seen him together:

We could have gone to him very gently,
And we would have caught him.

(She goes once more toward the harpsichord, but again stops
    and turns around.)

But how should I understand this?
She goes, and asks me not to come with her.
And as we were speaking of men,
She mentioned that she had made many mistakes,
And yet she did not describe any of them.
Perhaps she has left me here behind,
So that I won't see that man anymore,
Because she wants him for herself.
That old lady should be ashamed,
Trying to take this man away from me.
No, no, she can take anything else from me.
I will remain content; just don't take him![50]

For Lucinde the harpsichord was much more than a means of driving away displeasure; it represented a youthful idyll, a pre-lapsarian past. Having now been bewitched by the world's temptations, Lucinde is faced with the terrifying prospect of navigating an actual human relationship. She struggles to return to her instrument, but having fallen in love with a living, breathing man, she can no longer be satisfied by a surrogate.

&

Skillful performances by female keyboardists were frequently interpreted as reflecting well on the men in their lives. Perhaps Christiane Sibÿlla Bose had experiences like this one imagined by Friedrich Wilhelm Marpurg in 1749: "The young, charming Phyllis lets herself, after one polite refusal, be persuaded to play. The guests assemble themselves around the harpsichord according to the legal dress code. The skill of her hands is worthy of wonder. She does her master proud. Only her wooden listeners are unmoved. They honorably relax one after the next and slide to the backs of their chairs."[51] The audience in Marpurg's account is more absorbed in the stilted pageantry of the gathering than in the music itself. Phyllis's skilled hands could not sustain the attention of those ignorant of music, though they nonetheless raised her keyboard teacher in the audience's estimation.

Perhaps in her youth Fräulein Bose had experiences like that of the daughter of a wealthy merchant in Hamburg. On February 26, 1710, two brothers from Frankfurt—Johann Friedrich Armand von Uffenbach and Zacharias Conrad von Uffenbach—visited the home of her father, Henning Lochau, recording their experiences in a travel diary:

We went at nine in the morning to the home of Herr Licentiat Lochau, who first served us tea, which was poured by his intelligent and artful wife.[52] After we had imbibed a little, Herr Lochau led us up to his study, though he first showed us around the lower part of his house, and then up to a little room in which we found a number of really beautiful works of visual art. On the ground floor the most famous was a large piece by Rubens that depicted some nymphs and satyrs and for which he had been offered 800 reichstaler. [. . .] Also in the corner there were around 30 little tables of parchment, on which models with Augsburg costumes had been skillfully painted. In the study we first saw some books—mostly historical—but we moved quickly to see his collection of coins. These were in four little cases stacked in pairs of two, but which could be lifted for examination. Altogether there were perhaps five or six hundred reichstaler, including a large number of imperial exemplars, some of which were rare [. . .]. He also showed us a catalog of his collection thicker than a hand which he had made himself according to history and genealogy of the coins. [. . .] Finally Herr Lochau showed us a collection of around three hundred and seventy folios depicting flowers and plants, which had been drawn from life by a Dutchman on the basis of examplars in his gardens. They are certainly beautiful, and there are many rare plants among them. Herr Lochau, however, makes too much of these paintings, as he does of all of his possessions. He thinks that it is something truly special to use oil paints on paper, and acts as if this were his own invention. But here he is certainly wrong, since I have seen plenty of other examples. [. . .] He came to this pursuit by means of the four beautiful gardens which he inherited from his father-in-law, the mayor of Schafhausen. Lastly his daughter, who was about fifteen years old, had to sing for us, and to accompany herself with figured bass [at the keyboard], which she did quite well.[53]

All points in the Uffenbachs' choreographed tour of the Lochau household were calculated to draw attention to their host's wealth and intellectual acumen. The Rubens painting he had acquired for much less than its true value was a testament to his investment savvy. The renderings-in-oil of the foliage in his gardens were further proof of his extraordinary wealth but also vouched for his academic interest in the natural sciences. His ancient coins were more valuable than their contemporary counterparts and yet above the fray of modern commerce. Hoarding such largesse carried no implications of avarice and manifested Lochau's interest in ancient civilizations. His daughter's musical performance had certainly required a significant financial investment (for example, purchasing an instrument, paying for lessons, granting her time away from darning socks to practice), but his wealth alone was more effectively displayed by paintings and coins. The appeal of this performance, from Herr Lochau's perspective, was the display of his parenting skills. He and his wife had raised their daughter to spend her days sequestered, cultivating keyboard skills that could be displayed on his command.

A few years after their visit to Hamburg, on February 24, 1715, the brothers von Uffenbach found themselves in Venice at the home of the Prussian ambassador, Wilhelm von Willers, where they heard a performance by another talented woman:[54]

> In the afternoon we visited the Prussian ambassador to Venice, Herr von Willers, whose well-furnished apartments were decorated with many good, though mostly modern paintings. His best, though not his most beautiful piece of furniture was his wife, who is a real virtuosa in music. Her keyboard playing and her admirable voice—accompanied by an abbot on the bass— made the time pass incomparably. We stayed for quite a while.[55]

The description of Frau von Willers as her husband's "best, though not his most beautiful piece of furniture" suggested that her virtuosic performance compensated for her only modest beauty. The von Uffenbachs, and perhaps also visitors to the Bose household, evaluated musical performances in terms of the degree to which they raised a woman's teacher, father, or husband in the estimation of those who heard her perform.

❧

We might imagine Christiane Sibÿlla Bose, in the autumn of 1732, on the day of one of her keyboard lessons with Johann Gottlieb Görner. She probably came to her senses at around six o'clock in the morning. Perhaps she was awakened by tiny hammers pounding bells inside a gravity-driven alarm clock, by sunlight seeping in through windows of wavy glass, or by her mother, a sister, or a servant. Rolling off of a horsehair and straw-stuffed mattress, she would have splashed some water on her face and offered a prayer for God's continued forbearance:

Oh God in Heav'n with all Your might
You did create this sphere,
I have through the entire night,
Slept calmly, without fear;
I woke up feeling satisfied,
In health and without pain;
I look upon the sun outside,
And thank You for Your reign.
Allow me through this blessed day
To live according to Your way!
Help me to always keep my feet,
Upon Your path in place,
And give to all that I complete,
Your blessing and Your grace![56]

A servant woman would have helped Fräulein Bose to pin her hair and don some clothing, perhaps her housedress with the matching black nightcap.[57] Hurrying into one of the larger rooms in her home, she would have assumed an accustomed place next to her family members and servants, grateful for the warmth emanating from a wood-burning ceramic oven. More prayers would have been spoken and hymns sung before she received a chunk of heavy bread—mostly rye or bran with a few stray pieces of straw or hair from the threshing-room floor—which she probably washed down with a shot of brandy.[58]

Even affluent women like Christiane Sibÿlla Bose typically engaged in household chores. She may have spent part of the morning peeling apples, shelling peas, sorting seeds, plucking hops for beer, or twisting wicks for candles.[59] Perhaps she wove lace and spun wool, flax, hemp, or hards into yarn, keeping her feet warm by working the pedals of spinning wheels. The finished fabric could be used for nightgowns, tablecloths, napkins, and curtains. She, her mother, and her sisters may have devoted time to repairing worn-out materials: threadbare middle sections of sheets could be scrolled over to the side and cut out, socks were darned two or three times, and stains from wine or axel grease were removed with fatty candle wax and ash.[60] If it was the week of the "Big Wash" (*die große Wäsche*), a deep-cleaning process that involved coordinating the work of up to fifteen day laborers, Fräulein Bose might have guided the hired help in scrubbing washbasins in the courtyard, channeling water from wooden pipes into troughs, and soaking undershirts, wristbands, nightcaps, kitchen rags, and wool blankets in a mixture of lye, ash, and soap before they were hung out to dry on rented hills beyond the city walls. Perhaps she helped her mother make sure the laborers weren't wasting firewood, candles, or water, improperly folding laundry or stealing rags, or consuming too much veal, coleslaw, or beer.[61]

Fräulein Bose likely spent time on the day of a lesson caring for a sick family member. Disease was thought to spread primarily through the air, so the key to staying healthy was to avoid unpleasant odors. The Bose home had better plumbing than most houses of the era, but wooden tubs were probably used more often for salting fish than for bathing. The primary means of avoiding noxious fumes was to apply topical fragrances. Perhaps she mixed perfumes from rose hips, lemon extract, cinnamon, and nutmeg, or prepared fragrant skin balms from white bread crumbs, chopped lemons, black snails, melon seeds, and camphor.[62] Published manuals offered guidance in the preparation of elixirs and powders intended to cure everything from bleeding gums to indigestion.[63] If she was like other men and women of the era, she invited a barber-surgeon several times per year to drain her arm or leg of what was believed to be bad blood.

As she prepared for the arrival of her music teacher, Fräulein Bose probably spent some time practicing a clavichord or harpsichord in one of the larger rooms in her family's home, perhaps one of those with the bay windows overlooking the St. Thomas Church courtyard. Maybe she wore her pleated *Contouche* dress along with her matching black-and-white scarf and shoes. Surrounded by porcelain bowls and tea sets, fine oil paintings, and gleaming scientific instruments, she would have run through the chorale preludes and galanterien her teacher had copied for her over the past several weeks.[64]

At some point perhaps she took a break from practicing and opened the second-story window of her family's home on the St. Thomas Church courtyard in Leipzig. She would have heard sparrows on rooftops, nightingales whistling from balcony cages, and the gentle splashing sounds of water falling from the stone lion fountain in front of the St. Thomas Church.[65] She likely heard the grinding of iron wheels and the clopping of horses' hooves over cobblestone streets, accompanied by the shrill sound of a little horn signaling that the mail coach was departing. At the top of the hour, she certainly heard the bells of the Nikolaikirche followed by the much closer sound of the bells of the Thomaskirche.[66] Perhaps she also heard coachmen screeching down entire city blocks, trying to entice university boys into taking joyrides.[67] If she stood at the window long enough she might have heard a pest exterminator walking onto the courtyard chanting "Rat poison, Mouse poison! Here is the man!"; a knife sharpener calling out "Scissor sharpening, scissor and knife sharpening!"; or a Jewish merchant intoning "Lemons and limes! Autumn olives!"[68]

There was plenty of actual music that emanated from the streets as well. At ten o'clock she could have heard city pipers blowing stentorian brass chords from the balcony of the Renaissance city hall. At twelve or two o'clock she could have heard drum rolls and the piping of oboe bands accompanying military drills in front of the Pleissenburg castle behind her home.[69] Perhaps she heard ensembles of six to twelve black-robed boys from the St. Thomas School known as *Kurrende* (walking) groups singing hymns in the street, encouraging listeners to send a servant down to drop a few heavy coins into jangling donation boxes.[70] She likely also heard itinerant street musicians performing bizarre arrangements of opera arias on bagpipes, trumpets, and fiddles,[71] or a homeless beggar warbling through a Lutheran chorale melody, hoping to persuade pious listeners that he knew the suffering and redemption evoked in lyrics like "Whoever trusts in God will never again come to grief."[72]

From her window, Christiane Sibÿlla Bose could have watched Johann Gottlieb Görner exit the St. Thomas Church and walk past the stone lion fountain before disappearing beneath the arched entrance to her family home. He would have announced himself to the servants on the ground floor before ascending the winding, marble-lined staircase to the music room. Upon seeing Fräulein Bose, he would have bowed deeply, his powdered wig quivering as his right arm, hat in hand, swept out to the side.[73]

Herr Görner was thirty-five years old in 1732 and could already look back on a distinguished career in a highly competitive field. The son of an organist in a small town south of Leipzig, he had received a scholarship to attend the St. Thomas School under Bach's predecessor, Johann Kuhnau. He later studied at Leipzig University and while still a student had received a coveted appointment as university organist. From there he had moved through a series of increasingly prestigious positions: organist at the Church of St. Nicholas, music director at the Church of St. Paul, and—beginning in 1729—organist at the St. Thomas Church.

Not everyone was impressed with Görner's skills. One critic grumbled that his compositions were a horribly disorganized cacophony in which "the grossest blunders adorn every measure." The same writer alleged that his personality was characterized by "arrogance and crudeness [. . .] the former preventing him from knowing himself and the latter making him stand out in a very large crowd."[74] J. S. Bach was among those who was sometimes frustrated by Görner. The two men had bickered over royalties from a performance in the University Church. After they became colleagues at the St. Thomas Church, Bach had once become so irritated with Görner's playing that he ripped his own wig off and threw it at the organist's head, thundering that the man "should have been a shoe patcher" rather than a musician.[75]

Upon Herr Görner's arrival, Fräulein Bose would have curtsied politely, offered a pleasantry or two, and taken her place at the keyboard.[76] Lessons often began with some scales and arpeggios or other exercises intended to improve finger dexterity. If Görner was like other teachers of the era, he would have insisted that his student sit so that her upper arms were perfectly perpendicular to her forearms, which were to remain parallel to the floor. Her fingers were to curl slightly, perching gently on the ebony and ivory keys. As she concentrated on the notes and rhythms, he may have admonished her not to twist her mouth absentmindedly or allow her jaw to go slack.[77]

The repertoire she played would have consisted primarily of Lutheran chorale preludes. Her father was among the dedicatees of Daniel Vetter's two-volume "Musical Church and House Delight" (*Musicalische Kirch- und Hauß-Ergötzlichkeit*) published in 1709 and 1713.[78] The title page describes the contents as "consisting of the ordinary spiritual songs, sung throughout the year in public church services, set in an entirely comfortable and light manner [. . .] whereby each chorale is set for the organ and then in a broken variation to be played on the spinet or clavichord."

Fräulein Bose probably played galanterien as well. Other Görner pupils learned to play marches, arias, bourrées, sarabandes, gigues, courantes, allemandes, and passepieds, some of his own composition.[79] Bose's keyboard notebook likely included some secular songs as well, perhaps some even in the hand of her friend Anna Magdalena Bach. Given the close connections to the Bach family, it stands to reason that some of the music Fräulein Bose studied had been composed by Johann Sebastian himself. If she played a single movement by Bach, it was most likely the "Giga" from the first *Keyboard Partita* (BWV 825/7), which had appeared for the first time in 1726 and was fast becoming his best-known work. The "Giga" owed its popularity to hand-crossing: in nearly every measure, the left hand is required to leap over the right hand and back again, adding a visual element to the auditory entertainment. Perhaps Görner stood over Fräulein Bose and used a pencil to mark "l" (left hand) and "r" (right hand) over the pitches, as did other teachers of the era.[80]

After a while, the bells of the St. Thomas Church would have signaled the end of the lesson, and Görner would have taken his leave. Perhaps Fräulein Bose watched through the bay windows as her teacher exited the large gate to her home, passed the lion fountain again, and disappeared through the door of the St. Thomas Church. She might then have gone back to practicing, eager to improve the accuracy of her hand-crossing. Sometimes her fingers hit the right keys, but the next time they bungled things up again. Just as men and women pulled weeds and trimmed hedges in her family's opulent gardens on the outskirts of town, she honed the music until she felt it was ready for performance before friends, family, and guests. Only through discipline could raw nature be brought to a state of perfection.

Fräulein Bose's course of instruction in music was brought to an abrupt halt on February 1, 1733, by the death of August II, prince-elector of Saxony and king of Poland. The father of the country (*Landesvater*) was officially mourned for five months.[81] Church alters were draped in black.[82] Ordinary citizens avoided sumptuous meals and dressed modestly. Servants wore dark robes from dawn until dusk. Not a single musical tone was permitted anywhere in the realm from February until July. To celebrate life during a period of mourning was to insult the dead. Professional musicians, facing a dramatic loss of income, did what they could to get around such restrictions. Herr Görner himself was known to argue that the music he made with his *Collegium Musicum* was educational rather than merely entertaining and should therefore be exempt from the ban.[83] But Christiane Sibÿlla Bose is unlikely to have infringed upon the official period of silent mourning; the prince-elector and others in his dynastic line had personally done much to further the interests of her own family. In all likelihood, she was genuinely upset by the prince-elector's death and would have hung a black cloth over her instrument, proudly defying her own will to play. Perhaps in weaker moments, however, she followed the practice of other women of the era, perusing scores while lying in bed, fantasizing about accompanying famous opera singers while her fingers pressed imaginary keys.[84]

❧

Women were generally forbidden from becoming professional musicians. In rare cases, however, they were able to pursue professional careers in which music played a prominent role. One of the paths to doing so was to serve as governess to a wealthy family.[85] The character of this work varied widely from one context to the next, but it often involved a combination of looking after children, teaching, entertaining, cooking, and making music. In a quasi-fictional diary published by an English traveler named Thomas Lediard, the narrator describes visiting a wealthy man in Hamburg around 1727 whose governess not only cooked and served him tea but also made music: "*Madame la Gouvernante* play'd the Thorough-Bass, on the Harpsichord, and sung several Songs, which she accompanied herself, while my Friend play'd the Bass-Viol. However, she frequently rose, and surrender'd her Place to another, while she served us with Tea and Coffee, and, for the greater Variety, gave us two or three *Solo's* on the Lute."[86] In 1751 the playwright and translator Luise Adelgunde Victorie Gottsched wrote a letter to an unidentified acquaintance encouraging her to apply for work as a governess, suggesting, "Your beautiful handwriting, your talent in drawing, your skills at the keyboard, give you a rightful claim to the best of such positions, insofar as the perfection of the intellect is concerned."[87]

Professional opportunities for musically gifted women were occasionally available at court as well. In 1739 Frau Gottsched wrote a letter to a friend, Count Ernst Christoph von Manteuffel, on behalf of an unnamed young woman who sought employment as a lady-in-waiting (*Hofdame*) at the Prussian court in Berlin. Her chief selling point was rare skill on the lute:

> Now allow me to beg a favor of your Excellence. I ask not for myself, but rather on behalf of an art that has climbed so high it need not work for bread. There is a woman here who plays an excellent lute. I have never heard Weiss perform, but she outplays all masters that I know. The jealousy of others has robbed her of all hope for finding work in Dresden, where she has to this point been in the courtly service of a certain princely person. She would consider herself very lucky if she could find employment either with the queen or the crown princess. If I could entertain the hope that

your Excellence take up her cause by speaking with Herr Reinbeck, I would be beholden to you for the rest of my life. This woman is strong not only in music; she also draws very artfully, knits very beautifully, and knows everything that belongs to serving a high aristocrat. She desires nothing more than to stand among the ladies-in-waiting to such a princess. This would reduce the payment that she would otherwise require. She is prepared to come to Berlin and show herself if only she could entertain the hope that the journey would not be undertaken in vain.[88]

The Dresden court of Augustus the Strong, prince-elector of Saxony and king of Poland, occasionally employed female keyboardists. On February 23, 1728, Pierre Baron de Gaultier—Augustus's "Director of the Royal Pleasures" (*Directeur derer Königl. Plaisirs*)—submitted an order to a bureaucrat to pay an annual salary (beginning retroactively on January 1 of the same year) to a musician he described as "DuMasy, lady keyboard player" (*DuMasy, joueuse de Clavecin*).[90] The order was initialed by the prince-elector himself, but because Gaultier neglected to specify the payment amount, the musician in question did not receive her salary, and he noted some time later that "this matter remains open" (*cet article reste encore*). On April 12 of the same year, de Gaultier renewed his request:

> The king has ordered me to tell Your Excellence that he hopes that you will expedite the order sent to the Ministry of Finance to pay the lady harpsichord player, Demoiselle du Masis, an annual salary of 300 reichstaler beginning on January 1 of the current year and without discounting the first few months. This is the same du Masis of whom I made mention in the most recent list of orders which I had the honor of submitting to Your Excellence. It has been some time already, but the payment has not yet been made.[90]

The recipient of this note finally addressed the matter on April 14 by specifying that the "~~*Musicienne*~~ Musicantin, du Masis" was to be paid the specified salary "through the same means as the other foreign persons in our service."[91] The delay in processing this payment and confusion about her title likely stemmed from the rarity of a female instrumentalist receiving a salary from the court.

The best-documented woman to have worked professionally as a keyboard player in Bach's time is Barbara Kluntz. The daughter of a tailor, Kluntz joined a convent in the free imperial city of Ulm in 1704, when she was forty-four years old. Over the subsequent twenty-six years, she lived at the convent, preparing three manuscript chorale books, dated 1711, 1717, and 1720, which are filled with her own arrangements of Lutheran chorale tunes.[92] She is said to have given keyboard lessons to the children of a large number of families in Ulm.[93] In the dedication in one of her chorale books, her grateful students suggested that her faithful instruction would win her name a place in the "pantheon of heavenly music."[94] The arrangements themselves are full of parallel fifths and octaves, as well as other violations of basic voice-leading rules of the era, suggesting that she was self-taught. The impression that Kluntz was an autodidact is strengthened by the awkwardness of her handwriting, which is characterized by noteheads and clefs of radically different sizes and styles. Given the admiration she enjoyed in her time, however, it seems that her unorthodox approach to arranging chorale tunes did not hinder the enjoyment her admirers found in her music.[95]

The only women who regularly pursued professional careers in music were those who could sing. Though generally forbidden from performing in church, female vocalists were regularly employed by opera houses in courts and cities alike.[96] Pursuing such a career required not only talent and dedication but also the psychological fortitude to withstand a certain amount of opprobrium from their contemporaries. Many were revolted by the very idea of women displaying themselves on stage. Even Christiane Mariana von Ziegler, a passionate advocate for the emancipation of women and a defender of opera as an art form, admitted that those who argued that theatrical display was morally hazardous had a surfeit of evidence at their disposal:

> I cannot deny that at first glance theatrical productions might seem danger-ous or damaging to young people. They see all manner of beautiful and sumptuously dressed women before them, the exciting movements and poses of their bodies making a great impression on the spirits of the audi-ence members, their sweet countenances and flirtatious gestures causing listeners to lose control. Their pleasing voices mesmerize the human ear and heart through sweet and seductive tones; the so-called arias and boister-ous songs arouse all sorts of desires; their natural and artificial expressions cause vain and lusty drives such that the excited listener is almost robbed of his humanity. In summary the entire stage is transformed into a magic space in which the best behavioral customs are often undone.[97]

Some performances went well beyond sweet countenances and flirtatious gestures. Referring to the twenty-eight-year-old soprano Giovanna Astrua, one male opera lover in Potsdam wrote excitedly to another in 1748: "There will be six female singers, aside from the castratos, and twenty sultanesses, who will all be naked to the waist, which should make it possible to get a good look at Astrua's breasts."[98] The exhibitionism associated with singing on the stage—whether the female vocalists were fully clothed or not—in-spired rumors that they led hedonistic personal lives. Authors of behavioral guides for men strongly cautioned their readers against becoming romanti-cally involved with opera divas, for fear of contracting venereal disease.[99]

ॐ

From the perspective of Christiane Sibÿlla Bose, perhaps the most fascinating aspect of Anna Magdalena Bach was her background as a professional singer. Frau Bach likely regaled this "friend of her heart" with tales of having sung on stage. Engaged at age nineteen as a soprano at the court of Prince Leopold of Anhalt-Cöthen, she had been extraordinarily well paid, earning a salary of 300 reichstaler per year, just one hundred less than J. S. Bach himself, and considerably more than most of the other court musicians.[100] Her career slowed after her marriage in 1721, though she continued to perform professionally throughout the 1720s. Those who heard her recognized that she might well have enjoyed much greater success as a singer, perhaps even international fame, had she chosen not to marry.[101]

In 1732 Christiane Sibÿlla Bose was exactly the age Anna Magdalena Bach had been at the height of her professional career. No matter how excellent Bose's musical skills may have been, her high social class put a career as a professional musician out of reach. Perhaps she felt a bit like another young woman of the era who wanted more than anything to become a professional ballerina. She, too, was a prisoner of her high status:

> The more majestically I danced minuets, the more gracefully I made my *Entrechats* and softly moved my arms and body, the more swinging my *pas brisé* and *pas glissé*, the lighter my *pas frisé*, my *pas sur pas*, my *chassé en tournant*, my *volte*, the more sadly my father would call out: "Ah! Why is this not the daughter of a shoemaker! She would bring me at least 6,000 [reichstaler] per year and set the hearts of thousands of viewers aflame!" My stepmother enjoyed these comments. I made her tell me all about the national theater, and my young heart burned with desire to hear "Bravo" from one thousand tongues and deep sighs from inspired hearts. I even asked my stepmother if a person of noble status could not become a dancer at the theater in Vienna. In that case one would not need to marry in order to have bread and constantly stand at some man's beck and call. If one did not belong to a particular man, one could most easily be master of all men.[102]

For Fräulein Bose, Anna Magdalena Bach must have been a role model not only as an experienced wife and mother but also as a woman of the world. She had heard cries of "Bravo!" from throngs of appreciative listeners. She had known and worked with extremely skilled musicians not only as a helpmate but as a peer. Frau Bach had chosen to give up her professional career in order to marry and raise a family. Perhaps it was exciting for Fräulein Bose to consider that her friend could have decided otherwise.

CHAPTER 4

A Dark-Haired Dame
and Her Scottish Admirer

In 1764 an aristocrat from Edinburgh, Scotland, named James Boswell undertook a grand tour of the European continent. He would later achieve literary immortality as the author of *The Life of Samuel Johnson* (1791), but at age twenty-four he showed little promise. A self-absorbed oaf, he struggled with depression and what he viewed with some justification as destructive tendencies toward impoliteness and sexual overindulgence. His greatest aspiration was to become a man worthy of admiration, and his greatest anxiety was that he would never realize that aspiration.

In July, Boswell arrived in Berlin, where he had the good fortune to be offered an apartment in the home of the president of the city council, Carl David Kircheisen. The accommodations featured "a handsome parlour, gaily painted and looking to St. Peter's Church" as well as "a genteel, large alcove with a pretty silk bed."[1] Two days after moving in, Boswell was introduced to President Kircheisen's daughter, Caroline Henriette, and was immediately enamored.[2] That evening, he wrote in his diary:

> She was seventeen, comely, fresh, good-humoured, and gay, and had an ease of behavior that pleased me greatly. I was quite in pleasing frame. I must observe of myself that from my early years I have never seen an agreeable lady but my warm imagination has fancied as how I might marry her and has suggested a crowd of ideas. This is very true, but very, very absurd.[3]

Fräulein Kircheisen seemed not disinclined to the attentions of this Scottish visitor. Just a few days after meeting him, she offered him a tour of her books, her drawings, and her china collection. Sitting next to Boswell at dinner, she proclaimed herself impressed by his "Spanish" (in other words, stiff and pompous) manners, admitting she had expected the British to be "rude like Russians or Turks," a remark he found "excellent." Caroline's father, too, was quite taken with their houseguest, declaiming: "My dear Englishman, no man ever had a better heart. Your being sent to my house was an act of Providence."[4]

Two days later, Boswell attended a wedding and garden party with the Kircheisen family. Returning very late, Caroline performed for him at the keyboard. He excitedly recorded his impressions in his diary: "At one [a.m.] we went home. I made Mademoiselle play me a sweet air on the harpsichord to compose me for gentle slumbers. Happy man that I am!"[5] He sensed that with this performance Fräulein Kircheisen had initiated a new level of intimacy. This impression was encouraged the next morning by a thoughtful gift: "Scarcely had I got up when Mademoiselle sent me a rural present of luscious cherries."[6]

Caroline Kircheisen's nighttime harpsichord performances became a regular occurrence, further fanning the flames of Boswell's infatuation.[7] He found her intelligence, her generosity, and her music making tremendously alluring. How she herself intended her keyboard playing to be interpreted remains obscure. This chapter explores, on the basis of Boswell's diary and the letters they exchanged, the subtle ways music making influenced their relationship. First, however, I offer an account of music in eighteenth-century courtship more broadly.

❧

Although women like Caroline Kircheisen were encouraged to think of marriage as the key to personal happiness, few had much control over its fulfillment. Men prided themselves on the gifts they gave the women in their lives and the cleverness of their verbal appeals ("Beautiful one, it would be a cruelty to lock Cupid out of your worthy house when it's so cold and he's naked!"). Women, however, were to remain demure and largely silent courtship participants.[8] Respectable ladies could dress up and browse bookstore shelves or perch for hours in the bay windows of their homes in hopes of attracting admirers, but decorum prevented them from actually interacting with the men they encountered.[9]

The autobiography of Elisa von der Recke offers a sense for the ways in which boys and girls of Bach's Germany played at courtship. A graceful beauty at age eleven, Elisa became an object of fascination for a fourteen-year-old baron named Karl-Heinrich Hermann Benjamin von Heyking:

> When he looked at me with his big blue eyes, my glances meeting his and making him even more friendly, my little heart beat heavily; I blushed, and

became so comfortably bold when he kissed my hand. Two days had passed before my stepsister took me aside and told me with great joy the secret news that Heyking was mortally in love with me; he has no rest day or night, and my image followed him everywhere. This made him so happy, but it would make him very unhappy if I did not return his love. He had already written to his father about how beautiful and good I was, and he would like to learn much more about me, if he could entertain hopes that I might one day be his wife. As fond as I was of Heyking, and as much joy as this news brought me, I nonetheless hid my affections from my dear confidante. Why I did this I cannot say; I know only that I told my stepsister that I thought Heyking was among the dearest persons, but that I did not love him, and that he must not speak further of love if we were to remain friends and continue to see one another.[10]

Heyking agreed to her terms on the condition that she accept a gift of a little enamel box inscribed with the words "Proof of Sincere Friendship" (*Gage d'Amitié Sincère*):

> I hesitated to accept the gift, but had promised to assure him of my friendship [. . .]. [He explained that the box] possessed a unique quality. When I was alone and opened it to look inside, I would always see that which lives inside his heart, even if he was far, far away from me. [. . .] I was still undecided about whether to accept the gift, but my curiosity and the pleading of my stepsister and my brother brought me to fulfill Heyking's wish. With impatience I opened up the box and looked upon a mirror reflecting my own image. I was ashamed, I was overjoyed, cherished the giver and the box so much, and yet remained stiffly committed to regarding it only as a token of friendship. My grandmother and cousin were told that the box had come from my stepsister. This lie caused pangs of conscience, but whenever I opened it to look inside, the box, my admirer, and my own face became so dear to me that I would have told ten more lies on their behalf.[11]

The autobiography of Johann Stephan Pütter, a law professor in Göttingen, offers a sense for how actual marriages were negotiated. At age twenty-six, Pütter heard from one of his students about the daughter of a privy-counsellor in Braunfels who had a sterling reputation for household management. He wrote to her father asking whether he might visit the family home while in the area on business. With the help of the woman's brothers, Pütter received the coveted invitation, undertook the journey, and was surprised to find upon arrival that there were actually two daughters of marriageable age. He preferred the one he thought was younger, but fretted about offending her sister, who obviously stood first in line. That evening he learned, much to his delight, that his estimation of their ages had been incorrect: the sister whom he preferred was in fact the eldest. Pütter spent a few days conversing with the woman upon whom his designs had settled, after which he returned to Göttingen, wrote a letter to secure her father's permission, returned a few months later to collect his bride, and spent the next fifty years with her in holy matrimony.[12]

The autobiography of Johanna Eleonore Petersen offers a female perspective on marriage negotiations. The following account dates from the 1660s, when she was serving as a lady-in-waiting at the court in Lißberg:

> God deigned in His mercy to have the son of the Lieutenant Colonel to the Saxon Elector [. . .] fall in love with me. Through his father he let this be known to the count, who informed my late father, and "Yes" was heard from all quarters. [He] was to serve one year as a cornet and then take over his father's military company, which was at that time inactive in the countryside. After he went to war, I heard often from others that his life was not dedicated to God but rather to the mundane world, which troubled me secretly, and I prayed that either his spirit or our engagement might be changed. I did not know, however, that the Lord's plan involved allowing this engagement to drag on for a time to shield me from marriage proposals from other noblemen. I was still quite young at the time, but able to fend them off with the fact that I was already spoken for. Little did I know, however, that there had been some changes on his side, and he had engaged himself in my absence here and there with other women. This went on for several years, during which I had many secret worries, and my joy in life's pleasures was diminished.[13]

Petersen's fiancé eventually broke off the engagement, souring her entirely on the idea of marriage. But it was not long before she was approached by another suitor:

> After a while, a man of the cloth who held a high position became attracted to me, and traveled a great distance in order to move me to marry him. This caused a tempestuous struggle in my soul, which was then quite averse to the idea of marriage. After much internal conflict I turned my fate over to the Lord, putting the matter in the hands of my mortal father, from whom I wished to learn the will of my heavenly Father. Before doing this, however, I wrote letters to two God-abiding men, whom I knew to be true believers, and asked them a few questions, which they then answered, and my soul was at peace with whatever my heavenly Father decided by means of my earthly father. He asked our noble ruler [. . .] for approval, and the count notified my suitor of his consent. I again appealed to my earthly father, saying that I did not wish to answer "yes" or "no" but rather to turn the matter over to him: his "yes" would be my "yes," and his "no" my "no." He eventually decided against the marriage, said "no," and that was that.[14]

Girls learned early that premarital sex was strictly forbidden. When one six-year-old aristocrat found her mother weeping inconsolably, she was told by her older sister that their mother had recently learned of a "well known noblewoman" who had become a "whore." Years later, she recounted her reaction in her autobiography: "Though I did not know what a whore was, I thought to myself that it must be something really terrible, because it made my mother cry so much. So I went off by myself, fell to my knees, wept and prayed that God prevent me from becoming a whore."[15] Obviously not everyone observed the strict prohibitions against extramarital sex, and in an age without reliable contraception their behavior sometimes had consequences. During Bach's time in Leipzig, the parents of around 12 percent of the infants baptized in the two main churches were unmarried.[16] Sex outside the bonds of wedlock was not restricted to irresponsible soldiers, university students, and prostitutes. Noblewomen who became pregnant illicitly were swept off to isolated nunneries to give birth in secret. Some were able to parlay their extramarital trysts into political gain, but this came with serious risks.[17] All unmarried women who became pregnant were subject to social sanctions and faced financial penalties, beginning with double the ordinary baptismal fees. For a few reluctant mothers, the prospect of raising an unwanted child was too much to bear, and they suffocated their infants with pillows. Such behavior was the horrifying antithesis of all that was expected of women: giving death to a child instead of life. Perpetrators were imprisoned in squalid conditions for months before being ceremoniously marched out to the market square for public execution. The neighbors who had sold them bread, strewn sand on their floors, and begged outside their doors jeered as executioners swung their broadswords and sent shards of bone and sprays of blood flying into jeering crowds. Detailed reports of public beheadings, complete with engraved images, served as cautionary tales for women of all social classes.[18]

৵

Given the restrictions on active pursuit, women of Bach's era relied on indirect means of influencing their marital fates. Young ladies did their best to display both practical and galant skills in group settings where attractive eligible bachelors just happened to find themselves. The inclinations of potential suitors could be encouraged in subtle ways, from offering them the best cuts of meat at dinner, to letting them borrow cherished books, to giving them guided tours of carefully curated porcelain collections. Such favors could be defended as springing solely from the time-honored obligations of hospitality rather than from some unseemly desire to secure a mate.

Music offered a particularly effective means of indirect courtship. A performance for a male suitor could be excused as the byproduct of an innocent fascination with the art of tones rather than a calculated attempt to seduce. Such displays were made all the more effective by the keyboard's close association with domestic virtue. An impressive performance at the clavichord or harpsichord signaled that a young lady had spent countless hours at home, sequestered from the temptations of the sinful world. Music's galant image—its status as an idle pastime completely without practical application—served to both mask and enhance its utility in courtship.

The mysterious power of music, particularly its power to engage the body, gave a woman's practice room a distinctive frisson. Keyboards were frequently kept in bedrooms or dressing rooms, heightening the allure of inviting a suitor to hear a few innocent galanterien. The only man regularly granted access to the inviolate space of a woman's music room was her music teacher. The personality characteristics ascribed to such men—"warm and moist, tempted by lust, more womanly than manly, inconstant, weak-hearted, and timid, given to being pampered and eating fancy foods, submissive, open-hearted, and gullible"—are expressions of the palpable anxiety that stemmed from this easy access.[19] Parents worried that their daughters might be unmoored by the mysterious power of music and fall in love. A character in a play by Bach's frequent librettist Christian Friedrich Henrici (a.k.a. *Picander*) is so taken with her keyboard instructor that when he sings a particular song, she finds it "impossible to resist kissing him."[20] Friedrich Wilhelm Marpurg wrote of a music teacher who had "good hands" but "does not know [. . .] how to use them well, except when the chaperone installed by the mother steps into the next room and he is left alone with one of his female students."[21] In Wolfgang Caspar Printz's play *Battalus* from 1691 an organist named Lælius is arrested and is called before a tribunal (*Canzeley*) to defend himself against rumors of licentious behavior:

SECRETARY OF THE CANZELEY: Have you ever instructed women in music?
LÆLIUS: Yes.
SECRETARY: How many?
LÆLIUS: Two.
SECRETARY: Did you ever kiss them?
LÆLIUS: Yes.
SECRETARY: How often?
LÆLIUS: I don't know because I didn't count.
SECRETARY: Did you ever sleep with them?
LÆLIUS: Yes.
SECRETARY: How often?
LÆLIUS: I don't remember, though if you really need to know I could perhaps figure it out by looking at my calendar.
SECRETARY: That's enough![22]

It soon becomes clear that the female pupils in question were Lælius's first and second wives, but humorous exchanges like this gave release to the genuine fear that music could lead vulnerable women to ruin.

The contents of a woman's music room were fetishized by Bach's male contemporaries. Among the most important of these was the keyboard notebook (*Clavierbuch* or *Clavierbüchlein*), which served as a repository for repertoire copied by the teacher. Bound in velvet or leather and decorated with gold inlay, ribbons, or buckles, such books were designed to highlight the intimate character of the music within. They served as missives between the protected realm of the practice room and the dangerous world beyond. Inviting a friend, acquaintance, or potential suitor to contribute a poem, drawing, or piece of music to one's clavierbuch was an unmistakable sign of affection. One young woman of the era made this explicit on her note-book's cover: "A collection of various melodic songs copied into this book by high patrons and patronesses, as well as male and female friends, in order to show me, as owner, their respect, clemency, and friendship, for which I honor them my whole life with submissive and obedient thanks."[23]

Some girls and women treated their keyboard notebooks not only as collections of repertoire but also as repositories for sentimental thoughts. In the 1690s the teenage Countess Elisabeth Dorothea Landgräfin zu Hessen-Darmstadt interspersed the following aphorisms among the notes and rhythms copied by her music teacher:

> – Friendship which ends was never really friendship.
> – Nothing will change me, neither force nor good words.
> – I love you more than myself . . .
> – Always constant and faithful until death and never changing.
> – Friendship without end.
> – Virtue surpasses wealth.
> – Love is a strange beast.
> – When fortune torments me, hope will content me.
> – Love is the goal.
> – Love, honor, and my dearest are the three flames of my heart.
> – I abide by these bywords: constancy and sincerity.
> – Unwavering fidelity.
> – Desire and love for just one goal | Will bring all work under control.
> – Nothing by force, all with pleasure.
> – Contentment surpasses wealth.[24]

The countess presumably copied these mottos not only as an aid to her own memory but also to display her character for those with access to the book.[25] The impression she sought to evoke was one of a faithful, romantic, and innocent teenager. The appearance of these ideals in her music notebook heightened their believability. Paging through it was akin to the voyeuristic experience of reading someone's diary.

Romantic exchanges of music notebooks were often thematized in the literature of Bach's era. In a poem published by Johann Georg Gressel, the speaker claims not to know what to write into the music notebook of his beloved Dorimen. Confronted by the blank page, he opts to abandon conscious thought and allow his hand to write what it will:

"FOR DORIMEN'S SONG BOOK" (1716)

You wish that I should write something into your song book,
I set the feather down but know not what to pen,
I know myself not whether I should try again.
I let the keel go blindly and then take a long look.
It writes: Oh come now, *Dorimen*, it is well known.
It writes: I am your servant, yes, I'm yours alone.[26]

Gressel's poem expresses the pain of a male lover silenced by decorum. The speaker is grateful to Dorimen for offering him the opportunity to write in her songbook but recognizes the emotional and social perils of sharing his private thoughts. He solves the problem by disengaging his mind and turning the task over to his body.[27]

It was a gesture of still greater intimacy for a woman to grant a male admirer access to her practice room. It is not surprising that such experiences also set literary pens in motion, as in this poem by Johann Ulrich von König:

"TO *MADEMOISELLE S.* ON HER PERFECTION IN MUSIC" (1716)

When your fair hand does touch the keyboard's keys,
Then every chord finds passage to my heart with ease.
And when your dainty mouth with charm begins to sing,
Its lovely sound wins praises more than I can bring;
Still further when a lute performance you suggest,
Strange feelings are aroused in my enchanted breast,
My love is driven not by sight as usual,
But passes through my ears and straight into my soul.
In order that my sighing trouble you no more,
I beg you do not let me listen heretofore;
My sentiments are clearly in these words expressed:
Your wondrous playing's truly played away my rest.[28]

König emphasized not only the seductive effects of Mademoiselle S's music making but also her virtuous ignorance of those effects. The keyboard-playing woman's allure was innocently emanated rather than willfully directed: her "fair hand [. . .] does touch the clavier's keys"; her mouth "with charm begins to sing." The speaker suggests that the woman's body acted independently, without mindful direction, rhetorically shielding her from charges of agency.

In a more elaborate poem published in 1704, Christoph Gottehr Burghart suggested that the lady keyboardist might in fact be aware of the seductive effects of her music making:

"AS SHE PLAYED THE KEYBOARD AND SANG" (1704)

How long must I, your servant, beg of you this little favor,
Here in the realm of music one can't honor you enough;
A bungler seeks from judging ears invariably a waiver;
But you could stand with masters and their challenges rebuff.
Indeed your skills give you the right to set yourself still higher,
Although your modesty precludes your taking rightful praise:
You say: "My singing never sounds as good as I desire,
My playing at the keyboard must improve in many ways."
Ah, beauty! Do you really mean to say such things sincerely?
Forgive me—this time only—for refusing to believe;
For you will prove yourself these statements judge you too severely,
Your fingers at the keyboard won't allow you to deceive.
Your singing voice will also make my arguments persuasive,
And if I'm able to convince you to sit down and play,
Then you yourself will hear your sounds are not the least abrasive,
You'll know my praise is justified and true, just as I say.
As when we were most recently together all alone,
I found your clavichord there standing with an open lid,
I asked you then to play for me, a concert all my own,
With keyboard and with music book in hand you surely did.
Oh heavens! Oh, what wonders did your playing put on view,
What sounds did I on that day hear! I stood there mesmerized.
My freedom had long left me but was lost to you anew,
And here I cannot claim that I was in the least surprised.
Your playing was uncommon: runs and fugues were heard in turn,
The trickiest of all the chords you played with graceful ease,
Though fingers truly flew, one could each note you played discern,
You never failed to demonstrate the greatest expertise.
The proudest master here would have to forfeit you the prize,
Instead of trying to compete against your skilled white hands.
Yes, even great *Francesco* would be forced to lower his eyes.
And if the vain world deems him peerless, it misunderstands.
Still more was I enchanted by the beauty of your voice,
It was as if an angel had been sent to sing for me.

To spend all my time here with you would always be my choice,
This house a heav'nly kingdom to which you would hold the key.
Away, proud Italy! And take with you your women of song,
Whose reputation reaches to the sun and stars above;
The notion that they have no peer will henceforth be judged wrong,
As long as she does walk the earth: Divine *Lisette*, my love.
Away you bold castrati and away with coloratura!
The singing voice is there among you far too unrefined;
In contrast *Lisette*'s hands play at the keyboard with bravura,
The sound her lovely mouth makes is unique to all mankind.
So were my thoughts then, and I now must share them here in writing,
That you might know I feel that you possess rare quality,
So long as this our mundane world finds loveliness exciting,
The praise I give your name today will last eternally.
Strict politesse prevents you from accepting your due praise,
You scorn yourself, and do injustice to your great achievement;
In order that you in the future shun such sinful ways,
Your punishment will be a kiss from me, your loyal servant.
Farewell to you, my joyful thoughts now bid that I should finish,
And offer me the hope that I might kiss you one day near;
I know you will atone sincerely and this sin diminish,
I write to you with pleasure: fare thee well, my angel dear.[29]

The speaker of Burghart's poem credits his beloved Lisette with performing not only fast passagework at the keyboard but also tricky chords and fugues, surpassing even Francesco Canova da Milano, the Italian keyboardist whose name was a byword for musical greatness in Bach's Germany. Her allure, however, stems not only from her skills but also from her modesty. Many entreaties are required before she finally agrees to play ("How long must I, your servant, beg of you this little favor"), and she repeatedly denies that her talents are worthy of display ("My playing at the keyboard must improve in many ways"). Like König's Mademoiselle S, Burghart's Lisette is ostensibly ignorant of the strength of her abilities and must be persuaded by her own voice and fingers, as if these could operate without conscious direction. The separation between her "fair hands" and her mind facilitates an interpretation of her keyboard playing as fundamentally re-creative rather than creative. Burghart's rhetoric preserves Lisette's morality and intensifies her appeal by evading the implication that her actions are calculated to seduce. His poetic speaker hints, however, that her modesty is pretended, that she may in fact be aware of the power of her musical skills ("Forgive me—this time only—for refusing to believe") and therefore also cognizant of the effects her music has on this particular listener, a sin for which the speaker playfully suggests that she atone with a kiss.

It was only women of ill-repute who wielded their musical skills strategically. David Fassmann's novel *Des angenehmen Passe-Tems* (1742) includes the story of a woman who charmed men with her voice, her lute, and her clavier before enticing them to join her in bed.[30] In his novel *Le Saxe galante* (1735), Karl von Pöllnitz imagined the manipulation of the prince-elector of Saxony, Augustus the Strong, by Anna Aloysia Maximiliane von Lamberg, known as the Countess Esterle, who was upset about the elector's cold behavior after she had submitted to his advances:

> As she did not know the reason for his distance, she believed that he was being untrue to her [. . .]. She wrote to him and requested that he come to her chambers [. . .]. She dressed herself in a costly nightgown, her hair in a rather negligent state, though still galant, and she wore a portrait of the prince-elector in an armband. In this pose she awaited him. As he entered her chamber, she played upon a harpsichord and sang a very sad aria. When she saw him, she cried ample tears and could not be moved from her chair. The prince-elector was disturbed to find her in such a state, and asked her to reveal the reasons for this behavior. Sobbing incessantly, she responded: "How can you ask me the reason for my tears? Does your heart itself not tell you the answer, as it is the sole cause of my distress?"[31]

The Countess Esterle is portrayed as having staged every aspect of this scene, from her negligent attire to her immobility and tears. Her decision to position herself at the harpsichord was also calculated. She timed her performance to coincide with the elector's arrival, making him a voyeur witnessing an apparently spontaneous scene of emotional distress. Her conscious efforts to wield her sexual power—aided and abetted by the power of music—signaled unmistakably to readers that her agenda was impure.

The tension between virtue and seduction at the keyboard was thematized in a painting rendered in the 1750s by Johann Heinrich Tischbein the elder and reproduced in plate 7. The artist depicted himself at work on a scene of the ancient battle between Menelaus and Paris over Helen of Troy while his wife, Marie Sophie Tischbein (née Robert) plays a clavichord. Frau Tischbein's keyboard playing has caused her husband to stop painting, lean on the back of her chair, gaze in her direction, and listen. She appears to be wrapped up in the music, oblivious to her husband's fascination. The animals in the foreground, however, tell a different story. Tischbein draws a close parallel between himself and the dog (dark colored, standing, staring at the cat) and between his wife and the cat (light colored, sitting on a chair, deliberately avoiding the dog's gaze). The dog observes the cat intently, preparing an assault. The cat, by contrast, stares beyond the dog, pretending to be unmindful of his presence. There can be no question, however, that she is highly attuned to his behavior, her feline head extended warily beyond the edge of the chair, ears perked, legs tucked under her body. Though she looks artfully past the dog, the cat's body is prepared to take evasive action at any moment. The parallels suggest that Tischbein's wife's clavichord playing has aroused a powerful compulsion within him, a desire as natural as that which drives dogs to chase cats. Her obliviousness, by implication, is feigned. Just as the cat is fully aware of the dog's presence, Frau Tischbein knows that she has piqued her husband's desire, and yet plays on.

ॐ

In James Boswell's mind, Caroline Kircheisen made music in hopes of furthering their intimacy. He was flattered by the attention he had received from this attractive and talented young woman. The "sweet airs" she played at the harpsichord mollified his fears of inadequacy and helped him to sleep. From his perspective, every note she offered was a sign of her affection. Kircheisen, for her part, seems to have harbored rather more complex views.

About one week after Kircheisen's first private performance at the harpsichord, Boswell decided to spend a few weeks in the city of Braunschweig. He discussed his travel plans over tea, flirtatiously suggesting that he would not be taking Caroline with him because he "feared to tire of her in two or three days." The very idea of an unchaperoned trip with the teenage daughter of Berlin's city council president was ludicrous, but Boswell's comment seems to have offended her nonetheless. After describing the exchange in his diary, he noted: "I must really learn a little of that restraint which foreigners call politeness, and which after a certain time becomes quite easy."[32] The next day, he offended Caroline again by averring that he "would not marry any woman whose fortune was less than £10,000 [ca. 44,500 reichstaler]," suggesting boldly that she was financially beneath him. He acknowledged that this had "seriously shocked" Caroline and her mother and that he should not have said it, admonishing himself to "above all strive to attain easy reserve."[33] By the end of that week, he believed he had patched things up; he toured Berlin in a carriage with the Kircheisen women and reported that Caroline "looked sweet and cheerful and had her green silk parasol and looked like an Indian princess."[34] The ease of their earlier interactions, however, would never return.

The character of the relationship between Boswell and Kircheisen is vividly documented in the letters they exchanged while he was visiting Braunschweig. Their correspondence, like their conversation, was in French, a subject Boswell thematized at the outset of his first message:

> To show you, my dear friend, how completely I am a man of my word, I take
> the risk of exposing my ignorance of the French language. I have found ways
> of hiding it somehow or other in the volubility of conversation, but when
> you read at your leisure what I have written, you will see that your Scots
> Spaniard has such contempt for the frivolous nation that he has scorned
> to learn its language.
>
> Have you ever seen a man so vain as I am? I am sure you never have. I
> cannot divest myself of vanity for a single instant. I assure you that I began
> quite sincerely to make excuses for my bad French, and yet I could not get
> to the end of a sentence without taking a high tone and priding myself on
> my very ignorance. *Es bien?* You are good enough to pardon me all my faults;
> I am only too sure of it. If I correct them, it is more out of generosity than
> out of fear. You know it, my dear; and you behave toward me in a manner
> very different from the way I can only imagine that I would like to behave
> toward my wife, if I were so honored as to have one.[35]

Boswell's introspection reflects both his enormous ego and his vulnerability;
he lays himself bare with self-critical comments and trusts that Kircheisen
will not use them against him. He even asks her explicitly for absolution
("You are good enough to pardon me all my faults"). At the same time, he
exhibits little confidence that she would accept this guidance. Boswell's
blithe bravado suggests that his aristocratic status served as a buoy to his
self-esteem, that there was nothing she could say or do to hurt him. And yet
his wry observation that she behaves toward him in a manner very different
from the way he would behave toward his wife—reversing traditional gender
roles—suggests subtly that she was the dominant party in their relationship,
despite the fact that she was younger, female, and bourgeois.

Kircheisen's response reveals that Boswell's fears of emotional trauma at
her hands were not entirely unfounded. This was an extremely intelligent
woman who had little interest in absolving Boswell of his faults or assuaging
his anxieties. Indeed, she seeks rather to playfully exacerbate his insecurities
while maintaining a patina of easy cheer:

> Monsieur, you would not do honor to your nation if you were not a man of
> your word. I believe that this is the greatest motivation that has ever inspired
> you to send me news. I admire you, sir, for having forced yourself to give
> me this information in a language so far beneath the genius of the English.
> The mistakes you say you have made in your letter do you honor, for they
> prove that you need not reproach yourself for having wasted much of your
> time in study. [. . .] Perhaps in time your generosity will overcome your
> prejudice, and you will be motivated to perfect yourself in the language of
> the frivolous nation.[36]

In response to his report that he was dining regularly at the court in Braunschweig and was "beginning to become known" she wrote:

> I was very charmed to learn that the Court of Braunschweig does justice to your merits. Between ourselves, does this not nourish that slight tendency toward vanity that you have? Admit frankly that I have guessed correctly in thinking that it is nectar to you. I fancy you will return having perfected yourself as a Spaniard, and woe to whoever does not treat you humbly and respectfully. I shall already have prepared myself in advance.[37]

Caroline Kircheisen both flattered and mercilessly mocked Boswell, playfully poking at his insecurities while maintaining the letter of decorum. Only in a discussion of harpsichord playing did Boswell gain the upper hand. Turning briefly away from his favorite subject (himself), he asked rather provocatively:

> How goes the harpsichord? Labor to perfect your playing, I implore you. You will perform miracles one day. In the meantime, you have the satisfaction of contributing much to the happiness of a very worthy man, who (between ourselves) receives a rather large share of your admiration. How charming you are! Do not blush. You took it badly when I told you that you admired me. Perhaps you will not take it so badly when I put this in writing. I would like to try it and see.[38]

Boswell's bold assertion that Caroline "admired" him—in other words, that she harbored a romantic interest in him, and that her harpsichord performances had given voice to her true feelings—was one he expected to "offend." The "miracles" he predicted she would perform one day were clearly a reference to attracting suitors. He offered her the opportunity "in the meantime" to practice on him, while once again making clear that he was not interested in serving as more than a surrogate husband.

Boswell's cheeky commentary lifted the veil that shielded Caroline Kircheisen from charges of using music actively in the service of courtship. She had apparently taken this assertion "badly" on a previous occasion. By comparison with the vulnerable and self-deprecating tone he adopted elsewhere in the letter, his discussion of music is rather aggressive; it virtually demanded a response. Any strong reaction, whether positive or negative, would confirm what he desperately wanted to hear her express: that he was a man worthy of her desire.

Caroline Kircheisen did indeed respond to Boswell's provocative assertion, but her laconic answer could not have brought him much satisfaction: "You had the goodness to ask after the harpsichord; I am practicing

it but do not flatter myself to succeed in this realm as you believe I will."
By blithely ignoring Boswell's provocation, Kircheisen neither confirmed
nor denied her purported admiration. She managed nonetheless to make
clear that she did not expect to work the "miracles" he anticipated. The
response, perfunctory and uncharacteristically void of irony, suggests that
this topic made her feel vulnerable.

Upon returning to Berlin, Boswell and Kircheisen were pleased to meet
again, but he quickly became frustrated once more by her devastating
ability to mock him while remaining relentlessly upbeat: "In the afternoon
I talked much with Mademoiselle Kircheisen, whom I like much. She has
good sense and enough of vivacity, and she is comely. She is the only girl I
ever saw constantly agreeable. She has but one fault. She loves too much
to *badiner* [joke], and thence is now and then a little impolite. She is a
mimic, and that is dangerous."[39] Kircheisen was dangerous in the sense
that she was extremely skilled at turning Boswell's own words against him.
He wanted desperately for her to desire him yet found himself weak in her
presence, always feeling the sharp end of her wit. Their interactions drove
him to assert his social superiority in ever more blatant and aggravating
ways. In the wake of an argument with Kircheisen and her mother shortly
after his return, he wrote in his diary, "I raged in the cause of pride, and
said my greatest satisfaction was to have power over others, to have which
I would suffer many evils; and I thanked heaven for having given me noble
sentiments and the rule over lands. They talked of contentment. I said
it was a poor thing. Indeed, I was too fiery."[40] Boswell's interactions with
Caroline had once helped put his mind at ease, but he was now finding it
increasingly difficult to sleep. After lying awake one night, he abandoned
"the merit of a year's chastity" and accepted the services of a prostitute who
came to his apartment selling chocolate.[41] He would do so repeatedly over
the next few weeks as Fräulein Kircheisen continued to cause him pain.[42]
Frustrated by her unwillingness to accept his dominance, he sought to
reassert his sense of self by turning to more vulnerable women.[43]

Finally, on September 17, Boswell confessed his full frustration to
both Caroline and her mother: "At night I had a long chat with Madame
and Mademoiselle, and owned that I had the misfortune to be *changeant*
[moody] in a most unaccountable degree. 'You will not be able to believe
it, Mademoiselle, but sometimes it has given me great pain to see you in
the morning, and to hear you play.'"[44] Fräulein Kircheisen's harpsichord
serenades were no longer the tonic that had once helped Boswell to slumber.
Though she may well have played the same music she had performed when
he first arrived, it had taken on a different meaning. In July he had heard
each note as an emblem of her admiration; by September the music was

only reminding him of his inadequacies. Her playing had assumed the ironic tone characteristic of her correspondence and conversation.

Caroline's mother, at pains to console the young nobleman who was her family's guest, offered an account of her husband's struggles with depression and how they were overcome:

> "You must take care, or you will become hypochondriac. You must drink a great deal of water and take a great deal of exercise. My husband used to be very melancholy. He thought everyone had a grudge against him. He wanted to stay in this room. I had his bed brought here, and I lay on the settee. Then he would say, 'I should be better off on the settee,' and we would change. Well, I pretended to go to sleep. He would remain then without closing his eyes, get up, wander about the room; he was always restless. He tried to write. He couldn't. He was gloomy and complained bitterly. I would rise. I would talk to him. I would quote him consolatory passages from the Bible. He would be somewhat soothed. He would begin again. So I said to him, 'Why, you will kill me and yourself too, staying awake like this, and what will become of our family?' I would talk like that just to rouse him a little. Then he would be sorry. He made an effort. He conquered his humor. He began to sleep." This history gave me infinite pleasure. I wish I may have such a wife.[45]

Boswell desired a wife who was devoted to making her husband feel loved and supported. Caroline Kircheisen had all of the beauty, intelligence, and wit of the woman he wished to marry. She had no interest, however, in playing for him the role that her mother had played for her father.

On September 19, 1764, Boswell took leave of the Kircheisen women "very tenderly" and left Berlin for Italy. While on the way, he sent Caroline a letter in which he posed a series of questions designed to shore up some of the insecurities their relationship had engendered in him:

> Tell me, am I not a true philosopher? A solid man? A man who is master of himself? I am about to give you proof of it. After having tasted all the delights that an amiable stranger can taste at an amiable court, was I enfeebled? No. Not at all. I seated myself with perfect tranquility on the post-coach, and in spite of the rain, the wind, and the darkness of a wretched night, I made my way in excellent humor to Halle, where I am at present. Do you know that on the way I composed some French verses? You can well imagine what kind of French verses a man would make if the year before he did not have enough of the language to ask for food and drink. I shall write them down for you nevertheless. When has a man ever shown such boldness?[46]

Presented as ironic, self-deprecating, and even mock-heroic, the question of whether he was a worthy man genuinely plagued Boswell. He needed

Kircheisen to answer it—in the affirmative, naturally—and he hoped with his verses to provoke the reaction his efforts thus far had failed to elicit:

VERSES WRITTEN ON A POST-COACH
ADDRESSED TO MADEMOISELLE KIRCHEISEN

Formerly a poet, I
Was obsessed with a brunette.
Songs of love she did inspire;
Those were days I'll not forget.

She had quite a tender heart,
This galant and dark-haired dame;
Quoting Cavalcabo's art:
Her wild love I could not tame.

Like a shadow those days passed;
Bye my love, farewell my lyre!
Cold and somber now at last,
I am through with fair desire.

Ah! My pretty Caroline!
Who did charm me every eve:
From your sweet eyes I divine
You're *unwilling* to believe.[47]

Although Boswell deliberately left his poem free of identifying specifics, the "dark-haired dame" of the first three stanzas is implicitly identified with the "pretty Caroline" of the fourth. Indeed, she too was a brunette.[48] He hoped that readers, especially Kircheisen herself, would conflate the two. In his fantasy world, she had loved him passionately—*à la fureur*, as Cavalcabo, an Italian marquis, once wrote of a conquest.[49] She had entertained him "every eve" at the harpsichord, a memory he was still hoping to revise retrospectively into a sign of her affection.

Kircheisen's problem, according to Boswell, was that she was "unwilling" to believe. Indeed, he underlined this word in his manuscript of the poem: *Vous ne voulez pas me croire.* Her tendency to ironically use his own words against him not only hurt his self-esteem, it also hid her own true feelings. Again and again in his interactions with Kircheisen, he had sought to provoke an emotional reaction, and she had refused to oblige. Any heartfelt response could be interpreted as a sign of respect, which he could stretch in his mind into admiration. Not only had Kircheisen refused to accept his dominance, she had remained an amiable cypher, one who hid her genuine emotions behind clever galanterie.

Caroline Kircheisen responded to Boswell's letter a few months later, skillfully deploying the irony she had always maintained in their interactions. Not only did she ignore his provocative insinuation that she herself was the "dark-haired dame" of the poem, but she went so far as to ask for further news of his romantic escapades. Caroline downplayed her central role in his emotional suffering, presenting herself not as a participant but merely as an observer: "I will take advantage of this occasion, Monsieur, to thank you for the poetry that I found in your last letter; it gave me much pleasure to know that you were thinking of me on your recent journey. You have already seen all of the beauties of Germany, and are now occupied with admiring those of Italy. I am quite curious to know of the adventures you have experienced, and since we have not received any new verses, I flatter myself that you will furnish us with some more at your first opportunity."[50] Her extraordinary wit enabled her to skillfully hew to the limits of social decorum while expressing thoughts and feelings that would otherwise have brought offense. Harpsichord playing served the same purpose. Like the words she spoke, the notes she played were deployed to express the exact opposite of what Boswell wanted them to mean.

CHAPTER 5

Two Teenage Countesses

In 1968, during renovations of a castle near Frankfurt, workers happened upon a mysterious wooden chest filled with approximately seven hundred manuscripts of eighteenth-century music. The collection was quickly traced to Johann Karl Ludwig Christian, Baron von Pretlack, a military officer and diplomat to whom the castle had once belonged. Pretlack had been a music lover, and a few of the manuscripts bore his monogram. Many more manuscripts, however, bore the initials of his first wife, Friederika Sophie, Countess zu Epstein, and of her sister, Luise Charlotte, Countess zu Epstein. The collection was dominated by opera arias and music for keyboard solo. Judging by dates on the manuscripts, most were copied between 1742 and 1744, when the Countesses zu Epstein were between twelve to fourteen and fifteen to seventeen years old, respectively. Nearly all were in the hand of a single scribe who signed his work with a cryptic monogram: "Me."

The manuscripts were acquired in 1970 by the Staatsbibliothek zu Berlin, where today they constitute the *Sammlung Pretlack*.[1] Over the past half-century, scholars have examined specific works that once belonged to the Countesses zu Epstein. The collection, however, has never been studied comprehensively or recognized for what it truly is: the largest, best-preserved collection of music for teenage girls in J. S. Bach's Germany. This chapter is devoted to a thorough account of the keyboard music prepared for the Countesses zu Epstein. In order to establish the context, however, I will first discuss contemporary rhetoric about music for women.

❧

The musical lives of girls and women in Bach's Germany were bathed in a rhetoric of ease. In his 1687 treatise on organ playing, Daniel Speer included an appendix titled "Easy instructions for women on playing the keyboard."[2] The author had been inspired to devote some attention to this unusual subject by the surprising demands of an aristocratic lady who wished to learn "not only the names of the notes, but also multiple clefs and complex rhythms." Speer advised his organist colleagues to paste the note names on the keys of their female students' instruments and then present some simple repertoire:

> One can copy out for the lady short chorales, arias, ballets, courantes, gavottes, or sarabandes and teach them to her, but when one has given her one piece, it is important not to give her another until she can play the first well and in tempo with all the right notes. She should also be able to name all the notes on the page in both the right and the left hand, and she should be able to tell you how long each note is to be held. Only then should you give her a new piece, always making sure she can fulfill these requirements before moving on. In this way she will progress to greater perfection in a manner that will be enjoyable for both teacher and student [. . .]. After she has the basics of the keyboard in hand [. . .] use the collection of pieces that she has accumulated in her notebook to teach her music theory, paying special attention to the bass line, which can help her to cultivate a natural musical aptitude and will eventually lead to the proper study of figured bass.[3]

By ending his proposed training regimen with figured bass, Speer tacitly discouraged women from pursuing more creative aspects of music making; there is no hint that women might learn ornamentation, let alone improvisation or composition. Displaying such skills might undercut the image of fragile innocence and tractability Bach's female contemporaries were encouraged to embrace.

The many published collections of keyboard music marketed explicitly to female players (*vors Frauenzimmer*) featured minuets, polonaises, and other galanterien and were frequently advertised as "light" (*leicht*) or "playable" (*applicable*).[4] The music contained in these collections, like that Speer suggested fifty years earlier, was overwhelmingly quick and cheerful in character rather than slow and melancholy, and challenging enough to demonstrate discipline but not so difficult as to suggest independence. Johann Ludwig

Krebs, an organist in Zwickau, published several such collections, some of which were sold to customers by his former teacher, J. S. Bach.[5] He explained his goals in a preface: "It seems to me that I may annoy some people with this collection, since it appears that I am weighing down the musical world with such easy and non-artful works. But I did so only after careful consideration. Though it would have been possible for me to put difficult and artful works before the eyes of the world, I have decided rather to serve the majority of keyboard players by publishing easy pieces that can be played without difficulty by women, as well as beginners."[6] Krebs was not the only writer to treat male beginners and female keyboardists in general as roughly equivalent. Most writers in eighteenth-century Germany assumed that the ambitions of women were limited and that their lessons would cease as soon as they were married. The claims that this music was "easy" were intended not so much to reassure female players worried about having to practice too much as they were intended to reassure their parents and others who purchased keyboard music on their behalf that this repertoire would project an image of demure domesticity rather than overweening ambition.

While Speer's brief discussion of teaching women was a novelty in the late seventeenth century, the concept was so common by the mid-eighteenth century that it could be subjected to parody. In 1749 Friedrich Wilhelm Marpurg, a music theorist and friend of J. S. Bach, published the following fictional letter purportedly written by an aristocratic girl living not far from Berlin:

> In addition to singing, I enjoy playing the keyboard and have made much progress. My dear papa purchased an excellent clavichord for me at a certain auction for 15 groschen and 6 pfennige. A skillful man employed as organist on the outskirts of a neighboring city serves as my teacher. We invite him to come once every two weeks and he teaches me for thirty minutes on each visit. He is not at all expensive, and we pay him only two or three Ducats [five to eight reichstaler] per month. Additionally, my dear mama honors him each year with a scheffel [about fifty liters] of grain. Even if I had no aptitude for music, this man would certainly be capable of instilling one in me. He is very modest, and for a man of bourgeois blood knows well how to get along with people. He always sits to my left when I play, and never forgets after the lesson to bow deeply in the manner of a certain English dance. He marks all of the notes with letter names, thereby sparing my mind all unnecessary stress. By now I can already begin to read the first and second lines of the soprano clef pretty well. He cannot stand it when he sees the right hand part written in the treble clef, and says that this practice was invented at some untimely moment by a few musical free-thinkers, and that the grandfather of his former teacher was its sworn enemy. The choice of fingerings is, in his view, unimportant, and he leaves

it entirely up to me, though he would like to ban the use of my thumbs on the keyboard, and rails against the frequent use of these digits by today's keyboardists. Because he is so selfless and does not wish to hold me up for two or three years, he instructs me to avoid all ornamentation, claiming that it only hinders swiftness in playing. Beyond this he gives me hope that I might soon be able to play the latest arias. In addition to the *Schmiedecourante*, the *Gassenhauer*, and two Polish dances, I have already learned at least a half-dozen chorales and am thus well prepared to play the most difficult pieces. I must also not forget to mention that my diligent master always has his jaw harp [*Maultrommel*] or hollow branch flute [*Weiderpfeiffe*] with him, and he often plays along with me so that, as he says, I can develop a sense for what it is like to perform concertos.[7]

Marpurg's satire is aimed in part at the girl's keyboard teacher, a lazy, ignorant, and old-fashioned village organist. His incompetence is manifest in his lack of professional success, his suspicion of treble clef and use of the thumb (both of which had been common for decades), as well as his leaving fingering decisions to the whims of an inexperienced student. Marpurg also ridicules the student's parents for buying an instrument that was too cheap to be of much use and yet paying ten times too much for instruction from this foolish man. The primary subject of the parody, however, is the girl herself. She is mocked for enduring and reporting this deplorable situation without recognizing its problems. Charmed by frivolous nonsense such as her teacher's bow from an English dance, street songs, and the "concertos" he plays with her on woodsy folk instruments, her musical life is limited by what the author implies is a gender-based deficiency of critical acumen.

Without explicitly advocating change, Marpurg did imply that there was room for improvement in the education of female keyboardists. His fictional teacher's suggestion that the girl avoid all ornamentation is corroborated by other accounts from the time.[8] For serious keyboardists of the era, ornamentation was not an optional adornment but a primary interpretive tool, a means of making one's performance unique. To ignore this critical expressive element in order to play a little more quickly suggested unmistakably that this girl's musical life was restricted to mechanically following orders. Marpurg implies obliquely that female musicians should be taught not only re-creative but also creative skills.

Of course the musical lives of female keyboardists were far more complex than Marpurg's parody would imply. It is true that surviving keyboard notebooks of the era—for example, those of Princess Sophia Augusta of Anhalt-Zerbst (ca. 1685),[9] Princess Wilhelmine Amalia von Braunschweig-Lüneburg (ca. 1693),[10] Christiane Charlotte Amalie Trolle (ca. 1699),[11] and Sophie Charlotte Albertine von Brandenburg-Culmbach (ca. 1724)[12]—are dominated by chorale preludes and galanterien. These books, however, offer only a very limited picture of the musical lives of their owners. They were overwhelmingly prepared by music teachers and cannot be assumed to represent the preferences of the female players themselves.

The influence that gender-based obligations could have on a woman's musical life is documented in a keyboard notebook once owned by Anna Margaretha Stromer.[13] She wrote on the inside cover that her music lessons had "begun with God" (*mit Gott den Anfang gemacht*) on November 9, 1699. The earliest portion of the book is in German tabulature notation copied by a single experienced scribe, presumably her teacher. It includes sixty-three galanterien (primarily minuets but also a few sarabandes, courantes, and gavottes), as well as some chorales and other songs. On June 19, 1702, Fräulein Stromer married Johann Conrad Will, a pastor in Dinkelsbühl several decades her elder. For nearly twenty years, she accumulated no new repertoire in her keyboard notebook. At some point in the 1710s, her first husband died, and on January 22, 1720, she married a merchant in Nuremberg named Johann Nikolaus Bassi. On July 7, 1721—just one year and six months after her second wedding—she began once again to fill her keyboard notebook with new repertoire. The second section of her keyboard notebook is copied in Italian (in other words, modern) notation and presents harmony exercises, chorales, and sacred songs, as well as some preludes and more galanterien (primarily arias and minuets). These are copied by a different professional scribe, presumably her new teacher, who in some cases wrote the note names in red ink next to the note heads as an aid to his pupil. Clearly she was just beginning to familiarize herself with modern notation, suggesting that the hiatus in the book corresponded to an actual hiatus in her musical life. It is probably no coincidence that the nearly two-decade gap in her accumulation of repertoire corresponds exactly to the period of her marriage to Pastor Will. Perhaps he prevented her from making music, feeling that it was unbecoming of a pastor's wife. At least one other woman of the era is documented as having quit her keyboard lessons because she married a pastor.[14] Her second husband, the merchant Herr Bassi, seems not to have objected to his wife's music making.

Not all women of Bach's time were content to limit their musical lives to reflecting well on their parents and husbands. Christiane Mariane von Ziegler was a pioneer not only in the literary realm but also in the musical. She rejected the traditional constraints imposed on female musicians in choosing instruments. As she wrote in a letter to a female friend:

> You are curious to know whether I practice daily all of the instruments to which I refer in my letters. Indeed I do, though I do not pretend to be more

than a raw apprentice at them. You are quite amazed that I have also taken up the recorder and the flute, which seem to you strange choices. Hopefully the following explanation of my motivations for doing so will calm your mind. I am aware that those of our gender who evince a tendency toward and a love for learning music ordinarily end up playing the keyboard or the lute. I myself not only laid the foundation of my musical knowledge with these instruments, but attempt daily to strengthen my command of them; both require not only time and patience but also skillful and practiced fingers. But if I am to reveal the truth, I cannot deny that the instruments that borrow their sound and pleasing qualities from human breath and the stirring tongue have always been of far greater interest and value to me. They are obviously more difficult for a woman to learn than are the stringed instruments, but my uncommon affinity and enthusiasm for wind instruments helped to ease the difficulty and remove all the stones in my path. An additional reason for my preference stems from a perhaps not-so-noble desire for honor: many women can be heard performing the lute and keyboard every day, while the flute and recorder are seldom played by German ladies. That which is rare and strange always wins more acclamation and favor than that which is commonplace. Should you wish to make the objection that such instruments are inappropriate for a lady, as they are usually associated with men, I can assure you that French women of both noble and bourgeois blood—who are regarded by all nations as the most galant and artful creatures in all the world—often play the flute. [. . .] So please have your daughter learn this pleasurable and unusual instrument without further consideration in order that I might have a female comrade.[15]

In advocating for expanding the instrumental choices for girls and women, Frau von Ziegler confirmed the power of the traditional constraints she sought to break.

Christiane Mariane von Ziegler also eschewed easy galanterien, preferring slower, more heavily ornamented music that, in her view, was more interesting. As she wrote in a letter to a male friend who had sent her some compositions by mail:

The overture you included in the package, as well as the accompanying fugue, in which nearly all voices are heard throughout, are very beautiful. The art here brings credit to its creator, as do the two concertos, though I would have preferred that the works were somewhat more endearing and flattering to the ear, and not so serious. It seems to me that it takes a greater artist to play an adagio than an allegro, because the former is so much more enchanting and full of love. I know many who demonstrate great facility in their playing and for this reason are held to be great virtuosi by some, but when one seeks amenity and ornamentation, one is left searching among the rests. There is more art to be found in decoration than in speed, and those who see and hear only the springing notes seem to think more highly of a flighty minuet or polonaise than a concerto or an overture and prefer galanterien to those artful and serious works that take us much more trouble to learn. But to each his own taste.[16]

Princess Amalia of Prussia, younger sister of King Friedrich II, was another bold individualist who opted never to marry, instead becoming an abbess (or "Bride of Christ") in Quedlinburg. She visited the convent just twice in thirty-one years, preferring to spend her time in Berlin.[17] Amalia relentlessly cultivated musical skills, taking up instruments traditionally associated with men, such as the violin and the flute. She was also an avid keyboardist. At age thirty-two, she had Johann Peter Migendt build her a small organ.[18] Two letters she wrote in 1755 to her sister-in-law, Wilhelmine of Hessen-Kassel, reveal her obvious delight in crushing the notion of a women's music room as an inviolate space:

> Great news, my dear sister—interesting for me, though perhaps not for you. Today I played my organ for the first time. Countess Schwerin says that it is a bit noisy—that is natural, but the sound is charming—I beg you to tell this to my brothers—it gave me real pleasure—the boys of the street did not gather round, although the balcony was open—this proves that the instrument hasn't the volume typical of church organs—I really want to accompany each of my brothers in a solo and to be sure that their continuo part is not off by a semi-tone [. . .].[19]

> Guillaume will tell you that he was present at the inauguration of my organ—I trot over to it every day after dinner—it is the only exercise that I allow myself, the only thing that gives me pleasure. Then I am confident, like Orpheus who, when he played his lyre, assembled all the beasts to listen to him—under my windows, on the staircase, in the corridor, every place is full of a rabble that gathers round—this amuses me, for I am giving them a spectacle gratis.[20]

Amalia relished this opportunity to run roughshod over the precious image of the keyboard-playing lady cloistered in her practice room, biding her time until a man came along to marry her. She opted instead for promiscuity, giving noisy performances on a massive organ, hoping to draw even the attention of the "boys from the street." They were no doubt fascinated both by her performance and by the striking image of a princess unburdening herself of her assigned social role and adopting that of a professional organist.[21]

The rhetoric of ease associated with women at the keyboard suggested that they were less ambitious musicians than men. The music they were encouraged to play was simpleminded, more athletic exercise than means of genuine expression. They played in order to please their parents and potential suitors, who interpreted modest virtuosity as a sign of docility. As the examples of Frau von Ziegler and Princess Amalia demonstrate, however, some women took great exception to these conventions. Others pushed social boundaries in more subtle ways.

৵৯

The Countesses zu Epstein were the youngest daughters of Ernst Ludwig, Landgrave of Hessen-Darmstadt. The state their father ruled consisted of more than a dozen noncontiguous bits of land which stretched over three thousand square kilometers and was home to around fifty thousand people. Compared with the most illustrious states of the Holy Roman Empire—for example Prussia, Saxony, and Bavaria—Hessen-Darmstadt boasted few natural resources. Its capital city of Darmstadt was small and rural, with a population of perhaps three thousand.[22]

Ernst Ludwig nonetheless did what he could to keep up with his galant peers, and he was constantly tempted to live beyond his means. Already in 1707 his mother had complained of insurmountable debts and criticized her son for a "disorderly and corrupt" approach to finances. Decades before the Countesses zu Epstein were born, their father had commissioned a new palace, an opera house, and an orangerie, and introduced the colossally expensive practice of *par force* hunting. Throughout his tenure, his court (*Hofstaat*) employed some 260 people, including around sixty government bureaucrats, sixty horsemen, thirty huntsmen, twenty-five cooks, and twenty musicians.[23] By 1722 the Landgrave had accumulated unpaid bills amounting to 1.3 million reichsthaler.[24]

Ernst Ludwig had married early and sired five surviving children by his first wife. Since her death in 1705, he had been amorously involved with numerous women but had married no one. Things changed, however, in the 1720s, when he began a relationship with a widow more than two decades his junior, known as the Countess von Seiboldsdorf. Born Luise Sophie, Baroness (*Freiin*) von Spiegel zum Desenberg, she had raised herself to the level of countess (*Gräfin*) through her first marriage to a Count von Seiboldsdorf and was intent on raising herself still higher by marrying the aging Landgrave. Ernst Ludwig relented under some duress. The couple was married on January 20, 1727, just two months before the arrival of their first daughter, Luise Charlotte, who was born on March 22, 1727. Three years later, on July 27, 1730, the couple had a second daughter, Friederika Sophie.

Ernst Ludwig's grown children saw the Countess von Seiboldsdorf and her daughters as upstarts. As the court's debts reached into the millions of reichstaler, the Landgrave withdrew from courtly life and nervously sought to solve the state's financial problems by using alchemy to turn lead into gold.[25] His five older children did what they could to prevent their younger half-siblings from draining scant resources. They persuaded their father to have his second marriage officially designated morganatic. That is, the Countess von Seiboldsdorf and her offspring would remain outside the main line of inheritance, bearing the name "Countesses zu Epstein" (after a tiny corner of their father's territory) rather than "Landgravins von Hessen-Darmstadt." The Countess von Seiboldsdorf found the Epstein designation *trop odieuse* and complained generally of a lack of respect at court, alleging that whenever she arrived at the palace she was overrun by half-grown lackeys who did not even reach for their hats, let alone doff them in proper deference.[26]

The situation became still more difficult for the Countess von Seibolds-dorf after Landgrave Ernst Ludwig died in 1739. Rather than endure the affronts of her stepchildren and their allies, she opted to leave Darmstadt, taking up residence in the small town of Rauschenberg, several days' travel to the north, where she owned a modest estate left over from her first marriage. Her daughters, by now aged twelve and nine, were left to fend for themselves under the new Landgrave, their forty-eight-year-old half-brother Ludwig VIII von Hessen-Darmstadt. The girls had to beg him for virtually everything, from permission to travel to the sugar they mixed into their tea.[27] As they put it in a letter they wrote to him in 1742: "We feel it necessary to seek asylum with you, and very humbly ask that Your Highness remember Your Highness's oft-repeated promises to provide for us as a father and to keep us in mercy."[28]

The Countesses zu Epstein remained in Darmstadt, where they resided in the home of Christian Ludwig, Baron von Löwenstern, an amateur battle-scene painter and composer.[29] Their education was entrusted to governesses and private tutors with whom they had little rapport. In one letter to their half-brother, the girls charged that their governess, a certain Madame Ebel, was scarcely capable of governing herself and regularly subjected them to what they called an "unworthy slavery" (*unwürdige Sklaverÿ*).[30] The governess shot back, decrying the "pains and insults" she had been obliged to suffer at the hands of the Countesses zu Epstein and alleging that the girls, then fourteen and eleven, regarded her unjustly as "the most vile person in the world" (*la plus vil persone du monde*).

From faraway Rauschenberg, the Countess von Seiboldsdorf did her best to stay involved in her daughters' lives. Among her highest priorities was making sure they were well trained in the arts. In a letter to Ludwig VIII dated November 12, 1746, she cited their achievements in dance and sought further opportunities for them to show off their skills:

I take this opportunity to inform your Highness of the reasons why the two countesses have trained so much in dance with the Court Dancemaster, Monsieur de Moll, and have performed in the home of the equerry [*Stallmeister*], Herr von Schorockofski, to universal applause, but have not danced at court or in the opera house. Madame de Schade and Madame Ebel [the girls' governesses] regard dancing as uppity and sinful; they have discouraged and even forbidden the countesses from taking part, as the court lackey Andreas Leisler has confidentially informed me. Frau von Schorockofski has expressed her strong opposition to this ban on the countesses' dancing; she believes that they might well be the very best dancers at court, having seen how skillfully they performed in her home. [. . .] If your Serene Highness would mercifully permit the countesses as well as the girls of the von Minnigerode family and other young people to hold a ball in the large room on the top floor of my apartment, Your Highness could and would receive a more in-depth report, as Frau von Schorockofski would serve as inspector and presiding matron.[31]

The Countess von Seiboldsdorf recognized that her daughters might improve their standing at court by dancing and thereby overcome the limits of their morganatic status. Through spies, like the lackey she mentioned, and diplomatic letters like this one, she did what she could to undercut the influence of the governess and all others who she felt stood in the way of her daughters' advancement.

It was undoubtedly to this same end that the Countess von Seiboldsdorf arranged to have her daughters trained in music. By 1742, when they were twelve and fifteen years old, both girls already had a firm grasp of note reading and keyboard technique.[32] From 1742 to 1745 their mother arranged for a young man from Rauschenberg named Johannes Merle—the mysterious "Me" of the manuscript collection—to travel to Darmstadt and instruct them in both religion and music.[33] Merle was ideally suited to the job. He had studied theology at the University of Giessen beginning in 1729 and the University of Jena beginning in 1731, and he was an experienced musician.[34] As the son of the Countess von Seiboldsdorf's pastor in Rauschenberg, Merle was also unlikely to resist her control.

⁊ℰ

The keyboard manuscripts Johannes Merle prepared for the Countesses zu Epstein fall into two types: those presenting a variety of pieces by multiple composers extracted from larger works, and those presenting one multi-movement work by a single composer. Modern classical musicians tend to treat the music set down on paper by eighteenth-century composers as inviolate. Rarely is an individual movement of a suite or sonata left out or presented out of sequence in performance. Eighteenth-century musicians, by contrast, tended to treat the music much more roughly. Each work was like a buffet from which one could select some items and ignore others. In preparing multiple-composer manuscripts for the Countesses zu Epstein, Merle made some effort to keep movements of a single suite together, but he often left some movements out or presented them in an altered sequence. Examples are presented in chart 1:

Chart 1. Multiple-Composer Manuscripts for the Countesses zu Epstein

Composer's Original Presentation	Manuscripts for the Countesses zu Epstein
G. F. Händel: Suite Nr. 7 in G minor **(London, 1720) [HWV 432]** Ouverture 1. [Grave] 2. Presto *Andante* *Allegro* Sarabande Gique Passacaille	**F.S.C.Z.E. SONATINEN... ex clav. A dur et** **ex clave A moll del Sigl. Schmidt,** **Hirschman & Sorgen et. Hendel** **(Darmstadt, Jul. 1744)** Sonata del Sigl. Schmidt: Allegro temperat [A] Menuet [Schmidt] [A] Rejouissance [Schmidt] [A] Gique en Gallop [Schmidt] [A] *Allegro del Sigl. Hendel* [transposed from g to a] *Presto* [Händel] [transposed from g to a] Aria affectuosissim del Sigl. Hirschman [a] Menuet 1 [Hirschman] [a] Menuet 2 [Hirschman] [a] Sonatine del Sigl. Sorgen [Sorge] [a]
C. Graupner: Suite in A major **(Darmstadt, ca. 1720-30?) [GWV 147]** *Allemande* Courante Sarabande *Double* *Air* *Menuet* Menuet Air Air (Largo) *Gique*	**A Tonus von Allerhand Auctoribus aufs** **CLAVECIN vor F.S.C.Z.E. (Darmstadt, 1743)** Amoroso del Sigl. Telemann Capriccio del Sigl. Sagorsky Concerto del Sigl. Agrel Largo [Agrell] Menuet 1 [Agrell] Menuet 2 [Agrell] Gique [Agrell] *Menuet del Sigl. Graupner* *Aria del Sigl. Graupn.* Concerto del Seigr. Eberth Allegro [Eberth] *PARTIE del Sigl. Graupner	Allem:* *Double* [Graupner] *Gique* [Graupner]

Merle organized the multiple-composer manuscripts he prepared for the countesses by key.[35] Both examples in chart 1 were prepared for Friederika Sophie and are in the tonality of A (major and minor).[36] Two movements from the Suite by Händel had to be transposed from G minor up to A minor to accommodate them to the manuscript's other contents. Presumably this focus on key or tonality as primary organizing factor had something to do with temperament. Once the harpsichord was tuned to a particular key, the girls could play from this manuscript for hours.

The arrangement by tonality may also have had a pedagogical aim. Merle familiarized the student's hands with one key before moving on to the next. This would have the effect of orienting the student to the ways of functional harmony. After learning all twenty-four pieces in A major/minor, the pupil would have developed a good sense of the tonal polarities within one key and could have built on this knowledge when moving on to music in another key.

The second type of manuscript ordinarily presents one multimovement work by a single composer in its entirety, as in the two examples in chart 2. The composer's original conception (for example, in terms of the number and sequence of movements) remains, in these cases, unaltered.

Since the manuscripts are often dated by year and month, it is possible to determine, roughly, the sequence in which they were copied. On the graph presented in plate 8, each of the columns represents a manuscript, the height of which shows the number of movements within. Blue columns represent multiple-composer manuscripts, while red columns represent single-composer manuscripts. From left to right one can see the months and years in which Merle prepared them.

Chart 2. Single-Composer Manuscripts for the Countesses zu Epstein

---

CONCERTO à Cembalo Obligato, Violino Primo, Violino Secondo, Alto Viola, del Seigl. Graun ex clave C moll. L. C. C. Z. E. Dst: 1743 Jul. Me. [Bv: XIII: 50]
Allegro [c]
Larghetto [E-flat]
Allegro [c]

SONATA à Cembalo Solo ex clav. G mol. del Sigl. De Loewenstern. L. C. C. Z. E. Dst. 1744 Dec.
Les Plaintes [g]
Allegro [g]
Les Satyres [g]
Giga [g]
Les Nymphes [g]
Allegro [g]

The multi-composer and single-composer manuscripts cluster together chronologically. Just because a manuscript was copied in February 1744, however, does not necessarily mean that the music it contains was actually learned that month. It is more likely that Merle's copying activities reflected his access to materials that served him as models. That he copied none of the surviving manuscripts between February and July 1744, and that he copied so many in December 1744 (fifty-four movements in one month) likely reveals more about his schedule than it reveals about the musical lives of the Countesses zu Epstein.

The music Johannes Merle copied for the zu Epstein sisters is like that which was published with female players in mind: galanterien predominate. There is an emphasis on pieces of a quick, motoric character. Works originally composed in common time are often sped up to cut time, with eighth notes beamed in groups of four rather than groups of two. Two movements of the Suite by G. F. Händel cited above, for example, were titled "Andante" and "Allegro" by the composer, but in Merle's manuscript they are sped up to "Allegro" and "Presto."

Pieces with programmatic titles are also common. The few slow movements in the countesses' collection are not improvisational or melancholy in tone but rather evocative of a pastoral idyll, with pedal tones and quasi-programmatic titles like "Shepherding" (*Les Bergeries*) and "Lullaby-Minuet" (*Wiegen-Menuet*).[37] A substantial number of the quicker pieces feature hand-crossing, which added a theatrical element to musical performances.

The manuscripts Merle prepared for the Countesses zu Epstein are virtually free of works that have a contemplative or improvisatory character. Nor do they contain strict counterpoint. The countesses were not encouraged to cultivate their skills in these realms. Furthermore, there is a curious lack of progression in this collection; the pieces copied in 1744 are not technically more advanced than those copied in 1742.

The most popular movement types and titles are given in table 3, along with the frequency of their appearance in the combined collections of the sisters zu Epstein. The names of the composers whose music Merle copied for the Countesses zu Epstein are presented in table 4, along with the number of movements credited to each.[38] Much of the repertoire Merle copied for the countesses was composed by musicians in Darmstadt—for example, Christoph Graupner, Jacob Friedrich Greiss, Jacob Führer, and Christoph Bieler—suggesting that Merle received it from local colleagues or from the court library.[39] The presence of three works attributed to "Rasbach"— presumably Johann Lorenz Rasbach, organist at the Lutheran church in Marburg—suggests that at least some of the repertoire he copied for the

Table 3. Movement Titles for the Countesses zu Epstein

Nr./Mvts.	Most Popular Movement Titles
85	Allegro
85	Menuet
37	Aria [Air, Arioso]
36	Programmatic Title [e.g., *Les Bergeries, La Poule*, etc.]
22	Gigue
13	Sonata [Sonatine]
11	Andante
11	Presto
10	Allemande
10	Gavotte
7	Capriccio
7	Courante
7	Rondeau
4	Bourrée
2	Double
2	Prelude [Præludium]
2	Sarabande
351 Total	

Table 4. Composers Copied for the Countesses zu Epstein

Nr. of Mvts.	Merle Attribution	Corresponding Names
72	Agrel	Johan Joachim Agrell
42	Loewenstern	Christian Ludwig, Baron von Löwenstern
33	Anonymous	?
29	Chelleri	Fortunato Chelleri
25	Platti	Giovanni Platti
23	Graupner	Christoph Graupner
18	Foerster	Christoph Foerster?
17	Marcello	Benedetto Marcello
16	Telemann	Georg Philipp Telemann
12	Händel	Georg Friedrich Händel
12	Sorge	Georg Andreas Sorge
9	Hirschmann	?
9	Lerme	Johannes Merle?
7	Graun	Carl Heinrich Graun
7	Torner	Joseph Torner?
6	Kolborn	Ernst Kolborn
6	Schmidt	Balthasar Schmidt?
4	Bieler	Christoph Bieler?
4	Froberger	Johann Jacob Froberger
4	F.S.C.Z.E.	Friederica Sophie, Countess of Epstein
4	Führer	Jacob Führer?
4	Greiss	Jacob Friedrich Greiss?
4	Hasse	Johann Adolph Hasse
4	Kolbe	Anton Kolbe?
3	Heinichen	Johann David Heinichen?

Table 4. Continued

3	Kirchhoff	Gottfried Kirchhoff?
3	Rasbach	Johann Laurenz Rasbach
3	Sagorsky	?
2	Eberth	?
2	Fesch	?
2	Gelinek	Hermann Anton Gelinek?
2	Lapis	Santo Lapis?
1	Bach	Johann Sebastian Bach
1	Count de Buckebourg	Albrecht Wolfgang zu Schaumburg-Lippe?
1	Hasman	?
1	Pepusch	Johann Christoph Pepusch?
1	Ristori	Giovanni Alberto Ristori?
1	Scarlatti	Domenico Scarlatti
1	Schneider	?
1	Seybert	?
1	Zachau	Friedrich Wilhelm Zachau
400 Total		

Countesses zu Epstein was from his own personal library. Merle and his brother, August, must have come to know Rasbach's works while studying in Marburg. Rasbach is an entirely obscure figure whose music would not likely have found its way to Darmstadt if Merle had not brought it himself.[40] The appearance of works by Christian Ludwig, Baron von Loewenstern, comes as no surprise, since the Countesses zu Epstein lived in his home during the 1740s.[41]

One suspects that the works attributed to "Lerme" were composed by the teacher himself, since Lerme and Merle are anagrams.[42] The name is perhaps additionally a pun on the German word for noise (*Lärm*), suggesting a self-deprecating sense of humor and perhaps an inside joke between pupils and teacher. Lerme's music is indeed noisy in the sense that it is highly energetic and full of awkward leaps. It seems likely that these works were composed with the countesses in mind.

Johannes Merle apparently put only a single work by J. S. Bach before the Countesses zu Epstein. In 1742, while preparing a multiple-composer manuscript in B-flat major for Luise Charlotte, he copied the "Giga" from Bach's first *Keyboard Partita* (BWV 825/7), shown in chart 3. The work has a sunny, playful character, predictable four-bar phrasing, and hand-crossing. Such features are as typical of the zu Epstein sisters' music collection as they are atypical of Bach's œuvre. His slim representation in the countesses' music collection—one movement out of four hundred—is probably typical of the place he occupied in the musical lives of other teenage girls of his era.

Chart 3. The Only Bach Work to Be Copied for the Countesses zu Epstein

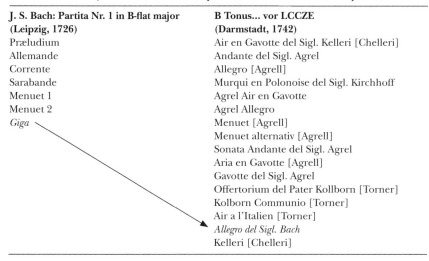

J. S. Bach: Partita Nr. 1 in B-flat major (Leipzig, 1726)	B Tonus... vor LCCZE (Darmstadt, 1742)
Præludium	Air en Gavotte del Sigl. Kelleri [Chelleri]
Allemande	Andante del Sigl. Agrel
Corrente	Allegro [Agrell]
Sarabande	Murqui en Polonoise del Sigl. Kirchhoff
Menuet 1	Agrel Air en Gavotte
Menuet 2	Agrel Allegro
Giga	Menuet [Agrell]
	Menuet alternativ [Agrell]
	Sonata Andante del Sigl. Agrel
	Aria en Gavotte [Agrell]
	Gavotte del Sigl. Agrel
	Offertorium del Pater Kollborn [Torner]
	Kolborn Communio [Torner]
	Air a l'Italien [Torner]
	Allegro del Sigl. Bach
	Kelleri [Chelleri]

Theoretically, the Countess zu Epstein might have been forced by their mother or their teacher to practice the keyboard. There are signs, however, that they were personally invested in their own musical education. The manuscript of a Sonata by Giovanni Platti bears the following indication in Merle's hand: "L.C.C.Z.E. cedes this manuscript to F.S.C.Z.E." (*L.C.C.Z.E. cedirt F.S.C.Z.E.*).[43] This remark is a sign that the girls kept their music collections separate and that changes in ownership were documented. It suggests that Luise Charlotte gave this work to her sister, perhaps as a gift. If the Countesses themselves cared about which manuscripts belonged to whom, they must have cared about the contents.

One can also sense active engagement from the countesses' own copying activities. Luise Charlotte herself copied manuscripts of keyboard works by Rasbach,[44] Seybert, and Sorge,[45] French songs,[46] and Italian opera arias.[47] Her work is rough and characterized by remarkable errors: a missing half-bar here, an incorrect number of beats there. For example, after a failed attempt to fit a hand-crossing piece by Seybert composed in 2/4 into bars of 3/8 (see musical example 6), she gave up and started over, copying the entire thing in the proper time signature on another sheet of paper.[48] She seems to have relished this mundane work, copying not only her own parts but sometimes those of her accompanying musicians. In October 1743, at age sixteen, she copied the viola part to an aria by Leonardo Vinci, adding the following remark at the bottom of the page: "NB. Here the second violin and alto [vocal part] still have to be written out separately."[49] Clearly this young woman was unwilling to wait for Merle or other professional scribes to copy everything on her behalf. She sought in this modest way to overstep the boundaries established for girls of her station.

More striking still, in October 1744 Johannes Merle copied the title page for an entire *Sonata* he credited to "Illustrious Madame F. S. C. Z. E."[50] The pages within have staff lines but are otherwise blank. It seems he was expecting the fourteen-year-old Friederika Sophie zu Epstein to provide music. The only movements that found their way onto the page are a pair of "Menuets," the first of which, in C major, is in Merle's hand. The second of these, in C minor, appears on a loose-leaf piece of paper in the hand of Friederika Sophie herself (see musical examples 1–4).

These two minuets are clearly the work of an inexperienced composer; the progression of phrases and harmonies is sometimes awkward. But if indeed Friederika Sophie composed these works at the age of fourteen, she already had a solid grasp of the style and construction of a minuet. There is a great deal of attention to motivic integration, and she comfortably moves from one key area to the next, perhaps a testament to the tonality-based pedagogy of her teacher. Of the eighty-odd minuets in this collection, Friederika Sophie's are most similar to those credited to "Lerme" (Merle), copied just one month earlier.[51]

One might suspect that Merle himself composed these minuets too and merely attributed them to Friederika Sophie out of affection or respect, or to flatter her. There are, however, good reasons to believe that Friederika Sophie herself actually composed this music. Her handwriting in the second minuet is modeled on Merle's, but it's extremely shaky: beams are forgotten, systems are awkwardly grouped in threes rather than in twos, and so on. If she were copying from a source prepared by another composer (Merle or anyone else), she would presumably have made fewer egregious mistakes, since tracing every element of a model manuscript is a strictly mechanical process. One might expect the occasional muffed time signature or missing bar, as one finds in her sister's manuscripts of music by other composers, but not consistently missing beams on groups of eighth notes.

That Friederika Sophie herself composed this music is suggested by another composition in her handwriting: a "March" in F major on a piece of scratch paper.[52] The march shows the same musical aptitude and the same notation problems. Friederika Sophie could not decide at the beginning if she should beam the faster notes as sixteenths or as eighths. This quandary suggests deliberation rather than mechanical copying. On the back of the page there is also a fragment of music based on the same march (see musical examples 5 and 6). It was obviously an attempt to further explore the work's motives. Clearly she was not simply copying from a model manuscript but was herself composing.

The discrepancy between the musical experience evident in Friederika Sophie's compositions and the awkward, untrained character of her handwritten notation reveals much about what was expected of her and how she navigated these expectations. Her musical life, like that of her sister, was expected to begin and end with the execution of charming, quick repertoire composed by others. No one anticipated that she would ever compose. If anyone had, she would have been taught to write music down on paper. Copying was among the primary tools young male composers used to master their craft, a means of accumulating repertoire and learning from "mute teachers" (*stumme Lehrmeister*).[53] Although the initiative to compose must have been her own, Friederika Sophie seems to have had the support of her teacher, who showed himself willing and even proud to copy the compositions of the "Illustrious Madame F. S. C. Z. E."

The zu Epstein sisters were not content to accept the strictures their society imposed on female musicians. Luise Charlotte wanted to engage in the process of choosing her own music and in the messy business of setting it down on paper. She enjoyed temporarily usurping the position ordinarily occupied by their teacher, Johannes Merle. Friederika Sophie sought not only to recreate music that had been written by others but also to create new music of her own. She sought to usurp not only the position of the teacher but also to see her own name in the spaces ordinarily occupied by those of famous composers such as Agrell, Chelleri, Platti, and Bach.

≈

Little is known about the circumstances in which the Countesses zu Epstein made music. However, a 1753 inventory of their mother's residence in Rauschenberg, which describes the contents of a small bedroom that contained a harpsichord (*Clavecin*), provides a sense of context. The instrument was surrounded by a fireplace with related implements (bellows, tongs, a little iron shovel, an iron grate for holding firewood); a cracked mirror above the fireplace; a bed with two mattresses of drill (heavy cotton) fabric stuffed with hay and a comforter lined with white linen and stuffed with silk; a little bobbin for winding yarn; two square tables (one of walnut and the other lacquered black and covered with leather); a large, brocade sun hat; two small, circular tables (*Guéridons*) with walnut inlay; four large portraits and four small portraits; and a florid, blue carpet.[54]

Musical Example 1. Friederika Sophie zu Epstein: Menuet 1 in C major. Transcribed by Andrew Talle.

Musical Example 2. Friederika Sophie zu Epstein: Menuet 1 in C major.
Copied ca. October 1744 by Johannes Merle. D-B: N.Mus.ms.BP95.

Musical Example 3. Friederika Sophie zu Epstein: Menuet 2 in C minor.

Musical Example 4. Friederika Sophie zu Epstein: Menuet 2 in C minor.
Copied ca. October 1744 by Friederika Sophie zu Epstein. D-B: N.Mus.ms.BP95.

Musical Example 5. Friederika Sophie zu Epstein: March and March Fragment in D major. Transcribed by Andrew Talle.

Musical Example 6. Friederika Sophie zu Epstein: March and March Fragment in D major. Copied by Friederika Sophie zu Epstein. At the top of the page is an abortive attempt by Luise Charlotte zu Epstein to copy a work designated "Allegro moderato" in F major attributed to "Seybert." D-B: N.Mus.ms.BP670.

The primary audience member whom the Countesses zu Epstein likely had in mind as they practiced was their half-brother, Landgrave Ludwig VIII von Hessen-Darmstadt. That they performed for him with some regularity is revealed by a letter of February 1, 1750, in which they request permission to attend a performance of J. A. Hasse's opera *Demofoonte* in Mannheim:

> Monseigneur! Having seen that Your Serene Highness takes some satisfaction in the little we have accomplished in music, we would like once again to have the inestimable pleasure of singing in the presence of Your Serene Highness, and will try to acquit ourselves better, in a fashion that is capable of contenting such an august auditor. And as the opera currently playing at Mannheim might help us to improve further, we would like to ask your permission to attend it incognito [. . .]. This favor would give us so much happiness.[55]

Performances like these would have taken place at court, in the presence not only of their half-brother but also of the entire court assembly. They were talented singers and keyboardists, but the environment must have made them nervous. There were other women of the court who they could tell wanted nothing more than to see them flub the hand-crossing or break a string.

All of their practicing, however, seems to have paid off. Musical performances at court must have been among the factors that led Ludwig VIII to assume the role of protector to the Countesses zu Epstein. A nineteenth-century source preserves the following anecdote, which relates a signal event of their lives:

> During the reign of Ludwig VIII, some noblewomen took the liberty of asserting their superiority over the two Countesses zu Epstein in the courtly hierarchy, and to consistently treat them rudely. When the Landgrave became aware of this behavior, he was very upset and decided to put a quick and decisive end to this embarrassing situation. For this purpose he invited a large number of courtly women and men to his table. After the guests had been assembled in a carefully chosen room of the castle in Darmstadt, the Landgrave appeared leading each of the two Countesses zu Epstein by the hand. With a bow to the guests Ludwig VIII presented the two countesses with the words: "Ladies and Gentlemen, I present to you my sisters, the Countesses zu Epstein" [*Mesdames et Messieurs, je vous presente mes soeurs, les Comtesses d'Epstein*]. This unambiguous introduction had a decisive effect, for after that time none of the courtly ladies dared to condescend to the two sisters or to strive to surpass them in the courtly hierarchy.[56]

੨ᴥ

In 1745, Johannes Merle left Darmstadt to take up duties as deacon in the nearby town of Groß-Gerau. On November 18 of the same year he married Anna Magdalena Elizabetha Schneider, with whom he would eventually have ten children. Two years later he was appointed pastor in Büttelborn, and in 1759 he became pastor in Ginsheim, a post he held for the rest of his life.[57]

Luise Charlotte, Countess zu Epstein died at the age of twenty-six. The music manuscripts that had once been hers were absorbed into her sister's collection. Friederika Sophie kept them for the rest of her life. Her interest in preserving this music must have extended well beyond the practical. The sight of these manuscripts, the sounds of the music recorded within them, even the feel and smell of the paper must have brought forth a flood of memories. They represented not just a collection of keyboard repertoire but relics of the lost world of her youth, including the tensions with other women at court, the supportive and charming Herr Merle, and especially the fond memories of Luise Charlotte—and the painful cleft in her life brought on by her early death. What must she have thought, years later, while playing through music her sister had ceremoniously ceded to her or copied with her own hand?

Friederika Sophie remained unmarried and lived at court throughout her twenties and early thirties. She continued to make music in later life. In the spring of 1760, a performance she gave at court impressed an anonymous aristocratic visitor, who wrote of their encounter: "The Countess zu Epstein sang a few Italian arias very beautifully and accompanied herself at the harpsichord. She is a natural daughter of the former count, a person of thirty years of extraordinarily great intelligence and accomplishments."[58] In 1764, at age thirty-four, Friederika Sophie married Ludwig von Pretlack, a general in her half-brother's army. Although Pretlack was only a baron—not a count, let alone a landgrave like her father—his family had long served the court of Hessen-Darmstadt in important diplomatic and military roles, and the marriage brought her credit. Pretlack loved music and supported his wife's continued cultivation of keyboard skills. A letter she sent on July 4, 1768, reveals that she was in touch, via intermediaries, with the kapellmeister in Darmstadt, Wilhelm Gottfried Enderle, as well as a bassoonist and scribe named Johann Christian Klotsch ("Glotsch") who prepared manuscripts on her behalf, much as Johannes Merle had done decades earlier:

And as to the two concertos for the harpsichord, it would be difficult to judge them on the basis of the themes, if they are beautiful and good as well, I ask you to tell Enderle that if they cost only the price of copying, I rely on his judgment to make me a copy of one or the other or both if they merit it, in which case you will have the goodness to hire Glotsch, who I hope will be able to use paper that is wider than it is high. The general asks me to send along his compliments and thanks for your trouble.[59]

The Baron and Baroness von Pretlack had two sons and one daughter, all of whom lived to adulthood. Sadly, they scarcely knew their mother. Friederika Sophie died in Paris on August 26, 1770, at age forty. Her eldest child at the time was just four years old. The Baron von Pretlack remarried but carefully kept the manuscripts that had meant so much to his first wife and her sister. They remained out of the public eye until their discovery in 1968.

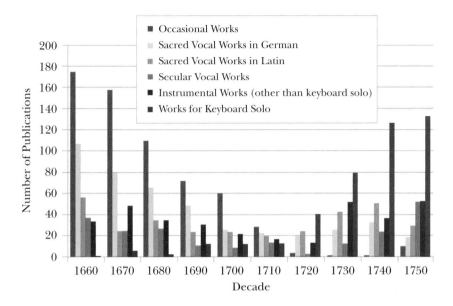

Plate 1. Music Printed in German-Speaking Lands, 1660–1759.

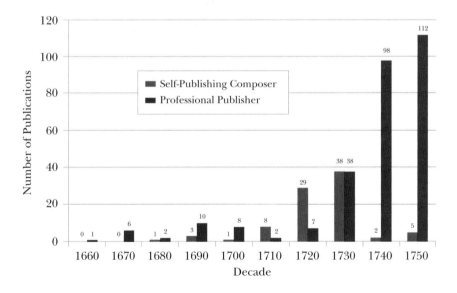

Plate 2. German Music for Keyboard Solo (for which the publisher is known), 1660–1759.

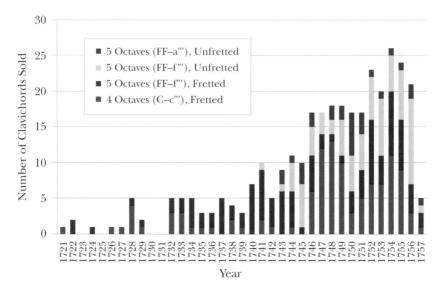

Plate 3. Barthold Fritz: Clavichord Sales, 1721–1757. The record for 1757 includes only the months January through March.

Plate 4. (4a.) Johann Christoph Eberling: Portrait of Barthold Fritz. Wolfenbüttel, Herzog August Bibliothek: Inv.Nr.7212. (4b.) Barthold Fritz: Signum from a Lost Clavichord. Braunschweig, Städtisches Museum.

Plate 5. Barthold Fritz: Clavichord for Johann Heinrich Heyne (1751). London, Victoria and Albert Museum: Inv.Nr.339–1882.

Plate 6. Johann Kuhnau: Frontispiece to *Musicalische Vorstellungen einige biblischer Historien* (1700). Staatsbibliothek zu Berlin: Mus.ant.pract.K385.

Plate 7. Johann
Heinrich Tischbein
the Elder (self-portrait
with the artist's first
wife, Marie Sophie
Tischbein, ca. 1757).
Gemäldegalerie Berlin,
Inv.Nr.1697.

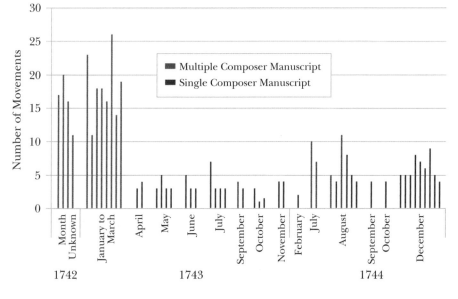

Plate 8. Johannes Merle: Keyboard Manuscripts for the Countesses zu Epstein,
1742–1744.

Plate 9. Anonymous: Portrait of Friederika Sophie, Countess zu Epstein. Schlossmuseum Darmstadt, Inv. Nr.B21320.

Plate 10. Elias Gottlob Haußmann: Portrait of Luise Adelgunde Viktorie Gottsched (1740). Custodie und Kunstsammlungen der Universität Leipzig. Inv. Nr.4691/90.

Plate 11. Leonhard
Schorer: Portrait of
Johann Christoph
Gottsched (1744).
Custodie und
Kunstsammlungen der
Universität Leipzig. Inv.
Nr.0699/90.

Plate 12. Detail from
Grundriß über die
Rittergüter Rötha
und Rüben (1681).
Sächsisches Staatsarchiv,
Staatsarchiv Leipzig,
20532 Rittergut Rötha,
K1.

Plate 13. Gottfried Silbermann: Organ for Rötha's Church of St. George (1721). Photograph courtesy of Jihoon Song.

Plate 14. Anonymous: Portrait of Christian August, Freiherr von Friesen. Photograph courtesy of Jihoon Song.

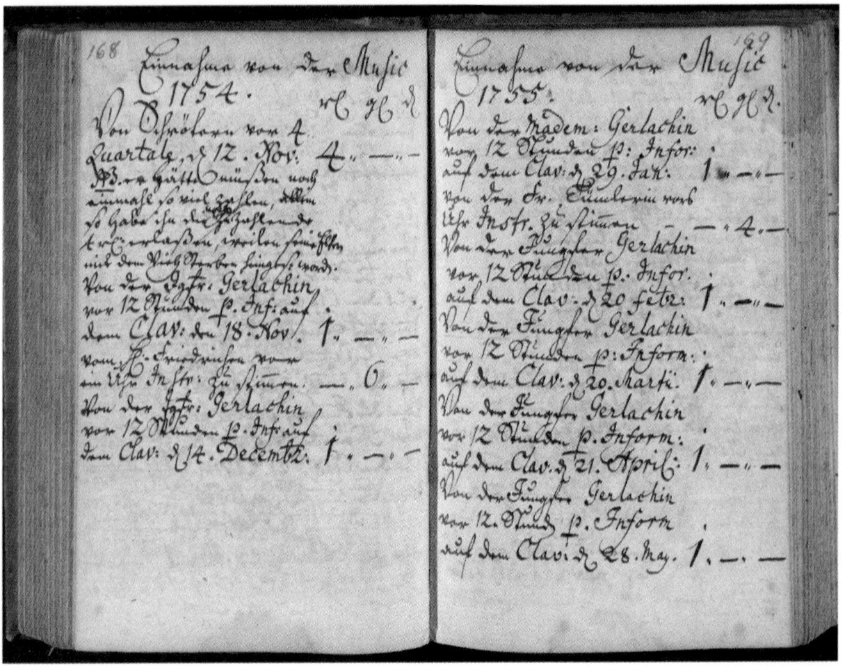

Plate 15. Carl August Hartung: Excerpt from *Kleine Wirthschafft Rechnung über Einnahme und Ausgabe.* D-BS: H III 3:99, 168–69.

Plate 16. Carl August Hartung: Excerpt from *Verzeichniß von Clavier-Piecen des seel. Herrn Joh: Seb: Bachs.* Staatsbibliothek zu Berlin: Mus. ms.theor.1215, f. 18r.

CHAPTER 6

A Marriage Rooted in Reason

Luise Adelgunde Victorie Gottsched (née Kulmus) was one of the most prolific and widely read writers and translators in J. S. Bach's Germany. Her life and that of her husband, Johann Christoph Gottsched, are unusually well documented, as they were both subjects of avid attention from their contemporaries. The couple's many surviving letters offer fascinating insight into their private lives.[1] In addition to her successful career as an author, Luise Gottsched was also an avid amateur musician. For much of her life, keyboard and lute playing served as a means of expressing optimism that human beings could improve themselves and the world around them by cultivating their unique rational faculties. In later years, as her relationship with her husband began to fray, her faith in rationalist philosophy suffered, and she endured a crisis of both body and spirit. This chapter presents an account of her musical activities within the framework of her courtship and marriage.

ॐ

One evening in the spring of 1729, the hands of a sixteen-year-old girl flitted across a harpsichord, dazzling guests assembled in her family's home in Danzig. Her powers of concentration were acute, though on this occasion she probably found it a bit difficult to focus. As colorful fugues and improvised caprices flowed from her fingers and mingled with the sounds of conversation and spoons stirring sugar into coffee, her mind was likely distracted by the presence of a stranger. A young man in the audience had traveled all the way from Leipzig in hopes of marrying her.

Luise Kulmus was tall and beautiful, with cherubic cheeks, a long nose, and enormous eyes. Under her mother's guidance she had mastered cooking, cleaning, knitting, calculating household finances, and all the other essentials of eighteenth-century homemaking. Her discipline was already becoming the stuff of legend. An early obsession with lace making had inspired her father, a physician, to burn her tools for fear that staring so intently for too long would damage her eyes. Luise turned her attention to literature, and it became her primary passion in life. She read plays, novels, and poetry in French and English, and later in Greek and Latin as well. Her zeal was such that she sometimes copied out pages, chapters, or entire books by hand. By age sixteen she had already written numerous short poems and translated Marie-Madeleine de La Fayette's four-hundred-page novel, *La Princesse de Clèves* (1678) into German.[2]

Fräulein Kulmus was also deeply interested in music. Her mother had arranged for her to receive proper instruction at the keyboard, and she had quickly excelled. On one occasion she had, in the attic of her home, found a lute her father had plucked during his university years; she had subsequently taught herself to play, nimbly navigating among the few strings that were still intact. Her father's colleagues, who regularly gathered to perform chamber music in the Kulmus home, offered a welcome audience.

The stranger distracting Luise this particular evening was Johann Christoph Gottsched, a twenty-nine-year-old assistant professor of poetry at the University of Leipzig. Gottsched was brilliant and diplomatic, though in discussions of philosophy or aesthetics he could become imperious. The force of his arguments was enhanced by his extraordinary size; he was usually the tallest and largest man in the room.

As those who conversed with Gottsched quickly learned, he was a firm believer in the rationalism of Gottfried Wilhelm Leibniz and Christian Wolff. The "new philosophy," as it was then called, held that the universe God created could be fully known only through careful observation and rational deduction. It was up to human beings to cultivate the discernment that would enable them to systematically consider and ultimately perfect the world around them. Gottsched was constitutionally opposed to assertions of truth that could not be explained in terms of logic, whether they came from superstitious peasants or from learned theologians. His special abomination was Pietism, a grassroots branch of Christianity whose moony adherents were more likely to weep and faint at the prospect of God's mercy than they were to think critically. Gottsched himself believed in natural religion, a universal spirituality of which historical religions were merely manifestations. A few years before visiting Danzig, he had delivered a speech titled "On the Poison of Religious Extremism and the Beneficial Tolerance of All Religions" in which he imagined an encounter between a Muslim, a Confucian, and a Catholic, asking each of them rhetorically: "Which of you is right? Which of you should have the power to oppress the others?"[3] The answer he offered—"No one"—was anathema to most religious and political authorities of the era, who regarded such thoughts as corrosive to civilization. The author defended himself by proclaiming Lutheranism to be the most rational religion, but his opponents rightly sensed that his allegiance to Gospel truth was weak.

Gottsched had come to Danzig after a visit to his hometown of Königsberg, where his parents still lived. He had decided to spend three months here on his way back to Leipzig, ostensibly to make professional contacts with like-minded intellectuals, including Luise's father, Johann Georg Kulmus. Luise herself no doubt suspected, however, that something else was afoot. She had received her first letter from him two years earlier. Gottsched had been inspired to write after a mutual acquaintance had shown him a few of her poems. Wanting to know if "fame's news could be believed," he had requested more of her work, and she had quickly obliged. As he later recalled: "Every line exceeded my expectations."[4]

For Gottsched, Luise Kulmus represented an ideal of enlightened womanhood he had devised theoretically some years earlier. He and two male colleagues had decided that the perfect woman was fastidious in her housework, virtuous in her dealings with others, intelligent, well educated, literary, and musical; she was also immune to vices such as vanity, pedantry, flattery, pretense, arrogance, selfishness, jealousy, coquettishness, pride, and gossipmongering. In Gottsched's eyes, Luise Kulmus possessed all of these feminine virtues and none of the vices.[5]

After hearing the young lady at music, Gottsched went back to his lodgings, sharpened a quill pen, and set to work on a poem. It began: "Victoria! you've won my heart, I am your knave, Victoria!" He praised her as beautiful but also sensitive, not "like a marble statue" but full of wit.[6] It was her music making, however, that had captivated his imagination. He could not stop thinking about her hands:

> Can you, soft hands, please let me know
> If Hermes ever made such haste
> When he to hell's dark streams did go
> And there the dead's lost souls displaced?
> Does Orpheus strike tones through you,

He who put Cerberus to sleep,
And did through Pluto's Hades creep,
His lovely bride's death to undo?
No! Phoebus and his choir alone,
Inspire and touch, they drive each tone.

You seem to conjure, not to play,
Whenever you take up the lute;
One's veins and marrow must obey,
When harpsichord is your pursuit.
Oh richness of new fantasies!
How quick, how skillful, full and fine,
The colors that your fugues entwine.
You seem to play them all with ease!
Because, as one can see and hear,
Divine force is your puppeteer.

O would that I could kiss them all!
I'd kiss and kiss 'til I reached ten!
My pangs of conscience I'd forestall,
By so profusely thanking them.
To daily sense with eye and ear,
Such wisdom know, such beauty see!
So long as I have breath in me
I'll honor them and hold you dear.
I long to gaze upon your face
And there perceive a glimpse of grace!

If I could but such hopes afford!
Has here my pen just run astray?
Has it behaved in ways untoward?
Be still now, stop this idle play!
Fair caution hides with darkened veil,
The traces of each person's fate;
It's often best to calmly wait,
And trust that favor will prevail.
Enough, I'm fully satisfied:
Fate's proved so far a steadfast guide.[7]

The man who hated magical thinking above all showed himself ready and willing to cast aside his principles in order to win Luise's affection. Her fingers seemed "to conjure, not to play," affecting not his rational faculties but rather his "veins and marrow." Leibniz and Wolff were jettisoned in favor of Hermes, Pluto, Orpheus, Cerberus, and Phoebus. Perhaps Fräulein Kulmus was troubled by Gottsched's willingness to abandon rationalism for the sake of flattering her. Either he was a pure philosopher who was uninterested in connecting theory and practice, or her music making was too trivial to interpret in terms of his actual belief system. Furthermore, his effusiveness must have seemed oddly theoretical; it was as if he had somehow fallen in love with her before their first meeting.

Despite her misgivings, Fräulein Kulmus must have been intrigued. She recognized that marrying the professor from Leipzig would offer an unrivaled opportunity to continue doing the things she liked to do—namely, read, write, and make music. Gottsched had long been in favor of improving education for women and had championed other female writers. He would be supportive of her ongoing intellectual development. There were practical as well as theoretical benefits to being held up as a model of womanhood. What other suitor could offer so much?

Regardless of how Luise Kulmus felt, no courtship would be possible without the approval of her family.[8] Her parents recognized that their daughter was a true prize, and they might have seen her married to a wealthy banker or even a member of the lower nobility. Though sympathetic to Gottsched, they were concerned about his future. He showed great promise but had not yet attained the rank of full professor, and there was no guarantee that he would advance socially or economically. Furthermore, his exuberant embrace of the "new philosophy," while in line with the thinking of the Kulmus clan, was professionally dangerous. The mutual acquaintance who had first introduced Luise's poems to Gottsched, Christian Gabriel Fischer, had been fired from his professorship at the University of Königsberg for presenting the theories of Leibniz and Wolff in his lectures. And firing was not the worst of it. He'd been threatened by the king with hanging if he did not leave Königsberg within twenty-four hours and Prussia within forty-eight. His mother, wife, and daughter had "frozen in terror at the news" and had not seen him since.[9] Naturally, Luise Kulmus's parents did not wish to see their daughter suffer a similar fate.

❧

Gottsched left Danzig in June 1729 aboard a ship called "Hope" (*Hoffnung*). Upon receiving word of his voyage's successful conclusion, Luise wrote to him enthusiastically:

> So you have arrived safely in Leipzig! See what a good result has been achieved by our wishes. They accompanied you both on water and on land. Their denial would certainly have marked the first time that heaven had rejected the wishes of true friends and the pleading of a lady friend. One, and certainly not the smallest of my hopes has thus been fulfilled. [. . .] Who knows whether the name of your ship might be an auspicious sign? Let us trust the prudent fate that brought us together. If it is her will, we

will develop the purest and sweetest friendship. Her blessing is given only to the most virtuous. Let us be virtuous too, so that we may have a claim to her assistance.[10]

The Kulmus family had granted Gottsched permission to correspond with Luise, but only as a mentor, not as a suitor. The role fit comfortably for a man with such firm ideas about femininity; it would enable him to mold the object of his affection into the wife he wished her to become. Luise Kulmus was probably a bit unnerved by this molding process, but she showed herself open to his advice, at least in the semi-public forum of their correspondence. In his first letter, he offered observations on feminine behavior and a positive assessment of women in Saxony, the state where he hoped she would one day live with him. Her response suggests a strong desire to live up to his philosophical ideals:

> All that you wrote in your letter constitutes a model for how a virtuous woman should be and is also a proof of how far I, and most others of my gender, fall short of this ideal. The description you give of Saxon women is beneficial. The land that can boast of so many such daughters is lucky indeed, and the women themselves must be pleased that their virtue is appreciated even by foreigners. I myself hope not to be waylaid but rather to travel steadfastly down the path to virtue.[11]

Luise Kulmus's pragmatic orientation led her to rebuff the professor's sending more overt tokens of his affection in his efforts to win her hand in marriage, recognizing that these might arouse the ire of her family. Whenever he seemed to veer into the realm of romance, she sought to steer their relationship back toward mentorship. On January 7, 1731, she wrote a gentle but unequivocal response to jewelry or some other gift more likely to be sent by a suitor than by a mentor:

> The gift you included with your letter leads me to suspect that you think I am selfish, a vice I loathe. No, my best friend! You will never win me with gifts. The merits of the intellect and the heart must take precedence; all the treasures of the world are meaningless to me, though their appeal may be magnetic to others. Lead my heart not into temptation, that I might come to enjoy things from which I have tried to wean myself. Writings that develop the mind and better the heart will for me always be a welcome gift. In the future, I hope to receive no presents other than these as products of your generosity.[12]

On November 6, 1731, Luise Kulmus's father died, sending her spiraling into financial uncertainty and deep depression. She wrote to her mentor: "I hope to soon follow him into the holy home, where perhaps he awaits me with fatherly joy. This is my only wish."[13] Though worried about the object of his affection, Gottsched recognized this as an opportunity; within a month of her father's funeral, he had sent a letter formally asking for her hand in marriage. She demurred, pleading with him to respect the traditional period of mourning: "The positive opinion you have of me is extraordinarily flattering, and your decision does me honor. How happy I would be if I felt I had earned these laurels. [. . .] I would ask one thing of you, however, and that is to permit me to fully grieve before I think of happier days."[14]

Although Gottsched did not receive the answer he was hoping for, it was not an outright refusal, and the occasion had enabled him to bring his intentions into the open. He began to shift more aggressively from mentor to suitor, offering gifts that were not strictly educational. Foremost among these were packets of sheet music. Unlike literature, pitches and rhythms specified a choreography to be enacted by the musician's body. Such gifts enabled Gottsched to place himself, as he had suggested in the first poem he had written for her, in the position of "divine puppeteer."

The first musical gift Gottsched sent consisted of keyboard works by Johann Sebastian Bach, cantor of the St. Thomas School and music director for the City of Leipzig. Bach and Gottsched were acquainted with one another. In 1727 the two had collaborated in presenting a funeral cantata occasioned by the death of the Electress of Saxony and Queen of Poland, Christiane Eberhardine.[15] Their work had been well received, and Gottsched had subsequently described Bach in print as "the greatest of all musicians in Saxony."[16] He undoubtedly hoped that some keyboard works by this luminary might help him win Fräulein Kulmus's heart. Her thoughts, however, were elsewhere. At the end of a letter dated January 9, 1732, she wrote: "My keyboard has been silent for four weeks. As soon as I touch it again, I will play the piece you sent and think of you."[17]

Refusing to be deterred, Gottsched sent Kulmus some works for lute composed by Johann Christian Weyrauch, who had studied with Bach and was then working as a notary in Leipzig. In a letter of May 30, 1732, she acknowledged both musical gifts, though she did not disguise a distinct lack of enthusiasm: "The pieces you sent by Bach for the keyboard and by Weyrauch for the lute are as difficult as they are beautiful. When I have played them ten times I still feel like a beginner. Among the works of these two great masters, everything pleases me more than their caprices; these are unfathomably difficult."[18] This assessment of Bach and Weyrauch reflects genuine frustration. Kulmus found the repertoire unrewarding to practice because it did not offer her much sense of progress. Worst of all were the movements she called "caprices," a term commonly used to refer to preludes.[19] The words "unfathomably difficult" (*unergründlich schwer*) constituted a true condemnation, particularly when directed at such a strong proponent of rationalist philosophy. She effectively meant to suggest that the challenges of this music exceeded that which could be justified by reason.[20]

Kulmus's criticism of Bach's music probably does not reflect an inability to perform it. Her extraordinary accomplishments served as a shield against charges that she was lazy or incapable of understanding or performing complex music. Despite modest protestations to the contrary, she was undoubtedly confident in her ability to come to terms with this music's challenges. What probably made her uncomfortable was the prospect of taxing her listeners. If she still felt like a beginner after playing Bach's work ten times, it was too much to expect that her audience members would comprehend this music after just one hearing.

The idea of imposing such challenges on listeners in order to showcase her intellectual ambitions held little appeal for Luise Kulmus. It is no coincidence that the next two lines of the same letter are devoted to a critique of Laura Maria Catarina Bassi, who just a few weeks earlier had become the second woman in history to achieve a university teaching post: "What do you think of Donna Laura Bassi, who has recently received her doctorate at Bologna? I suspect that when this young doctor gives her lectures, she will attract more spectators in the first hour than listeners for the rest of her career."[21] Kulmus had no objection to Bassi, or any other woman, cultivating her intellect. Indeed, she herself spent her days expanding her mind through reading, writing, and translating. She was offended rather by Bassi's effort to so spectacularly subvert traditional gender roles. Performing these extraordinarily difficult musical works would have projected an image that she found unbecoming.

Ironically, Kulmus seems to have been more troubled by women striving for public recognition than was Gottsched. The disparity in their views on this issue came into the open a few weeks later when he suggested that she might one day aspire to joining the ranks of the "German Society" (*Deutsche Gesellschaft*), a feat recently accomplished by Christiane Mariane von Ziegler.[22] Kulmus declared herself completely uninterested in such accolades:

> Frau von Ziegler is right to deem her admission into the German Society as highly as if she had received a doctorate from any university. But surely, you must think me very bold if you presume me capable of aspiring to similar honors. No, this idea shall never enter my head. I will permit my sex to take

a little detour; only where we lose sight of our limitations we end up in a labyrinth and lose the guiding light of our weak reason which was supposed to bring us to a happy ending. I will beware of ever being carried away by this current. For this reason I assure you that I never wish to see my name among those of the members of the German Society.[23]

Fräulein Kulmus adopted a very different approach from that of C. M. von Ziegler, not only to her literary career but also to her music making. Generally speaking, she preferred to cultivate her talents in the home rather than in public. The same letter in which she denigrates von Ziegler's desire for recognition as a poet contains a response to Gottsched's request that she send him one of her musical "caprices" in order that he might share it with a friend in Leipzig. She refused to do so on the grounds that the music she composed was for private rather than for public consumption:

> You recently asked me to send you, on behalf of a friend, a particular one of my caprices. The one you requested is the best and most tolerable of the lot. I will not send it, however. Why not?
>
> > A song I sing for you is meant for you alone,
> > It is not for the street, it shouldn't be widely known.
>
> Oh! I am more covetous of my caprices than any man could be of the most beautiful woman. I want to play them all for you upon your return to Danzig. How I long to hear you say that I am more accomplished in music than I was when you left. When will I be able to assure you of my devotion verbally and in all tonalities?[24]

A short time later, Gottsched finally sent a musical gift that Kulmus could fully appreciate: a "Sinfonia" by Johann Adolph Hasse—probably a keyboard arrangement of the orchestral overture to *Cleofide*, an opera premiered with great fanfare in Dresden on September 13, 1731. On October 15, 1732, she responded enthusiastically:

> Honored Sir, I wish to thank you above all for the music you sent. I am to perform the beautiful *Symphonie* by Hasse at the next concert. I will have to rehearse my fingers dutifully in order to avoid making the excellent piece unrecognizable.[25]

The music of Hasse—light, quick, melodic, and virtuosic—was repertoire with which Kulmus felt comfortable identifying herself. She was happy to practice endlessly in order to play a piece like this for friends and family. Unlike the works of Bach and Weyrauch, this was music that did not foreground her intellectual ambitions.

Gottsched too must have been elated to have finally sent a gift that aroused some excitement in Luise Kulmus. He could be confident that her audience in Danzig would know, not least from the work's Saxon origin, that she had received this music from him. The professor in Leipzig could not have hoped for a more effective means of appearing magnanimous to the Kulmus family members who controlled the fate of his marital aspirations.

Yet the plan seems to have backfired. The intimacy made palpable by Gottsched's serving publicly as Kulmus's divine puppeteer seems to have inflamed family anxieties. On January 16, 1733, Luise sat down at her writing desk and scrawled out some crushing news:

> My relatives do not wish for me to break off all contact with you, but they feel it would be best for me to write less often than before. This is the hardest test that one can ask of me.[26]

He wrote back immediately in frustration, calling her "cruel" and accusing her of "breaking her promise." She asked him to be patient:

> If our relationship was a fire that could be extinguished, it would have happened long ago [. . .]. So fear not where there is nothing to fear; let us pass this test of our patience, and we will be richly rewarded in the end.[27]

Eventually, Gottsched recovered his balance and began sending gifts again, though never again another work of music. He offered her instead a scholarly tome: Johann Gottfried Walther's *Musicalisches Lexicon* (Leipzig, 1732). In a letter dated March 7, 1733, Kulmus thanked him for the book in a chilly, formal letter likely written with family censors in mind:

> Honored Sir, you never cease to enrich my book collection. The *Musical Lexicon* was completely unknown to me. With its help I have been able to resolve many knots of doubt and each time I do so I think of your goodness in sending it to me.[28]

Like the works by Bach, Weyrauch, and Hasse, Walther's *Lexicon* was a recent product of Saxony's flourishing musical culture. The professor's faith in the theory that he and Luise would be happy together in Leipzig was unshakable. But what could he do to persuade her family?

Gottsched's courtship efforts received a decisive boost on January 17, 1734, when he was promoted to full professor at an elaborate ceremony in Dresden. The academic recognition, social stability, and higher salary calmed the nerves of Luise Kulmus's family. As her uncle would write (in English) not long after the promotion: "I must needs own, that the Beginning of your Courtship, mett with innumerable Difficultÿs, the small part I had to act in this affair was carried on with all manner of Sincerity, in Regard to the Conservation of the mutuale Good of the Concerned. And as it pleased Providence to provide wonderfulÿ for the new Couple, bÿ placing you into such honourable Post, you had the loud Consent of the whole Family."[29]

But theirs would prove to be a relationship in which things did not always go smoothly; more obstacles were to arise before the wedding could be arranged. The death of the Saxon Elector and King of Poland Augustus the Strong on February 1, 1733—the same event that put Christiane Sibÿlla Bose's keyboard lessons on hold for five months—started the War of the Polish Succession (1733–1738), and in 1734 Danzig was bombed from the sea. Luise and her family were forced to take refuge in quarters outside of town. Due to the deprivations of their provisional housing, her mother fell ill, and on May 10, 1734, she died. This devastating loss and the war, which raged in Danzig through July, temporarily rendered all marriage plans moot.

Finally, in early April 1735, Professor Gottsched was able to announce to the administration of Leipzig University that he would soon be traveling to Danzig to wed. The courtship had lasted six years; he was by now thirty-six years old. And on April 19, 1735, one week after her twenty-second birthday, Luise Adelgunde Victorie Kulmus became Luise Adelgunde Victorie Gottsched.

⁊❧

The Gottscheds arrived in Leipzig on May 14, 1735, and moved into a spacious apartment in a house known as the "Golden Bear." Their landlord was Herr Gottsched's publisher, Bernhard Christoph Breitkopf, whose offices occupied the ground floor of the same building. The apartment was modern and attractive, with the larger rooms covered in fashionable wallpaper. Two servants, one man and one woman, stood ready to serve their quotidian needs.[30]

Rationalist philosophy was manifest in every room of their apartment. Books were all over, bound in calf's leather with marbled endpapers and filed neatly into bookcases with double doors of wood and canvas. The shelves assigned to Frau Gottsched were painted blue and white with decorative gilded border patterns and glass doors. Because university classes met in their home, one of the largest rooms had an adjustable lectern at the front, and eight benches for students, each one about eight feet long. One of the smaller rooms contained scientific instruments, including a sundial on a stand, a magnifying glass, prisms of white and blue glass, a touchstone for assaying metals, a compass, and rulers of various sizes and shapes. Dozens of plaster and wax medallions immortalized the faces of various noble rulers and learned academics. An elegant cabinet of stained wood and golden knobs contained Herr Gottsched's collection of ancient coins. There were also natural specimens of diverse description: fossils from sandpits all over the Holy Roman Empire, sea snail shells and dried crab claws, the skin of a snake, a fly preserved in amber, a piece of elephant tusk, and five porcupine quills.[31]

Frau Gottsched was thrilled with her new circumstances, particularly the latitude she now enjoyed to pursue her passion for learning. A few months after the wedding, she wrote to an acquaintance in Danzig:

> At long last, you should know that I am still alive, that I am doing very, very well in the excellent city of Leipzig, and that in my marriage I have made the happiest and best choice. I spend my time very much according to my incli-nation. My husband has an excellent library of the best books, and he has access to all the other large libraries in town. Think of how much time and occasion I have to read; I will certainly take advantage of this opportunity.[32]

A month later, in another letter, she described how she and her husband spent their days:

> Our activities are, just like our thoughts, always similar. We read very much, discussing every passage of special interest. We often take different stand-points for the sake of debate, which allows us to assess the merits of a given idea to see if our opinions are well founded. I am daily made aware of the gaps in my knowledge and discover ever-greater deficits in my understanding. The only thing equal to the gravity of these faults is my will to improve myself.[33]

Herr Gottsched too was entirely content with his life as a married man. He loved his wife more every day and was pleased with the degree to which she carried his theoretical ideals into practice. He told the world as much in a book dedication penned on their third wedding anniversary:

> From my perspective, I can say that my regard for you has only grown as I have come to know your love, your understanding of household economy, your pleasant means of interaction, your wise counsel, your modesty in good fortune, your calm acceptance of misfortune, your freedom from all vanity and waste and, in summary, your unaffected tendency to embrace all that which is truly good and noble. And this is to say nothing of your lively spirit, your love of the arts, your insight into the sciences, your skill in music, your experience in foreign languages, your excellent accomplishments in our own mother tongue, your uncommon wit, and your exceptional company, which springs from all of these traits.[34]

A philosophical manifesto Herr Gottsched had written a few years before his marriage—the "First Principles of a Complete Knowledge of the World"

(*Erste Gründe einer gesammten Weltweisheit*)—had made him an academic luminary.[35] The book had been designed to introduce students in secondary schools and universities to the Leibniz-Wolff philosophy, but it had found tremendous popularity with the broader public as well. His higher profile had also earned him powerful new enemies who were, quite literally, determined to destroy him. In 1737 he was summoned to Dresden to defend himself before the *Oberconsistorium*, a phalanx of theologians who accused him of spreading anti-Christian doctrines. The professor was charged with corrupting youth by promoting *Indifferentismus*: the view that Christianity was fundamentally comparable with other religions. Through personal connections with influential supporters, he was spared disciplinary action. Outwardly he showed remorse, but he felt no inner compunction to change his behavior. His enthusiasm for the "new philosophy" was undiminished, and he continued to corrupt youth for the remainder of his long career.[36]

Frau Gottsched threw herself into the task of promoting her husband's philosophical agenda, as she felt it behooved a wife to do. In an editorial written a few years after arriving in Leipzig, she opined, "Our gender is a happy tool used to promote the lives, comfort, and pleasure of men. And how can we better use our energies than by tending to those duties which our wise creator has assigned us?"[37] Professor Gottsched needed not only philosophical support but also practical help. His wife gathered material for his diverse scholarly projects, corresponded on his behalf, and made copies of the letters he sent and received. In 1739 she wrote a summary of Leibniz-Wolff theories under the title "Triumph of Knowledge of the World" (*Triumph der Weltweisheit*), which sold well.[38] Her favorite work was preparing translations of literature and works of philosophy originally published in French, English, or Latin.[39] All of this had an adverse effect on her health, as she acknowledged to a friend:

> I spend most of my life doing work that most people of my gender would find strange, and my health would perhaps be better, if I moved around more and had more pleasurable distractions. This is what my physician says when I ask him for advice about the weakness of my body. My own inner drive says, on the other hand, that busying myself with activities that satisfy my affinities and gratify my soul cannot be harmful to my health. I will follow this inner drive, as long as my machine does not become completely decrepit.[40]

Frau Gottsched produced plays, mostly comedies, mocking what Herr Gottsched had long decried as the foibles of their contemporaries. In *Die Pietisterey in Fischbeinrock* (Pietists in Petticoats) she attacked adherents of the religious movement that was her husband's particular bête noire. When a father leaves the country on business, his weak-minded wife falls prey to a group of Pietists spouting gibberish. They take over the home, open a printing shop for Pietist literature, and persuade nearly everyone that Lutheran orthodoxy was drivel. Even the coachmen called his horses "orthodox" when they balked at his commands because he "could think of no more vile insult."[41] The villains were exposed in the end as greedy and ignorant hypocrites more interested in profits than in enlightenment.

In *Die Hausfranzösin* (The French Nanny) Luise Gottsched railed directly against the German weakness for all things galant. A family preparing to send a son on a grand tour to Paris is so consumed with French nonsense that its members neglect to notice that these foreign foods, fashions, and licentious activities were blinding them to good taste and corrupting their morals. Those enthralled by galanterie are ridiculed as slaves to effeminate foreign clowns.

The victims in Frau Gottsched's comedies are not evil but rather frustratingly irrational. Their fundamental ambitions in life are sound, but things go wrong when they engage in reflexive, unthinking behavior, following the herd rather than thinking for themselves. In her view, virtually all social ills could be attributed to the failure of human beings to cultivate their capacity for reason.

A standard character in all of Luise Gottsched's comedies is a young woman who does not participate in the action so much as she observes and offers wry commentary.[42] She asks penetrating questions of those who wield more influence, gradually bringing them around to her rational point of view. In *Die Hausfranzösin* and *Die Pietisterey in Fischbeinrock*, it is no coincidence that this character is called "Luischen," a diminutive form of her own name. She viewed her own power as stemming primarily from the trust placed in her by the most sympathetic male character, a wise mentor and obvious stand-in for her husband.

Frau Gottsched's plays were well received. *Pietisterey*, her most successful comedy, went through seven editions in its first two years.[43] The content, however, proved incendiary. Outraged Pietists had it banned in their strongholds of Berlin and Königsberg. No one knew the identity of the author because she had published the play anonymously, a common tactic for writers who expected controversy. In at least one case, Pietist vigilantes smashed the windows of a man they incorrectly believed to have authored the play.[44] Like "Luischen," Luise Gottsched mocked her enemies and enlightened her friends while keeping a safe distance from the action.

§

During the early years of their marriage, Frau Gottsched continued to devote many hours to practicing the lute and the keyboard. When one of her mother's old friends asked whether she might soon have a baby, she responded:

No, gracious lady, destiny has not yet seen fit to grant me a child. I would certainly regard it as a gift from Heaven, but in the event that I never receive one, I will accept this as the will of God. I have often heard that there is nothing more difficult than raising children, and raising them well; who knows if I possess the necessary skills? If destiny, for its own wise and beneficent reasons, does not bless me with a child, I will devote myself all the more assiduously to answering my true calling in other ways. I work a great deal, and study even more. I practice music and would like, if possible, to try my hand at composition. All of this would be impossible if I were a mother, because I would devote all of my time to my child.[45]

In the prime of her reproductive years, Luise Gottsched already had a prescient glimpse of her childless future. The prospect of becoming a mother was one that she could "accept as the will of God," but it was not a circumstance she seemed to desire. Exercising her mind brought the greatest rewards, and the thought of giving it up filled her with dread. She was pleased to be married to a professor to whom she could be more useful as an assistant to his academic work than as a mother to his children.

Frau Gottsched's well-being also depended on the free time she devoted to making music. Writing of the early years of their marriage, Herr Gottsched observed that his wife "continued to use music to diversify her leisure hours." He was pleased, too, that she wished to pursue composition—that is, to create new works rather than merely playing in a mechanical fashion. Her approach to music making was in this respect unusual:

> As in other realms, she endeavored here too to step beyond the bounds of a woman's common path. Figured bass she had already mastered in Danzig, but the art of setting music, or composing, was not yet in her grasp. Given her great aptitude and musical proclivity, there remained only this final step to take. Her husband chose a teacher for her from among the many in Leipzig who understood music: one of the most skillful students of Kapellmeister Bach, Herr Krebs, who has since become quite famous. In a short time, she understood enough of this art to still her desire. She composed not only an entire so-called suite, which she presented to her husband as a birthday gift, but also set one of his texts as a cantata commemorating their anniversary.[46]

Luise Gottsched's composition lessons with Johann Ludwig Krebs began sometime after November 1736 and continued until May 1737, when he left Leipzig to accept a post as organist in Zwickau. Krebs remembered her fondly and in 1740 dedicated one of his publications, a collection titled "First Piece, Consisting of Six Easy Preludes, Well Made According to Today's Taste," to Frau Gottsched, whom he described as a "precious heroine of our time." In a dedicatory poem, he highlighted his astonishment at her musical skills:

There was a time I thought I'd wisdom to impart,
But how? I quickly came to just admire your art,
To teach one who has ears so fine would be imprudent,
I heard you play just once and then became your student.
[...]
In you did art and nature build a masterpiece,
Let praises due your noble spirit never cease.
And this is well! You'll do what we've all failed to do.
Though art climbs high, she'll never see the likes of you.[47]

Luise Gottsched's only surviving musical work is a cantata for a female vocalist to perform while accompanying herself at the keyboard.[48] The words she chose were drawn from a poem written by her husband on the occasion of their marriage in 1735. She now sang them back to him accompanied by music of her own composition:

Lovely hour! Welcome now!
Let me kiss my dearest Frau!
Oh how gorgeous are the fields
Where our sheep can safely graze
After painful, long delays,
Endless patience finally yields,
Graceful *Galatea*'s vow![49]

Luise Gottsched's decision to set her husband's words to music can be understood as an allegory of their marriage. Her talents were at his disposal. Her role, as she understood it, was to enhance and further his agenda rather than to assert an independent voice. The tone of the cantata she composed is joyful and vivacious, with virtuosic runs and ebullient leaps. Only in occasional references to the suffering (*Leiden*) endured during their courtship did she indulge in brief moments of madrigalesque tone painting. But she never dwells on sorrow or suffering, and tensions dissipate quickly. Her cantata is unusually orderly, even by eighteenth-century standards, with phrases tightly cordoned off from one another rather than elided together in the Bachian manner. Her goal in this work, and in all of her music making, was to flatter listeners with sounds that were not only attractive but also readily comprehensible.

ᘒ

Over the course of her life, Luise Gottsched amassed a large music library.[50] Her collection of Italianate vocal music ranged from actual Italian composers like Giovanni Antonio Giay and Francesco Mancini to Germans who composed in the Italian manner, such as Carl Heinrich Graun and

Conrad Friedrich Hurlebusch.[51] She also owned copies of song collections by Lorenz Mizler and Johann Friedrich Gräfe that were dedicated to her.[52]

Frau Gottsched received lute repertoire from correspondents such as Adam Falckenhagen and Friedrich Melchior Grimm.[53] Her favorite lute composer, however, was Silvius Leopold Weiss, whom she met for the first time in 1740 when he visited Leipzig.[54] She eventually acquired an enormous collection of his music—fifty-three solos, sixteen duets, five trios, and ten concerti—which the composer himself edited on her behalf. He also sent her what he called a *Galanterie-Partie*, intended "for you and for you alone," advising her not to give it to anyone else "since as long as one keeps something for oneself, it is always beautiful and new."[55]

Luise Gottsched seems not to have acquired much keyboard music after her wedding. Most of the repertoire she performed in Leipzig she had learned already in Danzig, and much of it had been composed nearby; her library was heavy on works by composers active in eastern Europe, such as Christoph Schaffrath, Johann Georg Neidhardt, and her former keyboard teacher, Daniel Magnus Gronau.[56] She had a particular fondness for the keyboard music of Georg Friedrich Händel, who was already an international celebrity; her library included two books of his *Clavier-Stücken* as well as six of his *Clavier-Sonaten*.[57]

Although Luise Gottsched was J. S. Bach's neighbor for fifteen years and remained in Leipzig for twelve years after his death, she seems never to have found space on the shelves of her library for much of his music. The only piece she is documented as having owned was the one J. C. Gottsched had sent to Danzig as a gift in 1732.[58] Some of her reservations about Bach's music were probably philosophical. The cantor of St. Thomas was a devout orthodox Lutheran who had little patience for worshipers of reason. The following excerpt from a cantata text Bach set to music in 1724 probably reflects his opinion of rationalists like the Gottscheds:

> They teach but vain and false deceit,
> They aim to counter God, His truth unseat;
> The concepts which their minds envision
> Are heresies which lead to church derision,
> And seek to weaken gospel truth.
> One takes this side, the other one that side
> The foolishness of reason is their guide.[59]

But the absence of music by Bach in Luise Gottsched's library probably also had to do with the character of the music itself. It can be no coincidence that the four composers who dedicated collections to her all opted to make the works in those collections relatively light in character: Johann

Friedrich Gräfe and Lorenz Mizler offered her simple songs, Johann Ludwig Krebs offered her keyboard preludes advertised as "easy," and Silvius Leopold Weiss offered her a so-called Galanterie-Partie. All four of these men deeply admired Luise Gottsched's extraordinary intelligence and musical acumen and were capable of composing more intellectually challenging repertoire. Presumably it was their knowledge of her own preferences that led them to present music that aimed to charm rather than challenge the ear. Luise Gottsched was certainly up to the task of performing Bach's most difficult keyboard works. This music, however, did not evoke an image that she felt comfortable projecting.

Frau Gottsched's taste in music was very much akin to her taste in literature, which itself was closely aligned with that of her husband. In 1730 Herr Gottsched had published an "Essay on a Critical Poetic Art for the Germans" (*Versuch einer critischen Dichtkunst vor die Deutschen*), which sought to establish rational criteria for assessing literary quality.[60] He argued that art should imitate nature, but the natural world he imagined was not the one that surrounded him but rather the one that had preceded the Fall of Man. In paradise there were no mountains, hills, or even bumps. Everyone spoke a single language without the slightest hint of a dialect. Interactions were efficient, clear, and flawless. The goal of all art was to inspire humankind with a glimpse of this vanished state of perfection.[61]

The aesthetic violation Herr Gottsched most abhorred was what he called "turgidity" (*Schwülst*). A prime offender was Seneca the Younger, whose works Gottsched believed to be full of unnecessary verbiage. In a passage he liked to quote from *Hercules Oetaeus*, the title character tries to achieve godlike status by appealing directly to Jupiter:

> Why do you tarry so long, Jupiter? Are you perhaps afraid of me? Or will Atlas not bear the weight of both Hercules and the heavens at the same time? Give me, Jupiter, oh give me at least the duty of guarding the gods. Your thunderbolts will never be required in whatever part of the heavens you ask me to defend. Whether it be the cold north pole, or the torrid lands of the noonday sun, you can be assured that the gods under my protection will be safe.[62]

For Professor Gottsched, all of this bloviating made Hercules seem weak. His stilted style of speech ("Give me, Jupiter, oh give me . . .") was a relic of literary tradition unworthy of preservation. Modern heroes did not need to repeat themselves so much.

Herr Gottsched's greatest contempt, however, was reserved for the writer he referred to as the "German Seneca," Daniel Casper von Lohenstein.[63]

Lohenstein's chief crime, from Gottsched's perspective, was larding his plays with unnecessary similes, as in the following passage from *Ibrahim Sultan*:

> What new and unaccustomed beams do shimmer
> Atop the city, countryside, and mountain's crown?
> Is this a throne bedecked with crimson gown?
> Have myrtle wreaths replaced the Danube's glimmer?
> Have sand grains turned to gold and reeds to sugarcane?
> Have diamonds replaced ice, and pearl the river's foam?
> What sun now lights Tyrolia's terrain?
> Could rocks like these bring forth a blazing golden dome?[64]

For Gottsched, Lohenstein's verbosity had taken on a life of its own. The comparisons are indulgent; they served only to show off the author's vocabulary. One admired the effort but meaning was ultimately crushed under the weight of all those superfluous words.

In Herr Gottsched's mind, the ancestral hero of German poetry was Martin Opitz, in whose verses he found valuable arguments presented in orderly, unpretentious language:

> The ordinary creatures, each one knows his means,
> They are by nature guided to obey routines:
> But man alone, their lord, whose power comes from thought,
> Is only capable of things which he's been taught.
> He learns from others how to eat, drink, talk, and walk,
> To teach him how to sleep, one must his cradle rock.[65]

In Gottsched's view, human beings, unlike God's other creatures, were capable of intellectual improvement. From simple imitation they could progress to advanced learning and eventually to a state of rational perfection.

That which Herr Gottsched rejected in literature—the wasteful, artificial, and overwrought—he also rejected in music. In the original edition of his treatise on aesthetics, he devoted a few chapters to music, encouraging composers to avoid filling their scores with trills, unnecessary repetitions, and lurid text painting.[66] He derided opera in particular for its flowery singing, outsized emotions, and irrational plot twists, concluding that this was "the most incongruous artform ever conceived by humanity."[67] Herr Gottsched recognized, however, that he lacked the technical knowledge of music to justify his strong opinions. Shortly after his marriage, he assigned his wife the task of helping him prepare a new, updated edition of the book in which he had made these claims, hoping that she might be able to bolster his arguments. Frau Gottsched took the task very seriously.[68] All of the musical examples she added to the new edition of her husband's text were drawn from her own personal library. She praised the works of

Giovanni Antonio Giay, Carl Heinrich Graun, Georg Friedrich Händel, Johann Adolph Hasse, and Francesco Mancini.[69] Particularly rational, in Luise Gottsched's view, were the cantatas of Conrad Friedrich Hurlebusch: "He avoids all of the errors which one commonly finds in the works of other composers. The repetitions are sparing, namely never more than three times. The recitatives are full of melody, and not a single word is wrenched by the music. Everything is sung in quick succession, clearly and understandably."[70]

Johann Sebastian Bach, with whom Herr Gottsched had collaborated more than once, and whose cantatas the couple regularly heard during Leipzig worship services, was conspicuously mentioned nowhere in this aesthetic manifesto. His music espoused ideals antithetical to those of the Gottscheds. Far from being unencumbered, clear, and concise, it was aesthetically tense, repetitious, and overwrought, with challenging chromatic harmonies, thick counterpoint, and countless ornamental barnacles. Bach's music epitomized the turgidity the Gottscheds abhorred in art. But they could not say so in print except through omission and faint praise; this particular composer was the highest musical authority in their city and someone with whom Herr Gottsched occasionally had to collaborate.

و

The revised edition of Herr Gottsched's *Critische Dichtkunst*, with his wife's additions, appeared early in 1737 and was read with particular alacrity by a twenty-nine-year-old music theorist and composer in Hamburg named Johann Adolph Scheibe. Scheibe had spent his first twenty-eight years in Leipzig, where his father worked as an organ builder. His time there had been beset by frustrations. As a boy, he had lost an eye to the carelessness of one of his father's assistants. Perhaps as a result of his disfigurement, he had enjoyed little success with women, whom he described in misogynistic pamphlets as "beasts" filled with evil, jealousy, and deceitfulness.[71] As an aspiring organist, he had studied with J. S. Bach but suffered humiliation in 1729 when his former teacher rejected his bid for the organist post at Leipzig's St. Nicholas Church.[72] In 1736 he had packed up and moved to Hamburg, where he had established a journal on music modeled explicitly on Herr Gottsched's *Critische Dichtkunst*. He even called it "The Critical Musician" (*Der Critische Musikus*).

Paging through Luise Gottsched's expanded treatment of music in her husband's aesthetic manifesto, Scheibe was impressed anew by her emphasis on clarity and her denigration of "turgid" (*schwülstig*) writers like Seneca and Lohenstein. He recognized an implicit parallel between the literary style of these writers and the musical style of his former teacher, J. S. Bach.

No doubt emboldened by the fact that the Gottscheds had failed to mention Bach in their list of approved composers, the frustrated young man sensed an opportunity for the revenge he had long dreamed of exacting.

On May 14, 1737, Scheibe published an essay describing twelve living composers, only two of whom met his approval.[73] Those two—J. A. Hasse and C. H. Graun—were mentioned by name but the other ten were left anonymous. One of those left unnamed was easily identified as J. S. Bach:

> Herr _____ is the most eminent of the *Musicanten* in _____. He is an extraordinary artist on the clavier and on the organ, and he has until now encountered only one person with whom he must compete for the palm of superiority. I have heard this great man play on various occasions. One is amazed at his ability, and one can hardly conceive how it is possible for him to achieve such agility, with his fingers and with his feet, in the crossings, extensions, and extreme jumps that he manages, without mixing in a single wrong tone, or displacing his body by any violent movement.
>
> This great man would be the admiration of whole nations if he had more amenity [*Annehmlichkeit*], if he did not take away the natural element in his pieces by giving them a turgid [*schwülstig*] and confused style, and if he did not darken their beauty by an excess of art. Since he judges according to his own fingers, his pieces are extremely difficult to play; for he demands that singers and instrumentalists should be able to do with their throats and instruments whatever he can play on the keyboard. But this is impossible. Every ornament, every little grace, and everything that one thinks of as belonging to the method of playing, he expresses completely in notes: and this not only takes away from his pieces the beauty of harmony but completely covers the melody throughout. In short, he is in music what Herr von Lohenstein was in poetry. Turgidity [*Schwülstigkeit*] has led them both from the natural to the artificial, and from the lofty to the somber; and in both one admires the onerous labor and uncommon effort—which, however, are vainly employed, since they conflict with nature.[74]

Scheibe's critique deeply offended Bach and sent shockwaves throughout the musical world. The cantor of St. Thomas was defended in print the following year by Johann Abraham Birnbaum, a notary and sometime professor of rhetoric in Leipzig. Birnbaum asserted the value of Bach's learned counterpoint over "silly galanterien," concluding that "there is only one Bach, and no one else comes close."[75] The affair continued for years with fierce attacks and counterattacks from both sides.[76]

As the spark turned into a conflagration, Scheibe decided he needed not only the tacit support of Professor Gottsched's bestselling literary theory but also the active support of the author himself. Though the two men had spent more than a decade living in the same city, they had never actually met in person. On June 10, 1739, Scheibe wrote his first letter to Gottsched, beginning by acknowledging the intellectual debt he owed the distinguished professor:

> I count myself among the many who have gained much insight from Your Magnificence's philosophical writings. I have not only learned a great deal that was completely unknown to me, but I have also gained from your *Critische Dichtkunst* new and better-founded conceptions of poetry and criticism than I had previously possessed.[77]

Scheibe went on to humbly request that his literary hero publish a (positive) review of the *Critische Musikus* in his own journal, the "Contributions to the Critical History of the German Language, Poetry, and Rhetoric" (*Beyträge zur critischen Historie der Deutschen Sprache, Poesie und Beredsamkeit*).

Flattered by Scheibe's words, Professor Gottsched agreed to his request. Like all other music-related tasks, he sensibly turned this one over to his wife, who wrote and published a review the following year.[78] Writing under the ambiguous byline "Gottsched," Luise began by declaring her intention to steer clear of the raging debate about Scheibe's critique of Bach: "We do not wish to become involved in the dispute between the author and Herr Birnbaum."[79] There were personal and professional reasons to avoid this morass. Both Birnbaum and Bach were the Gottscheds' colleagues, and there was no incentive to burn the bridges connecting them by associating themselves with the young upstart in Hamburg.[80] Despite the stated goal of remaining neutral, however, Luise Gottsched effectively took Scheibe's side in the debate:

> We are pleased that good taste and particularly the purity of the German compositional style are spreading also in the realm of music, particularly since these days Germany can compete in practical music making with any other land. One honors a German Händel in England. Hasse is admired by the Italians. Telemann recently earned glory and accolades in Paris. Graun makes our fatherland proud in the minds of all those who know his pieces. What should I say about Bach and Weiss? All this is to say nothing of other skillful men who can also be compared favorably with foreigners. Music will reach great heights here in Germany if our musicians follow the rational suggestions of Herr Mattheson and Herr Scheibe for improving music theory and performance.[81]

Given that Luise Gottsched and her husband were personally, professionally, and geographically far more closely connected with Bach and Birnbaum than they were with Händel, Hasse, Graun, or Telemann, her endorsement of Scheibe's prescription for "rational" composition is certainly a ratification of his criticism of Bach. Her praise for him is faint ("What should I say about Bach and Weiss?"), not a sign of her own enthusiasm for his music but rather an acknowledgement of the esteem in which it was held by others. Although she would later come to greatly admire the music of S. L. Weiss, at the time she wrote these words she had not yet had any personal contact with him and probably knew little of his music.[82]

Luise Gottsched seems to have maintained this relatively negative assessment of Bach's music throughout her life. Many years later, in a letter of November 10, 1753, she responded to her friend Dorothea Henriette von Runckel's comparison of an unnamed "great composer" with Seneca:

> Your comparisons between a certain great composer and Seneca are matchless. Both are very much in love with their own ideas. I endure the repetitions of the ancient sage, however, more willingly than I do those of the musical Seneca. But let us speak very quietly of this; one would very much chide our taste.[83]

Given the parallels explicitly drawn by her husband between Seneca and Lohenstein, and by Scheibe between Lohenstein and Bach, the "musical Seneca" discussed here was almost certainly the recently deceased *Thomaskantor*. This interpretation is made all the more plausible by her plea for caution. Given the onslaught of criticism Scheibe had endured for having attacked Bach in 1737, Frau Gottsched knew well that it would be best to keep her opinion to herself.

❧

The wife of a professor in Leipzig enjoyed many opportunities to make music for houseguests. Admirers from near and far came to the "Golden Bear" to have the famous professor inscribe some wisdom into their friendship albums, stay for tea or dinner, discuss literature or the new philosophy, and hear his wife play the keyboard or lute. During Leipzig's tri-annual trade fairs, which lasted for two to three weeks each, the Gottscheds likely welcomed strangers into their home several times each day.

In November 1736 two English cousins—Jeremiah Milles and Richard Pococke—spent fourteen days in Leipzig on their continental "grand tour." Their local guide was Johann Ernst Hebenstreit, a medical professor of "great modesty, politeness, and affability"[84] who regaled them with tales of his recent expedition to Africa. The Englishmen visited the Bose family gardens and an Egyptian mummy in the local library before receiving an impromptu invitation to the Gottsched home. Milles described the experience in a travel diary:

> Mr. Gottsched Professor of Philosophy is a Polite Gentleman, speaks French well, and is a member of the Society for improving the German Language.

This Society meet[s] often. Mr. Gottsched shew'd me their Library, in which there was a collection of German Poetry, more by half, than I could ever have imagin'd to have been published in that language; I cannot boast much of the goodness of them. Everybody knows that the Germans never pretended to be Poets. Mr. Gottsched lately married a wife of great accomplishments. She is of Dantzich, and her name before marriage was Victoria Aligunda Kulmus. She is between 20, & 30, speaks French admirably well, understands Italian, & English, she has translated Mr. Addisons Cato into Dutch[85] and is very well versed in the Belles Lettres: what diverts her most is the study of Perspective, in which she has made great progress, and drawn out very fairly in a book all the figures that are in Chambers's perspective and has a very nice hand at it.[86] She plays delightfully on the Harpsichord; we heard her perform some of the hardest compositions of Mr. Handel with great dexterity. With all these accomplishments the lady is neither vain nor assuming; and seems to sett no extraordinary value on herself on this acc[oun]t. Her misfortune is that she is very sickly. We had great reason to be satisfy'd with the polite reception this Lady gave us.[87]

Pococke offered a corroborating report on the evening's experiences in a letter to his mother:

A Gentm. came to us [who] was in Africa wth Professor Hebenstreits, & introduced us to the Lady of Mr. Gottscheld Professor of Logick, she is young, very agreeable in every respect understands French, and English so as to talk as well to read, & I think Italian, she talk'd in French very modest & does not desire to appear knowing, she has applied much to perspective & drawing, & musick, we saw some things of the former like graving, she is indeed a very amiable woman, & in a particular way, but I know a certain Lady that lives retir'd with whom she is not to be named in point of learning. We drank tea she plaid on a fine harpsichord.[88]

The choreographed tour Milles and Pococke were given was probably typical; these were not particularly illustrious guests, and they had no prior connection with the Gottscheds. Whereas many galant-era families might have emphasized wealth, the professor and his wife emphasized the cultivation of their minds. They dazzled guests with their command of foreign languages and presented their library as a physical manifestation of their expansive knowledge. Drawings and musical performances by the lady of the house advertised her discipline and also gave guests a sense of intimacy.

Luise Gottsched's decision to perform of "some of the hardest compositions of Mr. Handel" for Milles and Pococke may have been inspired in part by these visitors' country of origin—the composer, too, lived in England. Her preference for Händel's music, however, extended well beyond this particular performance, as evidenced by its heavy presence in her music library. This repertoire evoked an image Frau Gottsched was comfortable projecting. It was difficult for performers to execute but not for audience members to appreciate. The music wears its learning lightly, avoiding ostentatious voice exchanges, canonic writing, and other forms of imitation like those found in works by Bach. There is a clearer distinction between melody and accompaniment. It seems to be more cognizant of its audience's attention span and interests, presenting a galant conversation rather than a learned monologue.

Modesty seems indeed to have been a value Frau Gottsched sought at all times to project. As Milles and Pococke observed, she was "neither vain nor assuming;" she "did not desire to appear knowing" and seemed "to sett no extraordinary value on herself." Herr Gottsched later wrote that his wife's personality was "characterized by simplicity or, to put it better, modesty":

> She appeared to promise little in company, but as a result accomplished that much more, after her trust had been won. All of her words and statements were carefully considered and so well expressed that they could have been written or printed immediately. She never sought to gleam in society with a shimmering witticism. She never sought to show off her learning, particularly in the company of women, for fear of arousing revulsion. Even scholars had trouble soliciting her participation in learned conversations.[89]

Bach's music was not incomprehensible to Luise Gottsched. Nor was it beyond her skills as a keyboardist. But Händel's music was better suited to the image of the modest and rational woman she aimed to publicly embrace.

Eighteen months after Milles and Pococke visited, on May 12, 1738, a young adherent of rationalism from Switzerland named Gabriel Hürner arrived at the Gottsched home. He was treated to a cantata performed by Adolph Carl Kuntzen, the son of a famous kapellmeister in Lübeck, and Pierre Coste, pastor of the reformed church in Leipzig, among others. Hürner recorded his impressions in a travel diary:

> This evening I saw everything that is beautiful to me about Leipzig. Herr Gottsched arranged a concert for me in his home and invited guests. Herr Coste, a master's student, and two other students were present, and played. The performance featured a young man from Lübeck, who is the son of Kapellmeister Kunzen and a great virtuoso. The first topic of conversation was the eloquence of Herr Coste. I charmed Herr Gottsched by saying that it must be difficult to follow Herr Coste at the pulpit, and indeed this is the case: he is an eloquent speaker. I looked at Herr Coste and said [in French] that it is easy to climb up to the pulpit but difficult to descend with honor. This pleased him. Herr Coste is a subtle man, but he believes firmly in natural religion. [. . .] Frau Gottsched tries to speak French but cannot

produce a single word, or in any case not a single complete phrase. She is very timid and worries at every moment that she will make a mistake. I saw that she glanced at me a few times and noticed that she quite resembles Mademoiselle Lambalet and is no less pleasing; she also possesses no less of that which a woman should have. Herr Coste is one of those who hears everything and weighs every word. I said to Frau Gottsched that Frau von Mosheim loves her writings and holds them in high esteem, which she found touching. After drinking coffee, we went to music, and this lasted, together with an evening meal of various dishes, until 10 P.M. Frau Gottsched cannot play everything effortlessly; she wants to perform only the pieces she already knows. She played for a long time at the harpsichord, but this was nothing compared to her performance on the lute; there I was enraptured. She noticed my astonishment and this inspired her to play more. She is admirable with the lute, and even more beautiful than Mademoiselle Ritter. I could not admire her enough. Herr Gottsched loves to show off his wife. He is not so ambitious for himself. He just wants to be passed by, but he wants his wife to be loved. She herself, however, wants only to be admired. Herr Gottsched invited me up to see the library of his wife, among other things. He considers the Christian religion to be merely an affirmation of natural religion, one that provides new grounds for belief. [. . .] This is the best day that I have spent in Leipzig. If I could make verses, I would sit and try to fashion some.[90]

Hürner was dazzled by Luise Gottsched's accomplishments, yet, unlike the English visitors, he remarked also upon her limitations. She was charming but timid and afraid of making mistakes in French. She could not play just anything at the keyboard but wanted to perform only the works she already knew. Hürner implies that Frau Gottsched was hiding something, that the image she presented was not all that it seemed. She sensed his skepticism and sought means of winning him over, chiefly through music.

The Swiss visitor's observations are also much more sexually charged than are those of Milles and Pococke. Hürner was taken with Frau Gottsched's beauty and charm, which he felt "every woman should have." He was most attuned to her allure at the moments that she noticed him. It was her glances that inspired his comment on her feminine graces. Her cognizance of his "astonishment" at her lute playing inspired him to remark upon her beauty.

Hürner's sense that Frau Gottsched's musical performance enhanced her allure is perhaps what Herr Gottsched hoped for when he married her. It was the otherworldly power of her fingers to "conjure, not to play," that had appealed to him when he first met sixteen-year-old Luise Kulmus. Now that she was his wife, Herr Gottsched himself was in a position to wield her mysterious musical power. He wanted her keyboard and lute playing to make everyone feel the way one of his correspondents felt in reading Luise's literary efforts: "No man other than Gottsched is worthy to possess her."[91] In Hürner's view, the professor hoped that his wife would be "loved" by listeners: a strong, emotional reaction. She herself, however, hoped only to inspire "admiration"—a more measured, rational reaction. The couple's individual aspirations would diverge further in subsequent years.

ॐ

By the 1740s the "new philosophy" was no longer so new. Due in part to the efforts of the Gottscheds, the faculties of many major German universities were dominated by advocates for the theories of Leibniz and Wolff. With the ascendance in 1740 of King Friedrich II, a formidable rationalist, the Pietists lost the fearsome political power they had once wielded.

The triumph of rationalism put the Gottscheds in the position of representing the intellectual status quo. Though objections from theologians became more muted, potent new counterarguments were put forward by younger philosophers like Christian August Crusius, who stressed the fallibility of reason and argued instead for empiricism, which held that reality was a phenomenon to which even the most brilliant human beings, with just five senses and imperfect minds, had only limited access. Philosophers like Crusius recognized that human cognition was not strictly rational but also fuzzy and magical. His position accorded well with Jean-Jacques Rousseau's assertion that as culture becomes more refined, the morality of its practitioners is diminished. Herr Gottsched regarded Crusius and Rousseau as learned contrarians whose ideals were a threat to civilization.

The most devastating attacks on Herr Gottsched's theories, however, came from two scholars based in Zürich: Johann Jakob Bodmer and Johann Jakob Breitinger. The Swiss pair rejected the aesthetic principles pronounced by a man they regarded as a literary dictator in Leipzig and argued instead that great writing flourished only when poets unleashed their irrational powers of imagination. They translated John Milton's epic *Paradise Lost* into (Swiss) German and championed the irregular meters and mysticism of Friedrich Gottlieb Klopstock. Beauty, in their view, was not subject to rules and regulations; it was purely in the eye of the beholder. The mountains of Switzerland, and the rough Swiss dialect, were not signs of God's displeasure—reminders of the Fall of Man—but rather phenomena that were beautiful in their own unique ways.[92]

Like her husband, Luise Gottsched found it difficult to come to terms with the aesthetics espoused by the younger generation of poets and philosophers. Their vaunted freedom from the strictures of reason resulted in what she saw as a pretentious and confusing style. In her final comedy,

Herr Witzling, she mocked their fuzzy thinking, but the work did little to salvage rationalism's sinking reputation. Eventually she gave up all hope of bringing her younger contemporaries to their senses. As she wrote to a friend: "I am writing no more poetry [. . .]. I am too old, too grumpy, and perhaps also incapable of teaching my muse to travel on the new paths. Taste, style, meter: everything has changed. And whoever does not follow the new trends is not lightly but rather savagely criticized."[93] Frau Gottsched's lack of influence in the new literary world eventually sent her into a deep depression. After spending countless hours preparing a "History of German Poetry from Its Origins to the End of the Seventeenth Century" (*Geschichte der Deutschen Lyrik von den Anfängen bis zum Ende des 17. Jahrhunderts*), she and her husband were unable to find a publisher and one evening, in a fit of dejection, she threw her precious manuscript into the fire.[94]

By the 1750s the Gottscheds' frustrations were increasingly noticeable to visitors. As one regular guest at their table wrote in 1754:

> We can have lunch and dinner at Leipzig's best restaurants for two reichstaler and 8 to 12 groschen, and the food we get is far better and healthier than that which we received from the Gottscheds. The food they serve there is plain, raw, and shamefully paltry. They still maintain the harsh eating habits of those from the coastal cities. [. . .] Furthermore, the Gottscheds act as if it is an incomparable generosity that they allow us to eat at their table, and like to praise this act of charity as something truly extraordinary, chewing out this opinion with every bite. They are unbearable: she for her arrogance and he for his rudeness.[95]

Professor Gottsched and his wife were no longer the charming hosts they had been to the likes of Milles, Pococke, and Hürner in the 1730s.

The tension in the Gottscheds' professional lives strained their marriage. His academic influence waning, Johann Christoph sought solace in the affections of a charming countess who moved to Leipzig in the midst of an ugly divorce. Luise, too, cultivated a friendship with this alluring woman but remained cautiously distant. Never immune to feminine charm, Professor Gottsched stepped over a line with the countess, writing her galant letters in which he spelled out in allegory what his sex organ—a "little Alexander the Great, which no one can resist"—hoped to accomplish.[96]

In the wake of her husband's failure to live up to his own rational ideals, Luise Gottsched's health rapidly deteriorated. She took comfort in an increasingly close relationship with a female friend, Dorothea Henriette von Runckel, the wife of an aristocratic military officer in Görlitz. The two women seldom met in person but they exchanged dozens of letters each year, referring to Herr Gottsched as *Asmodi,* the Persian god of infidelity.[97] In a letter of 1753 Luise Gottsched vented her frustration with her husband by criticizing his philosophical treatise, which is divided into two parts, one theoretical and the other practical:

> The entire practical portion remains only theory, and since you request it of me I will ask the author on your behalf how far he has fulfilled the obligations of his glorious teachings. I bet that he will not answer the question. Philosophers and moralists seem to claim for themselves the right to dictate to others how things should be, and believe that they have fulfilled their duties completely when they have taught their doctrines, without ever supporting or confirming these with corresponding actions.[98]

From the beginning, Luise Kulmus had suspected that J. C. Gottsched's theories were more important to him than reality itself. He had fallen in love with her before they had met. He had sought as mentor to bring her behavior in line with his ideals. She had always sought to follow his guidance faithfully, but what had this accomplished? With the increasing attacks on her husband's philosophical and aesthetic ideals, and particularly in light of his failure to live up to his own standards, she found herself questioning the principles that were the foundation of their life together.

In the midst of this crisis, Luise witnessed a scene that must have aroused mixed emotions. Ernestine Christine Müller, a twenty-year-old woman of tremendous scholarly and musical ability, visited the Gottscheds' home together with her brother, who was to be inducted into a new academic society founded by Professor Gottsched. The women gathered in Frau Gottsched's music room, where Ernestine played the harpsichord and sang. As she did so, another of that afternoon's inductees, a forty-nine-year-old orientalist named Johann Jacob Reiske, entered the room and was immediately entranced by the young lady at the keyboard.[99] Perhaps Frau Gottsched recognized a glint in his eye that she had seen many years earlier in Danzig. Whether or not she actively discouraged Ernestine from acquiescing to the old man's courtship efforts, Fräulein Müller did not agree to marry Herr Reiske until nine years later, immediately after Luise Gottsched's death.

えめ

In August 1756 the army of King Friedrich II of Prussia invaded Saxony. Leipzig suffered more in the ensuing Seven Years' War (1756–1763) than most cities: its center was occupied, its suburbs burned, and its residents raped and murdered by marauding Prussian troops. The destruction and agony that Luise Gottsched witnessed must have reminded her of the time shortly before her marriage, when her mother and thousands of others had perished during the siege of Danzig.

In the midst of Leipzig's destruction, Johann Christoph Gottsched struck up an improbable friendship with the king who had sacked his city. The weakened professor was desperate to reclaim his former prominence and would take support wherever he could find it. He had no compunctions about walking through the ruined streets and into the arms of the conqueror as long as that conqueror was a committed rationalist. Summoned on several occasions to the King's quarters in an elegant home on Leipzig's central square, the two discussed philosophy and literature, affirmed the value of reason, and derided Rousseau and Klopstock as deluded mystics.[100] In exchange for a long dedicatory poem Gottsched had penned in honor of his "hero," Friedrich presented the professor with a golden snuff box.

King Friedrich asked frequently about Herr Gottsched's famous wife, but Frau Gottsched refused to meet him, openly defying her husband's demands. In her mind, the monarch was anything but a hero, and her opinion of him sank as the Prussian occupation dragged on. Shortly after Johann Christoph received his snuff box, Luise wrote to a friend, asking rhetorically: "What pleasure can a golden box bring me when it comes from the hand of a man who is, in the eyes of my fellow citizens, as dreadful as he is great?"[101]

The episode confirmed Frau Gottsched's growing suspicion that her husband was less interested in reason than in power. Friedrich was a great leader in Herr Gottsched's eyes because his theoretical ideals were noble. But philosophy and literature were useless to her fellow Leipzigers who suffered through the dead of winter, their homes burned to ash by Prussian troops. The most prominent remaining adherents of rationalism in Germany—Professor Gottsched and Friedrich the Great—were unable or unwilling to put their philosophical ideals into practice. The moral anguish of this recognition would precipitate Luise Gottsched's death.

Johann Christoph wrote that the last two years of his wife's life could not really be called life at all; they were rather a constant stream of "grief and affliction." Luise herself described her condition in one of her final letters to Dorothea Henrietta von Runckel:

> Dearest Friend, I must give you some sad news: I have lost my eyesight almost completely. [. . .] May God soon give me the blessing of a painless death. How I long to hear the bell strike the hour of my passing! You ask about the reasons for my ill-health? Here they are: twenty-eight years of uninterrupted work, secret grief, and six years of countless tears with only God Himself as my witness, and the suffering and deprivations endured by me and so many innocents as a result of the war.[102]

Having lost the faith that had governed her life, Frau Gottsched found herself unable to play the harpsichord. As her husband noted of her final years: "Her music was completely forgotten, and she generally regarded it with revulsion."[103] While playing the keyboard had once been a source of comfort to her, as well as a means of expressing love and loyalty to her husband, it now seemed hopelessly naive.

Shortly before her death, Luise Gottsched wrote of an upcoming musical performance of a cantata celebrating the end of the war, to take place in the Bose family home. Herr Gottsched, who had been so cozy with the leader of the invading forces, had written a poem celebrating the return from exile of the prince and princess of Saxony. Luise described the preparations for the performance: "Today there will be a rehearsal of the cantata based on a text by my husband. Owing to my illness, I cannot appear. I have, however, made an offering that I would only make to the prince and princess of Saxony, and to no one else. I have asked that my harpsichord be transported to the concert room. It will play its role better than I could."[104] Bedridden and demoralized, Luise reflected upon her life at some remove. She now saw her younger self as an actress playing a role in a theatrical production of her husband's creation. She had done her best to live up to the ideal of the perfect woman but had finally come up against her own personal limits. Now only her harpsichord—an insensate machine, free of thoughts and feelings of its own—could embody the philosophical ideal she had once sought so eagerly to represent: "It will play its role better than I could."

Less than four months later, on June 26, 1762, Luise Adelgunde Victorie Gottsched died of a series of strokes, at age forty-nine. Her husband described her final moments in an obituary:

> The emotions that I felt as I listened to her breathing and sighing, and the weakening of her pulse in her hand, which I constantly held in my own, can only be understood by one who has watched a loved one die. Hers was the first death at which I was present, so the experience was doubly powerful. Her last sigh and pulse came at last, as I asked God to take her in His hand. And thus I lost a dearly loved friend, who showed me so much love and tenderness, particularly in the early years, and who brought me so much honor with persons of high and low status alike![105]

Luise Gottsched's own last thoughts, as her husband admired her hands one final time, remain unknown.

CHAPTER 7

Male Amateur Keyboardists

– Do not carve your name into your tin dinner plate.

– Do not talk to anyone while playing with a knife.

– If you find a piece of coal or hair in your food, just put it to the side; don't tell everyone at the table about it.

– Walk quietly and honorably, don't run wildly in the street, and never shout.

– Do not go around counting shingles or sparrows on rooftops.

– Resist the temptation to anoint your feet in the gutters, as described in scripture.

– Don't wipe your nose on your hat, like a farmer, or on your sleeve, like a herring monger.

– Do not urinate in public; it is a shameful affront to all good breeding.

– If gas builds up inside you, cough at the same time you release it to disguise the sound.[1]

The rules established for boys' behavior in Bach's time assume a degree of independence that was not ordinarily accorded their sisters. Counting sparrows on rooftops, running wildly in the street, dipping one's feet in sewage sluices, and urinating in public were infractions that could only be committed by autonomous creatures. Karl Friedrich Bahrdt, the son of a theology professor in Leipzig, proudly recounted in his autobiography how at age ten he had risked life and limb to climb out onto a ledge and peer into the bedroom window of an attractive neighbor girl. On another occasion, he had poured water on the floor of his room to reenact the Old Testament scene in which Joshua leads the children of Israel across the Jordan River, soaking his father's books in the study below. Though antics like these regularly earned him "as many blows as could be endured," they were regarded not only as violations but also as hallmarks of an adventurous spirit.[2]

While girls were generally encouraged to focus on moving from the homes of their fathers to the homes of their husbands—from one state of dependency to another—boys were expected to focus on developing skills that would win them prestigious and lucrative employment. Those of affluent families could find success in the military, at court, as lawyers, businessmen, scientists, physicians, or preachers. It was certainly hoped that they would one day wed and have children, but bachelors were less worrisome to Bach's contemporaries than were spinsters.

The academic education of boys was generally more extensive and systematic than that of girls. Fathers often took responsibility for sons on the grounds that "only a man can form the future man."[3] The politician and poet Johann Ludwig Huber recalled his own early intellectual training as follows:

> The first instruction of my father—even before reading and writing—came in the form of practical religion, the comprehensible teachings of an invisible higher being, who is all knowledge and goodness; of this being's care for his children, namely humankind; of our duty to put all trust in him and for his sake to love one another like a big family; of the natural consequences of a noble or an ignoble life, and of our rewards or punishments in the afterlife. In the winter evenings he sat with us and gave us each lessons through easily understood stories of good and evil men from the Bible and from world history. [. . .] My education in the arts and sciences was equally natural and unbound by ordinary methods. In my fourth year of life, I was taught the German, Latin, and Greek alphabets, partly through grammar books and partly through my father's own preparatory writings. He had, in these three languages, a particularly clear and legible hand, which I learned to imitate. In my sixth year I could read all three as well as any six-year-old boy can. This was followed by the sour work of memorizing the words and paradigms. Even in our native tongue I was made to decline and conjugate. [. . .] The rules of syntax were read alongside examples provided by my father, but they were not memorized. In my seventh year I began to translate Latin and Greek writings into German, thereby learning the rules of proper and elegant composition. Beyond these methods, the scholarly languages are best learned through regular exposure, just like their modern counterparts. My father always began with the easy cases and moved to the more difficult, from the historical writings of the classical

authors to philosophical and poetical works. Two techniques in particular saved at least half the time it ordinarily takes to learn these languages: when we were translating, my father never allowed me to look up a word I did not know, but rather—with indescribable patience—gave me one hundred different examples of how it could be used, and the translations were never written down, but delivered orally.[4]

Those whose fathers had less time or patience were often educated by private tutors (*Hofmeister*). Karl Friedrich Bahrdt was taught by a young man compensated with twenty-four to thirty reichstaler per year, in addition to heat, light, and a room in the house he shared with the boys in his charge. The low pay meant that Bahrdt's father was not able to attract the best and the brightest, but he did not much care.[5] His only advice to the tutor was to "teach the boys daily for so and so many hours, keep them in their room, and if they misbehave use the bull whip to make their fur fly."[6] His first tutor was a man named Banden, who Bahrdt asserted was "tall as a tree, gaunt as a windmill, poor as a church mouse, and stupid as a goose":

> He smoked tobacco incessantly, causing his face to break out in a sweat, with droplets collecting on his nose. He sat at the table, squished against my two brothers and me, forcing us to read and then explicate the texts he had selected, because he could do no more himself. [. . .] The worse we explicated, the more his knuckles rained down upon our heads, and the more insulting the names he called us [. . .]. We sought to compensate ourselves for these sufferings by whispering little jokes to one another, making fun of our pest of a teacher by speaking in reverse. My brother would murmur "Nednab si a loof" (Banden is a fool) and I would respond "Nednab si a yeknod" (Banden is a donkey). When our school monarch finally deciphered our secret language he beat us, which necessitated the invention of new games for teasing him, until after a while my father realized what a hero our Banden was and sent him away.[7]

Bahrdt eventually transferred to Leipzig's St. Nicholas School. Every morning, he left with a heavy pack of books at seven o'clock and returned at eleven "having learned nothing at all."[8] His primary instructor was a certain Herr Adami, a man whom "God, in His rage, had made a school teacher":

> Whether or not he possessed the learning of a scholar I cannot say. But I know for certain that there was no trace of it to be found in his teaching. His explications of the classical authors consisted either purely of barren grammar, or with annotations in Minelli's manner. His voice was so unpleasant, his air so pedantic, his mood so hypochondriac, that one would become sick from tedium, or fall asleep. The latter was more common among his

pupils. One often saw entire rows or benches of children with their heads nodding in sequence.[9]

Boarding schools offered more rigorous training in classical languages, religion, history, and math. Pupils also engaged in physical education, which in the summer meant hiking up a hill for forty-five minutes in direct sunlight while singing Lutheran hymns. Athletic boys played ball at the top, while their weaker schoolmates found shady spots to read Ovid.[10] The pupils lived in large, dimly lit dormitories, one older and one younger boy in each room. They were awakened by a bell in the morning at five o'clock, after which a scholarship student called the *Inspektor* knocked on their doors with a massive key signaling that it was time for everyone to dress and appear in the dining room with hymnbook in hand.[11] Meals consisted of "soup broth at noon, with two bowls of nearly rancid meat for each table, with a good half-pound bread, a big wooden pitcher of decent beer, grilled meat three times, and wine twice per week."[12] Boys who could not tolerate the dearth of vegetables felt lucky to be sent to the infirmary, where the menu was a bit more varied.[13] The pupils' clothing was mostly of their own choosing but had to include a *Schalaune* (a black cloak) and a *Spanier* (a round hat of soft fabric that could be folded and stuffed into the ample pockets of the day).[14] A Leipzig newspaper announcement from 1731 describes what one young man was wearing when he ran away from his boarding school near Dresden:

> On June 27 a young man of the aristocracy named Gottlob Benjamin von Berge, age 16, around 2½ ells [= ca. five feet] tall, a little overweight with a full face and freckles, reddish hair, but wearing a light-colored wig with a braid in back, and a hat with a red feather, a light-grey coat, a coffee-brown vest, knickers with decorative buttons, and blended grey stockings. He speaks and writes French well, and ran away because he skipped some physical education classes with the company cadets here in Dresden and was afraid of being punished. He fled Dresden and cannot be located. [. . .] If you find him, please tell him that everything is forgiven, and whether or not he wishes to attend the university will be left up to him.[15]

This young aristocrat may have had other reasons for running away from his boarding school. Some pupils were subjected to hazing at the hands of older boys, who forced them to act as servants and punished them mercilessly for tiny infringements. Years after graduation, some still had nightmares about forgetting their hymnals or accidentally putting their cloaks on backward.[16] The position of *Inspektor*, which rotated among the older pupils, was one of particular authority, and some who held it were positively sadistic. Karl Friedrich Bahrdt presented the following scene as typical:

A poor boy, whose late arrival is eagerly anticipated, steps into the dining hall. The Inspektor cries: "Stop, scoundrel! Why are you so late?" or "Where's your hat?" etc. etc. The boy is silent, and stands like a lamb, as straight as possible before his tyrant, because if he does not do so he will be kicked on the spot. Now the Inspektor holds his right hand out and slaps him as hard as he possibly can, so that the dining hall echoes with the sound, and red imprints of his fingers are left on his victim's cheek. The younger boy dodders to the side, and the Inspektor shouts: "Stand, scoundrel!" and gives him a slap with the left hand so hard that his cheek swells. "Stay, dog!"—then the right hand again. And so forth until the barbarian has had enough. Then the younger boy goes to his seat with a swollen face, nearly deaf from the blows, says not a single word, and is not permitted to act as if anything unpleasant had just happened to him, lest he earn further punishment from the student in charge of his table. To complain to the teachers would be a grave mistake.[17]

Things were even worse in the privacy of the dorm rooms, where sexual abuse was allegedly rampant:

The vice of pederasty was so common in our school, I doubt that [. . .] a single student who was there during my time was not affected by it. This most abhorrent and terrible of all vices—which ordinarily has lifelong consequences, disturbs digestion, weakens the intestines, shatters the nerves, blunts the powers of the soul, and makes people stupid—was not just practiced in secret at night; this atrocity took place even in the light of day. [. . .] As this vice was common, each pupil believed that every other pupil knew about it. So all of the boys thought that I too must have been affected. Indeed, it would have been regarded as the most absurd pretension had I attempted to persuade someone that a boy like myself—delicate, pale, well educated, and still pure—had remained to this point free from all temptation. In this frame of mind, a certain pupil named Hofmann—who had the bearish face and clumsy body of a bumpkin, and a physiognomy suggesting stupidity and the maliciousness that often goes with it—came to me in the dining room and ordered me to immediately come up to his dorm room. As he was in the class approaching graduation [*Primaner*], and I was several years behind him [*Untersekundaner*], I had to obey him without delay or protest. After he unlocked his room and led me inside, he locked the door again and sat down on the bed. I asked what he wished from me. "Nothing," was the answer; "you should just come and sit down next to me." I did this, and there followed an abundance of caresses, kisses, and the like, which made me blush, though I did not think his behavior evil. As this shameless older student began to accelerate his advances, I pulled shyly away. He became indignant. I remained bashful. He became gruff. Finally he saw that I was unresponsive and stood up with the words: slutty boy, you just don't want me! He then boxed my ears twice, so that I fell over nearly deaf. He threw me out of his room and threatened, as I was sitting on the ground trying to recover, that he would beat me half to death if I did not go immediately to my own room. I pulled myself together and with swollen face went to [an older student named] Pallmann. "What's wrong, poor boy?" he asked, as tears flowed in streams from my eyes. Finally I told him the whole story. He was pleased at my naïveté, and explained to me with dark expression the disgraceful goals of this person, described for me the unhappy consequences of this vice, taught me of the prevalence I described above, which was entirely unknown to me, warned me not to betray Hofmann for fear of inciting in him a desire for revenge, and gave me suggestions for avoiding situations like this in the future.[18]

Bahrdt escaped the trials and tribulations of his boarding school through diligent study and began university training at the age of fifteen, a few years earlier than was typical.[19]

ॐ

Music was not ordinarily featured in the lesson plans of private tutors, day schools, or boarding schools. Many parents and educators regarded it as a waste of time. Whereas girls were encouraged to indulge in music and other galant activities, boys were encouraged first and foremost to focus on more substantive pursuits. Training in mathematics, history, theology, law, and medicine could contribute to a young man's financial and social well-being. Music ordinarily could not fulfill this role, and overindulgence was sometimes seen as a threat to the future careers of otherwise promising boys. Behavior guides encouraged male readers to limit their musical activities to a secondary pursuit (*Nebenfach*). Johann Christof Wagenseil's 1705 recommendation that young men should focus more on the development of listening skills rather than playing skills is typical:

> To learn an instrument well enough to play in front of respectable people requires far too much energy and time. It is even worse to play poorly, and wound the ears of your listeners, because that can really lower your reputation [. . .]. It is best to learn enough about music that you are able to distinguish the voice types, to know a good performance from a bad one, and to recognize skill and quality. That way, when you are in the company of your peers, and beautiful music is performed, or when someone plays a *Serenade* or *Aubade* on your behalf, you will be able to speak rationally and skillfully about it. It is a pleasure to be able to know music, and it is only those who do not understand it who might prefer a mouth harp or wooden guffaw to the sound of a lute, or would rather hear a farmer's song than the most beautiful motet.[20]

As chief educator to the fifteen-year-old Karl Wilhelm Ferdinand, crown prince of Braunschweig-Wolfenbüttel, Johann Friedrich Wilhelm Jerusalem was charged with finding music's proper place in a prince's educational curriculum. He wrote the following report to the boy's father in 1750:

> The violin has taken too much time away from real activities. A musician named Herr Weinholtz comes to him every day from 6:00 until 8:00 P.M. For such a sensual activity this is far too long. They do not think during this time, and music makes too great an impression upon them. I have to give credit to Herr Weinholtz for not taking advantage of the high place his teaching enjoys in the prince's estimation, as one might fear from such a person, as I have often listened for a long time from the adjoining room, and he can speak of nothing other than music and musicians. Two hours of this material, however, is too much for a prince, as it is lost time during which there is a lack of any real learning.[21]

Jerusalem worried that the magical power of music might be used to extract political favors from a naive young prince, just as others worried that the same magic might be used to take sexual advantage of female keyboard pupils. In the minds of Bach's contemporaries, the sensual power of melody and harmony had to be strictly controlled, lest it threaten otherwise impermeable social boundaries.

Advocates for music argued that it could refresh a boy's spirits, so that he might return to more important studies with greater alacrity. Bach's colleague at the St. Thomas Church, organist Christian Gräbner, asked rhetorically in his 1711 book on childrearing whether it was appropriate for a theology student to study music and answered: "Though it is not a necessity, it seems nonetheless to be of good service to the young man [. . .] because it allows him, after a long day of challenges in his difficult line of work, to quicken his spirits by playing a sacred hymn on the keyboard or other instrument."[22] Composers often used this same line of reasoning to sell their printed collections, easing the minds of customers worried about their sons wasting precious time. The following quotations are drawn from the prefaces of published works by Esias Reussner and Bach's predecessor in Leipzig, Johann Kuhnau:

> Such an exercise as [making music] can, in my view, have a positive influence on young people, who might thus use their free time profitably, and avoid idleness. And through practicing they can refresh their spirits, when these have been exhausted through other studies and worthy activities.[23]

> I have composed these new partitas, and published them myself, in the hope that those whose spirits have been tired out through other studies might refresh them at the keyboard, and also in order to please those who have chosen music for their profession.[24]

Parents who were inclined to have their sons study music usually had to make the arrangements outside of ordinary educational structures. The following account, which documents negotiations between the aristocratic mother of a musically inclined boy and the local cantor, can be taken as typical:

> One day in 1712, while I was at school in Herford copying some parts for Cantor Fockerode, a noblewoman came to him to ask his advice. She had a son who bore such interest and love for playing the keyboard that she and her husband were determined to give him over to the local organist for lessons. The cantor made all kinds of protestations and unworthy interjections, saying that he had an apprentice who played the keyboard well, and would ask no more than one groschen per hour, whereas the organist would want two. The woman responded that money was no object as long as her son received a righteous musical education, and in time learned to play the organ well. At this point the cantor answered that [the apprentice] would certainly help bring this plan to fruition. After her son had learned enough at the keyboard to play figured bass and chorales, he could gain access to the organ to perfect his skills by simply offering the organist a gratuity now and then.[25]

A sense for the musical instruction of boys who did not aspire to become professional musicians is available from the surviving keyboard notebook of Friedrich III, duke of Saxe-Gotha-Altenburg. It was begun in 1709, when the duke was just ten years old.[26] The volume is bound in brown leather with colored paper (red, orange, blue, and beige) decorating the inside covers. The first pages are devoted to a basic account of how to read music, which was copied by Friedrich himself.[27] Subjects covered include clef reading ("Wherever this symbol sits, that is the line for the note C") and note values ("A dot after a note means that you add half again its normal value"). Friedrich then copied a series of simple galanterien, including minuets, sarabandes, bourrées, gavottes, and the like. The back of the book contains a series of six arrangements of Lutheran chorale melodies. The pages that separate the secular from the sacred works—the vast majority of the book—are blank, suggesting that Friedrich's interest in music proved more limited than he or his handlers expected.[28] The repertoire itself is virtually identical to that copied for female amateur keyboardists in Bach's era. It is telling, however, that the music in this notebook was copied not only by Friedrich's teacher, the court organist in Gotha, Christian Friedrich Witt, but also by the ten-year-old pupil himself.[29] In contrast to the Countesses zu Epstein, who were never expected to dirty their hands committing music to paper, Friedrich of Saxe-Gotha-Altenburg was trained from the beginning to set down notes and rhythms of his own.

ớ▲

Leaving for the university was a singular event in the lives of boys, their
parents, siblings, and other loved ones. It often meant a separation of two
to five years, beginning with a rather uncomfortable and perilous journey
in a horse-drawn carriage. One English visitor described the German post
coaches around 1727 as follows:

> What they call a Post-Waggon, which is the usual travelling Carriage in
> *Germany*, cannot be more adequately described, than by comparing it to a
> Country Dung-Cart, with Boards nail'd a-cross it for Seats; some of which
> Seats have Backs to them, about a Foot and a half high, but others are
> without any; and to these blessed Vehicles was I confined for twenty-seven
> Hours; cursing, at every Jolt, the Stupidity of the more ancient *Germans*, who
> could think of no better Conveniency, for the Accommodation of Strangers,
> and the Folly of the present Race, who will be A——s, for no other Reason,
> but because their Fathers were A——s before them.[30]

Twenty-seven hours aboard a bumpy post coach was not unusual, as the
vehicles traveled day and night, the drivers eager to take advantage of favorable weather. When coach wheels got stuck in the mud, university boys were
often made to help get them unstuck, or to walk for a while to lighten the
load. Private coaches provided somewhat more comfortable conveyance
and also afforded opportunities for young men to hear about the lives and
exploits of their coach drivers, who were known to pass around distilled
spirits, offer moral advice, and tell stories of adventure on the road.[31]

While traveling, university-age boys had to be vigilant, watching out not
only for bludgeon-wielding thieves but also for army recruiters, who were
legally authorized to draft any male of military age found in their territories. Tall boys were particularly sought after, not because their height
offered any particular advantages in battle but because they looked dash-
ing while standing guard before princely palaces. While recruiters were
in the area, many boys played it safe by staying in their homes and inns.[32]
Border crossings between the territories of the Holy Roman Empire were
particularly fraught, and potential recruits were known to hide under lug-
gage to avoid detection.[33]

Upon arrival at university, students found accommodation in local
homes. Boys from the same region typically stuck together, often sharing
rooms.[34] Wealthier students hired lackeys for one reichstaler per week to
run errands such as purchasing fruit, coffee, or beer, distributing tips to
musicians in restaurants, and making payments to book dealers.[35] But even
ordinary students often lived in accommodations that came complete with

servants, or at least paid caretakers, who carried heavy trunks upstairs, washed laundry, and emptied chamber pots.[36]

Academic work began with a student's official matriculation. The university rector would often ask the incoming student a few questions about his background and perhaps test his knowledge a bit before recording his name and place of birth in the official matriculation book. Students then generally handed over a fee of five reichstaler, though this could be waived in the case of financial hardship.[37]

Classes, known as *Collegia*, were held in rooms and auditoriums in diverse spaces spread around the city, some owned by the university, others rented. Schools employed a small number of regular ("ordinary") professors, but most of the teaching was done by unofficial ("extraordinary") professors. Professors of all ranks earned the bulk of their income by collecting fees directly from the boys who enrolled in their classes. It was the job of an assistant (*Famulus*) to take the names of the enrollees and to extract payments.[38] These could amount to eight reichstaler per course, along with a smaller payment of around one reichstaler to the Famulus. Such fees, too, were frequently reduced or waived in the case of financial need.[39] The number of students in each class varied from ten to two hundred.[40] Private classes with just three or four other boys could be arranged, but it was more expensive, as was private tutoring, which could cost up to one hundred reichstaler per semester.[41]

Three fundamental courses of study were available to university students in Bach's Germany: theology, law, and medicine. Theology students spent their time memorizing Hebrew, Latin, Greek, and other ancient languages, mastering the finer points of biblical exegesis, hermeneutics, and ancient Greek philosophy, and polishing their rhetorical skills in order one day to deliver moving orations from the pulpit. While still enrolled in university collegia, they commonly honed their skills by giving sermons in nearby village churches. Karl Friedrich Bahrdt was so nervous at his first preaching engagement, at age nineteen, that he raced through his hour-long text in fifteen minutes, awkwardly began a prayer before the choir had finished singing, and elicited laughter from the congregation when he woefully misread the handwritten names of bedridden parishioners.[42]

Law students studied public authority interest, ancient Roman legal theory, and feudal, civil, canonical, and criminal law. Some added courses in mathematics and experimental physics, according to their inclinations.[43] Lectures and class discussions were generally conducted in Latin. The most popular professors were engaging and widely read, citing not only case law but also historical and travel writing to support their arguments. Practical training was of particular value, and some professors offered students the opportunity to work with real court files.[44] The best lecturers spoke freely rather than reading from prepared texts.[45] The worst professors, overburdened with legal work in territories near and far and unprepared to teach, wasted class time complaining about mistakes in the textbooks.[46]

Medical students studied math and physics, but above all anatomy.[47] They learned what they could from examining livers, uteruses, lungs, tongues, and penises floating in preservative solutions.[48] Teachers and students alike were constantly on the lookout for fresh corpses but were legally restricted to dissecting the bodies of those who had been executed by the state as well as those of stillborn children with spectacular birth defects.[49] Occasionally, illegal bargains were struck with poor families to acquire the bodies of recently deceased relatives in exchange for financial support. In 1720 two Leipzig university medical students were apprehended carrying a large, unwieldy bag. They initially claimed to the police that they were transporting "an old double bass" but it soon became clear that the bag in fact contained the corpse of an elderly woman.[50]

All students, no matter their chosen field, faced the challenge of maintaining discipline. Karl Friedrich Bahrdt was probably not the only young man at the university in Leipzig who felt overwhelmed by the independence he was granted:

> I could never bring myself to steadiness or continuous study. I started thousands of times from scratch, trying to force myself to read or write down my thoughts. But I could never get anywhere. Whenever a new semester began, I made the most solemn vows and promised myself to buckle down to study with unwavering dedication. I selected a large number of *Collegia*. I prepared for myself a calendar, accounting for every hour of the day from early in the morning until late at night. I asked God in my morning and evening prayers to grant me perseverance. I started the semester full of fire, never missing any classes, studying into the evenings, and going to bed feeling proud of myself. But that only ever lasted a few weeks. After the fire dissipated, little hindrances forced me to miss a few *Collegia*. Then I granted myself the freedom to take an afternoon or evening off to attend a party with friends. But the next morning, when I sat down to study again, the academic work had lost all of its appeal. Then I missed more classes. And before four weeks were past, my course of study was full of holes, my calendar in tatters, my enthusiasm cooled, and another semester wasted—though always with the resolution that the next one would be better.[51]

The challenge of maintaining discipline was made all the more difficult by the availability of a wide range of leisure-time entertainments. Some university students spent hours every day in coffeehouses drinking "Ethiopian water," which was thought to be good for curing hangovers—or, as they put it, "driving out Beelzebub with Astharoth."[52] They played card games like *Lombre* and *Pharao*, learning to pepper their speech with foreign terms (die *Entree*, die *Spadille*, die *Manille*, die *Basta*, die *Ponto*, etc.). Smoking was so common at university that some boys deliberately built up their tolerance so as to sit in small rooms smoking until the haze in the air became so thick it snuffed out the candles.[53] Billiard tables were busy from morning to nightfall: each participant was assigned a single ball and spent the game trying to strike those of his opponents into the pockets or over the side. One Leipzig student argued facetiously that the coffeehouses were true "schools of all the humanities" in which it was possible to meet people of different social classes from all over the world, read the news, and talk politics. He encouraged his comrades to sell their books, save money on ink, feathers, and paper, and turn their education over to the coffeehouses, rhetorically asking the collective body of textbook authors: "Do you, in your many chapters on figures of speech, have a single curse that might be useful to a righteous *Lombre* or *Pharao* player, when the game doesn't go his way? And you claim nonetheless to have fully covered the speech of the affections!"[54]

Many university students spent their free time making themselves more galant in hopes of charming local women. The mindset of boys recently freed from parental oversight is elegantly recounted in Johann Leonhard Rost's 1710 novel *Amor auf Universitäten* (Love at Universities):

> As soon as I left home my entire behavior changed. Before I had always dressed plainly, and never spent much money on clothing, but as soon as I had my own apartment I began to behave differently. I dressed in a more courtly fashion, as my status demanded, went to the dance floors, practiced music, hung out with friends from home, and was always joking around. And then love snuck into my life. My landlord had a daughter of artful construction and galant manner, who did not have many chores to do at home and had plenty of time to devote herself to galanterien. She played the harp beautifully, spoke French, danced well, and developed such an artful style of conversation through reading novels that it was a pleasure to spend time with her.[55]

University boys flirted with local daughters by exchanging letters or seeking them out at church or in the theater.[56] On Sunday mornings they tried to get girls' attention by dropping objects on their heads from church balconies.

The most readily available women were servants, with whom university students often lived in close proximity.[57] Karl Friedrich Bahrdt's autobiography includes the following account of the downfall of his favorite private tutor, a university student named Jäger:

Unfamiliar with all that which one calls sin, and having no experience with danger and temptation, he lived with us for three months without a single evil thought desecrating his soul. One day, however, he was invited to a feast celebrating someone's successful completion of a master's degree, where his too-strict virtue inspired not admiration but rather a prurient desire to corrupt him. "Hey," said one, "let's drink that sissy Jäger under the table tonight." They agreed and poor Jäger succumbed. Not drunk, but nonetheless loaded with an unaccustomed portion of alcohol, and tipsy enough that he would not have flinched if someone had brandished a sword in his face, Jäger came home late, and found everyone asleep except for our old maidservant, a woman of forty who was as ugly as the night. She brought him up to his room, noticed his extraordinary joviality, offered to make him a cup of tea, entered into conversation and—the poor, unlucky man—forgot herself. I still have a tear in my eye when I think of this dreadful case [. . .]. In one evening, completely independent of any intention on his part, the evil of those who envied his virtue, the power of drink, and his virtue itself—that is, his naive ignorance of vice—united themselves against him, ruined his innocence, destroyed his happiness, and annihilated a man who could have brought so much good to the world. Poor Jäger received a vocation early, and cried tears of joy before God and his patrons, but on that very evening the abominable woman announced to him that she was pregnant. A deathly fear came over him, he turned down the position he'd been offered, left Leipzig [. . .] and died of anxiety the next year.[58]

Bahrdt's account of his tutor's fall is delivered with a measure of ironic wit; the man's hopeless naïveté, his drunken courage, and the housekeeper's homeliness are intended to entertain. The "abominable" maidservant is blamed for having "forgotten herself" in the tryst with Jäger, whereas the drunken tutor is portrayed as a tragic figure. Such liaisons were not unusual and sometimes resulted in newborn babies turning up dead on the doorsteps of university buildings bearing notes from their mothers indicating that they were "student property" (*Studentengut*).[59] Public sympathy was generally reserved for the fathers and the babies.

Prostitutes could be found in Leipzig and all other university towns, accommodating the illicit sexual desires of university boys. Madams were known to deliberately bump into students on the street. When the boys turned around expecting an apology, the women instead offered them enticing descriptions of attractive young ladies "from head to foot, not forgetting to describe those things which they believed most essential."[60]

እ&

Music was benign by comparison with most other pastimes in which university students were tempted to indulge. Beyond merely refreshing the spirits for more important work, notes and rhythms were believed to have an inoculative effect not unlike the effect they had on girls. The following anonymous poem, which appeared in the university town of Jena in the 1740s, encapsulates this perspective:

> Some men opt to chase amour,
> Some are drawn to village life,
> Some esteem the gold's allure,
> Some love drink and end in strife.
> I instead play on the lute,
> And enjoy a lovely song,
> Violins, bass and my flute:
> These I could play all day long.[61]

Music offered university students an emotional outlet and a means of tempering bouts of melancholy. As for women, the keyboard could serve as surrogate companion, offering both an emotional outlet and an uncritical sounding board. Felix Christian Weiße revealed as much in the following poem, written while he was a student at Leipzig University in the 1740s:

> You, sweet-sounding dear clavier,
> What great joy you bring my ear!
> I admire your every tone
> When I sit at home alone;
> You are what I wish to be,
> Both revival and esprit.
>
> When I'm gay you play along
> Offering a joking song;
> Should my spirits be laid low,
> You can comfort pain and woe.
> And when I with God commune,
> You strike up a pious tune.
>
> Never in my breast ignite
> Sinful lust for false delight!
> Pleasure must remain demure,
> Just as all your strings are pure,
> And my life will never be
> Lacking in sweet harmony.[62]

More than most musical instruments, the keyboard was associated with domesticity. As such, it was viewed as among the best tools for keeping university students out of trouble. In 1753 Johann Christoph Gottsched wrote in a letter to the father of a boy who had come from Altenburg to begin university studies:

Recently [your son] hired a keyboard teacher, who comes to him every week for a few hours [. . .]. This much is clear: he has a natural inclination toward music, and has already laid the foundations for this in Altenburg. If this kind of activity keeps him in his apartment, the money is well spent. This has been my view regarding poetry and oratory as well; because these pleasant activities bring young people to working and reading, they are also brought to sit still and stay home.[63]

The account book of a student at Leipzig University in the early 1730s includes payments for "picking up the keyboard (two groschen)," "keyboard rental and transportation cost (two reichstaler, two groschen)," "binding a music notebook," and expenditures for lessons (two reichstaler, eighteen groschen per month), which went to Johann Schneider, the former Bach student and organist of the St. Nicholas Church.[64] Teachers often gave four lessons per week, though this could be reduced as necessary in times of academic stress.[65] The diary of Johann Christian Schuchardt, a student at Leipzig University in 1743–1744, reveals that he had keyboard lessons from a fellow student he called "Hr. Opitz." Schuchardt seems to have wanted four lessons per week, but his teacher was unwilling because he believed his student "could not really use more than two hours [per week]."[66] Schuchardt paid two groschen per hour, apparently the standard rate for teachers in large cities who did not inhabit professional organist positions. Lessons were given primarily at his teacher's apartment, but occasionally at his own.[67] When Mr. Opitz left town, Schuchardt studied with another student who borrowed Opitz's keyboard. The repertoire he played apparently consisted of dances (a "Bourrée" and "Bourlesque" are referenced in his diary) and chorale preludes ("Komm süßer Tod," "Herr Jesu Christ du höchstes gut," among others). He was particularly excited to find a print of the most popular song collection of the era—Johann Sigismund Scholze's *Sperontes Singende Muse an der Pleiße*—which he examined "in its entirety" in a local bookstore.[68]

Some young men hoped that the musical skills they cultivated might bring them success with women. At the very least, music was an excuse for gathering together in mixed company. A Leipzig periodical edited by Johann Christoph Gottsched published an issue in 1725 that described two men who intended to use music to help celebrate the birthday and nameday of two young beauties in order to "persuade them of their admiration."[69] The future physiologist Albrecht von Haller wrote when he was sixteen years old that the women in Tübingen were "mostly white-skinned and pleasant, and very well dressed" but he found those in Stuttgart more attractive not only because of their beauty but also because they "are not so prudish, are easier to see, and do not refuse invitations to snacks or music."[70]

Novels of the era offer insight into the fantasy world of libidinous university students and the role they hoped music would play in the satisfaction of their desires. In a novel by Michael Erich Frank published in 1715, *Die rachgierige Fleurie*, a young man visits the home of his would-be lover, an English woman named Susanne. After she serves him some food, he sets out to impress her with his musical skills:

> The wine was rather delicious, and the bread equally so, and as I looked around the room I noticed a harpsichord, so I left my wine glass standing and asked permission to go over and play this musical instrument. I knew Susanne's favorite minuet, and because I could play a little at the keyboard I performed it for her. As I brought the piece to its conclusion I saw a book of cantatas and arias on the side. I flipped through for a while until I found one that I knew, and I began to play and sing it immediately:
>
>> Have you, dearest, finally chosen
>> Never to grant love to me?
>> Is the heart inside you frozen
>> Or from hatred never free?
>> Have you, dearest, now decided,
>> To discard the love confided?
>> Must I now in bitter pain
>> Constantly from joy abstain?[71]

Susanne, unable to resist a man with such excellent keyboard skills, eventually accedes to his bold advances. His active seduction distances this protagonist and virtually all other male musicians in the novels of Bach's Germany from their female counterparts, who were supposed to make music solely for their own edification.

In Christoph Gottlieb Wend's 1713 novel *Der närrische und doch beliebte Cupido* (The Foolish and yet Beloved Cupid) a young keyboard teacher, Daferno, meets one of his doe-eyed pupils, Amalia, at a party. The aristocrat who employed Daferno is infatuated with Amalia, but after having lessons with Daferno and now hearing him perform at this gathering, Amalia falls hopelessly in love with the galant musician rather than the nobleman for whom she was intended:

> Amalia took much trouble to hide her dizziness when she was in Daferno's presence, and was grateful for the sympathy, and all of the goodness that he had demonstrated in shortening her long hours through his music-making. Now, at the party, he had to take his place at the clavier, and tried to satisfy the desires of his listeners. He improvised [*phantasirte*] for a while, and proved with his pleasing ideas that he was no mere student of this instrument. He then added his beguiling voice to the well-sounding strings and

set Amalia in charmed wonder with an aria, which he sang in his alluring manner [. . .]. The pure and extraordinary voice, the salacious ornaments, and the poignant gestures to which Daferno treated the ears and eyes of those present moved this artful young woman in her innermost heart, and she lost all the freedom that remained to her. The yearning to exchange her feelings with him drove her to a few stolen sighs, which lightened her sensitive breast a bit, and the more Daferno continued to please her ears, the more he unknowingly hurt the chances of his Lord, whom the enflamed Amalia now fully renounced in her heart, dedicating her full passion to Daferno.[72]

For male amateur musicians, to a greater extent than for their female counterparts, music offered opportunities to socialize. University students often banded together to form ensembles known as *Collegia Musica*. Once or twice per week, such clubs met to run through works for large ensemble in private homes, rented rooms, or local coffeehouses. By comparison with other clubs, these were seen as relatively harmless. As one who enjoyed performances of a *Collegium Musicum* in Jena in the 1720s wrote in his autobiography: "I went with pleasure whenever my friends held *Collegia Musica*, where things remained relatively respectable, and the inhuman drunkenness, which always bothered me tremendously, had no place."[73]

The character of such gatherings can be gleaned from surviving bylaws. The following set comes from a Collegium Musicum founded in Greiz in 1746:

1. Rehearsals take place from 3 to 5 o'clock on Wednesdays (or from 2 to 4 o'clock in the winter). At least five works are to be played and rehearsed until there are no mistakes. We begin with an overture and end with a symphony.

2. Members are to be fined one groschen for every fifteen minutes they are late.

3. Everyone is to play his correct instrument, unless otherwise directed.

4. If members do not play a given piece, they should remain quiet or be fined one groschen.

5. There is a four-groschen fine for skipping rehearsal, except as excused by illness or duties to aristocratic authorities.

6. Members are to keep their instruments in good shape, or be fined one groschen.

7. Fighting or arguing is to be punished with a two-groschen fine.

8. Members should tune carefully to the harpsichord.

9. The "unpleasant habit" of musicians fantasizing around on their instruments between pieces, particularly during recitatives in church music, is to be avoided as it creates a mish-mash for the listeners. Furthermore, "for those who understand music, this kind of mischief causes cramps and

toothaches" [*einem Musikverständigen das Seitenstechen und Zahnweh verursachen möchte*].

10. Pay careful attention to the much adored piano and forte [*das sehr beliebte Piano und forte*]. Play only the notes written down by the composer, and do not add any arpeggios of your own.

11. Those who do not learn their parts or disrupt the ensemble are to be fined four groschen the first time and eight groschen the second time. Further violations may result in expulsion.

12. Do not drink or smoke until the proper time [*bis es die Zeit erlaubet*] lest you be fined one groschen.

13. Any person of standing is free to attend the meetings of the *Collegium Musicum*, but will be required to pay two groschen as well.

14. Fines and other fees collected are to be paid into a "well guarded box" [*wohlverwahrte Büchße*].

15. A celebratory banquet will be held every year on the day on which the *Collegium Musicum* was founded.

16. Now and then the *Collegium Musicum* will purchase new instruments. Members should not lend them out to anyone else.

17. All members are obliged to perform in public worship ceremonies as necessary. The primary goal of the *Collegium Musicum* is to serve our neighbors and our noble rulers.[74]

These and other sets of bylaws draw no sharp distinction between rehearsals and performances. Works were likely run through several times in relative private before opening the doors for a paying public, but the practice sessions, too, seem to have been accessible to those willing to part with a few groschen. Such ensembles emphasized participation, with musicians likely outnumbering audience members.

Though the emphasis was on ensemble music, solo repertoire was sometimes featured as well. The art historian Jacob von Staehlin wrote in his memoires that while studying at Leipzig University in the 1730s he had occasionally played "a solo or a concerto" (*ein Solo oder ein Concert*) in the Collegium Musicum led by J. S. Bach.[75] Lorenz Mizler observed in 1736 that in Bach's Collegium Musicum "every musician is permitted to be heard before the public, and there are often many listeners present who are able to judge the worth of a skilled musician."[76] Contemporary reports suggest that the solo music performed was of a particularly virtuosic character. In 1742 an anonymous writer described the distinction between church and Collegium Musicum repertoire: "The music performed in the churches is not so difficult as that performed in the Collegium Musicum, which all the boys know. Because if one wishes to make oneself heard in a Collegium Musicum, one ordinarily chooses the most challenging pieces."[77] The following cantata text by Christian Friedrich Hunold takes as its subject the performance of a solo suite by a viola da gambist at a Collegium Musicum concert, offering a sense for the convivial atmosphere at such gatherings:

(A viola da gamba player is heard.)

Is that a viol' da gamb' I hear?
Let's see what he can do.

(The gambist plays a *Preludium* and the singer joins in
    when the meter becomes regular.)

Oh what amazing loveliness!
Which mesmerizes and delights me.
How gently the bow strokes the strings!
How artful the accords!
And listen to that quick passagework . . .

(Here the *Preludium* comes to an end.)

Thus dissipates the fog of my anxieties,
The music offers harmonies
As sweet as I could desire.
My friend, I beg of you,
Please play a full Partita.
Now, how would
The *Allemande* sound?

(The *Allemande* is played.)

Nice!
And the *Courante* would sound not bad right here.
Let's hear how it goes.

(*Courante.*)

How beautiful!
The *Sarabande*, with its noble qualities,
Would sound incomparably good at this point.

(*Sarabande.*)

Yes, yes, this is how to drive away resentments.
Through music my grief is put to rest.
Let the *Gigue* now conclude this performance.

(*Gigue.*)

Sa sa!
Tedium is far away,
Nagging thoughts have retreated.
I feel that my heart
Is no longer beset by melancholy,
But rather calmed by pleasure.[78]

The emphasis in Collegia Musica like this one was on active participation, even for those who were not actually playing instruments or singing. The pleasure of involvement came largely from the sense that one was surrounded by calm and like-minded individuals who were intent on pursuing honest entertainment.

Whereas female musicians were encouraged in Bach's Germany to obediently play what was written, male musicians were expected to depart from the confines of the page. The bylaws of Collegium Musicum ensembles typically admonished participants to avoid adding arpeggios and fantasies to preexisting works. Male musicians impressed women at parties by improvising clever new lyrics to hymn tunes: "As the deer who's seeking water cries aloud with his desire" became "As a tailor who wants oatmeal cries aloud with his desire," and "To God alone the glory be" became "The empty pipe demands its meat."[79] Male musicians in novels of the era did not merely present what was written before them but delighted their listeners by "fantasizing on various chords."[80] That such experiences were not confined to the realm of fantasy is suggested by J. F. A. von Uffenbach, whose diary includes an account of a raucous dinner at the University of Tübingen in 1712. The meal was followed by a musical performance from scholarship recipients who "pulled their instruments from closets" in the dining hall. Uffenbach was then ushered up to one of the apartments of a particularly affluent student. They had already enjoyed quite a bit of alcohol—apparently "no one ever left this dining hall without a buzz"; the boys gathered in an alcove, which offered a lovely view of the city. An unidentified fellow student was called upon to demonstrate his skills:

> We could scarcely hear the sound of his clavichord over the din of glasses clinking, but he wanted to demonstrate to us his accomplishments in the realm of composition. To this end he invited us to name any Lutheran hymn tune. This he promised to present in various guises, including that of a minuet, a gigue, and finally a sarabande. We suggested the well known hymn *Freu dich sehr o meine Seele* and he did indeed execute this tune in all of these various forms.[81]

Cultivating skills in improvisation and composition required a solid knowledge of music theory. This too was viewed as a realm more suitable for men than for women. While composers sometimes marketed collections of keyboard music explicitly to female customers, the authors of music theory books assumed their words would be read almost exclusively by men. This chapter concludes with two case studies of lawyers who exemplify the social and intellectual ambitions associated with male amateur music making in Bach's time.

❧

Johann Stephan Pütter was born in Iserlohn near Dortmund in 1725. From his earliest years, education occupied an unusually prominent place in his life, not least because his extended family consisted largely of merchants and doctors of law. From age eight he studied Latin, Greek, Hebrew, geography, and history with private tutors, one of whom was a convert to the philosophies of Christian Wolff and another of whom was a Calvinist preacher.[82] He was unusually gifted at Latin and was asked to deliver speeches at parties and at the nearby castle of Count Moritz Casimir I von Bentheim-Tecklenburg. At age thirteen Pütter began studying law at the university in Marburg, though he soon transferred to the university in Halle. On a visit to nearby Leipzig in 1740, he asked Johann Christoph Gottsched to sign his *Album Amicorum,* and the famous professor offered the following words to live by: "Not for yourself but for the world you are born."[83] He soon transferred to the university of Jena, assuming the position of Famulus for a well-known law professor. In 1744, at age nineteen, Pütter obtained the degree of *Licentiat,* which authorized him to teach courses in Marburg; two years later, at the astonishingly young age of twenty-one, he was appointed professor of law in Göttingen, a post he held for half a century.

A voluminous autobiography Pütter published in 1798 contains a number of passages detailing his musical development and interests. The first of these occurred around 1737, when he was twelve years old, at the count's residence. Pütter and other members of the community were invited to participate in fishing and hunting festivals and on occasion to make music at Bentheim-Tecklenburg's palace at the top of a heavily forested hill:

> As is the often case at smaller courts, the servants were musical. The count himself played the cello and devoted an hour of nearly every day to a little concert, which ordinarily took place just before the meal. I had already learned to play the keyboard a bit at home, and one of the count's servants gave me an hour of instruction per day. Gradually I developed a taste for music, though nature would otherwise have never guided me in this direction. In addition, the daily climb up the hill was good for my health. The count included me in his concerts and gave me the modest task of turning pages.[84]

Pütter continued to cultivate his musical skills as a twenty-year-old professor at the university in Marburg. He devoted one hour per day to studies with a violinist from Hungary. Every Sunday afternoon his mentor and professor, Johann Georg Estor, held a concert in his visitors' room. Pütter typically played the viola, favoring strings over wind instruments because they "presented no danger for the lungs."[85]

After Pütter's appointment as a professor in Göttingen in 1747, music began to play a more prominent role in his leisure time. His autobiography includes the following account, in which he mentions fellow lawyers Jacob Schuback and Gottfried Achenwall:

> The pleasure that I found in music was among my greatest diversions. Because others occasionally found me playing the keyboard, the violin, or the flute, my interest did not remain secret for long and brought me together with others of like mind. Among these was my friend and table-mate, Schuback, from Hamburg, who held a private concert in his own apartment every week. At his invitation, I took part and eventually allowed myself to be persuaded to hold the concerts in my own home. In the end it came to be a general concert held in rented rooms and has improved greatly since that time.
>
> As for myself, I continued to devote an hour to music on most days. Achenwall was my partner in such endeavors and there was a good harmony between us, as he could play figured bass at the keyboard. With the addition of another violinist we could practice duets or solo pieces. In order to play trios, I eventually added a cellist, for quartets or symphonies a violist, and finally a pair of flutes or oboes. In this manner a private concert series began in my home and I have maintained it ever since. For many years, however, the only time I had to hold a violin in my hands was on Monday afternoons when this gathering took place. Although my own artistry is limited to a basic ability to play the violin part of a symphony, it brings me great pleasure and exhilaration to do so. My aforementioned friend Schuback studied composition in Hamburg with Telemann and put together a little society that included me and took on the form of a Collegium, which made music still more dear to me, and offered me insight into its theoretical workings.[86]

Not everyone was impressed with the results. Joseph Martin Kraus, a composer in Göttingen whose works Pütter's ensemble once sightread, had little positive to say about the experience:

> I brought my first symphony to be read in a private concert series that took place on Mondays and Thursdays at the home of Professor Pütter. Pütter himself directed. *Holla!* He was beating time with his bow! They started! The group had not even made it twenty measures before completely falling apart. The violin was chasing the bass, the bass chasing the viola, the viola chasing the second violin, the oboes quacked a little underneath it all, and the horn opted wisely to just keep quiet. So it went! The best part was this: that the men firmly believed they had performed beautifully! On to the second symphony. They spit into their hands and readied themselves. Oh, my poor symphony! The first had been presented in a sort of broken dialect but the next was mercilessly burned alive by these law men.[87]

As Pütter acknowledged of his relationship with music, "nature would have never guided me in this direction," and he rarely practiced. The joy in music making came less from earning the admiration of connoisseurs than from the pleasure of collaboration with colleagues, students, and friends.

❧

Sometime in the spring of 1775, a lawyer and government bureaucrat in Fulda named Johann Heinrich Fischer contracted a catarrhal inflammation in his chest. Such ailments were not ordinarily taken seriously by doctors or patients, but this one would not go away. At around 6:30 in the morning on May 2, 1775, Fischer died "just in the moment he was about to take some medicine."[88] Over the next few days, bureaucrats charged with cataloging the contents of his apartment found, among many other items, an oak podium for reading and writing, various prayer stools and kneelers, a green wardrobe with yellow trim, a grandfather clock, and "an oakwood commode with a clavichord and a bookshelf on top."[89]

At the time of his death, Fischer was sixty-four years old and widely regarded as "an archetype and model of an active businessman."[90] He had been born in Hilders on March 8, 1711[91] and had led an extraordinarily successful career in Fulda's government bureaucracy. One of the northernmost strongholds of Catholicism in the Holy Roman Empire, Fulda was run by ecclesiastical authorities—prince-abbots and prince-bishops—who constructed palaces, went on hunts, and surrounded themselves with courtly servants and bureaucracies that rivaled those of secular authorities.[92] The city's glory days as a medieval center of power were long past, but its economy had begun to thrive again with the dawn of the galant era. Fischer had devoted his talent and energy to improving his city's fortunes, serving as "sacred home secretary" (*geistlicher Geheimer Rath*) and as "Vicar of the Bishop in Contentious Legal Matters" (*Vicar des Bischofs in streitigen Rechtssachen*).

In his leisure hours, Fischer cultivated an abiding passion for music. According to an account published shortly after his death: "In musical matters, Fischer was very experienced both in theory and in practice, and he enjoyed teaching others. He possessed a substantial and select book collection, and during his lifetime donated 109 volumes to the library in Fulda."[93] The public library referenced here had been founded in 1769, just six years before Fischer's death, by an enterprising librarian named Father Petrus Böhm. It contained more than six thousand books, combining the materials of the *Konventsbibliothek* (4,204 volumes), the *Hofbibliothek* (1,460 volumes), the *Jesuiten- und Seminariumsbibliothek* (218 volumes), and various private collections (249 volumes). Böhm had established strict protocols for patrons: the library was open to ministers, officials, and professors, but no dogs or children were allowed; borrowers agreed to fill out proper forms and to bring all materials back in an undamaged state.[94] Fischer had deemed this a worthy project and around 1770 had donated his library of music and books to the public good.

A substantial number of books on music Fischer donated are preserved today in Fulda's *Hochschul- und Landesbibliothek* (table 5).[95] He evidently enjoyed a good debate. His music theory collection includes numerous works by authors who publically opposed one another—for example, Sorge vs. Marpurg, Sorge vs. Fritz, Mattheson vs. Scheibe, and Mattheson vs.

Table 5. Johann Heinrich Fischer's Books about Music

Author	Abbreviated Title	Date	Call Number
Anonymous	*Sammlung einiger Nachrichten von Orgel-Wercken*	1757	K.W.F. 15/10
Anonymous	*Musikalische Erwegungs- und Übungs-Wahrheiten*	17??	K.W.F. 21/63
Adlung, J.	*Anleitung zur musikalischen Gelahrtheit*	1758	K.W.F. 7/14
Buttstedt, J.	*Ut, re, mi, fa, sol, la, Tota Musica*	1715	K.W.F. 21/18
Fritz, B.	*Anweisung wie man Claviere stimmen könne*	1757	K.W.F. 14/85
Hartung, P. C.	*Musicus theoretico practicus*	1749	K.W.F. 21/61
Hertel, J. W.	*Sammlung musikalischer Schriften*	1757	K.W.F. 2/21
Lingke, G. F.	*Die Sitze der musicalischen Haupt-Sätze*	1766	K.W.F. 21/83
Marpurg, F. W.	*Die Kunst das Klavier zu spielen*	1750	K.W.F. 101/5
Marpurg, F. W.	*Abhandlung von der Fuge* [vol. 2]	1754	K.W.F. 21/68
Marpurg, F. W.	*Handbuch bey dem Generalbass* [vols. 1, 2, 3]	1757	K.W.F. 21/71
Marpurg, F. W.	*Anfangsgründe der Theoretischen Music*	1757	K.W.F. 21/74
Marpurg, F. W.	*Kritische Einleitung in die Geschichte der Music*	1759	K.W.F. 7/15
Mattheson, J.	*Grosse Generalbass Schule*	1731	K.W.F. 21/36
Mattheson, J.	*Kleine Generalbass Schule*	1735	K.W.F. 21/45
Mattheson, J.	*Kern melodischer Wissenschaft*	1737	K.W.F. 21/48
Mattheson, J.	*Behauptung der Himmlischen Musik*	1747	K.W.F. 6/23
Mattheson, J.	*Mithridat wider den Gift*	1749	K.W.F. 6/20
Mattheson, J.	*Bewährte Panacea* [vol. 1]	1750	K.W.F. 6/21
Mattheson, J.	*Bewährte Panacea* [vol. 2]	1750	K.W.F. 6/22
Mattheson, J.	*Plus Ultra* [vol. 1]	1754	K.W.F. 2/19
Mattheson, J.	*Plus Ultra* [vol. 3]	1755	K.W.F. 2/19
Mizler, L.	*Neu-Eröffnete Musicalische Bibliothek* [vol. 1]	1739	K.W.F. 2/15
Mizler, L.	*Neu-Eröffnete Musicalische Bibliothek* [vol. 2]	1746	K.W.F. 2/15
Murschhauser, F.	*Academia Musico-Poetica*	1721	K.W.F. 21/30
Neidhardt, J. G.	*Gäntzlich erschöpfte Mathematische Abtheilung*	1734	K.W.F. 21/40
Riepel, J.	*Anfangsgründe zur musicalischen Setzkunst*	1754	K.W.F. 21/65
Riepel, J.	*Grundregeln zur Tonordnung*	1755	K.W.F. 21/69
Riepel, J.	*Gründliche Erklärung der Tonordnung*	1757	K.W.F. 21/75
Samber, J. B.	*Manuductio ad Organum*	1704	K.W.F. 21/24
Samber, J. B.	*Elucidatio musicæ choralis*	1710	K.W.F. 21/27
Scheibe, J. A.	*Gültige Zeugnisse über die Musical. Kern-Schrift*	1738	K.W.F. 21/48
Sorge, G.	*Zuverlässige Anweisung Claviere zu stimmen*	1758	K.W.F. 14/87
Sorge, G.	*Compendium harmonicum*	1760	K.W.F. 21/79

Table 5. Continued

Author	Abbreviated Title	Date	Call Number
Sorge, G.	*Anleitung zum Generalbass*	1760	K.W.F. 21/81
Spiess, M.	*Tractatus Musicus Compositorio-Practicus*	1746	K.W.F. 21/60
Walther, J. G.	*Musikalisches Lexikon*	1732	K.W.F. 4/15
Werckmeister, A.	*Cribrum Musicum oder Musicalisches Sieb*	1700	K.W.F. 21/20
Werckmeister, A.	*Harmonologia Musica oder kurtze Anleitung*	1702	K.W.F. 21/22
Werckmeister, A.	*Musicalische Paradoxal-Discourse*	1707	K.W.F. 6/10

Buttstedt. Those who perused this collection in the eighteenth century remarked upon the "sound and astute judgments" he had written in the margins.[96] On the inside cover of his copy of the anonymous "Some Clarified Musical Considerations and Other Easily Applied Truths of Practice" (*Musikalische Erwegungs- und Übungs-Wahrheiten*), Fischer remarked: "Mattheson writes somewhere that this treatise contains note-powder that one can also use to kill rats and mice."[97] Other annotations reveal him to be extraordinarily well informed. He wrote in the margin of Georg Sorge's "Harmonic Compendium" (*Compendium harmonicum*) that Marpurg had refuted these arguments already in 1760.[98] In the inside front cover of Marpurg's "Handbook of Thoroughbass and Composition" Fischer remarked that "it should be noted that what the author teaches in his *Critischer Musicus* is for the most part repeated here, though also improved. Whoever has this book can do without the *Critischer Musicus*."[99] Fischer also owned a copy of Barthold Fritz's guide to tuning keyboards, but he was not impressed, noting on one page that the proposed method "is completely impractical on the clavichord."[100]

Fischer's annotations also suggest a business-oriented mind. In his copy of the anonymous "Collection of Information on Famous Organs in Germany," he added check marks in pencil next to the prices of various organs—for example, 850 reichstaler for the organ in the evangelischen Bethause zu Neumarckt and ten thousand reichstaler for the organ in the Pfarr-Kirche in Schweidniß. But he knew more than prices, as revealed by the extensive descriptions of the registrations of the two organs in Fulda's *Domkirche* he himself scrawled on the back pages of the book.

Fischer's library also included numerous printed musical works, some of which are preserved today (Table 6). Judging from a cataloging system initiated by Fischer himself, the collection originally contained around fifty music prints.[101] The print of keyboard music by R. P. Justini (a.k.a. Justinus a Desponsatione) is divided into two parts: "Work for Two Hands" (basic information about playing the keyboard and realizing figured bass) and "Entertainment for Two Hands" (a variety of partitas, marches, arias, caprices, and the like, in two voices). It was explicitly aimed at appealing

Table 6. Johann Heinrich Fischer's Music Prints

Author	Abbreviated Title	Date	Call Number	Old Catalog
Bach, J. S.	*Clavier-Übung* I [BWV 825—830]	1731	[Morgan Library]	N. 3
Bach, J. S.	*Clavier-Übung* II [BWV 971, 831]	1735	[Lost since 1964]	.
Bach, J. S.	*Musikalisches Opfer* [BWV 1079]	1747	K.W.F. 138/84	N. 5
Justini, R. P.	*Musicalische Arbeith und Kurtz-Weil*	1723	K.W.F. 21/32	.
Nichelmann, C.	*Brevi Sonate da Cembalo* [I]	1745	K.W.F. 233/10	Nro. 25
Nichelmann, C.	*Brevi Sonate da Cembalo* [II]	1748?	K.W.F. 233/11	.

to both pre-professional and amateur keyboard players. The title pages of the two volumes of Nichelmann sonatas proclaim that they are intended "primarily for the use of women" (*massime all'uso delle dame*). Both collections seem to confirm the contemporary observation that Fischer "enjoyed teaching others."

The fact that Fischer owned the Nichelmann sonatas may imply that some of his pupils were women. These same prints, however, were apparently also borrowed by Benedictine monks. The first volume bears an annotation in Fischer's own handwriting referring to "Fr. [= Frater] Hazarinus Greser."[102] Both volumes of the Nichelmann sonatas, as well as Fischer's prints of J. S. Bach's Keyboard Partitas and Musical Offering, bear similar annotations on the title pages: "ad usum Fr. Fructuosus Röder. Prof. O. S. B. Fulda."[103] Even before donating his entire collection to Fulda's public library, Fischer seems to have managed his own musical lending library.

While nothing is known of Hazarinus Greser, Fructuosus Röder's biography is relatively well documented. He was baptized Johannes Theophilus Bernhardus Röder on March 5, 1747, in the small town of Simmershausen, just west of Fulda. His father, Johann Georg Adam Röder, was a teacher and organist at the *Hofkapelle* in the *Fasanerie* castle.[104] He entered the Benedictine order as a novice in 1763 and professed in 1764. Röder had music instruction with father Bernardus Beck, organist of Fulda's Cathedral, and also taught himself with the aid of C. P. E. Bach's *On the True Manner of Playing the Keyboard*. In 1767 Röder was sent for further musical instruction to Father Peregrinus Poegl in Neustadt (Hessen), where he studied counterpoint on the basis of Fux's *Gradus ad Parnassum*. On October 24, 1770, the day after Bernardus Beck's death, Röder took his place as organist and *Rector Chori* of Fulda's cathedral. He went on to compose settings of the Mass, Psalms, and Vespers, which were allegedly much beloved in their time. His "excellent manner of accompanying the choir, which aroused astonishment both among the singers and in the audience," led to an appointment in 1776 in Neusohl, where he taught for several years as *Instructor Clericorum*. Röder suffered chronically from hemorrhoids and his condition became particularly acute in 1781 on his journey back to Fulda. Upon reaching Regensburg he decided to turn south in hopes that the milder climate would improve his health. He stayed briefly at the monastery in Castellana before moving on to Naples, where he served for his remaining years as *deutscher Beichtvater, Novizenmeister,* and *Schuldirector* at the monastery of St. Lorenzo zu Aversa, dying on October 7, 1789, at age forty-two.[105]

Fructuosus Röder was apparently not the only musician in Fulda to have been inspired by the works of J. S. Bach in Fischer's collection. Like Röder, Fulda's *Hofkapellmeister,* Johann Baptiste Pauli, also seems to have been in regular contact with Fischer.[106] On February 13, 1750, Pauli mailed a print of Bach's Musical Offering and a manuscript in his own hand of four movements from Bach's sixth Keyboard Partita to the Franciscan organist and music theorist in Bologna Padre Giovanni Battista Martini.[107] In an accompanying letter, the hofkapellmeister wrote to Martini that Bach is esteemed and regarded "in the entire Empire" (*in quest' Imperio*) as "the only organist in the world" (*l'onico organista del Mondo*) and notes that, although he himself had not had occasion to meet Bach personally, he was able to recognize through his works that this was a composer with unusual "dexterity of the hands" (*portamento di mano*).[108] The works Pauli included with his letter were clearly intended to illustrate Bach's skills. In an earlier letter, he had requested that Martini send a sample of his own work, specifically asking for the *difficile* Sonata, by which he meant challenging contrapuntal works, not the *facile* sonatas Martini had already given him on his recent trip to Bologna.[109] In a letter written on June 25, 1748, Pauli fondly recalled conversations in which he and Martini argued for the strict style against more liberal views.[110] He undoubtedly chose the Musical Offering and the sixth Partita because of their grave, serious character and wealth of strict counterpoint. Within the sixth Partita he selected the Toccata, Allemanda, Corrente, and Gigue (tellingly labeled *Fuga* in the letter), leaving out the Air, Sarabande, and Tempo di Gavotta, probably because they lacked the contrapuntal gravitas integral to the image Pauli wished to project. Given Fischer's interest in the theoretical aspects of music, and the fact that both works by Bach were also in his own library, one suspects that he had similar convictions.

Although Fischer, Röder, and Pauli were Catholics, they were not deaf to the beauties of keyboard music by the quintessential Lutheran composer, J. S. Bach. They even proudly claimed him as a national representative in interactions with fellow Catholics abroad, allowing their patriotic and musical identities to take precedence over their religious affiliation. One suspects that their contact with Bach and his music was more extensive than the sparse documentation would suggest. In 1764, J. S. Bach's eldest son, Wilhelm Friedemann Bach, abandoned his post as an organist in

Halle to "go to Fulda."[111] Perhaps Fischer, Pauli, and/or Röder had a role in recruiting him.

Apparently not everyone in eighteenth-century Fulda was as enamoured of Bach's music as were Fischer and his friends. His print of J. S. Bach's *Keyboard Partitas* is highly unusual in that it is missing sixty of the original seventy-three pages. Of the forty-one movements, only five are preserved:

Table 7. Movements in the Print of Bach's *Clavier-Übung I* which Once Belonged to J. H. Fischer

Partita II: Allemande
Partita III: Gigue
Partita IV: Gigue
Partita VI: Toccata and Air

The missing pages were not simply lost to the ravages of time; they were ripped out deliberately. Whoever so drastically edited this print carefully crossed out the music on the backsides of even some of the surviving pages, including two complete movements: the Scherzo of Partita III and the Menuet of Partita IV.

And yet the editor of this print did not apparently wish simply to destroy Bach's entire collection. Manuscript repeat signs and the indication *2: volte* ("on the repeat") appear within the Air of Partita VI in a slightly iridescent black ink that closely matches that of the diagonal cross-hatching used to obscure the surviving pages. It thus seems that the editor was a musician, not just an ideologue who relied on titles alone for his or her pruning. Sometime before this radical editing took place, the words *Laus Deo* ("Praise God") were written in thick brown ink at the ends of the Gigues of Partitas III and IV and also at the end of the (crossed-out) Gigue of Partita V.[112] One presumes these words appeared at the end of each of the Partitas.

This radical editing suggests discomfort with the contents of Bach's collection. The *Laus Deo* indications were perhaps a first attempt to sanctify this secular music, or to purify the music of a Lutheran composer. The print was subsequently purged in a more draconian way, by tearing out pages and crossing out the backsides of what remained. One struggles to imagine a scenario that could credibly explain the damaging of this print, which was was not ideological in nature. Whether the editor's objection was rooted in Bach's religious orientation, by the perceived secular nature of the collection, or by the musical style cannot be known.

What is certain, however, is that the ideology that destroyed this print of Bach's music was not shared by Fischer, Röder, or Pauli. None of the other surviving prints from Fischer's library were similarly purged. Most likely the editor owned the print before or after Fischer. Perhaps it was a patron of the public library who ignored the librarian's directive not to damage borrowed materials. Perhaps it was someone who borrowed the print directly from Fischer before the public library opened in 1769.

Johann Heinrich Fischer did not feel his admiration for the music of J. S. Bach to be at odds with his Catholic faith. He made his collection of Bach's works available to other Catholic music lovers like Fructuosus Röder and Johann Baptist Pauli. These men appreciated this repertoire in part because it proved that notes and rhythms could do more than entertain. For them, Bach was a role model who transcended confessional boundaries.

CHAPTER 8

A Blacksmith's Son

The archive of the Stralsund town council contains a 1,554-page auto-biography handwritten by J. C. Müller, a local pastor.[1] This document, which covers nearly all of the author's fifty-two years, was prepared on the basis of lost diaries. Müller described in lavish and often astonishing detail his childhood, his university years, his time as a private tutor, and his career. He also wrote about the time he spent at the keyboard. Music played a particularly important role in his life during the years he spent studying at the University of Jena (1739–1743) and working as a teacher in Pomerania (1746–1755). This chapter presents an account of how Müller used his abilities at the keyboard to cultivate and maintain relationships with his friends, acquaintances, patrons, and a particular young woman who found a special place in his heart.

❧

Throughout the summer of 1739, eighteen-year-old Johann Christian Müller steeled himself for separation from everything he had ever known. In September he would leave his native Stralsund to begin university studies in Jena, a two-week journey to the south. His father, Christian Müller—a blacksmith who had been elevated to alderman and represented Stralsund's craftsmen in negotiations with the government—and his mother, Ilsabe, had raised him with great care and in comfortable circumstances. They were deeply concerned, however, about how their son would fare so far from home. Müller recounted the final days before his departure as follows:

It took me eight full days to bid farewell to all of the school and church authorities, the aldermen, a few businessmen, my father's patrons, friends, and acquaintances, so that only on my final day in Stralsund, Tuesday, September 22, at three o'clock in the afternoon, was I finally able to sit down and eat with my parents, who were waiting for me. Around four o'clock the wig-maker came with two new wigs, and cut off my natural hair, which I had always groomed so carefully. My uncle came by to see me off; my aunt and her daughters, who had already been with us for several weeks, helped my sisters wash the clothing I would be bringing on my journey. With the silent consent of my father, I gave them each a few reichstaler for their trouble, drawn from the money I had saved. The rest I gave to my father himself because I believed he deserved it for the love and the care he had taken in raising me. He left the room but shortly thereafter told the maid that an unknown person wished to speak with me. I was directed to a back room where I found both of my parents waiting. My father then said approximately these words to me: "My son, the hour of our separation nears, and your mother and I want to speak to you alone before you go. I have not had a chance until now, since you were so seldom at home, so I set down my advice and God's demands in writing and put my letter on top of your trunk. Do that which pleases God and man, and expect the best of yourself. I am sending you into the world at such a young age. The seductions are many, so look after yourself. Never think or act against God's command, and take care that you do not return with an unclean conscience. Learn something righteous, and do not be complacent, lest the costs and bitter sweat I have devoted to your education be spent in vain. From the money you saved, and which you wanted to give back to me, I exchanged the large showpieces you collected for smaller coins, and laid them together with the rest of the money in your trunk. Do not worry about us; I am old and you may never see me, your mother, or your beloved siblings ever again. Yet God may also choose to preserve us, and if it pleases Him, He will provide us all with a joyful reunion." With this he hugged and kissed me, and tears welled up in his eyes, revealing a tenderness that he did not often show. "I must return to the others," he said, "God's mercy be with you." Then my most tender mother put her arms around me. Tears prevented her from speaking. Finally she was able to say: "Now, my son, your father has said everything you must hear, and I find that there is nothing I wish to add. Sorrow prevents me from doing so anyway. O God! How difficult it is for a mother to see her innocent child travel into the world! O my dear son, do not forget God or your conscience, or the love of your parents. Ah, that we might one day joyously see you again! God will hear my prayer." The coachman came in and reminded us that it would soon be time to leave. My mother then said to me: "Travel safely, may God's angel guide you." Then woeful feelings again prevented her from expressing what was in her heart. My siblings, some of whom were still small, added their good wishes and wept. I then took leave of my assembled friends and accepted their farewells. Again the coachman came to remind us that the time for departure approached, and I had to hurry. Previously dull and apprehensive, I now seized control of myself, said goodbye to everyone in the house, and set off with my father and uncle for the post station. My first nanny, who was retired now and living in an apartment my father provided for her, waited for us on the corner with tearful eyes. I could hear her shouting good wishes down the entire length of the street.[2]

Over the next eleven days, Müller would spend more than one hundred hours in an open-air post-coach. A fabric pillow stuffed with flax became his most agreeable companion, as he sat on it all day and laid his head on it all night, sleeping on straw beds in roadside inns. He conversed with other university-bound boys and admired the unfamiliar landscapes and towns along the way.

After passing through Rostock, Güstrow, Havelberg, and Delitsch, Müller and his companions arrived on September 30 in the famously opulent city of Leipzig. Church spires in most towns were easily visible, but here they were lost amid the tall and elegant houses. At around forty thousand inhabitants, Leipzig was the largest city Müller had ever seen, and it was stuffed to the bursting point with merchants and visitors who had arrived for the autumn trade fair:

> The pretty Saxon ladies and galant Leipzig men mingled with all manner of foreigners—Hungarians, Transylvanians, Jews, Turks, Greeks, Arabs, Armenians, Chinese, Persians, Moors, Russians, Dutchmen, Englishmen, etc.—some in strange long gowns of colorful and florid silk with bejeweled daggers in their belts, or with long beards, and suntanned chests. It astonished my eyes and inspired wonder to see everyone transacting business with one another in such a friendly manner.[3]

Müller remained in Leipzig until Friday, October 2, 1739, the day J. S. Bach led a much-anticipated performance of his Collegium Musicum in a local coffeehouse.[4] The performance, however, did not take place until 8:00 P.M., and the young traveler was gone by noon.

Around the time Bach's students began tuning up their instruments in Leipzig, Müller and his traveling companions were disembarking from their coach in faraway Weissenfels. They slept that night on beds supplied by the wife of the court caterer. The next morning at 6:00, they continued their journey, riding nervously through Thuringian mountains on one-lane passes, sometimes with just a hand's breadth separating the coach's wheel from the edge of a steep cliff. By the late afternoon, they had at last reached their final destination.

With a population of around four thousand, Jena was just half the size of Stralsund and one-tenth the size of Leipzig. The houses were a mixture of small and large, old and new. The Saale river, which bisected the town, was regularly diverted to flow through the city's streets, carrying away the raw waste dried in sewage sluices, which servant girls cleared with brooms in front of their patrons' homes. A castle built by the dukes of Saxony-Jena in the fourteenth century stood in one corner of the city, a relic to a line that had died out in 1690. By 1739 the town had become utterly dependent, both culturally and economically, upon its renowned university.[5]

Müller opted to rent an apartment from a professor, despite concerns that it might be more expensive and less comfortable than one offered by a landlord not affiliated with the university. Living with professors often came with curfews and annoying obligations such as offering money and poems for birthdays and baptisms. But Johann Gottfried Tympe, who taught oriental languages, made Müller an offer he could not refuse: an attractive, two-room apartment with stone floors, plaster ceilings, and two windows that offered him an excellent view of the street below. The living room was furnished with a large mirror, two half-circular tables that could be put together to form a whole, a little tea table covered in oilcloth, six chairs with green fabric covers tied on with yellow ribbons, and a wardrobe built to accommodate both clothing and books. The apartment had the advantage of being adjacent to the kitchen, so he did not have to rely too heavily on the iron oven in his own living room, which could heat the room quickly in the winter but seldom maintain a comfortable temperature after the firewood burned down. He had to get used to his thin Saxon feather bed and also to the coarse sand on the floor, which pained the soles of his feet. To use the restroom, he had to climb two sets of stairs and walk down a long hallway, past the doorways of nearly thirty other university boys.[6]

In the days immediately after his arrival, Müller had his maid buy four bowls, a pair of plates, and a spoon, all of tin. He also acquired the essentials of domestic life: a glass pitcher, a few beer glasses, an iron lantern for studying at night, a pair of scissors for clipping candle wicks, bronze sugar and milk canisters, and coffee paraphernalia (a roaster, a mill, and a brass pot), as well as a stand for two wigs, and a wooden alarm clock with a glass bell. He opted not to eat with the professor's family but rather to have food brought up to his room, beginning each morning with a plate of fresh fruit. On the market square, he enjoyed huge sausages made from pigs' stomachs, slices of which Jena's residents ate cold with vinegar.[7]

First-year university students like Müller tried in vain to blend in, hoping to avoid being recognized as "foxes," the derogatory term used for fresh arrivals. They sought to rid themselves of their regional dialects and had the clothes they had brought from home modified.[8] As Müller wrote in his diary:

> The first thing I had to do was to have my clothing adjusted to local taste, so that I could disguise the fact that I had recently arrived. I had brought two pairs of shoes with me, the laces of which were high, up on the ankle, whereas fashion in Jena demanded that the laces be lower, down closer to the toes. The blue coat that I had worn while traveling was now too shabby for use in town, but the other two cloaks I had brought from home did not suit the local taste, nor did my wigs. So right away I had to request visits from a tailor, a shoemaker, and a wig-maker. I ordered a dark green coat for everyday use, as well as a flowered red vest and pants. I had round lapels with buttons added to my dark red coat, and had the yellow buttons removed. My dark ash-grey coat I just hung up in the closet for future use. I had rolled bangs and long braids added to my two new wigs at a cost of 1 reichstaler each.[9]

Finally ready to appear in public, Müller began his course of study in theology. His landlord, Professor Tympe, advised him to attend the lectures of a variety of instructors, staying with those whose style he liked best. Müller would eventually take classes in ethics, logic, physics and metaphysics, exegesis, the Psalms, Paul's Epistle to the Hebrews, dogmatics, the New Testament, Luther's ecclesiastical writings, the art of delivering sermons, the study of sacred beings, literary history, and French. An adjunct professor named Johann Andreas Fabricius, with whom Müller had some family connections in Stralsund, became his mentor, going over his notes from class and taking him on walks to discuss philosophy. It was Professor Georg Christoph Stellwag, however, who made the greatest first impression. Stellwag was particularly beloved not so much for the substance of his lectures but rather for his sense of humor. He pilloried the "Nature of Things" formulated by Leibniz and Wolff as the "Thing-Doctrine" (*Dingerlehre*), regaling his auditors with sexually tinged commentaries on "things" of all sizes. The students laughed uproariously at his witticisms, stomping their feet to express approval. When Stellwag asserted that he himself had never been like the reckless boys who "shot their powder" during their university years, his students chuckled and shuffled their feet on the floor to signal doubt.

Müller had absolutely no experience with women, and Professor Stellwag's insinuation that hedonistic sex was somehow normal for university students struck him as a revelation. His sheltered world developed cracks through which he found himself eager to peer. The same professor's wife was a key figure in this development. As Müller confided in his autobiography:

Not long after my arrival, I began walking regularly outside the city gates in order to get to know the area better. One time when I was in a suburb near the Johannis Vorstadt, a woman stepped out from the city and immediately drew my eyes and admiration. She was tall and slim and her countenance was round, white, and lively. Her clothing made her still more fetching. Over a large crinoline hoop skirt she wore a thin blue dress with an embroidered floral pattern. Her hair hung in short curls, and she wore a green summer hat decorated with a beautiful bouquet of flowers, which matched the corsage on her breast. I greeted her with the greatest respect and received her thanks with an agreeable friendliness. I was unaccustomed to seeing such women. Those I had known in my native city were still extremely constrained in their behavior. Daughters were held in isolation. Even close friends of the family could expect nothing in conversation beyond "yes" or "no;" they constantly looked to their mothers, who ordinarily spoke for them. If one happened to encounter a girl outside the gates and greet her, she would not know whether she should dare acknowledge the salutation and might well run away. Their education was as simple as their lifestyle; escorting a young lady to visit someone else's house was out of the question. In Rostock and other university towns, the women struck me as much more lively and polite. I followed the beautiful woman I had seen to the end of the road, at which point she disappeared through a garden door. I waited until I had a chance to ask someone, and then learned that the garden house belonged to a bookbinder, and that the lady in question was the wife of Professor Stellwag. I walked around the area for a few hours suspecting that she would at some point reemerge, and eventually she did so in the company of her husband. Because he was short and stout, his head barely reached to the top buckle of her dress. Nature had given him a sour face, and when he wanted to gaze into her eyes, he had to look up and smile through his furrowed brow as she glanced down pleasantly. Though all of this was new to me at the time, I became accustomed to it from seeing so many beautiful women out in public.[10]

While the students in Leipzig were known as skirt-chasing galants hommes, those in Jena were more famous for their pugnaciousness. In his diary, Müller recorded a line that tripped frequently off the tongues of his cohort:

A Jena boy who gains no scars,
At home can count his lucky stars.[11]

Dueling was a common occurrence that university and civic governments did their best to discourage, mostly without success. In the first half of the eighteenth century, when virtually all students carried swords or daggers, even the most innocuous offenses—for example, failing to doff one's hat while passing another boy on the street—could have dire consequences.[12] A few months after his arrival in Jena, Müller saw a large group of people streaming by his window, so he threw on his coat and followed them to a field outside of town where students frequently fought. A boy of noble ancestry lay dead on the ground, having been mortally wounded in a duel. The scene left an impression, as Müller later confessed to his diary: "I shuddered to think of how suddenly this person had been wrested from his mortal and eternal salvation, and what sorrow the news of his death would bring to his parents."[13]

Müller's own parents were deeply concerned about their son's well-being in Jena, frequently sending money and advice: where to eat, which classes to take, which books to buy, and so on. As Müller confided in his diary:

> During the first year, I rarely went out except to attend my classes because I dreaded to be recognized as a "fox." For this reason, I was often afflicted by loneliness and melancholy. Perhaps I was suffering from homesickness, but beyond tender concerns about the well-being of my parents and siblings I worried about my own future, though I trusted at all times in God's providence and mercy. In his letters, my father tried by every means to cheer me up and suggested that I might wish to find a roommate. I answered: "Yes, but only if we are like-minded; otherwise, no."[14]

Unable to persuade his son to take a roommate, Müller's father emphatically suggested that he acquire the next best thing: a clavichord. As the old man wrote in a letter sent six months after Müller's arrival in Jena:

> You have been safely—thank God!—away from home for half a year already; in this amount of time one can become a good deal more brazen and plucky, and also more shrewd. So it has been with the clavichord. Although I asked you to buy a good instrument, and promised to cover the cost, you still haven't gotten around to acquiring one.[15]

Between ages nine and thirteen, Müller's father had paid for him to study the flute, the violin, singing, and "especially the keyboard."[16] Now the elderly blacksmith hoped to persuade his nineteen-year-old son to take up music once again. Filling the role of perpetually like-minded roommate, a clavichord might offer companionship, temper melancholy, and help his son to avoid the "lusts of youth" and "seductive sirens" of which he had warned in the letter attached to the boy's traveling trunk.[17]

Müller eventually purchased a clavichord from a saddle maker just outside Jena's city gates. He soon found that it lent a certain focus to his social life. A small coterie of students from Stralsund, including the future pastor Immanuel Justus von Essen and the future notary Hermann Albert Sledanus, regularly gathered in his apartment to play the instrument and teach one another new pieces and performance techniques:

> Shortly after Christmas, at the repeated urging of my father, I purchased a beautiful, full-range clavichord with a lute stop [. . .].[18] It was brand new, and came with a large stand. Herr von Essen was a good musician and Herr Sledanus played this instrument quite well, and I was pleased that when they visited me they asked which pieces I liked and I would learn to play them, at first plainly, but then later with ornaments (*Manieren*) and with graceful motions (*angenehme Touren*); after they left I would try to imitate them. I also heard that the wife of Professor Tympe would sometimes leave the door to her kitchen open so that she could listen to us as we played, and now and then she sang an aria when we were together, or even when I was with her alone. She and my other landlords were always glad to have me for this reason: my friends were orderly and calm people, and we busied ourselves with honest entertainments. It also pleased them that I paid my rent and my tuition in advance, and in good currency—that is, in 2/3 or 2 groschen coins—that my clothing was orderly, that I was friendly and helpful to everyone.[19]

The new clavichord enabled Müller to attract and bond with musically inclined friends, thus helping him to overcome the loneliness and insecurity that afflicted him during his time as a "fox." Like most male amateur keyboardists, he and his friends were interested not only in playing the notes on the page but also in adding ornaments and employing graceful motions.

Müller's keyboard playing endeared him not only to his friends but also to his landlords. The clavichord in his room was an unmistakable sign of tractability, entirely of a piece with his reliably paying the rent. While other students stayed up late singing drinking songs, fighting, chasing women, dumping their chamber pots on the floor, or conducting volatile chemistry experiments in enclosed spaces, Müller and his friends just made music quietly at home.[20] Musical ability was a primary factor in the special treatment he received from Professor Tympe and his wife. They would eventually come to serve in loco parentis, exchanging gifts—smoked eel from Stralsund for smoked ox tongue from Thuringia—and constantly checking to make sure he felt comfortable.[21]

༜

After a time, Professor Tympe and his family moved to another house, forcing Müller to relocate. He weighed the benefits of joining them in their new location but decided to try his luck elsewhere, settling on a room on Jena's market square. His landlady was an elderly widow whose eighteen-year-old granddaughter Sophie served as his *Aufwärterin*, shopping, cooking, and cleaning on his behalf. She was an object of some fascination for Müller:

> The girl was of medium height, with fleshy curves, mischievous dark eyes, black hair that she wore in curls, and pinkish white skin. Her cunning

enabled her to feign simplicity and innocence. Despite being rather lusty, she was compliant and loyal, and kept my room tidy. When I sent her out to get things, I noticed that the other students called her by name, or smiled at her, and she acknowledged their attention. In conversation, I made reference one time to the maidens [i.e., virgins] of Jena and she began to laugh. I asked: why? Do you really think, she asked me, that there are maidens here in Jena?[22]

Sophie had a bad reputation. Her grandmother asked Müller, the aspiring pastor, to offer some advice that would bring her back to the straight and narrow. But he recognized that she was incorrigible and too clever to be dissuaded by his words or those of anyone else:

> I learned that she was once made to do public penance in church, kneeling in the chancel during the sermon on one of those green benches that are ordinarily used for communion. Afterward, the pastor stepped up to the altar and called this lost sheep to the attention of the congregants, many of whom had gathered in the chancel. She acknowledged her sins and transgressions, for which he then forgave her in God's name, gently admonishing her not to backslide and to accept God lovingly just as He had accepted her. The pastor then offered her holy communion as the choir sang *Erbarm dich meiner o Herre Gott* [Have Mercy on Me, O Lord God]. Some time later, when she was home roasting coffee beans in my kitchen, I asked her which transgressions she had perpetrated, and why she had sought absolution. Though she had wept the entire time in church, she now answered me rather cheerfully: "Because as soon as all of that is over, I am Maiden Sophie again, just like before." I reminded her of her promise to the congregation and the admonitions of the pastor, and the spiritual dangers of an immoral lifestyle, but I recognized that my words were falling on deaf ears.[23]

Sometimes singing to herself and dancing alone in the hallways, Sophie eventually began making more or less veiled allusions to her sexual availability to Müller himself. At one point, he knocked on her door late at night to retrieve a key and found her topless.[24] As he pretended to be oblivious to her lusty overtures, she coquettishly accused him of having a "cold nature." Over time, however, she came to recognize that his innocence was a ruse: Müller was not so much repulsed by her transgressions as he was titillated. As she put it, he was as hypocritical as the Pietists he and his friends so mercilessly mocked.[25]

During his years in Jena, Müller's cold nature was tested in other ways as well. As he moved beyond his time as a fox (officially one year, six months, and six days), he and his friends traveled to villages like Dorndorf and Dornburg, and to more distant cities such as Halle and Erfurt, where they sought adventure in unfamiliar settings such as Catholic churches, Jewish synagogues, castles, and public execution sites. The specter of violence, too, reared its head. Müller was at one point challenged to a duel by a former housemate named Johann Schlichtkrull:

> The chosen battleground was on a path between two fences, and I was there first. Shortly thereafter, I saw Herr Schlichtkrull and Herr Kercher, an artful Swiss who served as his second, hurrying toward us. We drew the swords from our leather scabbards at the same moment. Herr Kercher was on my right while Herr Tielcke, my second, was at my left. Herr Schlichtkrull snorted with rage and came after me in the most violent manner. I simply tried to defend myself, as it is not in my character to injure another person, and because I had a cool temper I was able to hold him off, forcing him to cease his attack three times. His fourth attempt to restore his honor by wounding me was so fierce that he foamed at the mouth, and his aggression caused me to become emotional, parrying him so strongly that my sword got stuck in the walking stick that Herr Kercher had sensibly laid on the ground in front of him, thus leaving me completely vulnerable to attack. [Herr Schlichtkrull] could easily have achieved his goal, if he had fought with cold blood. But luckily I had recovered by the time he attacked, and I held him off until he tired. At some point he said he had had enough, returned his sword to its scabbard, came to me, hugged me as usual, said to me that everything was forgotten and forgiven, that he had achieved revenge enough, and asked me to be his friend again. I answered that I had never considered myself his enemy, had never intended to insult him, much less injure him, that I hoped this episode would teach him to live more peaceably, and promised him my continued friendship.[26]

In Müller's view, it was his temperament that preserved him from the sexual temptation and violence that proved the undoing of so many other university boys his age, enabling him to explore the limits of appropriate behavior without getting into serious trouble.

In his later Jena years, Müller nonetheless felt compelled to test social boundaries, sometimes in the realm of music. While a "fox," he had occupied himself primarily with the clavichord, but in later years he took up a bass lute with twelve metal strings known as the "pandora" (*Pandor Zitter*). A fellow student named Johann Ehrgott Fabri gave him lessons, and the sounds of their music making sometimes attracted the attention of a law professor named Johann Christian Waitz who lived in the same rooming house:

> In addition to regularly attending my classes and devoting the necessary diligence to preparation and study, I was no enemy of permissible pleasures [*erlaubte Ergötzligkeiten*]. Beyond spending my time frequently at the clavichord, I had a pandora built for me for twelve reichstaler and learned how to play it

from a Silesian student named Fabri. With this instrument, I often drew the attention of Dr. Waitz and others whose doors were near mine.[27]

In some respects the pandora was a more social instrument than was the clavichord; it was typically used not for solo playing but to accompany oneself or others in song. Its flat body enabled sounds to project well in convivial settings. Clavichord playing no longer suited Müller's musical needs. His mechanical roommate's new position in his social life is reflected in an account of a spontaneous visit he made to the saddle maker who had built it some years earlier. The scene took place when he and his friends were on their way to Erfurt:

> We mounted our horses at four in the morning and left the city through the Johannis gate. When we had barely gotten out of town, one of my stirrups ripped loose from the saddle. I couldn't ride with just one stirrup, so I had to go back. In an area just outside the city lived the saddle maker from whom I had purchased my beautiful clavichord, which he himself had built. I knew that here I would be able to find help. I knocked for a while, and finally his elderly wife came out and opened the bottom half of the Dutch door. As soon as she saw me, and heard about my problem, she rushed off to wake an apprentice, leaving the bottom half of the door ajar. I held onto the wall but before I knew it my horse was ducking under the open bottom-half of the door, and if I hadn't immediately laid down flat on his back I would have been squashed, or the top half of the door destroyed. I cannot believe how I managed to escape unharmed, since those doors were quite low, and the decision to flatten myself was made so instantaneously. The wife of the saddle maker, who was upstairs in the small loft, stood up and screamed, because a beautiful harpsichord was sitting in that entryway waiting to be strung, but luckily my horse stopped and just stood quietly beside it. The apprentice fixed my stirrup expertly, I gave him a nice tip, he led my horse out, and held the animal until I was upon it again. He had barely let go of the reins to tighten the saddle, however, when the horse took me a second time under the half door and into the house; somehow once again I managed to escape without injury.[28]

This story, with its central image of the protagonist sitting astride a horse next to a harpsichord, is emblematic of Müller's relationship to keyboard playing. He did not visit the saddle maker to have his clavichord repaired but rather to have his saddle adjusted. By this point in his university career, it was no longer stimulating enough simply to stay home and make music.

The way in which Müller framed this story, however, also suggests that he felt a kinship with the keyboard. His horse's unpredictable behavior threatened two entities: Müller himself and the harpsichord in the entryway. Both were innocent and vulnerable. Like the instrument waiting to be strung, Müller was half-formed. He recognized, if only subconsciously, that he was not by nature an adventurer; he was fortunate that his testing of boundaries had not yet done him any lasting harm. At some level, he took pride in his innocence.

Shortly before Easter in 1743, having spent three-and-a-half years in Jena, Müller was ordered by his father to quit the city and continue his studies at the University of Leipzig. The decision came as a surprise. He enjoyed Jena and had already made preparations to receive a university degree by writing and defending a thesis. Perhaps his father was worried about the young man becoming too comfortable in this environment, letting his guard down, and succumbing to entertainments beyond the permissible; keeping his son in a perpetual "fox" state was a viable solution to this problem. Müller described his departure from Jena as follows:

> Herr Rüllmann helped me to pack up my bed and bookcase. In the three-and-a-half years I had spent here, my books and other possessions had become much more numerous. The cover of my large trunk broke in two so that I had to bind it with rope. I therefore called for Buch, the old and honorable book dealer from the orphanage, and entrusted the trunk to him, as well as my other boxes, and my pandora, and asked him to bring them to Leipzig for me. I gave my friends from Stralsund the things I could not easily bring with me: my wooden alarm clock with the glass bell, glasses and things purchased to make my apartment comfortable. My water canister for putting out fires, my tea kettle, and my other household effects I gave to Sophie, to whom I also offered a small monetary gift. I gave my landlady's grandson a pair of good boots, a few pairs of shoes, stockings and my leftover firewood. I entrusted Herr Kniephof with the task of selling my clavichord, though I never heard anything about what happened to it.[29]

Müller expected that music would continue to play a role in his life but his instrument of choice by now was the pandora. He did not even bother to find out what had happened to the clavichord which had once been the focal point of his social life.

၄◢

Upon arrival in Leipzig, Müller rented an apartment from a wealthy spice merchant. From his window, he could admire the fashionable galants hommes of Leipzig, who were so intent on showing off their wigs that they carried their hats exclusively under their arms. He ate his daily midday meal at a table with fellow university students. For between four and ten groschen per meal, they enjoyed game meat, fish, baked goods, and on Thursdays "a nice piece of calf's liver."[30] As they dined, women came around to their table selling fragrant soaps and waters.[31]

Müller studied Biblical exegesis, hermeneutics, Aristotelian philosophy, and took a class on German oratory from "the great Gottsched." At one point, he read a translation by that professor's "famous wife."[32] Müller enjoyed spending his leisure hours sipping coffee and playing billiards in Leipzig's well-known coffeehouses. He also enjoyed walking along the crooked paths of the gardens donated by the family of Christiane Sibÿlla Bose, admiring the exotic foreign plants and curiosity cabinets.[33] On Sundays he attended services in the churches of St. Thomas, St. Nicholas, and St. Peter, ordinarily visiting more than one on a single day in order to hear sermons from multiple pastors. Thereafter he often participated in the *Kirchenparade*, when congregants from all the city's churches paraded around the city together to see and be seen.

Music was not forgotten. Although he had left his clavichord behind in Jena, Müller quickly found friends in Leipzig who shared his musical inclinations, including Theodor Johann Quistorp and Christian Jakob Wilhelm Fischer:[34] "I found myself with Mr. Quistorp at the home of a friend from Sangerhausen named Fischer, who ate at our table and was also a good fellow. He played the lyre and his roommate the violin, and we sang to their accompaniment."[35] Müller described one particularly entertaining evening as follows:

> Because Herr Zeidler was up late and feeling rowdy, we had him put on Herr Fischer's black funeral frock, to which I added some scraps of paper to serve as a collar, and we borrowed a round wig from my neighbor's room. Sitting in the window and greeting everyone who passed, he looked exactly like a village preacher. There was a powerful storm that night that brought lightning, thunder, and rain, but we nonetheless left all of our large windows open. Herr St-ch went around in shirtsleeves with his socks hanging down; he grabbed my pandora, plucked it a bit, and sang:
>
>> When I my good fortune inspect
>> My heart fills with laughter unchecked.
>> [Substituting the lyrics:
>> When I my own calves do inspect
>> My heart fills with laughter unchecked.]
>
> Everyone must have thought we were wild men.[36]

On evenings like this, Müller and his friends cautiously abandoned decorum. Impersonating a village pastor mocked not only rural culture and urban sumptuary laws but also Christianity. Opening all of the windows during a heavy thunderstorm embraced an irrational desire to court danger and property damage. Plucking the pandora and singing this lyric, which was drawn from a play satirizing capitalism, mocked the enterprise of earning a living.[37] The text was made all the more ridiculous by their modifying the lyrics to highlight the fact that the singer's stockings were pulled down, exposing his calves. Despite Müller's obvious pride in behaving like "wild men," such jokes were harmless when compared with the panoply of truly dangerous activities available to him in Leipzig.

Though Müller does not mention any of the other songs he and his friends sang on such occasions, he must certainly have learned a few from the bestselling collection of the era, Johann Sigismund Scholze's *Singende Muse an der Pleiße* (Singing Muse on the Pleiße). Named for the river that flowed through Leipzig, this collection was beloved among university boys for its bawdy character. The following song, published shortly before Müller's arrival, might have been profitably accompanied by the harp and violin, or perhaps by the pandora alone:

> How I love to kiss you sweetly,
> When your soft tongue touches mine!
> Playing all around discreetly
> On your humid lips divine.
> Such a ticklish in and out,
> Gives a taste of heav'n, no doubt.[38]

On one evening when they met to sing songs like this one, Müller and his friend Quistorp were inspired by a bright moon and an adventurous spirit to take a walk to Connewitz, a village to the south of Leipzig:

> Along the broad highway there were two guesthouses, each two stories high and yellow in color. [. . .] My companion knew the place, and we climbed the steps to a little living room. After we had sat for a while a tall woman came to us dressed in the most elegant manner. She wore a little cap made of gold lace over her long, curly locks, large pearl earrings, a pearl necklace hanging in many rows on her chest, a dark green shirt with lapels, and a matching skirt made of satin, both of which were decorated with gilded lace, and a diamond ring, all of which made her slim figure and free character that much more attractive. I greeted her politely, though my companion was rather brash, offering no compliments. She led us into a brightly lit room that was full of music. I had never seen a woman dance with such art and skill, with such turns, slides, and gestures, and yet so effortlessly [. . .]. Watching her would have drawn anyone in. After a few dances we set off on our way. On the road, my friend asked me whom I believed this galant person to be. I answered that it must have been the daughter of the house owner. "Nothing could be further from the truth," he said. "She is one of those frolicsome people who sells her body for a few coins. I could tell that you didn't recognize this, because you were so polite. You must be more careful in the future, because they recognize immediately that you are still

a fox and will try to rob you. She would certainly have had a good time at your expense if there had not been so many other people around."[39]

The experience stayed with Müller, and he found himself increasingly preoccupied with temptations of the flesh. In Jena, he had avoided the crass and poorly dressed prostitutes and pitied the university boys who forfeited to them "their time, their money, and their health." In Leipzig, however, "this vice began to show me a galant side." The appeal of the city's women of ill-repute lay not only in their beauty and charm but also in the engaging atmosphere of the brothels, promoted by "the seductive tones of a skillful and lively music." According to his own diary, Müller found the strength to escape the clutches of sin by appealing to God's grace and by thinking of the note that his father had pasted to the top of his trunk. Among other advice, the old man had warned his son to beware the "lusts of youth, and to run away from seductive sirens" and had underscored this advice with quotations from the Bible.[40]

Perhaps out of concern that his son might succumb to temptation, Müller's father called upon him to leave Leipzig after just one year. At Easter 1744, he set out for Hamburg, where he spent a few weeks living with a cousin. Finally, after five years away from home, he returned to Stralsund and was reunited with his family:

> One can easily imagine the feelings that welled up in me as I crossed the border to Pomerania and came ever closer to my hometown and loved ones. [. . .] At last I saw the final destination of my trip and stepped out of the post coach, where I was met by my eldest brother-in-law and my middle brother, who were waiting for me. We walked along the parapet of the city toward my parents' home. My youngest sister is reported to have observed that a strange man in traveling clothes was coming from the city gate and told my mother, who immediately jumped up and ran to my father to tell him the news. As soon as I stepped into the room, both of my dear parents hugged me. The joy was so great that it took us a long time to come to our senses.[41]

෫෯

Upon returning to his hometown, Johann Christian Müller was still too young and inexperienced to fulfill his dream of becoming a pastor. He lacked connections to the government officials who might further his career. Since the end of the Thirty Years' War, the official head of government in Pomerania had been the king of Sweden, who was represented in Stralsund, the capital city, by a *Generalgouverneur*. His aristocratic ministers typically lived on rural estates, traveling into town as necessary. Many had children and employed resident house tutors (*Hofmeister*). By getting to know the families, young university graduates acquired experience and made connections that could subsequently further their careers.[42]

Müller resolved in 1746 to accept a position as tutor to the von Engelbrecht family on their rural estate in nearby Wendisch-Baggendorf. The head of the family, Joachim Friedrich von Engelbrecht, had served as government advisor (*Regierungs Rath*) to Pomerania's *Generalgouverneur,* and in this capacity he had come into contact with and earned the admiration of Müller's father. The *Regierungs Rath* had died in 1740, but his fifty-two-year-old widow, Anna Margaretha von Engelbrecht, to whom he referred by the feminine form of her husband's title as the *Frau Regierungs Räthin,* was socially well connected. She had two daughters at home, but Müller's primary job was educating her thirteen-year-old son, Johann Gustav Friedrich von Engelbrecht, known as Fritz:

> He was to be prepared for university study, not only in theology but also in Latin and other subjects, and taught good manners. For this work I was promised 50 reichstaler as well as free tea, coffee, sugar, laundry, and my own servant—a condition upon which I particularly insisted because my friends told me that it was difficult to find good help in the countryside, especially during the harvest time—as well as a riding horse, my own room, and freedom to travel into town whenever I wished.[43]

Müller threw himself into this work with alacrity, teaching Fritz for six hours per day rather than the four for which he was contracted. In addition to religion and Latin, he instructed the boy in poetry, Greek and Roman mythology, letter writing, and politics. He also enjoyed visiting the garden with Fritz, calling his pupil's attention to the activities of insects, examining their weapons and skills, admiring their diligence, and drawing moral lessons by reverse-engineering the work of the all-knowing Creator.[44]

Serving as tutor offered Müller an opportunity to test his own power as an intellectual and as a teacher. It was rewarding for him to see the positive effects of his instruction on a diligent pupil. The experience and learning Müller had acquired over his university years were manifest in daily interactions and persuaded him that he himself possessed a certain wisdom.

The other members of the household staff were chiefly of anthropological interest to Müller. The woman in charge of the Frau Regierungs Räthin's two daughters, known as the *Ausgeberin,* was given to trysts with visiting aristocrats.[45] A retired farmer named Fleck, whom the family kept as a coachman, was comically uncouth; while with a hunting party, he slipped and fell full length into a morass, covering his new white frock in mud and prompting him to worry aloud for several hours about what his wife would say.[46] Interacting with these poorly educated staff members was another new experience for Müller; he gained confidence from their deference and willingness to listen to him.

Some of the listening they did was musical. The von Engelbrecht family owned a clavichord that they kept in the largest room of their home. In his autobiography, Müller recounted the musical events that followed a coachman's wedding:

> The wedding guests were in the dining room next to the large hall. After we had eaten, I remained alone with the Frau Regierungs Räthin. While I was playing a clavichord in the meantime, and she was sitting directly in front of the double doors, one of which was slightly open, she noticed that someone outside the door was listening. She called to the eavesdropper and he showed himself to be the farmer Fleck [. . .]. The old man then came in and acknowledged that he was very much enchanted by the music of the clavichord. I had to play a few well-known minuets and polonaises for him. He subsequently told me when we were outside that back when he had served as coach driver to the late Regierungs Rath, he had sometimes been in my parents' home while I was having my keyboard lessons. He had listened secretly with tireless attentiveness as my teacher played the violin and I sang along. I thus saw how the wildest spirits can be stirred and captivated by music. Because when the Frau Regierungs Räthin was traveling, the Ausgeberin and the other staff members prevailed upon her daughters to make me play, until finally I satisfied their desire. They would have listened all night if I myself had not tired.[47]

The primary audience for Müller's keyboard playing in the von Engelbrecht home was not the Frau Regierungs Räthin, who was rather aloof, or her son Fritz, who was more interested in outdoor activities, but rather the household staff. Though they loved music, they were not in a position to demand that Müller perform for them: Farmer Fleck had to eavesdrop from beyond the door; the Ausgeberin and other staff members had to prevail upon the aristocratic daughters to ask Müller to play, and this was possible only when the Frau Regierungs Räthin was away from home. From the perspective of the household staff, the appeal of Müller's playing was not only the pleasure of hearing minuets and polonaises but also in the satisfaction of persuading a young man from the university to entertain them.

Müller was fascinated that the music he played could tame even "wild" spirits like these. Just as his father had used the keyboard to moderate his own behavior during the early years in Jena, Müller had used the keyboard to endear himself to his friends and landlords. His revelation in this first assignment as house tutor was that he could influence people of both higher and lower status. His use of the keyboard in this context was a microcosm of his broader aspirations.

ใ&

After several years in Wendisch-Baggendorf, Müller transferred in 1753
to the nearby town of Eixen. Here he was employed as tutor to the large
family of Gustav Peter von Lillieström, whom he invariably called by his
title, *Hofrath* (court advisor). The Hofrath was an impulsive and rather
bizarre character. He liked to invite Müller over for coffee, regaling him
with tales from the world of politics and praising his own skills of diplomacy:

> At every opportunity he looked at me and asked: Was that not clever? Was
> that not sly? Was that not politic? Was that not foresighted? and other
> such questions. I answered either with a brief "yes" or by simply nodding
> my head. He would then smile, full of amazement at himself, curling the
> fingers on both hands and pulling with his thumb and forefinger on his
> wig; the flour powder would then fall onto his shoulders and he would lick
> it off his fingers.[48]

The Hofrath was quick to anger but always eager for reconciliation, terribly
concerned if he felt that Müller was miffed about something he had said
or done.

The Hofrath's wife, Barbara Maria von Lillieström, had died six years
earlier and left him with twelve children, ten of whom were living at home
when Müller began his tenure as hofmeister. They are listed in table 8 along
with their nicknames and ages at the time Müller arrived.[49]

Table 8. Siblings of the Family von Lillieström, 1753

Sons	Daughters
Gustav Julius ("*Cornet*") [age 34]	.
Philipp Erich ("*Fähnrich*") [age 27]	.
.	Christina Wilhelmina ("Stienchen") [age 25]
.	Charlotte Magdalena ("Lotchen") [age 20]
.	Margarethe Agnesa ("Graetchen") [age 19]
.	Brigitte Hedwig ("Brigittchen") [age 17]
.	Barbara Maria ("Barbchen") [age 16]
.	Juliana Elisabeth ("Julchen") [age 14]
Thuro Diedrich [age 13]	.
Johann Jonas ("Hans") [age 11]	.

The von Lillieström house was rather shabby, though its natural setting
was of great appeal to Müller, who enjoyed taking long walks in the countryside, smoking a pipe and reading under shady trees:

The house lay directly across from the entryway and was accessed by a path that led over a long dam, on the left side of which was a pond and on the right side of which was the stockyard for animals. In front of the house was a large free space. The house itself was small, insofar as it had just one story [above the ground floor] and a little hallway on each side led to a room with two windows and a little chamber with a single window. One would not expect that a family could live in such a house, much less a large family.[50]

Müller's room was among the most rustic in the entire house. It had not been painted for years so that the clay lattice work was visible and full of holes. There were two windows but no curtains, so that anyone on the courtyard could see directly into his room. The furniture included several tables and chairs, a bookshelf, an old black oven for heating, a large double bed for the two youngest boys, and a small bed for Müller himself, all of which lacked canopies.

The hofmeister's primary obligation was to instruct the two youngest boys, Thuro and Hans. They made a poor first impression, appearing before Müller dressed in worn green shirts with tears at the elbows, wool stockings with holes, and shoes with soles in dire need of replacement. After bowing perfunctorily in his direction, they gave one-word answers to all of his questions. Müller was shocked at the neglect these children had suffered in the care of the previous hofmeister, a Swede who was apparently unable to speak proper German and preferred not to talk at all.[51]

The two older boys, whom Müller called by their military ranks, *Cornet* ("Officer Candidate") and *Fähnrich* ("Ensign"), tried to befriend Müller but the effort did not come naturally to them. The Cornet mostly kept quiet, but his twenty-seven-year-old brother, the Fähnrich was a sophomoric braggart. The food was never good enough for him, and he had the habit of moving on to the next course before the others had finished, securing the best pieces of meat for himself. He arrogantly threatened to beat servants who did not follow his commands to the letter and had the locks on his room changed so that no one could enter without his knowledge.[52]

The girls of the von Lillieström family made a far better impression than did their brothers. Of particular interest was twenty-year-old Charlotte Magdalena, whom Müller called by the diminutive Lotchen:

> The only things that made my stay here bearable were the beautiful natural surroundings and my pleasant dealings with the young ladies, who enthusiastically competed to outdo one another in friendliness toward me. Fräulein Lotchen in particular took it upon herself to please me and she, in my eyes, had the greatest merits of all her siblings. I had permission to visit the room in which she stayed with the French nanny [*Französinn*], Fräulein Barbchen, and Fräulein Julchen as often as I wished, and I used

this privilege liberally. The hours passed quickly as we chatted and played cards with the Französinn. At such times I was cheerful, joking, agreeable, and helpful, so they were glad to have me. [. . .] Although I was friendly with all of them, everyone could see that I liked Fräulein Lotchen the best. Now and then I also visited the room in which Fräulein Stienchen, Fräulein Grætchen, and Fräulein Brigittchen stayed. I frequently spent time in the garden. On my own behalf I never touched a single tree, but if one of the young ladies was there I did everything I could to pick some mulberries, pears, apples, cherries, grapes, peaches or whatever else was available. The old gardener was a rascal who had persuaded the Hofrath that the girls were spoiling the garden, and they were thereafter forbidden from touching any of the fruit. But because this prohibition had not yet been issued to me, I was free to pick whatever I wished and was happy to endure the gardener's disfavor on their behalf.[53]

The taste for forbidden fruit grew in Herr Müller and Fräulein Lotchen over the next weeks and months. It was her task to serve the food at mealtimes, and she routinely upset the Cornet and the Fähnrich by giving Müller the choice pieces of meat. When he caught a fever and was confined to bed for a few days, she sent him "a warm cherry soup with thick cream" which she knew he particularly liked. He was a little ashamed at this attention but also flattered, returning her favors by collecting large bouquets of flowers for her on his long walks in the countryside.[54]

Their interactions were intensified by a mutual interest in music. When Fräulein Lotchen learned that Herr Müller played the keyboard, she began asking for lessons. He was only too glad to oblige:

> For some time, Fräulein Lotchen von Lillieström had expressed an interest in learning to play the keyboard, and I encouraged her in this pursuit. One day, the oldest of my little pupils told me that Papa did not want to spend any money on lessons. I let Fräulein Lotchen know that she should not let this hinder her, but simply find a means of securing an instrument. She traveled shortly thereafter to Tribsees and brought back a clavichord. I began teaching her on December 5 [1754]. For this purpose, I had a beautiful music notebook in large format with golden decorations bound in brown leather, had the back gilded, and her initials printed on the side between two palm leaves and under a crown, and on the cover the year, also between two palm leaves of gold. Within the book itself, I copied out an orderly title page with large letters, and transcribed the keyboard pieces so cleanly that they looked almost as if they had been printed. This I asked her to accept as a memento from me. It was a pleasure to put so much effort into teaching her. Her agreeable talent for music made this job easy, and it did not take long for her to achieve good results. Her older sister, Fräulein Stienchen, who had been promised to the cloister in Barth, then also developed an interest in learning to play this instrument and asked

for a similar notebook. So I had to have another book bound in the same way as the first, to write the notes just as cleanly and to decorate it with a similar inscription. But she lacked an ear for music, and it was impossible for her to move her fingers in an orderly manner. They were always going crosswise and I could see that all of my efforts were in vain. I had to continue teaching her nonetheless because she was very envious and jealous of her sister. She even asked for better pieces than I gave to Fräulein Lotchen, so that my good will in agreeing to teach her eventually became a burden.[55]

Keyboard lessons provided a perfect excuse for Fräulein Lotchen and Herr Müller to spend time together. Her desire for lessons, and his willingness to teach, were easily defended as the products of an innocent love of music. Below the fig leaf of musical aspirations, however, lay a host of unmentionable motivations. The son of a blacksmith could never marry the daughter of a court advisor. And if their obvious affection for one another could not lead to marriage, where could it lead?

Fräulein Stienchen was jealous of her sister and eager to spend time with the charming tutor. Perhaps she was embittered by her father's early decision to have her sent to a cloister. In order to keep up the pretense that Fräulein Lotchen's music lessons were actually about notes and rhythms, Müller was forced to scrupulously treat Fräulein Stienchen exactly the same way. The fact that the latter was so disagreeable made this pretense all the more challenging to maintain.

For Fräulein Lotchen and Herr Müller, the keyboard lessons provided a kind of inner sanctum. Her clavichord offered opportunities to interact intimately, even in the midst of a room full of other girls engaged in various distracting activities. Müller described a typical scene, referring to most of the girls by their ages but to Fräulein Lotchen by name:

Every midday, when I was finished eating lunch, I went up to Fräulein Lotchen's room where both she and her older sister would play the keyboard. I usually stayed from 12:45 or 1:00 P.M. until 4:00 or 5:00 P.M. We played the clavichord, sang, talked, and drank coffee. They prepared the coffee for me every afternoon, no matter how often I forbade them from going to the trouble. The young ladies always enjoyed this time because whichever one had received that morning's leftover milk would drink it while I sipped my coffee. All of them were involved in the preparations: one took care that the beans were roasted; Fräulein Lotchen then ground them while sitting with the mill on her lap; another boiled the grounds; a fourth fetched some fresh milk; a fifth poured the coffee. If the oldest girl was playing the keyboard, Fräulein Lotchen brought me my coffee cup, as I liked to be near the keyboard, or if she was playing then the eldest one brought my coffee. Now and then one of the older girls would drink a cup with me. They bought the beans with their own allowance money. A few times the Fähnrich came up and must have been annoyed by what he saw. Often, and especially on Sundays, I had to drink coffee with the Hofrath in his room, particularly when he believed that I was somehow upset with him; in such cases, I went directly from the lunch table to his room. Now and then, I went in the evenings to the prayer hour, and after that went back upstairs to the ladies, where I remained until around midnight. In order to avoid waking the old man, whose room was between the house door and the stairs, I left by way of the living room and garden.[56]

The pretense of treating the sisters equally eventually became threadbare. Matters came to a head on July 5, 1755, when Fräulein Stienchen was driven to despair by Herr Müller's favorable treatment of her sister: "I spent all morning with Fräulein Lotchen, and went through the keyboard pieces, which later brought me into disfavor with her sister, Fräulein Stienchen. Despite her cantankerous and impolite behavior, she always wanted me to spend the most time with her."[57] From this point forward, Fräulein Stienchen abandoned all politesse, putting new locks on the garden door so that the Hofmeister could no longer bring her younger sister flowers or fruit. When he nonetheless presented Fräulein Lotchen with a bouquet of forget-me-nots and carnations he had received as a gift from Stralsund, Fräulein Stienchen came to the dining table with a large and awkward bouquet of the same flowers she had made for herself. She also poisoned the minds of the two younger sisters who shared her bedroom and began to spread scandalous rumors that her sister and Herr Müller were having an affair.

Others, too, had the impression that something illicit was going on between the hofmeister and Fräulein Lotchen. Gossip eventually reached Müller's former employer, the Frau Regierungs Räthin, who counseled caution when he was briefly back for a visit in Wendisch-Baggendorf:

> The Frau Regierungs Räthin revealed to me that people believed that a certain love relationship [*ein gewißes Liebes Verständnis*] had been established between me and Fräulein Lotchen in Eixen. The older Herr von Gadow had told of this suspicion in the Herr Assessor von Corsvant's house in Greifswald. She advised me to be careful and expressed her full confidence in my wisdom. I answered that I had great respect for such a well-mannered and loveable Fräulein as this one but that I would never forget what I owed her as well as that which I owed myself [*was ich ihr und mir schuldig*].[58]

Müller's pledge that he would not violate his obligations did little to calm the anxieties of those who knew of the keyboard lessons. Not long thereafter, the Herr Assessor Carl Friedrich von Corsvant, in whose home the discussion of the "love relationship" between Müller and Fräulein Lotchen had taken place, visited the von Lilleström household, no doubt in order to investigate the situation up close. The Herr von Corsvant was well equipped to penetrate the inner sanctum of the music lessons because he himself was a gifted keyboardist. Müller came home one afternoon to discover the Herr Assessor sitting at the clavichord in Fräulein Lotchen's bedroom:

> The assessor laid a handkerchief over the keys of the clavichord and played nonetheless pleasingly and with his usual skill. Fräulein Lotchen von Lillieström marveled at this. I convinced her finally to give it a try with assurances that she too would be able to achieve the same feat. I laid my handkerchief over the keys, named a particular piece, and she played it equally artfully and without hitting any wrong notes.[59]

Fräulein Lotchen was surprised at her own ability to play accurately while unable to see the keys. More than any of the participants realized, there was more to these music lessons than met the eye. They were blindly following instinct. Witnessing their close interactions at the keyboard is unlikely to have calmed the fears of the assessor sent to check up on them.

❧

Events in the household soon offered Fräulein Lotchen and Herr Müller an opportunity to live out their fantasies vicariously. In the summer of 1755 Müller found a love letter to an unnamed woman wedged into the Bible of his youngest pupil, Hans von Lillieström. The thirteen-year-old boy had written it in block letters rather than cursive, suggesting that the object of his affection possessed only a limited education. When confronted, Hans's face turned red and after much ado he was forced to admit that the addressee was Angreth, a servant girl several years his senior. Over the past weeks, the two had exchanged some gifts (shoe buckles, shirt buttons) and had kissed one another in the Hofrath's bedroom.[60] Müller felt there was only one person to whom he could turn with this delicate information:

> I could not talk about this with anyone other than Fräulein Lotchen, with whom I spoke at the earliest opportunity. The Hofrath himself would have laughed about it, pleased that his boy was already showing signs of galanterie. I showed Fräulein Lotchen the letter, which she read with astonishment, recalling that she had often seen her youngest brother in the dark hallways in front of the Hofrath's room and had once found him in the Fähnrich's room sitting on Angreth's lap.[61]

Fräulein Lotchen began interrogating Angreth and eventually learned the whole, dark truth. For some time, the servant girl had engaged in sexual liaisons with the Hofrath and even with his son, the Fähnrich. All of this might have gone on without attracting notice, but young Hans had seen too much through the keyhole. In order to keep the boy quiet, Angreth had begun to flirt with him too, allowing him to sit on her lap and kiss her. She was eventually sent to another town where she was provided with a bed to give birth to a child out of wedlock. Whether the baby belonged to the Hofrath or the Fähnrich no one knew.[62]

This sordid business was kept officially secret, but it strained relationships within the von Lillieström family. From this point on, the thirteen-year-old Hans absolutely loathed his older brother, the Fähnrich, blaming him for Angreth's banishment. Fräulein Lotchen was undoubtedly disappointed in both her father and older brother for their grievous offenses against both decorum and Christian doctrine.

The exposure of this misbehavior, however, undoubtedly strengthened the relationship between Herr Müller and Fräulein Lotchen. They assumed the role of adults in this debacle, holding not only Hans, Angreth, and the Fähnrich accountable for their misdeeds but also the hofrath himself. For all of their professed concern, they were titillated by this scandal and must have recognized parallels with their own relationship. It must have been liberating to experience, through surrogates, the thrill of romantic transgression between the aristocratic family and the household staff.

The Hofrath and Fähnrich were certainly embarrassed by these events. True to form, the old man sought reconciliation in his own awkward way. Not long after the affairs with Angreth came to light, he and his equally culpable son made an unusual appearance in Fräulein Lotchen's bedroom while she was having a keyboard lesson with Herr Müller. The two men had until that point displayed an aversion to her music making. The Hofrath had refused to pay for the lessons and the Fähnrich had been "annoyed" on the few previous occasions he had heard her play. Things changed, however, in the wake of the Angreth affair:

> On the 6th [of October, 1755], the Hofrath was in a very cheerful mood at lunch, so afterward I had to go drink coffee with him. He told me much and kept me for about an hour talking about his work. Thereafter I went back up to Fräulein Lotchen. We played the keyboard, sang, talked, and the time passed quickly. I remained there until 1:00 P.M. The Hofrath came upstairs too and listened to our music making together with his son Philipp. One could see the pleasure in his eyes as he observed Fräulein Lotchen's skill at the keyboard. I myself then had to play, and this pleased him even more, because I performed a minuet with thoroughbass, and thus a fuller harmony. Thereafter, I instructed Fräulein Lotchen in playing figured bass, and gave her a few galanterie pieces especially for this purpose, so that she would be able to teach herself.[63]

Suddenly offering support for Fräulein Lotchen's music lessons was perhaps the Hofrath's means of asking forgiveness for his recent misconduct. This spontaneous visit, however, may also have had threatening undertones. Both the Hofrath and the Fähnrich knew that Fräulein Lotchen and Herr Müller had become quite close, inspiring gossip within the household and beyond. Perhaps by violating their inner sanctum, these men wished to send a message that the keyboard lovers were vulnerable to discovery too.

It is entirely suitable that Herr Müller offered Fräulein Lotchen a few galanterien. The galant aesthetic was one of feigned innocence; the vaunted "ease" of this music was superficial. At its core, the music was substantive, and had effects in the real world. Keyboard playing had been successfully deployed to keep Müller out of trouble during his early years in Jena. He himself had used it to tame "wild" spirits in Wendisch-Baggendorf. Now, in Eixen, he had managed to use the innocence associated with keyboard playing as cover for an emotional, if not a physical, affair.

ॐ

On October 6, 1755, the same day the Hofrath and the Fähnrich visited the music room, Müller learned that he would soon be departing the von Lillieström household. His application to serve as pastor at the Heilig-Geist Church in Stralsund had been approved, in part through the advocacy of the Hofrath. Fräulein Lotchen was pleased for his success but deeply sorry that he would be leaving. Müller's account of her reaction to the news is telling: "Fräulein Lotchen looked at me and turned red, then congratulated me. That evening at nine o'clock we had a walk in the garden by moonlight and she expressed her sincere pleasure at this development."[64] In a congratulatory letter, the melancholy Fräulein wrote that she had always hoped he would achieve such a post. She conspicuously referred to him as the "high-born" Herr Müller, a form of address entirely inappropriate for the son of a blacksmith; she clearly preferred to think of him as a fellow aristocrat.[65] Müller described their final moments together in Eixen as follows: "I prepared for my departure in the morning, taking leave of the Hofrath and of Fräulein Lotchen. One can easily imagine that my parting from the latter was moving."[66]

Snapped out of their reverie, Herr Müller and Fräulein Lotchen realigned their behavior to accord more closely with reality. The future was now clear to them both. She would remain in Eixen and eventually marry a military officer of the aristocracy.[67] He would accept the position as pastor in Stralsund and, out of obligation to the city fathers, would marry his deceased predecessor's eldest daughter, twenty-six-year-old Anna Dorothea Geismar.[68] Not long after the wedding, Frau Müller told her husband that she too had heard the rumors about his past and had not actually believed he would marry "anyone but the Fräulein Lotchen von Lillieström."[69]

CHAPTER 9

May God Protect
This Beautiful Organ

On Sunday, November 9, 1721, the citizens of Rötha awoke with a keen sense of anticipation. Men whose backs hurt from harvesting beans and drying barley lit tallow candles that faintly sweetened the thick scent of damp hay in the air. They donned their best rockaleur cloaks and pants, untangled their powdered wigs, and pulled triangular hats from velvet cases. Their wives awoke from stress dreams about unshearable sheep to step into black cotton dresses, drape striped linen scarves over their shoulders, and tie bonnet laces beneath their chins. They checked to make sure their honeybee colonies had not frozen overnight before admonishing their children to set piglets back into the straw of living-room pens and prepare themselves for church.[1]

Closing their front gates behind them, Rötha's roughly three hundred residents walked along dirt paths toward the tallest spire in town.[2] They passed fields of wooden poles to which hearty hops vines still clung. Sheep, known in the local dialect as *Nösern*, were everywhere, wandering aimlessly across the broad meadows of what outsiders called "Sheep-Rötha" (*Schafrete*).[3] Some passed by a vast wasteland of burned-out lots where homes had once stood, a melancholy reminder of the fire that had devastated their town the previous February.[4]

From a distance the high tower on the north side of St. George's Church gave Rötha a grand appearance. Closer inspection revealed a curious lack of symmetry: the medieval town fathers had intended to build a second tower but had apparently run out of money.[5] A row of large, pointed windows flooded the sanctuary with light, illuminating pillars painted to resemble green palm fronds.[6] High atop the altar, a comically small statue of mustachioed St. George menaced a plaster dragon.[7]

Almost no one paid attention to the usual decorations today. Residents and visiting dignitaries craned their necks toward the back balcony in order to behold the greatest local philanthropic project of their lifetimes: a spectacular new church organ. One awed attendee described his impressions as follows:

> The outward appearance of the instrument pleases the eye with the symmetry of its architecture, as well as its decorative sculpture and carpentry. The case is painted a shade of white tending toward yellow, richly gilded with the most lustrous gold [. . .]. The pipes are forged of the best hardened and hammered English tin, polished to a matte finish. Large and small pipes stand in the most beautiful order and are so spaciously mounted that one who approaches can easily appreciate them individually.[8]

The present chapter explores the construction of this particular instrument as a window into the social importance of church organs in J. S. Bach's Germany.

ॐ

Of all Rötha's citizens, the most excited about this new instrument was Christian Langbein, the local organist. Every Sunday morning for the previous thirty-two years, he had martyred himself at the console of an instrument built by Josias Ibach in 1614. Ibach's organ had probably never been a joy to play, but more than a century after its construction, it was in such a deplorable state that the Langbein family referred to it as an "old clump of lead."[9] For the organist's entire career, it had been a dead weight on his musical inspiration.[10]

The son of a local blacksmith, Langbein knew the levers of power as only the lifelong resident of a small town can. He was smart and ambitious. No other organist in Rötha's history had obtained an appointment as schoolteacher. No other organist had managed to have his wife appointed mistress of the girls' school.[11] He had sought for decades to have a new organ built in his church, applying the full weight of his diplomatic skills toward this end. Knowing that his own judgment would be attributed to self-interest, Langbein had solicited the opinions of outside experts, who confirmed his view regarding the old organ that "no repair could possibly help."[12] These efforts had persuaded two influential men—the superintendent of churches in far-off Leipzig, Johann Dornfeld, and

Rötha's resident aristocrat, Otto Heinrich, Baron von Friesen—that the Church of St. George desperately needed a new instrument. Unfortunately, both were old and feeble, and the project languished as their health and influence waned.

Finally, in 1717 the old Baron von Friesen died and Rötha came into the possession of his nephew, Christian August. After taking up residence in the moated castle in Rötha, just a few steps from the door of the Church of St. George, Christian August had set about improving the lives of his town's residents, virtually all of whom rented plots of his land for farming and animal husbandry.[13] He had donated a library, paid to have books read aloud to illiterate farmers,[14] and doled out money to "poor schoolboys that they might buy books and other necessary supplies." He had also supported destitute occupants of "the woman's house," and other widows, orphans, and "miserable" folk.[15]

Sitting through church services, the younger Baron von Friesen had been annoyed by "violent howling" from the old organ.[16] Whether or not this was strategic howling engineered by Christian Langbein from the organ bench, the baron made up his mind that this instrument would be replaced. Von Friesen was a military man who had served for decades in the Saxon army of Augustus the Strong. Unlike many aristocratic commanders, he had personally led his soldiers into battle and had the scars to prove it. His body bore a 1706 stab wound from a Swedish dagger and a 1709 wound in the stomach from a French musket ball.[17] Once he committed to building a new organ in Rötha, no one was going to talk him out of it.

The Baron von Friesen spent his winters in Dresden, where he owned a home in the *Seestraße*, a short walk from the famous Church of St. Sophie, which was then in the midst of its own organ-construction project. The builder who had been entrusted with the new instrument in Dresden was a young man from Freiberg named Gottfried Silbermann. Having first trained as a bookbinder and carpenter, he had learned to construct organs from his brother in Strassburg. The ten instruments Silbermann had built since completing his apprenticeship were of exceedingly high quality. Though only thirty-eight years old, he was already being named alongside the many Saxons who had "distinguished themselves in the realm of music."[18]

Through their connection in Dresden, the Baron von Friesen had invited Silbermann to Rötha at the end of 1718 to sketch out a plan for building an instrument in the Church of St. George. On December 22 of that year, they had signed a contract that specified Silbermann was to remove the old organ and replace it with a new one in exchange for a flat fee of 1,000 reichstaler. Building supplies and subcontracting work were to be covered by the organ maker:

All materials—whether tin, wood, leather, clay, iron, bronze, wire, or what-ever else is necessary—are to be supplied [by Silbermann] and all other craftsmen—whether sculptors, carpenters, locksmiths, blacksmiths, nailers, belt-makers, or whatever names they may have, with the exception of painters and the carpenters who make the bellows—are to be subcontracted by the builder. The pipes are to be made of the best English tin, metal, and wood, and the housing cleanly and skillfully sculpted according to the design.[19]

Silbermann had been offered an additional 400 reichstaler for travel ex-penses, room, board, and firewood in Rötha for himself, three apprentices, and one pupil, as well as the availability of a calcant to pump the bellows. An additional 150 reichstaler had been allocated to Johann Christian Butze, a painter of hunting scenes from Dresden, who was charged with painting and gilding the façade and balcony railings so that they "accord well with the altar and pulpit."[20]

The total cost of the organ had come to 1,550 reichstaler, 600 of which was covered by the Baron von Friesen "in order to honor God and to save the church some money." The remaining 800 reichstaler had been offered by the Baron as an interest-free loan to the church. Rötha's Church of St. George took in 428 reichstaler every year in interest on investments and was thus well positioned to pay back the loan over the next few years. The Baron von Friesen, however, magnanimously declared himself willing to wait a bit longer so as not to cut into the budgets of the other institutions supported by the church, including the girls' and boys' schools and the women's house.[21]

Though the contract had specified that Silbermann was to finish the new organ by September 1719, this deadline eventually proved unrealistic. Only after November 15, 1720, the day he had completed the instrument for the Church of St. Sophie, was the maker able to turn his undivided at-tention to fulfilling his obligations in Rötha. After constructing the organ's main components in his workshop in Freiberg, Silbermann had taken up residence in Rötha in May 1721. He and his assistants spent the next twenty-five weeks unloading tin pipes from straw-laden horse carts, carrying bellows up winding church balcony stairs, and installing the organ housing in the rear balcony of the church.

Rötha was a trifling little hamlet by comparison with glorious Dresden, but Silbermann had refused to skimp on materials, employing the same high quality tin, brass, and wood he had used in the Saxon capital. He had even generously donated elements above and beyond those specified in the contract: a *Sesquialtera* third to fill out triadic harmonies at the pull of a stop, and twenty-three "blind" (non-sounding) pipes to balance the organ's visual impression.[22]

It was not until the late autumn that Rötha's new organ was finally ready for inspection and dedication. On Saturday, November 8, 1721, the day before the instrument's unveiling, Johann Kuhnau, J. S. Bach's predecessor as cantor of St. Thomas School in Leipzig, and Gottfried Ernst Bestell, court organist in Altenburg, were brought in to offer their opinions of the instrument's capabilities and faults. The two old men spent much of that Saturday playing the instrument and listening as others, including Christian Petzold, organist at the Church of St. Sophie in Dresden, explored its merits and sought to find its limitations. In the end, they judged Silbermann's latest creation an unmitigated success and announced that it was indeed ready for the public presentation planned for the following day.[23]

᠅

The grand church organ was not only the king of musical instruments, it was also among the most complicated pieces of technology in existence. Bridges, buildings, and pumps for removing water from the bottom of mine shafts required heavier lifting. Clock designs were sometimes dazzlingly complex. But no other machine was simultaneously so imposing and yet so intricate.

Impressive church instruments like the one in Rötha were spectacular feats of engineering and artistry. There was something promethean about the work of organ builders. Their task came as close as human beings ever did to fabricating fellow living creatures. The wind-chest of an organ was likened to a heart, and the wind itself to blood.[24] Whereas humans sang and played trumpets and flutes with the air God had breathed into them, the organ was said to sing with artificial lungs.[25] The most successful makers were revered for their creative power and likened to mythological characters who aspired to God-like status. As one of Gottfried Silbermann's admirers wrote in 1737:

> The science [of organ construction] requires such a broad base of knowledge in musical, mathematical, architectural, and mechanical secrets that it would take one who is not a natural master multiple lifetimes to acquire a thorough grounding in the necessary skills. Vulcan stood as a mortal among the heathen gods because he built a chariot for the sun. Dædalus was regarded as a wonder of his time because he was able to use quicksilver to make a wooden sculpture of Venus move as if it were alive. Callicrates and Architas aroused amazement by fashioning worms and doves that moved in actual flight. What would the venerators of such accomplishments say about the beauty of a Silbermann organ, in which everything laughs and lives, and which can produce the sound of the human voice, almost to the point of articulating actual words [. . .] [?][26]

As the world's most complex and lifelike machine, the church organ played a prominent role in philosophical debates of the era. Philosophers opposed to the radical materialism of Spinoza used the organ to make their case that there were exceptions to the laws of physics. The instrument, a physical body whose processes could be explained in terms of cause and effect, could do nothing without the direction of an organist, a soul whose actions physical laws could never fully explain. Ludwig von Holberg recognized that this argument, though popular, would not hold up to the challenges of those who saw the universe as entirely physical:

> The [. . .] argument that almost everyone uses when they wish to prove that the soul and the body are separate entities—and indeed this is an argument with which many have so fallen in love that they regard it as unimpeachable—goes as follows: in order to show that the body with all of its artful organization has and can have no life of its own, they compare it with an organ, and the soul with an organist. They say: just as an organ, no matter how complex it may be, can produce no sound—let alone tones in harmony—unless an organist touches it, so is the machine of the body life-less when not set in motion by the soul. This argument would be excellent and the comparison well conceived if experience did not reveal that when a bodily organ is damaged, and the flesh falls into confusion and insensibil-ity, that the soul also loses consciousness, whereas the organist, no matter what confusion and disorder his instrument may be in, loses nothing of his ability to make music. No one can accuse me of seeking to strengthen the materialist argument: my intention is only to show through careful examination that such counterarguments are weak, and that depending on them makes a good thing seem dubious.[27]

Most eighteenth-century Germans who devoted so much time, energy, and money to having organs built in their churches had little interest in this philosophical debate. They did not lie awake at night wondering whether the materialists or antimaterialists had the upper hand. Both positions depended on human reason and were thus inevitably flawed. They trusted that their fate was in God's hands and devoted their resources to building organs in hopes of inspiring His mercy.

The relative prosperity of the galant era notwithstanding, the vast major-ity of Bach's contemporaries remained deeply concerned about survival. Half of all children—the offspring of the peasantry, the bourgeoisie, and the nobility alike—died of mysterious ailments during their first few years. Fires, floods, and epidemic diseases decimated entire communities. The obscure logic behind such disasters was painstakingly explained by pastors and other theologians, and their words offered some comfort, but in the end cause-and-effect reasoning inevitably felt unsatisfying. God's judgments remained unfathomable. The only relief came by way of blind faith that He knew what He was doing. This worldview depended on the firm conviction that God's efforts were and would always be vastly superior to those of even the most brilliant humans. If there was value to an analogy between the Lord and an organ builder, it was simply to show that God's work was infinitely superior, as one writer of the time put it in a poem:

> Let it be clearly seen, that you've been fabricated,
> The greatest organ known, you were by God created.
> Though human makers build with splendid skill and care,
> Their organs simply prove God's work beyond compare.[28]

By dedicating their greatest intellectual efforts to praising God through music, most of J. S. Bach's contemporaries hoped not to usurp His throne but rather to cultivate His favor. The church organ—the most complex machine in the world, the product of the best and brightest minds—was a prayer machine. Church organists were professionals employed to appeal to God on behalf of their congregations. The success of this appeal, and nothing less, was at stake every Sunday morning.

਻੺

Anticipation grew as both the male and female sides of Rötha's Church of St. George filled to capacity. Residents found their way to the wooden seats and pews that their families had rented for generations. In the balcony, a group of choir boys from the St. Thomas School and Leipzig city pipers milled about the new organ. Johann Kuhnau, Bach's predecessor as *Thomaskantor*, had brought these musicians on the four-hour journey from Leipzig to celebrate this momentous occasion.

As the sound of church bells dissipated, the congregants settled into an expectant silence. Kuhnau arranged his musicians and led them into a chorus on Psalm 100, verse 4 ("Enter into His gates with thanksgiving, and into His courts with praise: be thankful unto Him, and bless His name"). The opening choral movement was followed by a recitative thanking the Lord for His generosity in creating the world ("What a beautiful harmony our God has brought into all things!").[29] The first half of the cantata ended with another chorus particularly appropriate for the people of Schafrete: "Lord, we are your people and the sheep of your meadow."[30]

The text of this cantata had been written by Johann Christian Langbein, son of Rötha's organist. A deacon in the nearby town of Borna, the younger Langbein had prepared a pamphlet for this occasion in which he defended music as a force for good in the world, expressing the view that it was a gift from the Creator that men had developed "in part for their own pleasure and use, but more importantly in order to praise God."[31] He regaled his readers with the history of the organ, an ancient instrument powered by wind that had already been introduced into the church in the eighth century. He noted that these early efforts had been improved upon in the "Latin churches" of France and Italy but brought to perfection in Protestant Germany "and especially in our beloved Saxony."[32]

After the sermon, Christian Petzold sat down at the console and offered the assembled congregants their first experience of the new organ's power. He likely improvised a prelude on Psalm 98, which began the second half of the cantata. The farmers, bakers, sheep shearers, glass blowers, and virtually everyone else in attendance knew the text of this psalm by heart: "O sing unto the Lord a new song; for he hath done marvelous things." At first only obliquely referencing the chorale tune, Petzold would have built up the music to a point at which it was unmistakable. The crystalline melody floated over thickets of fast passagework. The silvery peel of trumpets, the warm glow of stringed instruments, and the ethereal whistling of flutes echoed between the stone walls and pillars of the church. By the end, bass pedal tones pounded out the chorale tune, rattling loose window frames.[33]

Kuhnau gathered his forces and brought them in on the next verse of the same psalm: "Make a joyful noise unto the Lord, all the earth: make a loud noise, and rejoice, and sing praise." The recitative that followed invited "everyone in Rötha" to add his or her voice to the dedication of this "newly built instrument of God."[34] The pews creaked as parishioners rose to do their part.

Listening to the new organ, the people of Rötha likely felt a sense of proud resilience, even resurrection. They had recently been reminded how quickly fortunes could change. Nine months earlier, on a winter's night, around one-quarter of Rötha's homes had burned to the ground. Nearly every person in town—men, women, children, visitors and residents alike—had spent the night passing buckets of water from a frozen-over pond from one pair of numb hands to the next, trying to quell the flames of a growing conflagration. Their efforts, led by a local judge, had failed.[35] Many congregants hearing the organ for the first time this morning had lost everything they owned and spent months living in school buildings, barns, and spare rooms, dependent on the hospitality of their families, friends, and neighbors.

The glorious sound of Silbermann's organ was evidence that Rötha had passed this test of its faith.[36] God had not forsaken their town. Through the leadership of their patron, Christian August, Baron von Friesen, they had constructed a prayer machine and dedicated it to God's glory. The congregants now trusted that this sacrifice would inspire mercy in the only judge who had the power to actually protect them.

The Baron von Friesen was entirely pleased with Silbermann's accomplishment. The positive opinions of the experts he had hired to test the instrument were confirmed by the "complete approbation" he saw on the faces all around him. The original plan had been to move Ibach's "old clump of lead" over to Rötha's smaller house of worship, the Church of St. Mary. Hearing the power of Silbermann's new instrument, however, the Baron von Friesen resolved to commission the maker to remain in town for a few more months and build a second new instrument in the Marienkirche.[37]

To conclude the performance, one of the most talented St. Thomas School pupils stepped to the freshly painted balcony railing in Rötha's Church of St. George and sang the following aria:

> Rötha, in this way you can
> Bring great joy to God and man:
> Simply love sweet harmony.
> When you praise the Lord with song,
> Let the organ sing along.
> God, its safety guarantee![38]

This prayer for the organ's safety was echoed by Kuhnau and Bestell in the official report they filed the following Monday. Recognizing that the instrument would likely outlive them by centuries, they wrote: "May God protect this beautiful organ from all damage, and allow it to be performed in peaceful, sacred worship for a very long time."[39] An extraordinary example of baroque craftsmanship, Silberman's organ can be heard in Rötha to this day.

CHAPTER 10

How Professional Musicians Were Compensated

Boys who dreamed of becoming organists, cantors, and kapellmeisters in eighteenth-century Germany often endured discouragement and even contempt from the authority figures in their lives. Johann August Ernesti, rector of Leipzig's St. Thomas School and sworn enemy of J. S. Bach, liked to provoke pupils he found making music with the mocking question: "So you want to be a beerfiddler too?"[1] The composer Gottfried Heinrich Stölzel wrote in his 1740 autobiography that those who felt they had his best interests at heart had discouraged him from pursuing a musical career "nearly by force."[2] Georg Philipp Telemann's autobiography includes an account of his widowed mother's reaction to the successful performance of his first opera, *Sigismundus* (1693). Until this point, the twelve-year-old prodigy had received nothing but encouragement for his musical pursuits, but the prospect that he might now turn professional changed everything:

> Ah! What a storm this opera caused! The enemies of music descended upon my mother and had her imagine that I would become a sideshow artist, a tightrope-walker, a minstrel, a marmot-trainer, etc. if music were not removed from my life. Sooner done than said! Sheet music, instruments, and with them half my life were taken away. So that I would not be distracted by them further I was sent to a boarding school in Zellerfeld, perhaps because these tyrants believed that back behind the Blocksberg mountain no music would be tolerated.[3]

Men like Stölzel and Telemann could proudly recount harrowing tales of the obstacles they had overcome because subsequent success had proved their tormentors so misguided. It is true, however, that for most aspiring professional musicians fame was illusory and fortune all but nonexistent. The decision to abandon music in favor of a career in law, medicine, or jurisprudence was not an irrational one.

In a world where the prestige of a profession depended on the degree to which it insulated practitioners from the natural world, musicians were difficult to classify. On the extreme physical end were itinerant buskers who juggled, walked tightropes, trained wild beasts, and played popular songs on the street, their socks soaking through in the rain and their freezing fingers barely able to beat a triangle in tempo. When musicians like these were invited indoors, it was to play as beerfiddlers in rowdy taverns. In such contexts, trumpeters were known to blow lively tunes in support of one side in a drunken political debate and foul laments to discourage the other.[4] Somewhat higher on the totem pole of music professionals were dance musicians hired to play student parties. Their position was more favorable insofar as they had greater latitude in negotiating payments and choosing repertoire. Here too, however, things could get physical. Shouts of "You want to be paid for this dog-food music?!" could be followed by threats to smash double basses and end with physicians stitching up the head wounds of inebriated young men at four o'clock in the morning.[5] The musicians who plucked lutes, sang opera arias, and performed concertos in coffeehouses exhibited more refined physical movements, and their patrons mostly just sipped hot chocolate, shot billiards, and cursed at one another.[6] Musicians invited to participate in subscription concerts were regularly appreciated not only for their virtuosity but also for their ability to challenge audiences intellectually. Their insulation from the physical world was underscored by the reverent silence in which their performances were received. Those who wished to insult professional musicians deliberately conflated these diverse groups.

The relative prestige of professional musicians sometimes came to the fore in public disputes. Christian Caspar Müthel, a friend of Telemann's and the father of a Bach student, found himself in the midst of one such conflict shortly after accepting an organist post in the town of Mölln. Traditionally, the men who had held his position were required not only to play the organ but also to serve as secretary to the *Feuergreven*, the town's largely honorific fire department. Müthel refused to engage in these ancillary activities, feeling that they were beneath his dignity, and opted to pay a colleague twenty reichstaler per year to do them in his stead. This posed no particular problem until it came time to organize a parade. Müthel insisted on marching directly behind the mayor and aldermen and in front of the Feuergreven. The firemen, however, objected strenuously to his asserting precedence over them. His position, after all, demanded that he serve as their secretary; the fact that he paid someone else to fulfill this duty did not raise his status. When confronted, Müthel responded by arguing that it "would hardly be appropriate for a musician and organist to be ranked among the lowest citizens and day laborers."[7] The mayor of Mölln initially offered support, fearing that it would be impossible to find another organist of Müthel's caliber if he decided to quit. Eventually, however, he yielded to the petitioners and decreed that the organist take up a position behind the firemen in future parades.[8]

Wedding receptions could also lay bare a musician's position in the complex social hierarchies of the day. In 1725 Heinrich Lorenz Hurlebusch—a sixty-year-old organist in Braunschweig—was charged by a local couple with dereliction of duty for having sent an assistant to provide music at their wedding. He had held his post for thirty-six years without ever hearing a complaint and in response to these accusations felt compelled to write a letter to the town council to plead his case. Hurlebusch had sent an assistant for one primary reason: "The citizenry treats organists and cantors too poorly at weddings." He did not hesitate to provide details:

> When one arrives in the wedding house, most grooms and brides are so impolite that they not only do not properly receive one, but also make the cantor and the organist stand around and wait in the hallway (sometimes more than an hour) together with girls, boys, and all manner of riff-raff, which is hard to take for an honor-loving spirit, particularly when one's social position is as high as that of most citizens, businessmen, brewers, or whatever names they may have. When a citizen is of character, he knows how he compares with others in terms of his status, and I certainly have nothing but due respect for those above me, of which there are a great many. In my defense, however, I must dutifully report—without vainly wishing to praise myself—that I had the honor for three years to offer musical instruction to our most gracious duke, and to respectfully perform for him at other opportunities, either by myself or with others. On such occasions his Highness granted me entry into his ante-chamber so that I would not have to wait around with all manner of servants and court boys, and this arrangement was also mercifully allowed by the other members of the nobility. I will not even mention the respect with which such high persons treat me when I am called to provide chamber music, for fear of trying the patience of the honorable members of the town council. How can an ordinary citizen, who is at best my equal, not show me the same respect that is shown to me out of mercy and goodness by our gracious rulers, noble ministers, and other high persons? Ordinary citizens owe

me this respect. Musicians tolerate such poor treatment so well simply because they have become accustomed to it; since time immemorial it has been attached to their profession. They have to perform at weddings for even the lowest of the low. A musician has to play serenades on the street for those of the nethermost status, as long as they are not criminals, and must basically perform for whoever asks him, again with the exception of criminals, at whatever time and place that person demands. But this type of treatment cannot and must not be tolerated by any reputable organist, whose primary job it is to provide music for the church. [. . .] I request that if the highborn, noble, and learned town council would, for the many and true reasons outlined above, pass an ordinance [. . .] that would require wedding parties in the future to treat the organist like the other guests: in other words, by allowing him to wait in a room with the other guests, rather than in the hallway, before the ceremony begins and, if coaches are required to pick up the guests and ferry them to the wedding house, that they should do the same for the organist.[9]

In the end the members of the town council refused to produce the requested ordinance, but they did grant Hurlebusch the right to send substitutes as he saw fit.

In one way or another, Bach and his professional colleagues faced fundamental questions about the value of their work every day. Whereas bakers, butchers, and blacksmiths could certainly do their jobs badly, no one denied the fundamental value of work aimed at producing bread, meat, and tools. Music's value, by contrast, was ephemeral. Justifications for its existence often depended on metaphysical evidence that not everyone found persuasive. Music's ambiguous status was a burden for its practitioners, from boys first approaching their parents about pursuing professional careers to elderly retirees. This chapter explores the rhetoric around music making for money in Bach's time, as well as the family background, education, and career paths of professional musicians. It also considers the rewards that came to those who persevered in this socially and financially unstable line of work.

 ༚

Professional musicians of Bach's time tended to come from the artisan classes. Some of the most successful organists of the era had fathers who were weavers,[10] fabric-makers,[11] lampblack salesmen,[12] and shoemakers.[13] Many were driven to play keyboards, lutes, and violins not only by an innate love of music but also by a powerful aversion to taking up their fathers' trades. The organist Johann Georg Hoffmann wrote in his autobiography that he had felt "not the slightest inclination" to learn to weave like his father, because he "saw daily how he slaved over the evil yarn, torturing and martyring himself for a tiny living."[14] Convincing his parents to allow him to pursue a career in music, however, was not easy:

> In my eleventh year, after much pleading, I received a violin from my father. Despite his poverty, he arranged for me to have some lessons as well. And this was supposed to be the end of it. Upon turning twelve, I was compelled to choose a profession in order to serve my neighbor and earn my bread. When my father heard my resolution that I wished to become a musician and organist in this world and nothing else, he was not pleased [. . .]. But I kept begging, and told my parents that I expected dear God to find a way to support me. When I finally received their permission, I was overjoyed.[15]

Michael Kirsten was the son of a poor shoemaker who showed an aptitude for music at around the same age. His parents supported his musical inclinations to an extent but were reluctant to see him abandon the shoemaker's last:

> My father bought me a hammered dulcimer, on which I tried my best to play all manner of dances, and I pleaded with my father to let me study with a village bandsman, so that I might be a learned bandsman rather than just a natural one. But my father had no desire to facilitate such a thing, and rather devoted all of his strength to persuading me to go into his trade, in which I had no interest. Eventually a merchant who admired my playing and also my handwriting spoke with my father, promising to make all manner of good things out of me. This struck my father as not a bad idea, as he would much rather have seen me become a rural judge than a musician.[16]

At some point, Kirsten gained access to a spinet and began teaching himself Lutheran chorales:

> I went into the countryside, wherever there was an organ in a church, so that I might play upon it. One can easily imagine how excellent I sounded. My first formal appearance took place in a village called Böhmischdorf [today Ceská Ves in the Czech Republic]. After the sermon the organist was nowhere to be found, so I dared, with fear and trembling, to perform in his stead. The chorale I had to play was "When We Are in Deepest Need" [*Wenn wir in höchsten Nöten sein*]. I knew this chorale best in C major, so the farmers were forced to gamely scream up to a high G.[17]

Many of those who pursued musical careers were like J. S. Bach in that they had grandfathers, fathers, brothers, and uncles who already played professionally. Supervision, contacts, and career advice from family members gave these boys advantages that were difficult to overcome for those born to weavers and shoemakers. If nothing else, the presence of instruments around the home could inspire the interest of younger family members. Ernst Wilhelm Wolf, later organist and kapellmeister at the court in Weimar, told the story of his musical beginnings as follows:

> When I was around four years old [1739], there was a keyboard in my room. My father asked me: "You? Do you want to learn to play the keyboard?" My older brother was studying composition with Kapellmeister Stölzel in Gotha. When he returned home for a visit my father said to him: "Do you know what? Ernst Wilhelm would like you to teach him to play the keyboard." He sat down at the instrument and taught me the keys and notes, as well as a minuet, which I can still play today, at age fifty-six. [. . .] Things continued to progress, and I learned so quickly that in no time I could perform on the organ. When I was thirteen, my brother came back to Behringen from Kahla, where he was then living. I was made to play the keyboard for him. He was so pleased by my performance that he invited me to return with him to Kahla and stay. Four weeks later I traveled there with my father, and because my brother had an organ in his room, I could "organ" away the hours in great comfort.[18]

The most common route to a career in music was to apprentice oneself to a professional musician. Those without family connections had to make their own arrangements. Michael Kirsten was brave enough as a teenager to pool all of his money—half a dozen reichstaler—and travel to Brieg, where he apprenticed himself to a local organist who he hoped would teach him all he needed to know about music:

> The organist, however, was unwilling to take me for only a few months; I had to promise to stay two whole years. I did it, though he did not trouble himself to teach me very much beyond note reading and basic keyboard technique, as well as the violin and viola da gamba. The best part was that he gave me the responsibility of serving as organist in a village called Groß-Jenkwitz, where a new organ with pedals had recently been built, which was of great advantage to me as a practice instrument. At the same time, I diligently read books about music, which guided me along the proper path. That I was also expected to act as schoolmaster was a source of some discomfort, however, because some of the pupils were not much younger than I was.[19]

Johann Georg Hoffmann's apprenticeship experience was somewhat more positive:

> In my thirteenth year, because I was a weak little boy, I was sent shortly after Easter to begin a five-year apprenticeship with the organist Herr Quiel, who was paid a paltry tuition to take me in. He taught me to play all of the string and wind instruments, including trumpets and hunting horns, though these I abandoned as soon as I could, because of my feeble lungs.

Still, it was good to familiarize myself with their features. The evening hours, particularly during the winter, were spent examining writings on music, especially those by Werckmeister and Printz. Quiel did what he could to explain these texts to me and his two other apprentices. [. . .] When my teacher returned in 1714 from the Easter Fair in Breslau, he brought with him Johann Mattheson's *Neu-eröffnete Orchester* [1713], Johann David Heinichen's *Neu erfundene und gründliche Anweisung zu vollkommener Erlernung des General-Basses* [1711], and Reinhard Keiser's *Musikalische Land-Lust* [1714]. He gave us the first of these to read, and the second formed the basis of our figured bass training. The [*Neu-eröffnete Orchester*] pleased me so much because of its clear organization and all of the new things within (though I did not understand everything), that I pooled all of my money, begged the rest from my parents, and bought it from my teacher. I carried this little book with me day and night and read it so often that I came to know the text as well as I knew the catechism.[20]

An alternative to the apprenticeship path was to attend a choir school, of which the St. Thomas School in Leipzig was by far the most famous. Boys came from all over to audition, often with their fathers or mothers, in hopes of receiving full scholarships. Admission rested largely upon musical skill, as the school depended upon income and donations from wealthy Leipzig families, who appreciated the choir's services not just in church but also at weddings, funerals, and other celebrations. The choir members spent many hours each day performing and rehearsing for upcoming performances under the tutelage of the most accomplished musicians in Germany, most famously J. S. Bach.[21]

Although university training was not a prerequisite for professional musicians, many chose to spend a year or two studying theology or law. Those who anticipated musical careers tended not to have much disposable income. The Leipzig University student and future organist Johann Paul Kuntzen was obliged by financial circumstances to live in the *Paulinum*, a cheap dormitory where the food was an abomination and the rooms were situated in close proximity to the medical division's anatomy chambers, where human and animal body parts floated in preservative solutions or simply rotted in wooden cabinets.[22] Another resident found it impossible to stay in the Paulinum for more than one night: "The experience seemed no different to me than sleeping in a latrine. The smell prevented me from falling asleep, and it was so thick in my throat that I felt I might suffocate."[23] Kuntzen breathed this toxic air for several months before a local family took him in.[24]

The capstone of a musician's training was often a period of travel, following the journeyman model of other artisan professions. Visiting new cities offered one the opportunity to make connections with future colleagues, assist with performances at churches and courts, and familiarize oneself with a wide range of performance styles in the years before family and employment obligations curtailed one's mobility. This was particularly important for organists since instruments varied so much from church to church and city to city. As Bach's friend Jacob Adlung observed:

> One can learn to play figured bass, to fantasize, to perform chorales, and to read music notation from principles, and pick up the rest on one's own. But in playing the organ—particularly in matters of registration—there is a great deal that one has to learn through experience, and one can never amass all of the necessary knowledge in a single city, which is why it is important to seek that knowledge elsewhere.[25]

Young musicians—like young lawyers, preachers, bureaucrats, cooks, horsemen, and practitioners of myriad other professions—dreamed of attaining prestigious posts at the noble courts of the Holy Roman Empire. Georg Philipp Telemann wrote in 1718 that gaining "the grace of great lords, the courtesy of nobles, and the love and deep respect of other servants" in a court *Kapelle* was the best motivation for improving one's musical skills, "especially when one is still young enough to have the necessary fire for such undertakings."[26]

The leader of a court musical establishment ordinarily held the title of *Kapellmeister* (chapel master). He had under his direction all musical employees, most immediately the court chamber musicians. Only occasionally were celebrity musicians—particularly opera divas—better paid. Trumpeters and timpanists were absolutely indispensable at virtually all courts, and their services were required more often than those of most other musicians.[27] Members of the court chapel (*Hofkapelle*) were regularly called upon to entertain guests in concerts or at meals, in addition to providing music for religious services.

In the hierarchy of most courts, musicians were of relatively low rank. Even the kapellmeister was ordinarily consigned to the lower third of the ceremonial ranking system, behind the *Ceremonienmeister* (master of ceremonies), the *Hof-Jägermeister* (master of hunts), *Hofärtzten* (court medical doctors), and the *Bau-Director* (court architect). He usually outranked the *Küchenmeister* (master chef) the *Hof-Fechtmeister* (court fencing master), and the *Hoforganist* (court organist).[28] The official, salaried musicians were often supplemented by outsiders: local boys, journeymen, or sons of other court employees, whose skills and pay were often quite meager. Organists who received their salaries from town churches were sometimes brought in to perform at services in the court chapel or at assemblies,[29] and a few held dual appointments.[30]

Music was often performed privately for members of the ruling family. The works on offer ranged from elaborate concertos prepared for visiting dignitaries to simple spiritual songs that served as background music while a potentate kissed the cheeks of his grandchildren.[31] In 1710 Georg Friedrich Händel spent some time at the court in Hannover, where he was admired for being "so learned in music" and "surpassing everyone who has ever been heard in harpsichord-playing."[32] The contexts in which he performed are unclear, but Bach's former student Heinrich Nicholas Gerber, in the employ of Prince Günther of Schwarzburg-Sondershausen, was said to have "weekly performed at the harpsichord in two court assemblies, in addition to his duties performing in church on Sundays and during the week."[33]

A musician with an aptitude for diplomacy could sometimes attain non-musical appointments. Johann Christian Edelmann wrote that because his father "had an excellent alto voice and could play the lute well," he was appointed chamber musician to Duke Christian of Saxe-Weißenfels, but when the duke moved to Sangerhausen in 1711, he was promoted "to serve as court secretary."[34] H. N. Gerber, too, was obliged late in his career to take on a bureaucratic position. Much to his regret, this post required him to spend most of his time calculating bills and left him barely half-an-hour per day to practice the keyboard.[35]

Working at court was stressful because so much depended on political winds, which could abruptly shift. Telemann acknowledged that "at court one is worked too hard, the masters are not all music lovers, and one can all too easily fall into disfavor."[36] Johann Beer wrote of how musicians were mistreated at court:

> Today he must go there with the court, tomorrow somewhere else. Day or night, heavy gale, rain, or sunshine, it makes no difference. Today he must be at church, tomorrow at the table, the day after in the theatre [. . .]. The more excellent he is, the more he will be obliged to remain at the same rank at which he was hired, all the feathers plucked from his wings so that he cannot rise any higher [. . .]. He can hope for stipends for his children from city appointments (which is a great thing), but very seldom, if ever, from courts.[37]

Relationships between musicians and patrons at court were sharply asymmetrical; court musicians were at the mercy of the wild mood swings of inbred potentates, subjected to abuse of all kinds, and not always paid.[38] Musicians and other employees deemed unfaithful, recalcitrant, or simply too talkative could be interrogated, jailed, or worse.[39]

ર૦

The primary alternative to working for a court was working for a city. Talented keyboardists often aspired to become church organists. Some were awarded such positions on the basis of reputation alone.[40] Others were aided by family connections; it was not unusual for an elderly organist to request an "expectancy" that his son would take over upon his retirement or death.[41] In some cities, priority was given to candidates who promised to marry the widow or daughter of a deceased organist; this reduced the strain on municipal welfare rolls.[42] In other cities it was customary for public officials, including organists, simply to buy their positions; jobs were awarded to whomever among the qualified candidates offered the largest cash donations.[43] J. S. Bach himself was famously denied an organist post in Hamburg in 1720 because one of the other candidates displayed more virtuosity in dispensing reichstaler than he did at improvising preludes.[44]

Musical ability was not always foremost in the minds of committees charged with hiring organists. In 1725 a pastor in Neukirchen wrote that he and the rest of the committee had chosen a particular candidate not because he was a great musician—"We do not need an artist here"—but because he had clear handwriting, was an experienced teacher, behaved well, and was already beloved by the congregation.[45] Even those who held prestigious positions were often expected to serve in nonmusical capacities. When Johann Paul Kuntzen was appointed organist in 1732 at St. Mary's Church in Lübeck, he was simultaneously made the town's *Werckmeister*, which required him to keep track of church expenditures, look after the church building, and distribute salaries.[46] Other organists were responsible for waiting on preachers, preparing and delivering handwritten lists of the sick and shut-in so they might receive the prayers of the congregation, setting up communion tables, bringing candles to the altars, and filling baptismal fonts.[47]

For many of the most coveted organist positions, it was necessary to pass a rigorous audition. Unlike musicians today who are typically expected to perform previously written compositions, auditionees were expected in Bach's time to create new music on the spot. The following protocol, documenting an organ audition that took place at the St. Johannis Church in Lüneburg in 1737, includes not only the various challenges presented but also commentary on how one candidate came to terms with these challenges:

> The candidate will be asked to improvise for two minutes, moving from B-flat major to B minor before introducing and extemporizing upon the following theme:

Result: Instead of beginning in B-flat and ending in B minor, the candidate began in B minor and continued in that key for six minutes, revealing that he knew no more than what he had memorized in advance.

After this he was asked to play the chorale *Wir glauben all an einen Gott* [We All Believe in One God] in C-sharp minor. He then accompanied a singer performing the opera aria *Ihr tunkeln Schatten ihr* ["You Dark Shadows"]. He was subsequently asked to improvise on the fugue theme below:

The candidate was finally asked to improvise upon a chorale of his choice and present a fantasy of his own making.

Result: The first fugue theme was executed poorly, moving only through B minor and F-sharp minor, the other key areas not even touched upon. The chorale he began in C-sharp minor as asked, but because he could not handle the footwork in this key, he moved quickly to D minor, where he seemed more comfortable, and did quite well. The aria he accompanied poorly and played many wrong notes; he had no control of tempo so that the singer had to stop singing. He seems to be a poor student of figured bass. The fugue he did not even try to play, and instead closed with a fantasy, which brought more agony than pleasure to his listeners.[48]

This level of incompetence was apparently not unusual. Carl Philipp Emanuel Bach was among the examiners at a 1741 audition in Berlin at which it became clear that one of the finalists could not even read music.[49] But the fact that the demands remained consistently high suggests that successful candidates were able to meet them.[50]

The musical duties of organists varied somewhat from one locality to the next, but they shared foundational elements. The contract Johann Buttstedt signed when he became organist at Erfurt's *Predigerkirche* in 1693 was typical in requiring him to look after the organ, to let his superiors know if it needed any repairs, and to prevent others from playing or damaging it. He was to receive approval for all travel plans well in advance and "lead a devout, pious, calm and modest life, at all times avoiding invidious company and excessive drink."[51] Contractual details relating to his musical duties offer rare insight into the performance schedule of a professional organist in Bach's time:

He is to play the instrument—to the best of his understanding, knowledge, and conscience—on the mornings and afternoons of Sundays and Feast Days, after the primary sermon, on Saturdays or whenever Vespers services are held, and during weekday church services whenever celebratory music is required. He is to appear punctually and remain at his post until the end of the service, playing the organ as required. He is to accompany chorale singing on the portable reed organ [*Regal*] outside the church, and at the beginnings and ends of both school examination periods. He is not to allow any trouble, cold, or other obstacle to hinder him in performing his duties at the appointed times, except in case of emergency. Nor is he to ask another to stand in for him, but is rather to appear in person in every case, in order to honor God and bring praise to the Christian congregation [. . .]. He is also to perform once per year at the Festival of John the Baptist [June 24], in the afternoon following the service, using the entire organ, all registers and voices in a well sounding harmony, for half an hour, in order to demonstrate to the congregation how his skills had improved.[52]

Preludes and postludes offered organists the most regular opportunities to display their creativity. Johann Mattheson remarked that a musician has more freedom in a postlude than in a prelude because there was no time limit, suggesting that they relished such opportunities.[53] The contract Johann Andreas Leonhard signed when he was appointed organist in Kiel in 1733 offered some specific guidance based on bitter experience:

He is to accompany *Allein Gott in der Höh* (God Alone on High) and all other chorales sung on Sundays and Feast Days in the morning and afternoon services. During communion the organist is to prelude before the first chorale begins, which the cantor will then sing alone. If further chorales are necessary, the organist should play along with the second psalm and thereafter play in alternation [with the cantor]. It shall remain up to the organist whether he merely introduces the chorales after communion or accompanies them. Further, the organist is ordered never to prelude on the chorales without using their melodies, to avoid all unknown melodies, and to use only those that are familiar to the congregation. For short chorales, the entire verse should be performed; for longer chorales just the beginning of the melody.[54]

As noted here, communion offered organists another opportunity for musical display. Practices varied widely from city to city and church to church, but organists were frequently expected to provide appropriate background music as congregants took the holy sacrament. In 1736 two visitors described the atmosphere at a communion service at Leipzig's St. Nicholas Church for which J. S. Bach likely led the music:

Sunday, August 5, we were led to the large and beautiful St. Nicholas Church, where we witnessed the Lutheran worship from beginning to end, noting many similarities with papal [= Catholic] practices. Not only were the preachers dressed mostly in white choir shirts, but there were also two large wax candles on the altar, where people communed. Before the communion, they were blessed as one would be during a Catholic Mass. During communion the organ was played constantly, both with voices and with all manner of other instruments.[55]

Organists had to know how to use music to engineer the appropriate emotional tone for each moment in a church service. Mattheson suggested in 1739 that they take their cues from the texts of the Lutheran chorales upon which they improvised:

Because there are so many different church pieces and chorale tunes that contain widely different emotions, for example: exalted joy, quiet satisfaction, undisguised humility, moving melancholy, deep remorse, bitter pain, fervent longing, urgent desire, firm trust, faultless devotion, victorious generosity, tawdry contempt, holy defiance, etc. [. . .]. So a player must be sure that he knows the intended affect very well, and that he is able to express it clearly in his prelude. He must not invite his audience to cry when they should be joyful, or move anyone to laughter whose heart should rather be moved to contrition. Unfortunately, there have been many examples, noticed by almost no one, in which an organist who never really took the trouble to cultivate his creativity always confidently plays the same music he memorized as a youth, whether it is appropriate or not.[56]

Those who were uncomfortable improvising sometimes tried to cheat by simply rehashing materials they had culled from disparate sources. Lorenz Mizler, in his *Musikalischer Staarstecher* of 1740, offered some colorful commentary on the importance of presenting a coherent musical experience to the congregation:

A beautiful woman's face is not unappealing. The neck of a horse is not unnatural. A goat is nothing unusual. A fish tail is not disgusting. If a painter, however, decides to set a beautiful woman's face on a horse's neck, make the body like that of a goat, and the tail that of a fish, the resulting artwork is unappealing, unnatural, unusual, and disgusting. Is it any different when organists present all of their ideas on top of one another capriciously, borrowing one theme from a funeral cantata, one from a wedding ode, and mixing everything together indiscriminately? Truly it is something unnatural, unusual, disgusting, and—for those whose ears are governed by reason—unappealing. The irrational admirers of such artifices enflame the false ambitions and multiply the numbers of the artists guilty of these unnatural acts.[57]

The most consistent complaints about organists were that they did not intone the melody of chorale tunes long enough, so that the congregation had trouble finding the proper pitch, and that they dropped out and forced the congregation to sing *a cappella*. Such musical innovations, however well intentioned, tended to cause confusion and strife.[58] An organist in Glückstädt, Johann Conrad Rosenbusch, was attacked in 1718 for allegedly playing "very many completely unnecessary, indulgent, secular-sounding passages" that were deemed inappropriate for a service honoring God. After his superiors demanded that he play nothing more than an orderly chorale, he "annoyed and disturbed the congregation" the following week by "making creaks, rattles, and cries of misery with the organ."[59]

Other organists came into conflict with their superiors by setting sacred texts to tunes "with which farm girls might dance themselves to death in village inns."[60] It was acceptable to compose joyous arias to evoke joyful passages in the Bible, but musicians needed to check themselves to make sure they were not simply trying to "make themselves beloved in the galant world" by inciting their congregations to dance.[61] An anonymous author writing in 1742 described a substitute organist playing "an uppity passepied full of Polish phrases," hacking and racing around for nearly half an hour before finally intoning the chorale tune *Warum betrübst du dich mein Herz?* (Why, My Heart, Are You So Afflicted?):

> He then wildly fought his way with the entire instrument, making frightening leaps with his hands, his absurd and inappropriate progressions finally causing the congregation to fall silent, and, against their will, they were forced to sit and listen to this arrogant artist's machinations. Does this type of mania really honor our great God? Does it not defile, profane, and mock the sacred chorale tunes?[62]

At smaller churches, organists were responsible not only for accompanying worship services but also for training boy choristers to sing and preparing cantatas for performance every Sunday.[63] At larger churches, tasks like these were typically entrusted to a cantor. Of the two posts, that of the cantor was generally ranked higher, though the organist provided him with his chief source of musical support.[64] Given their structurally unequal relationships, tensions between cantors and organists sometimes ran high. The cantor was nominally more powerful, but an organist held at his fingertips the power to rudely bring whatever the cantor was doing to a brusque conclusion with a few massive chords from God's own instrument.[65]

❧

German archives are full of letters from both court and city musicians begging their employers for more money. When an organist in Kiel who had served for thirty years asked for a salary increase, he reminded his superiors that his predecessor had died 700 reichstaler in debt and observed that he would likely suffer a similar fate, since it was impossible to support his wife and child on such a paltry income. The position he held required him to serve not only as organist but also as church scribe, a task for which he received five reichstaler per year. The scribal work, however, took many hours and he calculated that he could earn three times as much if he spent those same hours teaching privately. Serious illness could mean financial ruin for an organist, and death could thrust his family into abject poverty.[66]

Musicians routinely supplemented their salaries with ancillary sources of income. Many earned additional funds by playing weddings and baptisms, and teaching Latin, arithmetic, or the catechism. Some built folding wooden chairs onto their instruments and rented them out for use during church services.[67] Those with university experience sometimes offered spiritual, medical, or legal advice for hire.[68] Less-well-educated organists found nonmusical means of supplementing their income, though town councils were known to step in if they felt the ancillary work might embarrass the church; organists were forbidden in some places from farming, raising animals, gardening, threshing, or from selling candles, twine, beer, or brandy.[69] It was important that leading musicians not be associated with work that was seen as demeaning, lest it damage their reputations and, by extension, the reputations of those who had hired them.

The most common means through which musicians earned ancillary income, and endeared themselves to the communities that supported them, was teaching. While organists frequently tutored pupils in nonmusical subjects such as mathematics, history, and theology, the most lucrative teaching was musical in nature. In Bach's time, keyboard students were given hourly private lessons between two and four times per week. The going rate of two or three groschen per hour enabled organists to supplement their income significantly, depending on how many pupils they could attract. Bach's distant cousin in Weimar, Johann Gottfried Walther, wrote that in good times he regularly taught fifteen to eighteen students.[70] A former Bach student named Johann Gotthilf Ziegler allegedly had to turn away thirty-three potential students in 1730 because he was already busy teaching from six every morning until nine every evening.[71] Most organists earned far more income from teaching than they did from performing. Professional connections with churches and courts were valuable not so much for the salaries they offered, which were often meager, as for the prestige and visibility they accorded, which in turn enabled organists to attract more students and charge higher fees.

Teaching was also the primary means by which organists and other professional musicians engaged socially with the communities that surrounded them. The relationships they cultivated with students and their families often went beyond the strictly commercial. A sense of intimacy could be expected given the many hours teachers and students spent in close proximity, but the emotional nature of music itself played a role too. A former Bach student named Hinrich Conrad Kreising wrote the following poem in 1742 upon the death of one of his pupils, Catharina Louise Müller, the wife of a school rector:

> Her joyful face I still can see inside my mind,
> When I would play and she to listening was inclined,
> She heard no other sound, no strange noise could upset her,
> Entranced by music's power, she liked nothing better
> Than sitting nearly still for hours at a time,
> Her eyes would sparkle, radiating joy sublime.
> I'll think now on those days with pain and disbelief!
> In lieu of pleasure and instead of the acclaim
> She did on such occasions boundlessly proclaim,
> The music I played then now brings me only grief.[72]

The bonds between Herr Kreising and Frau Müller, and by extension between other professional musicians and their students, were rooted not only in the ability of music to "entrance" and offer "joy sublime." Keyboard lessons offered a measure of emotional fulfillment less characteristic of lessons in theology, mathematics, or Latin.

The death of an organist could be devastating to the community he served. The obituary of Johann Adam Münzer, an organist in Neustadt an der Aisch, is revealing in this regard:

> He instructed children very diligently and with great gentleness, and was much beloved by them. He was very humble, agreeable, dutiful, and pious, but also of a spirited humor. He could sing in a variety of different vocal ranges, accompanying himself on the spinet, so that one would have thought that a large number of singers were present. For this reason he was welcome at all parties, and made himself useful elsewhere as well. When advanced age prevented the old organist, Herr Haueißen, from playing the keyboard, Herr Münzer was made his assistant, and from then on he was responsible for the organ in church, an instrument he completely understood and could artfully play, and he did this in a praiseworthy manner for four years. On April 3, 1706—the night before Easter Sunday—he died at age thirty-six of a hot stomach fever, leaving behind eight small children, which he had with his wife, Margaretha Theobald. On the third day of Easter, in his honor, a solemn and extraordinarily well-attended funeral sermon and procession were held in the church; there was general sorrow and many tears were shed. A few weeks before his death, mysterious organ sounds were heard from

the church, and Herr Münzer was called to see what instrument was being played and by whom. He went in and checked the organ but found nothing. A few people who lived near the church claimed that the music they had heard was none other than a funeral song, *Hertzlich thut mich verlangen* [My Heart Yearns for a Peaceful End], though the matter was never resolved. In recognition of his service, Herr Münzer's widow and poor orphaned children were provided an allotment of grain and a rent-free apartment.[73]

Though Münzer's relationship with his community was rooted in commerce—he earned his living from performing and teaching music—the tears shed at his "extraordinarily well-attended" funeral reveal the emotional bonds that grew out of this relationship. The sense of community that made his death so poignant no doubt also sustained him in life. His compensation was not only financial but also spiritual. The tale of ghostly premonition the people of Neustadt an der Aisch told one another in the wake of Münzer's death was a testament to the intensity of their pain; it comforted them to believe that this horrible event was somehow part of God's plan. But the story is also a testament to their understanding of music as a mysterious force in the universe. More than bakers, butchers, or lawyers, professional musicians were expected to interface with that which was ultimately incomprehensible.

It was the irrational character of music's appeal that gave professional musicians a bad name. The labor of farmers, ranchers, and physicians was rational in the sense that it promoted survival; it was unimpeachably valuable. The value of music, by contrast, was ephemeral and therefore more dubious. For many of Bach's contemporaries, music itself was a galanterie that had no merit beyond refreshing the spirits between bouts of more substantive work. It was permissible in the context of worship, but even here it was not strictly necessary, and some believers prided themselves on doing without. The only members of society who depended on music for survival were professional musicians. Like tightrope walkers and marmot trainers, their existence was secured through the provision of superfluous services.

For musicians and those who supported them, music's inability to promote survival was a source not of shame but rather of pride. Those who pursued musical careers were frustrated by the low remuneration, but they valued being able to spend their days doing what they most enjoyed. More than practitioners of most other professions, musicians were encouraged to create and thereby to develop themselves personally. Music offered an opportunity to grapple with mysterious forces of expression and meaning that did not wholly submit to rational analysis.

CHAPTER II

The Daily Life of an Organist

In an autobiography written not long before his death in 1859, the world-famous violinist and composer Louis Spohr described his early musical training as follows:

> I took up my studies in music and other subjects with alacrity. Violin lessons were given to me by the chamber musician Herr Kunisch, a thorough and friendly teacher, for whom I have much to thank. Not so friendly was my harmony and counterpoint teacher, an elderly organist named Hartung, and I still remember how, shortly after beginning my studies, he once angrily flew in my face when I showed him some early attempts at composition. "There will be plenty of time for that; first you have to learn something!" After a few months, he himself encouraged me to try my hand at composition but then corrected my attempts mercilessly, crossing out many of the ideas I felt were so magnificent and thereby causing me to lose all interest in showing him anything further. My lessons came to an end not long thereafter, when the old man became too ill to teach. He remains the only music theory teacher I ever had.[1]

Spohr had already achieved international fame by the time he wrote these words, and he chose them to highlight his autodidactic genius. He understood himself as a Romantic rebelling against the strictures of eighteenth-century tradition. His teacher, Herr Hartung, who died in 1800, was the embodiment of that oppressive old world.

But Carl August Hartung was much more than a pedant who once brushed elbows with a child prodigy. He was also an organist and teacher, a colleague and friend, a husband and father. His life was rich and varied, animated by an abiding love for music, particularly that of J. S. Bach. Hartung's career was typical of most musicians of his era in that he achieved neither fame nor fortune. His relatively ordinary life, however, is extraordinarily well documented. From 1752 to 1765, he kept a detailed account book, bound in green leather, which is preserved today in Braunschweig's City Archive.[2] On its 358 pristine pages, he recorded nearly all of the financial transactions he made between ages twenty-nine and forty-two. No other document offers such a wealth of information about the daily life of a musician in eighteenth-century Germany. The present chapter uses this previously unknown source to explore the ways in which Hartung, and by extension other professional musicians of his time, went about their daily lives. Although the records are financial, they offer insight into the many forms of nonmonetary compensation that motivated men like Hartung to pursue musical careers.

૨₰

Little is known about Carl August Hartung's early life. He entered the world on October 13, 1723, in Harzgerode, the eldest of six children born to Albertina Charlotta Hartung (née Schmid) and Johann Christoph Hartung, a brewer.[3] The family was Calvinist. At age eleven he was a student in the second grade class of cantor Johann Nicolaus Schroeter, who probably provided some early musical instruction.[4] It is likely that he also studied music with his maternal uncle, Johann Christoph Schmid, a provincial judge (*Landrichter*) known to have collected keyboard works by J. S. Bach.[5] A surviving manuscript of a "Præludium" by Händel was begun by Schmid and completed by a young Hartung, who clearly attempted to model his music handwriting on that of his uncle.[6]

When Hartung began his account book, on January 2, 1752, he was twenty-nine years old and living in Cöthen, the residential city of the princes of Anhalt-Cöthen. From 1717 until 1723, Bach himself had served here as kapellmeister to Prince Leopold. Upon Leopold's death in 1728 the territory had come into the possession of his brother, August Ludwig, who remained in power until his own death in 1755, after which it was ruled by his son, Karl Georg Lebrecht. The princely palace, surrounded by gardens of exotic fruit trees, was by far the most impressive structure in town. Cöthen's five thousand residents lived in around six hundred houses, which, unlike those in larger cities, were built low to the ground.[7] It was only a few years before Hartung began his account book that home owners were first required to hang lanterns outside their doors to illuminate the streets.[8] By way of comparison, Leipzig had installed street lanterns and a team of twenty men to tend them nearly half a century earlier.[9]

Hartung may have been drawn to Cöthen by his younger brother, Johann Christoph Marcus, who worked as a chef in the princely palace.[10] In any case, he seems to have arrived not long before beginning his account book. During the first two months of 1752, he taught no keyboard lessons, whereas beginning in March he taught virtually without interruption for the next eight years. The fact that he had no students in January and February of 1752 makes it likely that he was new in town.

Hartung's primary institutional affiliation in Cöthen was with the local orphanage, where he was paid a modest salary to serve as one of two instructors (*Informator*). He also held an unpaid position as cantor at the palace chapel (*Schlosskapelle*). The bulk of his income came from private teaching. He offered instruction in mathematics, Latin, history, and religion in his apartment at the orphanage and keyboard lessons in the homes of Cöthen's musically inclined residents.

Hartung's primary ambition in life was to become a full-time professional organist. He wished to obtain a post that would enable him to earn enough money to marry and support a family. Work at the orphanage paid the bills, but he must have regarded his time here as transitional, a way station on the path to achieving his long-term goal.

Cöthen's orphanage had been established in 1723 by Bach's patron, Prince Leopold, as a means of educating children whose parents had died or for some other reason were unable to provide for them.[11] Hartung's pupils were between six and sixteen years old, and of both Lutheran and Calvinist persuasions. They numbered around forty, judging from the number of vests and shoes the institution ordered each year.[12] The boys were to enter a profession to which they felt themselves suited, though they were particularly encouraged to become rural schoolteachers, which were then in short supply. The girls were expected to go into service as maids in the homes of wealthy families; they spent their days mastering skills such as knitting, sewing, cooking, and cleaning. Both boys and girls received instruction in reading, writing, arithmetic, and the catechism. The children paid no fees, but whatever free time remained to them was spent in productive pursuits intended to benefit the institution financially: the boys generated money through choral singing on the street, the girls through making and selling textiles.

As one of two male instructors, Hartung was charged with instructing his pupils for four hours per day, taking them on walks outdoors, leading them in prayer, and keeping them quiet in church.[13] He probably used a book in his library—Martin Hensel's "Evangelical Heart-Awakener" (*Evangelischer Hertzens-Wecker*)—as a guide for helping him turn unruly boys into pious village schoolmasters. Perhaps Hartung, following Hensel, told his pupils that becoming a teacher required an unusually high level of personal discipline: "Not many of you should become teachers, my fellow believers, because you know that we who teach will be judged more severely than others."[14] Hartung himself took this biblical paraphrase to heart, working diligently to earn the respect of his pupils, his colleagues, and his community.

Hartung enjoyed cultivating his mind through extensive reading. Though he owned at least one board game—a set of checkers, featuring turned-metal playing pieces—he seems to have spent most of his leisure hours with his books. Many of those he acquired in Cöthen were analytical works of theology,[15] but he also bought books on geography,[16] arithmetic,[17] history,[18] and medicine,[19] as well as works of literature by C. F. Gellert[20] and Ludwig von Holberg.[21] He frequented the bookshops of Johann Christoph Cörner[22] and Thomas Stückel, "an Italian Catholic who deals in small wares,"[23] and had his books bound in cardboard or leather.[24] He liked to remain informed about current events and subscribed to a wide variety of newspapers, not only from the region but also from Berlin, Halle, Hamburg, and Altona, as well as a periodical titled the "Newly Opened World and State Theater" (*Neu-eröffnetes Welt- und Staats-Theatrum*), which promised "news of war, peace, and government from all parts of the world, particularly Europe."[25]

Hartung furnished his apartment in the orphanage in accordance with the image he wished to project. His living room was heated during the winter by a fireplace, for which he had to purchase wood, a grate, and tongs, and pay a chimney sweep to clean. The apartment had three windows, all of which were protected by metal grates. At night the rooms were lit by tallow or wax candles, or a tin whale-oil lamp. He paid local woodworkers to build him a bed and a large secretary cabinet with desk and commode.[26] He covered his walls with two large mirrors and nearly forty copper engravings, including representations of the months of the year. He also hung framed portraits of Princess Albertine of Anhalt-Bernburg and Cöthen's Calvinist pastor, Christian Ludwig Schlichter. His rooms contained two flowerpots and small, practical items such as scissors for trimming wax candles, a spittoon, an hourglass, a magnifying glass, a mousetrap, and a flyswatter. Figurines of a lion, a camel, a rabbit, and a violin adorned his apartment, and three plaster dogs sat upon his writing desk.[27]

Hartung and the guests he invited into his home snacked on marzipan, fruits (lemons and several different varieties of apples), Italian nuts, pretzels, hazelnuts, pancakes, honey cakes, and sheep's cheese. They drank tea from cups of blue and yellow Meißner porcelain, pinching clumps of white sugarloaf with sugar tongs and stirring them into their tea with silver spoons. Hartung paid a "night watchman and grave digger" to scour his tin plates, bowls, and the canisters he used to contain tea, coffee, and milk.[28] He smoked a range of tobacco products, from snuff he kept in a red-lacquered box, to tobacco stuffed in pipes coated in silver and stored in fancy cases. He sometimes splurged on hemp tobacco known as canaster (*Knaster*), which cost twice as much as ordinary tobacco and likely induced some of the psychotropic effects associated with marijuana.[29]

Hartung cultivated a galant appearance. His account book includes payments of twelve groschen every three months to Wilhelm Gottfried Scheibe, a local barber-surgeon; the fixed rate covered hair trimming and face shaving at regular intervals.[30] The haircuts were designed to simply "accommodate" his hair since Hartung, like every other man of his time and social class, wore a powdered wig in public. He owned two pairs of black leather pants (*Lederhosen*) and also a hat, which he regularly had "blackened" to maintain water resistance.[31] The woven stockings he wore were of wool, fulled to remove impurities. He bought a new pair of shoes about twice each year and regularly had older pairs resoled. Sometimes he paid to have thick horse or ox leather added to the heels. He also purchased elegant fabrics such as white Silesian canvas, *Barchent* (a wool/linen blend), white flannel, black silk with colorful flowers, wool canvas with blue flowers, taffeta with gold flecks, and *Calamanque*, an extremely costly shiny wool fabric with a cross-hatch pattern.[32] He regularly hired local tailors to make the fabric he purchased into overshirts, undershirts, sleeves, and cuffs. Goldsmiths constructed cufflinks for him, as well as a belt with a silver buckle and buttons of silver, mother of pearl, and combed wool (*Casieng*).[33] Hartung liked to carry a walking stick with a colorful, decorative band around the handle. When he needed to look his best, he wore white leather gloves, red handkerchiefs, and a silver pocket watch worth an astonishing twenty-seven reichstaler.

The value of Hartung's pocket watch was substantially more than his annual salary at the orphanage, which amounted to twenty-two reichstaler.[34] Perhaps he himself had saved for years to purchase it. Perhaps it was a gift from a wealthy patron, or a family heirloom. In any case, he did not feel the need to pawn it for food, clothing, or shelter. The watch is indicative of how Hartung wished to present himself. It expressed not so much what he was but what he wished to become: a comfortably situated, tastefully dressed, God-fearing intellectual and musician.

Hartung's colleagues at the orphanage included a maid named Magdalena, who earned a meager salary (ten reichstaler) for keeping things tidy and

Table 9. Carl August Hartung's Income and Expenses in Cöthen, 1752–1760

(All figures in groschen unless otherwise noted)

Total income over 8.5 years (January 1752 to July 1760) = 17,806

Average income per year = 2,095 [= 87 reichstaler, 7 groschen]

Non-music-related income = 10,155	57%

Salary at the orphanage = 4,488	25.2%
Non-musical teaching = 5,460	30.7%
Non-musical scribal services = 60	0.3%
Gifts = 147	0.8%
From pupils = 89	
From others = 58	

Music-related income = 7,651	43%

Offerings at the Palace Chapel = 136	0.8%
Music lessons = 5,215	29.3%
Composing = 1,178	6.6%
Performing = 741	4.2%
Baptisms = 510	
Weddings = 228	
Organ Demonstration = 3	
Music sales = 233	1.3%
Prints = 82	
Music scribal services = 119	
Unknown = 32	
Instrument sales and repairs = 148	0.8%
Sales = 42	
Tuning = 90	
Repairs = 16	

Total expenses over 8.5 years = 15,058

Average expenses per year = 1,775 [= 73 reichstaler, 23 groschen]

Non-music-related expenses = 14,483	96.2%

Household Items = 2,844	18.9%
Art (paintings, figurines, etc.) = 109	
Kitchen-related expenses = 362	
Lighting = 89	
Household (unspecified) = 1,325	
Tobacco = 117	
Firewood = 8	
Writing-related expenses = 340	
Paper = 303	
Pencils/feathers/feather knives = 12	
Sealing wax/wax stamp = 25	
Other = 494	
Textiles = 1,282	8.5%
Canvas = 660	
Yarn = 12	
Flannel = 19	
Buttons = 339	
Other = 252	

Table 9. Continued

Tailoring = 546	3.6%
Pants = 195	
Tailoring = 83	
Repair = 112	
Shirts = 58	
Tailoring = 51	
Repair = 7	
Nightgown = 5	
Undershirts = 24	
Other = 264	
Accessories = 2,053	13.6%
Pocket watches (incl. repairs) = 780	
Buckles = 27	
Belts = 4	
Gloves (white leather) = 10	
Hat = 99	
Handkerchiefs = 66	
Stockings = 380	
Shoes = 687	
Entertaining Guests = 111	0.7%
Food = 216	1.4%
Gifts = 2,532	16.8%
Friends/Relatives = 1,837	
Hannichen = 233	
Baptisms = 324	
Tips = 120	
Charitable donations = 18	
Hygiene/Medicine = 426	2.8%
Barbering/shaving = 354	
Blood-letting = 52	
Other = 20	
Travel = 378	2.5%
Newspapers = 320	2.1%
Book-related expenditures = 885	5.9%
Books = 662	
Bindings = 223	
Printing services = 42	0.3%
Postage for letters and packages = 76	0.5%
Unspecified bills = 2772	18.4%
Music-related expenses = 575	3.8%
Music equipment (strings, rastra, rosin, etc.) = 75	0.5%
Sheet music = 500	3.3%
Manuscript = 62	
Printed = 438	

leading instruction of the girls and Johann Jakob Rindfleisch, the manager (*Inspektor*) of the orphanage, who earned a very large salary (100 and later 150 reichstaler). Between 1752 and 1756, Rindfleisch paid him a total of more than five reichstaler for giving sixty-four hours of keyboard lessons to his son. Hartung's closest colleague was the other male instructor, a certain

Herr Hütter, who earned the same annual salary (twenty-two reichstaler).[35] Presumably, the two men discussed curriculum plans and teaching schedules, but their ties went beyond the professional. Hartung purchased Bibles as well as a version of the Song of Solomon in verse from Hütter.[36] In 1758, Hartung "was laid low by a hard sickness." While recuperating, he bought four doses of "vital powder" (*Pulv: Vital*) and paid twelve groschen to the orphanage maid, Magdalena, for "looking after me in my illness."[37] He eventually recovered completely, but his colleague, Herr Hütter, was not so fortunate; he died the same year, presumably of the same ailment.[38] He was replaced by a certain Herr Voigt, with whom Hartung also cultivated a friendly relationship. Voigt sold him a book of theatrical comedies, borrowed a few reichstaler, and studied the keyboard with him for more than a year.[39]

It was probably through his boss Herr Rindfleisch that Hartung was offered the opportunity to serve as cantor at Cöthen's palace chapel. The position was paid only through modest free-will offerings,[40] but it offered him the opportunity to display his musical skills in a public setting.[41] Among Hartung's possessions were twelve identical baskets, presumably used to collect donations from congregants.[42] A request the court chaplain made in 1759 to visiting preachers offers some insight into Hartung's duties at the chapel: "Please let me know of your arrival one day before [the worship service] so that the palace cantor can pick up the hymns."[43] One presumes that Hartung performed arrangements of these hymns during the services, either at the organ or with diverse vocal and instrumental forces. He made assorted references in his account book to paraphernalia for stringed instruments: two violin bridges,[44] a number of violin mutes purchased from a comb-maker,[45] rosin,[46] and strings for a "David's Harp."[47] At the beginning of his time in Cöthen he owned a cello, which he later agreed to sell for two reichstaler, though he was frustrated to receive only one reichstaler and eighteen groschen from the buyer.[48] Hartung seems to have played the organ regularly. Every New Year's Day, he gave a gratuity of between eight pfennige and two groschen to Martin Bettzieche, the man who pumped the bellows of the palace chapel's organ.[49] On other occasions, Hartung loaned Bettzieche a few groschen, carefully recording in each case the date of the loan, the amount, and the date of reimbursement.[50] In 1756 Hartung himself was given a tip of three groschen by "a stranger, to whom I had to give a tour of the organ" in the *Schlosskapelle*.[51]

During the first years documented by the account book, Hartung performed regularly at baptisms and weddings at the palace chapel. He did not, however, relish this work, because dealing with the clientele was sometimes aggravating. Of the sixty-two baptism services for which he provided music between 1752 and 1760, slightly more than half were for the children of enlisted soldiers (*Musquetiers, Grenadiers, Hajduks*). He usually charged the parents of such children six groschen, though the fee went up for those employed by the court: lackeys, cooks, and servants paid eight to twelve groschen, while secretaries, advisors, and military officers paid sixteen to twenty-four groschen. Occasionally, the fee was increased for other reasons. After having provided music at the baptism of the child of "Eisenberg, the equerry's lackey," Hartung noted in the account book that the father and mother "had been found in dishonor [*Unehren*], and married just fourteen days before the child was born." Following the standard practice of the day, he charged the errant couple twelve groschen instead of the usual six.[52]

Each wedding in the palace chapel generally brought Hartung eight to twelve groschen.[53] Here, too, most of those who hired him were soldiers. Only occasionally did he perform at the weddings of couples who could afford larger fees—for example, a cook and a "chamber consultant" (*Cammer Consulent*).[54] Getting paid by the military men was sometimes a hassle. Next to a 1754 wedding record, he added the following note: "[I received] 4 groschen from the Grenedier Sergeant Pillgram, for the wedding. I was due 8, but he refused to give it to me."[55] Following this negative experience, Hartung avoided weddings. His performances at baptisms briefly surged around this time, perhaps in order to compensate for the missing wedding income, but then dropped off sharply too, as shown in table 10.

Table 10. Carl August Hartung's Baptism and Wedding Performances

Year	Baptisms	Weddings
1752	15	5
1753	12	4
1754	12	6
1755	21	—
1756	—	—
1757	—	1
1758	1	—
1759	1	2
1760	—	—

Hartung restricted his wedding and baptism performances after 1755 to those of prestigious patrons who could pay high fees. The money he earned from providing this service for those of lower standing was evidently not worth the trouble. Like many organists of the era, he probably felt that he was not accorded enough respect on such occasions. Bickering with enlisted men over a few groschen was degrading; he preferred to forego the income and protect his pride.

Perhaps it was his performances at the palace chapel that earned Hartung commissions from Cöthen's Calvinist School (*Reformierte Schule*). Twice per year, the rector, August Ernst Renthe, invited him to compose new music for a school event, typically a cantata around the New Year (*Neue-Jahrs Cantata*) and a ceremonial work (*Actus Music*) in August. He was ordinarily paid quite well on such occasions—between two and six reichstaler—though he also had to cover some significant costs associated with the productions; the paper alone could cost sixteen groschen.[56] On some occasions it was also difficult to collect the money he had been promised. Hartung noted in his account book that his fee for the 1757 New Year's Cantata had been four reichstaler but that he had received only three.[57] In 1758 he was offered ten reichstaler for the *Actus Music* but noted that he had endured "a lot of vexation and annoyance to get the money."[58] As in the case of the weddings and baptisms, the frustration likely stemmed less from the financial loss than from the feeling that his work was unappreciated. He felt passionately that providing music was a valuable service, and he was sensitive to perceived slights.

It is no coincidence that Hartung's closest friends were musicians. Working as Palace Cantor brought him into contact with members of the Cöthen court cappella. Emanuel Heinrich Gottlieb Freytag, a violinist who had performed decades earlier under J. S. Bach's direction, paid Hartung one reichstaler to copy a set of chorales for him in 1759. Hartung himself commissioned the princely bassoonist, Carl Ludwig Tourlee—son of Bach's former bassoonist Johann Christoph Tourlee—to copy thirty-four sheets of music in 1752 and two cantatas in 1753.[59]

Hartung's closest colleague at the palace chapel was the organist, Bernhard Christian Kayser.[60] Kayser was a native of Cöthen who had studied with J. S. Bach as a teenager in the early 1720s and then followed him to Leipzig, enrolling at the university in 1724. He had copied manuscripts of at least two cantatas for Bach (BWV 154, 186) as well as keyboard works such as the *Inventions and Sinfonias* (BWV 771–801), the *Well Tempered Clavier*, Book I (BWV 846–869), the *French Suites* (BWV 812–819), and the *English Suites* (BWV 806–811). Kayser's manuscript of the *English Suites* was prepared with the composer's help.

After concluding his studies with Bach in 1729, Kayser had returned to Cöthen, where he had served for years as "princely commissary as well as local court and government lawyer" (*fürstl. Anhältl. Commissarius, wie auch Hof- und Regierungs Advocat*).[61] He received payments of one hundred reichstaler per year to play chamber music and organ in the palace chapel. He remained in this post throughout the 1730s and 1740s but in 1753 his patron—Prince August Ludwig von Anhalt-Cöthen, an unstable hypochondriac who refused to see anyone, even his own children, for months at a time[62]—abruptly fired all of the court musicians. Kayser retained his position, though his salary was reduced by half, from one hundred to just fifty reichstaler per year.[63]

Immediately after this disastrous development, Kayser sold Hartung a large number of books on music theory, probably in an effort to shore up his finances. The books Hartung bought included portions of Lorenz Mizler's *Musicalische Bibliothek*, Niedt's *Generalbassschule*, Mattheson's *Der vollkommene Capellmeister* and one of his *Orchester* books, as well as Scheibe's *Critischer Musicus*.[64] From Kayser, Hartung was also able to acquire seven cantatas by Christoph Foerster and a bound set of secular cantatas by an unnamed composer (or composers), as well as unspecified *Carmina* and *Musical[ien]*. At some point Hartung also acquired Kayser's manuscript of Bach's *Inventions and Sinfonias*.[65] In 1757 Hartung recorded a payment of two groschen "to the commissary Kayser for the Bach cantatas."[66] The extremely low price may suggest that these manuscripts were rented rather than purchased. Clearly the friendship between these two men was founded upon their mutual love for music, particularly that of J. S. Bach. Hartung was no doubt eager to hear Kayser's stories about his years studying under their recently deceased hero.

Kayser died in April 1758, around the time Hartung himself became seriously ill, and his colleague Herr Hütter died. Following his recovery, he took pains to maintain a friendly relationship with Kayser's family. In 1759 his account book records payments to "Kayser for neck scarves with jewels and little coral stones," "the orphan boy Kayser for two pairs of ear muffs," and "to the orphan boy Kayser for making one neck scarf."[67] The boy in question was Kayser's fifteen-year-old son, Marcus Bernhard Ludwig. Having lost both parents, he may have resided in Cöthen's orphanage. In any event, given that Hartung never purchased neck scarves or ear muffs on any other occasion, he must have done so in order to support his deceased friend's son. The friendship of these two men, rooted in a mutual admiration of J. S. Bach, endured even in death.

Hartung was known among local families not only as an orphanage instructor and a musician but also as the head of a "corner school" (*Win-kelschule*). Non-orphans came several days per week to Hartung's lodgings for instruction in arithmetic, German, Latin, and the catechism.[68] Their parents were generally day laborers, cellar workers, horsemen, coachmen, messengers, lackeys, chamber servants, or soldiers, but Hartung also taught the sons and daughters of craftsmen, such as hat makers, shoemakers, tailors, printers, court carpenters, and bakers.[69] Standard tuition was eight groschen for three months of group instruction. A small number of his pupils—for example, the son of a court and chamber advisor (*Hoff- und Cammer Rath*)—came from more-affluent families and paid two or three times as much for private tutoring.[70] Some of the less-affluent students paid not in cash but in equivalent goods. In exchange for instructing the daughter of a metal worker, for example, he received a fireplace grate.[71]

Much of the teaching Hartung did was intended to help girls pass their communion examinations.[72] He probably took as his manual in this endeavor a book in his library, Gotthilf August Laurentius's 1731 "Guide to Raising Christian Youth" (*Anweisung zu Christl. Erziehung der Jugend*), which emphasized the positive influence of such teaching: parents would be more proud of their children, children would eventually thank their parents for insisting on the measure of discipline required, and society in general would benefit from having more docile and conscientious citizens.[73] Because this type of instruction had a clear goal—formal admission into the community of Christian believers—the pupils had a palpable sense of accomplishment and relief when they achieved it. Hartung's grateful pupils and their parents visited his apartment, where he served them coffee, milk, eggs, zwieback, pickled vegetables, and wine.[74] The new communicants presented him with a diverse array of gifts, including a fine beaver hat, a pair of Moroccan leather pants, and a purse with silver lace.[75]

Not all of Hartung's teaching experiences ended so well. When he was seriously ill in 1758, he could not work for six weeks. His teaching income for that quarter amounted to just seventy-six groschen (as opposed to 112 groschen for the previous quarter and 154 groschen for the following quarter). While he was recovering, some of his students transferred to other schools, and Hartung's anger at having been abandoned fairly bristles from the pages of his account book: "The following students went to a different school and thus cheated me out of half a quarter's tuition: Grundmann, and the four children of Kersten, the baker."[76] One senses that the loss of income—a total of one reichstaler—was less significant than the injury to Hartung's pride. As in the case of the frustrating wedding and baptism experiences, he likely had the distinct impression he had been disrespected by social inferiors.

※

The private teaching that Hartung found most rewarding was musical in nature. He earned approximately 30 percent of his income from providing keyboard lessons. Beyond the financial benefits, this was work that was close to his heart. If he was ever able to attain a full-time position as an organist, he fully expected to give up many of the ancillary sources of income, such as walking orphans to church and teaching the children of bakers to read. Keyboard teaching, however, was an activity he no doubt expected to continue throughout his life.

Hartung's standard rate for keyboard lessons in Cöthen was two groschen per hour. Ordinarily he was paid retrospectively, and the payments generally covered one month or one quarter. Sometimes students paid for a specific number of hours (typically twelve, twenty-four, or forty-eight), which could be stretched over longer or shorter time spans as desired. A certain Monsieur Böttcher, for example, paid him four reichstaler "for 48 hours of lessons on the keyboard" on five separate occasions, but the payments were separated by intervals of between three and six months.[77] Students typically had keyboard lessons for two to four hours per week, but this also varied from case to case. Giesela Friederica Gerlach, for example, paid one reichstaler at regular one-month intervals "for 12 hours of lessons on the keyboard" in 1753, 1754, and 1755: an average of three one-hour lessons per week. In 1756, however, these payments dwindled to once every two or three months: just one or two hours per week. Finally, toward the end of that year, Hartung recorded the final stage in this downward trajectory, noting that Mademoiselle Gerlach "has now quit completely."[78]

Table 11 presents what is known about the identities of Hartung's keyboard students in Cöthen. The majority were boys between ages twelve and sixteen. Most, if not all, were unmarried at the time of instruction.[79] Some studied in hopes of pursuing musical careers, and at least two eventually obtained music-related posts.[80] Others initially planned musical careers but later changed their minds. Hartung noted in his account book that sixteen-year-old Johann Gottlieb Gebhard quit the keyboard "because he will become a button maker" (*weil er ein Knopfmacher wird*).[81] The causal relationship suggested by the word "because" reveals that choosing to become a professional button maker was a logical reason to break off a course of study in music.

Gebhard the future button maker is typical of Hartung's male keyboard students in that he came from relatively modest circumstances. The fathers of his other students were schoolteachers, brewers, and farmers. Hartung consistently referred to these boys by their last names only—for example, "Fitzau," "Gebhard," and "Geißler." The orphans who studied music with him were likewise referred to by their last names, though with the additional designation *Waisenknabe* (orphan boy)—"Waisenknabe Allihn."

A few of Hartung's male keyboard students were of more elevated social status. This group included two sons of a court administrator named

Table 11. Carl August Hartung's Keyboard Students in Cöthen, 1752–60

Hartung's Designation	Name	Dates	Age	Hours	Family (S=Self, F=Father, H=Husband)
Schulmeister Allihn in Elderitz sein Sohn	Allihn, Johann Heinrich	1758–60	12~16	148	Schoolmaster (F), Cantor (S)
Waisenknabe Allihn	Allihn	1759	≤16	36	Orphan (S)
Bieler	Bieler, Lebrecht Gottfried	1755	∞1763	31	Chancellory Assistant (F)
Monsieur Böttger	Böttger	1753–54	?	240	?
Frau Cantzeley Rath Clæpius	Clæpius, Augusta Friederica	1754	24	31	Merchant, Chancellory Advisor (H)
Jungfer Erxleben aus Badegast	Erxleben, Christiana Marie Regine	1756	13	27	Bailiff (F), Bureaucrat (H)
Fitzau	Fitzau, Johann Philipp?	1758–59	13–14	132	Baker (F)?
Gebhardt	Gebhard, Johann Gottlieb	1759–60	15–16	80	Weaver (F), Button Maker (S)
Kleiner Geißler	Geißler, Carl Heinrich Christian	1752–53	12–13	129	Cup Bearer (F)
Jungfer Gerlach	Gerlach, Giesela Friederica	1753–56	16–19	372	Consistorial Secretary (F)
Jungfer Hummel	Hummel	1757	?	8	?
Waisenknabe Huthmann	Huthmann	1759–60	≤16	72	Orphan (S)
Monsieur Kreßler	Kreßler	1753–54	?	83	?
Kreysch	Kreysch	1757	?	12	?
Jungfer Lezius / Frau Kretschmar	Lezius, Maria Friederica	1752–54	∞1754	93	Pastor (F), Merchant (H)
Monsieur Lezius	Lezius	1752–57	?	219	?
Monsieur Lüdicke	Lüdicke, Johann August	1752–53	15–16	42	Brewer, Nailsmith (F)
Die beiden Nordmänner	Nordmann	1757	?	[24]	Regional Court Administrator (F)
Monsieur Nordmann aus Wärmsdorff	Nordmann	1757–60	?	[216]	Regional Court Administrator (F)
Schulmeister Proft in Wulfen sein Sohn	Proft, Johann Gottlieb Heinrich	1752–56	18–22	162	Schoolmaster (F, S)
Reipsch	Reipsch, Georg David?	1757–60	14–17	96	Saddler (F)? Furrier (F)?
Monsieur Jonathan Rindfleisch	Rindfleisch, Johann Jonathan?	1752–56	13–17	64	Pastor (F, S)
Schröter	Schröter, Johann Martin	1753–54	15–16	120	Farmer, Butcher (F)
Waisenknabe Schwartz	Schwartz	1758–59	≤16	72	Orphan (S)
Mademoiselle Theuerkauf	Theuerkauf	1758	?	24	?
Monsieur August Friedrich Vierthaler	Vierthaler, August Friedrich	1757–60	12–15	152	Court Chamber Advisor (F), Lawyer (S)
Mein College Herr Voigt	Voigt	1759–60	Adult	66	Teacher at the Orphanage (S)

Nordmann, the son of Johann Jakob Rindfleisch (Hartung's boss at the orphanage and in the *Schlosskapelle*), and August Friedrich Vierthaler, the son of a wealthy businessman. The latter paid Hartung not only for keyboard lessons but also three times the usual rate for instruction—presumably private tutoring—in reading, writing, math, and Latin. In his account book, Hartung invariably prefaced the names of these boys with *Monsieur* or *Herr*. These respectful terms of address signaled that unlike the orphans and the sons of craftsmen, farmers, and schoolteachers, these boys would not be pursuing careers as cantors and organists. Their interest in music was purely recreational.

The same must have been true of Hartung's female students, who were barred from pursing professional careers in music. They tended to be around the same age as his male students but came from more affluent families; their fathers and husbands were court officials, pastors, and merchants rather than schoolmasters or craftsmen. Hartung taught no orphan girls. Only one of his six female students, Augusta Friederica Clæpius, was married at the time she began her lessons with him. She was twenty-four years old, and her lessons continued for just thirty-one hours before Hartung noted that she had "stopped the lessons because she moved to Dessau," presumably to follow her husband, who took a job there as chancellory advisor.[82] Another student, Maria Friederica Kretschmar (née Lezius), was single at the time she began her lessons with Hartung but married by the end. Tellingly, she had eighty-four hours of lessons before her wedding and only nine thereafter.

Hartung's account book offers few clues as to what went on before, during, and after the lessons. He seems to have taught at the homes of his students. Some time was likely spent tuning their instruments, as this was apparently included in the price of tuition.[83] He sold his students prints and manuscripts of sonatas, suites, and sacred chorales. In 1752, for example, Lebrecht Gottfried Bieler purchased a print of sonatas by Johan Joachim Agrell,[84] and in 1754 Maria Friederica Kretschmar purchased a manuscript copy of Daniel Wolleb's published psalm settings.[85] Presumably repertoire like this was central to his pedagogical approach.

One of the most important services Hartung offered his keyboard students, and the community at large, was supplying sheet music. He devoted substantial time and energy to cultivating relationships with music dealers in Cöthen and beyond. The most frequent recipient of Hartung's manuscripts was a lawyer and family friend in Harzgerode named Gottfried Paessler, who in 1756 and 1757 paid him sixteen groschen on five separate occasions "as a gift" (*zum Geschenck*) for unspecified sheet music.[86] Most of his customers were in Cöthen. In 1753, for example, Hartung purchased a print of "1753 Dresden Polonaises and Minuets"[87] for fourteen groschen from a music dealer in Dresden named Rose, copied it, and sold his copy to a local assessor named Herrmann for twelve groschen.[88] Herrmann could theoretically have purchased the original print for just two groschen more but he chose instead to pay Hartung to copy it by hand, perhaps because he liked the look of manuscript music better, or perhaps because he simply lacked the necessary connections to find a print. In 1757 Hartung recorded a payment of "postage money sent to Berlin for the musician Meyer" from whom he acquired a "catalog," presumably of music for sale.[89]

When he was paid to copy music, Hartung generally charged per sheet of paper (*Bogen*), which usually amounted to either four or eight pages of music. Frau Kretschmar, for example, was charged one reichstaler (twenty-four groschen) for a manuscript copy in Hartung's hand of Wolleb's *Die Psalmen Davids*, which consisted of about four hundred pages of music (= fifty sheets of paper). This suggests that his rate was about one groschen for every two sheets of paper. Two years earlier, he had paid eight groschen to Christoph Cörner, a book dealer and lieutenant in the Cöthen palace guard, for the Wolleb print, which served as the model for the copy he sold Kretschmar.[90] Hartung had the print bound in calf's leather for six groschen.[91] Acquiring and binding the original music thus cost a total of fourteen groschen, and he was able to sell his manuscript copy for twenty-four groschen, turning a profit of ten groschen. This assessment ignores costs only indirectly documented in the account book. The fifty sheets of paper were probably worth five or six groschen. And he also had to contend with standing costs for quills from turkeys or geese (around one groschen each), knives for sharpening the quills (three groschen each), and rastra for putting staff lines on the page (one to four groschen each). Hartung's profit margin was thus more likely two or three groschen, though economies of scale could have raised this number if he sold additional manuscripts of the same print.

Hartung's relationships with his keyboard students extended into realms beyond the musical. He noted in his account book that the pupil he called "Little Geißler"—Carl Heinrich Christian Geißler[92]—paid only one quarter of the usual tuition rate "because his father is a good friend of mine."[93] Johann Wilhelm Geißler was the court wine steward (*Mundschenk*) and likely a colleague of Hartung's brother, Johann Christian Marcus Hartung, the court cook.

Another Hartung keyboard student, Johann Martin Schröter, was the son of a farmer and butcher in Groß-Paschleben, a village on the outskirts of Cöthen.[94] Schröter began keyboard lessons at the end of 1753, probably with the expectation of becoming a village organist or schoolmaster. On

November 12, 1754, he owed his teacher eight reichstaler for an entire year of lessons but could come up with only four. Hartung noted in his account book that Schröter "was supposed to pay twice as much, but I forgave him the remaining four reichstaler because animal death was visited upon his parents" (*seine Eltern mit dem Vieh Sterben heimges[ucht] worden*).[95] Around the same time, Hartung purchased six geese from Schröter's family in Groß-Paschleben for a total of nearly two reichstaler. He noted in his account book that he gave the geese as a gift to his brother the cook but added: "I helped eat them too."[96]

Hartung was motivated to discount Schröter's lessons so dramatically because he felt pity for his student's family in their time of need. He was far more magnanimous in this case than he had been in the case of the soldier who had cheated him out of wedding income or in the case of the baker who withdrew his children from school without paying tuition. His bond with Schröter was not only economic but also musical. More than many relationships in his life, Hartung's ties to fellow musicians were rooted in mutual respect and a spirit of shared purpose.

≥▲

While living in Cöthen, Hartung placed a great deal of importance upon spending time with his family. He saw his brother the cook on a regular basis and occasionally offered gifts, such as two silver spoons as a wedding present and a German translation of John Milton's *Paradise Lost*.[97] A substantial proportion of his income was spent on traveling back to his hometown of Harzgerode to visit his parents, siblings, and other relatives at the holidays. Adding together expenses on the road, barber's bills in the new city, food, gifts, and entertainments such as bird hunting and target shooting, such trips typically cost around four reichstaler.[98] While in Harzgerode, Hartung must have visited with his uncle Johann Christoph Schmid, to whom he sent a hand basket and a set of violin strings.[99] He brought his father cash and a yellow snuff box, his younger brother a pair of shoes, his nephew a bowling pin, and his niece a hand basket full of apples.[100]

Beginning in 1758, Carl August Hartung's account book documents regular contact with a cantor and organist in Bernburg named Johann Marius Christoph Hartung.[101] The familial relationship between these two men is unclear; they were probably cousins.[102] In any case, they had known one another for a long time, having attended primary school together in Harzgerode.[103] J. M. C. Hartung had served in their hometown as choir prefect before accepting a position in 1750 as rector in Aschersleben and then moving in 1753 to take up duties as cantor and organist in Bernburg, allegedly because he was "more inclined to music than to academic work."[104]

The pages of the account book dated 1758 and 1759 are filled with payments documenting the relationship between these two men: "Cantor Hartung was here from Bernburg with his beloved wife and daughter,"[105] a "courier for sparkling wine sent by the Cantor Herr Hartung from Bernburg,"[106] and various monies spent to act as godfather to one of the cantor's children.[107]

Hartung's budding relationship with one particular person in Cöthen deserves special attention because it became the most important of his life. Already at the beginning of the account book, amid the names in a list of pupils who studied nonmusical subjects with him, he recorded the name "Jokel." The reference is probably to August Ludwig Jokel, the fourteen-year-old son of the court tailor, brewer, and Cöthen town council member Christian August Jokel, and his wife, Catharina Elisabeth.[108] From 1753 to 1756 the name "Jokelin" appears on the same list, referring most likely to August Ludwig's sister, Maria Christina Jokel, who was then in her mid-teens.[109] Perhaps through his instruction of these two siblings, Hartung came to know the Jokel family, and at some point he began to take an interest in his pupils' older sister, Johanna Sophie, known by the diminutive "Hannichen."[110] In 1758, when he was thirty-five and she was twenty-seven, Hartung recorded payments of one groschen and four pfennige for "a blue ribbon for Hannichen's apron." Later the same year, he spent two reichstaler on "a decorative box intended for Hannichen." In 1759 Hartung twice offered two or three groschen to "Marichen, Jokel's maid," suggesting that he visited the Jokel home regularly. He later paid a basket weaver "for adding a handle to Hannichen's tea kettle," bought "white lace for Hannichen," "a pair of white cotton gloves from the seasonal market for Hannichen," "velvet ribbon for Hannichen," "four ells of cotton fabric for Hannichen," "one ell of red taffeta ribbon for Hannichen," and "five-and-a-half ells of fabric for a body belt for Hannichen."[111] Clearly, this young woman had found a special place in his heart. As an orphanage instructor and cantor, however, it was impossible to support a wife and children. If he ever wanted to marry Hannichen, he needed to find a more lucrative, full-time position.

❧

At some point in the late 1750s Hartung learned that an organist position had become vacant at the Church of St. Bartholomew (*Bartholomäuskirche*) in Braunschweig. The city was five times larger than Cöthen and had a much more affluent population.[112] Braunschweig was comparable to Leipzig in that it owed its prosperity to trade fairs, but it was like Cöthen insofar as it served as the residential city of a high aristocratic family. Most of its leading citizens were courtiers and bureaucrats. The city was famous throughout the German-speaking world for its intellectual life, boasting a well-regarded boarding school and a large concentration of influential writers.

The Bartholomäuskirche was a modest and rather nondescript structure in Braunschweig's *Schützenstraße*, near the city center. It had been built in the middle ages but reconsecrated as a church only in 1709, after a period of use as a military depot and a school.[113] It housed two Calvinist congregations—one German speaking and one French speaking—both of which were served by the same organist. The church had recently commissioned a new organ from the court organ builder, Johann Christoph Hüsemann. The instrument was not large; it had just one manual and pedals and a modest range of tone colors in accordance with the Calvinists' conflicted views about music in worship.[114] Its façade bore a clock donated by the church's director (*Kirchen-Vorsteher*), Johann Herrmann Diekmeier, intended to remind parishioners that their time on Earth was limited.[115]

The post was very attractive to Hartung, and he had a family connection to the same Herr Diekmeier who had donated the organ's clock. A citizen in Braunschweig Hartung referred to as "Cousin Liebau" (*Vetter Liebau*) was likely related to Diekmeier's wife, Johanna Catharina Diekmeier (née Liebau).[116] In any case, Hartung apparently did not audition for the post, perhaps because of the family connections or perhaps because of the Seven Years' War, which raged from 1756 to 1763 and restricted travel.[117]

Sometime in the spring of 1760, Hartung received a letter from Braunschweig, which would be among the most momentous he would ever open. The leadership of the Bartholomäuskirche had decided to offer him the coveted position as full-time organist. The two congregations would pay him a combined salary of eighty-five reichstaler, four times what he was earning at the orphanage.[118] The German congregation promised to cover moving expenses while the French congregation offered a generous signing bonus of ten reichstaler. His sense of elation comes through clearly in the response he wrote to the pastor and other church dignitaries in Braunschweig on April 18, 1760:

> Highly honored and highly learned, highly noble and greatly admired, especially highly distinguished sirs, as you have deigned to send my lowliness a written invitation to serve as the organist of your congregation, I wish to thank you most kindly for the love and good intentions this act displays. I will seek to fulfill the duties of this new office, to the extent that God allows, and to completely satisfy both congregations with my playing and my behavior. Furthermore I live in the joyful and pleasing hope that you eternally honored sirs will continue to regard me with favor. May great God preserve you and your families in comfort and pleasure. I recommend

myself to your continued support and remain with the greatest respect, your honorable, noble, and my highly distinguished sirs' most devoted servant, Carl August Hartung.[119]

Thrilled with his good fortune, Hartung immediately proposed marriage to Johanna Sophie Jokel. She and her family agreed, and from then on he referred to her as "my Hannichen."[120]

As he was to begin working in Braunschweig already in mid-summer, Hartung stored most of his belongings in the homes of his fiancée's family and his brother the cook. In July he moved to the new city alone and spent the next few months getting acclimated. He would return in the autumn for the wedding, which took place on October 14, 1760, in the Church of St. Jacob on Cöthen's central market square.[121] Hartung's account book gives a vivid sense for the pageantry and costs associated with a musician's wedding. It includes payments for shaving his beard and making his suit, for three pairs of stockings for the bride's sisters and the maid, for the bride's earrings, and for a hairdresser "to make the bride's head right" (*vor die Brautkopf zu rechte zu machen*). Hartung's total expenditures for the wedding alone amounted to around twenty-three reichstaler, slightly more than his old annual salary at the orphanage.[122]

Upon moving to Braunschweig, Carl August and Johanna Sophie Hartung settled into married life. They furnished their rooms with a new kitchen cabinet, wooden frames for curtains on the windows, and some decorative plaster lions. Following common practice, they covered the floor of their home with sand (used as a cleaning agent), which was swept out with a new broom they purchased.[123] On November 11, 1760, Carl August bought firewood to heat his home, relying on advice from a local baker, who helped him negotiate the price. He then paid a certain Herr Schäfer, the man who pumped the bellows of the organ at the Bartholomäuskirche, to chop the wood into small pieces.[124] The Hartungs slept atop an elegant bed he had commissioned for four reichstaler from a carpenter in Cöthen, as well as a mattress they kept stuffed with fresh straw. The Hartungs also purchased a bedspread and comforter worth more than ten reichstaler.[125]

Unlike in Cöthen, Hartung organized his expenditures in Braunschweig by day. Table 12 indicates how he earned and spent his money during the first two weeks of March 1761.[126] Food purchases represent the most significant change in Hartung's daily economy. In Cöthen his job included board, but in Braunschweig he and Hannichen had to buy groceries and prepare their own meals. The two weeks cited in table 12 coincide with Easter, which is why the Hartungs ordered such a large cut of veal on Good Friday and paid the cook who roasted it a few days later. In other weeks, they spent their

Table 12. Carl August Hartung's Income and Expenditures, March 17–31, 1761

Tuesday, March 17	Rthl.	Gr.	Pf.
Bread	.	–2	–4
Coffee	.	–2	–8
Milk	.	.	–4
Herring	.	.	–8
16 hours of lessons for Ms. Lambalet	+2	.	.

Wednesday, March 18	Rthl.	Gr.	Pf.
Mr. Ballhorn's bill	–3	–8	.
Olive oil	–1	–4	.
Sugar	.	–2	–4
Pickled vegetables	.	–1	–4
Starch	.	–1	–8
Butter	.	–2	–8
Mr. Bosse for copying the Fehre Passion	+4	.	.

Thursday, March 19	Rthl.	Gr.	Pf.
To the tailor Mr. Zastro for making the black *Andrienne* dress	–1	–20	.
Bread	.	–2	.
Pastries	.	.	–4
Bratwurst	.	–3	–8
Milk	.	.	–4
Hulled grains	.	–5	.
Butter	.	–2	–8

Friday, March 20 [Good Friday]	Rthl.	Gr.	Pf.
Beer	.	–4	.
Bread and pastries	.	–1	.
Frau Holz for a cabinet for bowls	–3	–6	.
The same for 3 window boards for curtains	.	–12	.
Candles	.	–1	–4
Olive oil	.	–1	–4
Bread	.	–4	–8
Butter	.	–5	–4
Garden plants	.	.	–6
Milk	.	–	–4
2 pounds of beef	.	–4	.
8 1/4 pounds of veal for roasting	.	–14	.
Veal sausage [*Weisswurst*]	.	–3	.
Pearl Barley	.	–1	.
Beer	.	–1	–9
Sugar	.	–2	–4
For 3 scarves sent to Cöthen	.	–14	.
2 lions made of plaster	.	–2	.
Postage for sheet music from Cöthen	.	–4	–8
A tip for Liesebett for the cake	.	–3	.

Saturday, March 21	Rthl.	Gr.	Pf.
From Rector Renthe for composing the New Year's Cantata for the choir of the Calvinist School in Cöthen	+3	.	.

Sunday, March 22 [Easter Sunday]

Table 12. Continued

Monday, March 23	Rthl.	Gr.	Pf.
Milk	.	.	−6
For roasting the meat [veal on Easter]	.	−1	.
Candles	.	−2	.

Tuesday, March 24	Rthl.	Gr.	Pf.
Olive oil	−1	.	.
Sugar and coffee	.	−5	−4
2 bottles of wine	.	−12	.
3 pipes	.	−2	.

Wednesday, March 25	Rthl.	Gr.	Pf.
Milk	.	.	−4
Bread	.	−2	.
Beer	.	−5	.
Coffee	.	−2	−8
Tobacco	.	−1	.

Thursday, March 26	Rthl.	Gr.	Pf.
A bed frame	−1	−16	.
For delivery [of the bed frame]	.	−2	.
Bread	.	.	−8

Friday, March 27	Rthl.	Gr.	Pf.
Bread and rolls	.	−2	−4
Milk	.	.	−4
Dried cod	.	−1	.
Tobacco	.	−1	.
Wurst	.	−2	.
Candles	.	−2	−8
Sugar	.	−2	−8

Saturday, March 28	Rthl.	Gr.	Pf.
2 1/2 pounds of veal	.	−3	−9
Butter	.	−2	−4
Eggs	.	−1	−8
Bread	.	−2	.
Garden Plants	.	−1	.
Rice	.	−1	.
Milk	.	.	−4
Beer	.	−3	.
Tea	.	−1	4
Two pipes	.	−1	4
Tobacco	.	−1	.
Bread rolls	.	.	−4
Olive oil	.	.	−9
Sugar and coffee	.	−5	−4

Sunday, March 29			

Monday, March 30			

Table 12. Continued

Tuesday, March 31	Rthl.	Gr.	Pf.
Butter	.	–2	–8
Bread	.	–3	.
2 1/2 pounds of pork	.	–5	–4
Lard	.	–2	–4
Milk	.	–4	.
Beer	.	–4	–3
For chopping wood	.	–1	–4
To repair Herr Ahldefeld's keyboard	.	–8	.
Fräulein Bausen for one month of lessons	+2	.	.
Herr Bausen for one month of lessons	+2	.	.
Keyboard lessons for Fräulein von Blücher as well as for the eldest Herr von Blücher,			
February 25–March 25, 1761	+4	.	.

money on mutton, lamb, and smoked meats. Their fish purchases included herring, dried or cured cod, and smelt. They supplemented their diet with grains (barley, bran, farina, flour, and millet), vegetables (beans, cabbage, celery, peas, lettuce, turnips, and onions), and fruits (plums, raisins, baked pears, and especially apples). Their primary starch was bread (including pretzels, zwieback, and pastries) but they occasionally ate rice or noodles instead. The Hartungs bought at least one *Nößel* (about half a liter) of milk nearly every day and occasionally also cheese or cream. They cooked with butter, olive oil, or lard and seasoned their food with horseradish, nutmeg, and salt. While they sometimes drank aquavit, brandy, and wine, their most common beverage by far was beer, which they paid to have a woman deliver to their home.[127] The most typical nonalcoholic beverages were coffee and tea, which they drank with milk and sugar.[128]

Herr Hartung's new position demanded that he dress more elegantly than he had as an orphanage instructor. Shortly after arriving in Braunschweig, he spent four reichstaler on a single pair of stockings, by far the most expensive item of clothing he ever purchased.[129] He also did his best to keep his clothes in respectable shape, hiring a washing service to clean his shirts. Whereas he had never spent any money on wigs in Cöthen, twice in his first few years in Braunschweig he invested two reichstaler in new wigs and generously tipped the wigmaker's apprentices.[130] His wife regularly purchased shoes, lace, and headgear, as well as perfumes of linden blossoms and rose water. She presumably spent some of her time at a spinning wheel the couple purchased, making yarn and knitting it into garments.

Frau Hartung did at least some of the shopping in Braunschweig. She even briefly took over her husband's account book, covering half a page with purchases of milk, a shoe brush, shoe wax, pork, bread rolls, butter, cheese, apples, and postage for a letter from Cöthen.[131] Eighteenth-century German orthography was not very systematic, but her misspellings—she rendered *Brief* (letter) as *Brif* and *Äpfel* (apples) as *ebffel*—suggest that her education was limited. She regularly kept up with friends and family in Cöthen, sending them letters and gifts such as the three scarves listed in table 12.[132] Carl August took all September 1764 off from teaching so that he and Hannichen could travel back to her hometown.[133]

Sometime in the winter of 1761, Hannichen became pregnant, and in the summer she gave birth to a baby girl the couple named Johanna Rahel Henriette.[134] The baptism took place on August 1, but the birth itself occurred a few days earlier, probably on July 28, the day Carl August uncharacteristically purchased a bouquet of carnations.[135] Other baby-related expenses followed: the baptism itself, "Rahel's shoes," diapers, cotton fabric for cradle pillows, baby balsam, and for a wet nurse who was paid to "take her breasts out."[136] The Hartungs were of a social status and income level that enabled them to hire a servant to ease the burdens of daily life. A woman named Dorothea Utschen earned four groschen per week to do chores and babysit.[137] The Hartungs had two more daughters in the next few years: Henriette Conradine in 1765,[138] and Johanna Sophia Carolina in 1767.[139] Sadly, their first daughter died at age four and their third daughter at just three months. Only their middle child, Henriette Conradine, survived to adulthood.[140]

Hartung's account book reveals little about his work inside the Church of St. Bartholomew. At one point he spent one reichstaler and four groschen on a coal pan on a tripod and a little shovel to go with it, probably for use in the organ loft, where he needed to keep his hands warm during the winter months.[141] The account book documents the purchase and binding of diverse printed keyboard works, some of which he likely performed during Sunday services.[142] He may also have performed works he had copied in Cöthen by composers such as Arnold Melchoir Brunckhorst, Johann Gotthilf Jænichen, Georg Friedrich Händel, Johann Adolf Hasse, Christian Bernhard Linigke, Christian Ernst Rolle, Georg Philipp Telemann, Georg Tegetmeyer, and Johann Gotthilf Ziegler.[143]

Even after Hartung moved to Braunschweig, he continued to fulfill commissions to write the New Year's Cantata and the *Actus Music* for the Reformed Church in Cöthen. He also received lucrative commissions in his new city, including "a gold ducat" from the English ambassador for composing six partitas for the harp in 1762.[144] In the spring of 1763 the congregation in Braunschweig paid him thirty-five reichstaler for composing "Peace Music" (*Friedens Music*) to celebrate the end of the Seven Years' War.[145] Prince Ferdinand and Duke Karl Wilhelm Ferdinand of Braunschweig-Wolfenbüttel had served as field marshals to King Friedrich II of Prussia, and their leadership was decisive in the Anglo-German army's victories over the French. A certain Herr Lambelet, whose wife and daughters studied the keyboard with Hartung, was so pleased with the "Peace Music" that he presented the organist with a gift of one reichstaler.[146]

Hartung apparently did not perform at many baptisms or weddings in Braunschweig. The only such gig he played was the wedding of his former keyboard student, Charlotte Rahel Ehrhardt, who married a merchant from Magdeburg named Peter Favreau on June 14, 1764.[147] On this occasion, he was paid the astronomical sum of thirty-six reichstaler for composing and presumably also performing a wedding cantata (*Hochzeit Carmen*).

In Braunschweig Hartung spent much less time teaching nonmusical subjects than he had in Cöthen. He did, however, offer sixteen hours per month of instruction in reading and arithmetic to the children of a painter at a rate of two groschen per hour, and instruction in reading, writing, and Christianity to the daughters of an aristocratic riding master (*Rittmeister*), who paid slightly more.[148] Between November 17, 1760, and April 10, 1761, Hartung instructed Bernhard and Fritz Ahldefeld—sons of the merchant, confectioner, and director of the church, Johann Wilhelm Engelbert Ahldefeld, and his wife Friderike Albertine—for "two hours daily" in reading and writing.[149] The rate they paid was suspiciously low.[150] Tellingly, Hartung gave a New Year's gratuity to Ahldefeld's wood chopper (*Holzhacker*) and paid eight groschen on March 31, 1761, to have the Ahldefeld family's harpsichord repaired.[151] Perhaps the Hartungs lived during this period with the Ahldefeld family, and part of his compensation came in the form of free rent. In April 1761 Hartung's instruction of the Ahldefeld boys came to an abrupt halt, perhaps because he moved out of their home. By 1764 at the latest—the year his salary from the German congregation was increased from sixty to one hundred reichstaler per year—the Hartung family was living in a place that enabled them to rent a room to a merchant from Lübeck who visited Braunschweig to attend the trade fairs.[152]

Even after Hartung stopped teaching the Ahldefeld boys nonmusical subjects, he maintained good relations with their family, receiving gifts of sugarloaf at the New Year and at one point borrowing around five reichstaler from their father, which he paid back one year later. And in December 1762—more than a year after having the family harpsichord repaired— Hartung began giving keyboard lessons to ten-year-old Bernhard. When Fritz turned ten two years later, he too began lessons. The Ahldefeld boys were typical of Hartung's keyboard students in Braunschweig insofar as they were the sons of an affluent merchant who belonged to the congregation of the Bartholomäuskirche. The biographical information known about Hartung's keyboard pupils in Braunschweig is presented in table 13:

Table 13. Carl August Hartung's Keyboard Students in Braunschweig, 1760–1765

Hartung's Designation	Name	Dates	Age	Hours	Family (S=Self, F=Father, H=Husband)
Monsieur Bernhard Ahldefeld	Ahldefeld, Bernhard	1762–65	10–13	448	Merchant and Confectioner (F)
Monsieur Friedrich Ahldefeld	Ahldefeld, Friedrich ("Fritz")	1764–65	10–11	160	Merchant and Confectioner (F)
Kleine Madem. Anna Catharina Bausen	Bausen, Anna Catharina	1764–65	12–13	256	Merchant (F, H)
Monsieur Engelbert Bausen	Bausen, Engelbert	1763–65	18–20	120	Merchant (F, S)
Monsieur Bausen	Bausen, Herrmann?	1761–64	16–19	528	Merchant (F)
Mademoiselle Bausen	Bausen, Maria Helena	1761–65	20–24	736	Merchant (F, H)
Der älteste Herr von Blücher	Blücher, Adam Friedrich von	1760–61	15–16	176	Aristocrat, Military (S)
Fräulein von Blücher	Blücher, Elisabeth von?	1760–61	17–20	160	Aristocrat, Military (H)
Mademoiselle Burchardi	Burchardi, Johanna Catharina	1762–63	31–32	224	Merchant (F), Pastor (H)
Engl. Magazin Inspector Herr Chenal	Chenal	1762	Adult	76	English Military Officer (S)
Mademoiselle Daniels	Daniels, Johanna Catharina?	1760–61	17–18?	192	Money Changer (F)?
Kleine Mademoiselle Daniels	Daniels, Charlotte Philippine?	1762–63	8–9?	64	Money Changer (F)?
Frau Diekmeier	Diekmeier, Johanna Catharina	1762	22	80	Merchant (H)
Mademoiselle Ehrhardt	Ehrhardt, Charlotte Rahel	1762–63	23–24	128	Merchant (H)
Kleine Mademoiselle Jonas	Jonas, Anna Margaretha Rahel	1762–65	10–13	624	Merchant (F, H)
Monsieur Jonas	Jonas, Georg	1761–64	13–16	560	Merchant (F, S)
Monsieur Jordan aus Berlin	Jordan	1761	?	32	?
Kirchhofs Kinder	Kirchhof, Johann Engelbert?	1760	14?	[4]	Pastor (F)
Kirchhofs Kinder	Kirchhof, Johanna Augusta?	1760	12?	[4]	Pastor (F)
Mademoiselle Kneins	Kneins	1761–63	?	325	?
Älteste Mademoiselle Krüger	Krüger	1762–63	16–17?	236	Court Carpenter (F)
Kleine Mademoiselle Krüger	Krüger	1762–63	?	236	Court Carpenter (F)
Älteste Mademoiselle Lambelet	Lambelet, Anna Elisabeth Louise	1761–64	12–15	552	Merchant (F), Hat Merchant (H)
Kleine Mademoiselle Lambelet	Lambelet, Charlotte Margaretha	1762–64	10–13	[256]	Merchant (F, H)
Madame Lambelet	Lambelet, Magdalena Elisabeth	1762	Adult	[56]	Merchant (H)
Herr von Lieven	Lieven, Friederich George von	1764	16	40	Aristocrat from Courland (F, S)
Herr von Lingen	Lingen, Johann Philipp von	1764–65	14	112	Aristocrat from Bremen (F, S)
Mademoiselle Meisen aus Elberfeld	Meisen	1764–65	?	32	?
Mademoiselle Proah	Proah, Eleonore Louise?	1764–65	∞1768?	96	Pastor (H)?
Fräulein von Schwartzkopf	Schwartzkoppen, Caroline Sophie?	1761	6?	[23]	Aristocratic Military Officer (F)?
Fräulein von Schwartzkopf	Schwartzkoppen, Christine Louise?	1761	5?	[23]	Aristocratic Military Officer (F)?
Monsieur Spitta	Spittau, Carl L. or Heinrich G.	1761	15/16	74	Brewer (F)

Carl August Hartung made considerably more money from teaching private keyboard lessons as an organist than he had as an orphanage instructor. His students were generally more affluent, so he charged them more per hour, and taught them for many more hours, as shown in table 14:

Table 14. Carl August Hartung's Keyboard Teaching in Cöthen and Braunschweig

Cöthen, 1752–1760

Months documented = 98 (March 1752 to April 1760)
Average teaching hours per month = ~28
Total students = 27 [2,751 hours]
Female students = 6 [555 hours] (married = 1 [40 hours]; unmarried = 5 [515 hours])
Male students = 21 [2,196 hours] (married = 0–3; unmarried = 18–21)
Average teaching hours per student = ~102 (female students = ~93; male students = ~105)
Average number of students in a given quarter = 4.75 (most = 10, least = 1)

Braunschweig, 1760–1765

Months documented = 54 (November 1760 to May 1765)[1]
Average teaching hours per month = ~123
Total students = 32 [6,633 hours]
Female students = 20 [4,303 hours] (married = 2 [136 hours]; unmarried = 18 [4,167 hours])
Male students = 12 [2,330 hours] (married = 0–2; unmarried = 10–12)
Average teaching hours per student = ~207 (female students = ~215; male students = ~194)
Average number of students in a given quarter = 8.45 (most =13, least = 2)

Note: 1. Hartung did not teach in September 1764 because he was on vacation visiting Cöthen.

While some teachers of the era taught between fifteen and eighteen students at a time,[153] Hartung taught a maximum of twelve or thirteen students, and more often just eight or nine.

The prestige of Hartung's new position and the wealth of the congregation enabled him to raise his rate from two groschen per hour up to three groschen per hour. Whereas in Cöthen his keyboard teaching had yielded an average of just under two-and-a-half reichstaler per month, in Braunschweig it brought him an average of around fifteen reichstaler and could sometimes reach twenty.[154] As in Cöthen, however, his music students sometimes paid him in goods rather than in cash: a pair of shirt cuffs, handkerchiefs, a bowl of butter, or a nightgown.[155] At the new year he sometimes received up to ten reichstaler in gratuities from his music students, in addition to gifts such as tea, coffee, and sugarloaf.[156]

Whereas in Cöthen Hartung's music students had been overwhelmingly boys, in Braunschweig they were mostly girls.[157] He was now serving a more affluent clientele whose children sought to pursue music primarily for recreational purposes, not to become professionals. In Braunschweig as in Cöthen, Hartung's students were usually unmarried. Between 1752 and

1765 he gave 4,858 hours of lessons to female musicians in these two cities, but only 176 hours (less than 4 percent of the total) to married women. As in Cöthen, marriage seems to have precipitated a cessation of keyboard lessons. At one point, Hartung noted in his account book that a longtime female student, Johann Catharina Burchardi, had decided to stop having lessons "because she married Pastor Gericke" (*hat aufgehört, weilen sie den Hr. Pastor Gericke heÿrathet*).[158] The word "because" here suggests a causal relationship; it was self-evident that a woman who married (or at least a woman who married a pastor) would cease to study the keyboard.[159]

In Braunschweig Hartung's pupils were more often related to one another than were his pupils in Cöthen. Twenty-three of his thirty-two students (72 percent) had a close relative who had studied with him, as opposed to just four of twenty-seven (15 percent) in Cöthen. The Braunschweig merchant, Peter Bausen, sent at least four of his children to study the keyboard (and in one case, the cello) with Hartung.[160] The Bausen family commissioned him to copy chamber music, keyboard sonatas, songs, chorales, and an entire opera by the court kapellmeister in Braunschweig, Johann Gottfried Schwanberg. They also loaned him money and regularly gave him gifts at the New Year, including tea and coffee beans. One year, "Madame Bausen, who lives in the *Breite* street" presented him with a colorful blue woman's scarf, presumably as a gift for Hannichen.[161]

As in Cöthen, Hartung seems to have traveled to the homes of his students, rather than having them come to him. When they lived unusually far away, he was compensated for travel costs. For example, in addition to the two reichstaler per month he was paid for teaching two daughters of the Daniels family on Wednesdays and Saturdays, Hartung was paid 16 groschen "horse money" (*Roß-Geld*).[162]

Hartung's dealings with his pupil Johanna Catharina Diekmeier, wife of Johann Herrmann Diekmeier, the merchant and director of the German Reformed Church in Braunschweig, were unusual insofar as Frau Diekmeier often presented Hartung his official church salary when he came to her home to give her keyboard lessons.[163] As noted above, she was closely related to a certain "Cousin Liebau," with whom Hartung was also familiar. The account book documents a tip to Liebau's maid for preparing a sausage and a payment of nearly three groschen to a glazier for repairing Liebau's lantern, "which I broke in two."[164]

Another family with whom Hartung had particularly close relations was that of the merchant Johann Ludwig Lambelet. His first wife, Maria Elisabeth, died before Hartung's arrival in Braunschweig, but their daughters Anna Elisabeth Louise and Charlotte Margaretha Hermina Lambalet studied the keyboard with Hartung. Herr Lambelet's second wife, Magdalena

Elisabeth Lambelet had keyboard lessons with him as well.[165] Hartung
bought firewood from Herr Lambelet in 1762, and he borrowed one *Louis
d'or* (the equivalent of five reichstaler) from him in 1763. Upon the death
of a certain Herr Leidenroth, prefect of the choir at St. Martin's Church,
Hartung arranged to purchase the deceased's keyboard on behalf of Herr
Lambelet, fronting the money and receiving a tip of one reichstaler for his
trouble.[166] In addition to teaching Lambelet's daughters over an extended
period, Hartung sold the family (via a servant) several collections of printed
galanterien marketed explicitly to female keyboardists.[167] Hartung also
copied psalms and hymns for the Lambelets, presumably for use in their
home devotional services.

Hartung earned far more money from copying music in Braunschweig
than he had in Cöthen. His students commissioned him to write out chorale
books, chamber music, sacred vocal works, and entire operas. The boys
asked for more music than did the girls (thirty-three commissions from
twelve boys as opposed to six commissions from twenty girls). Hartung also
copied music for court musicians in Braunschweig,[168] and in one case he
sent a collection of six sinfonias by J. G. Schwanberg to the crown prince
of Anhalt-Bernburg.[169] He also copied "various Sinfonias" and sold them
for three reichstaler to a man he described as the "Moor and Timpanist
Pauli," presumably a court musician of African heritage.[170] Altogether,
copying music constituted around 10 percent of his total income, a far
higher proportion than it had in Cöthen.

Comparing Hartung's sources of income in Cöthen and Braunschweig is
complicated by the fact that records for Braunschweig thin out after 1761.
However, comparing two well-documented quarters—the first quarter of
1755 in Cöthen and the first quarter of 1761 in Braunschweig—offers a
sense for Hartung's lifestyle change in the new city.

As shown in table 16, C. A. Hartung's expenditures, as a proportion of
his income, were far higher in Braunschweig than they had been in Cöthen.
In order to support his family in Braunschweig, Herr Hartung repeatedly
felt compelled to borrow money from the wealthy families with whom he
had close relationships, particularly the Ahldefelds and the Lambelets.
Hartung spent substantial sums playing the lottery, no doubt fantasizing
about resolving a variety of financial challenges in one fell swoop.[171] He
also liquefied some of his assets, including the "silver minute watch" he
had acquired at some point, selling it to a horn player for more than
27 Reichstaler.[172] In Braunschweig he had actually achieved his dream of
becoming a well-regarded and well-paid musician and teacher. He no longer
felt such a powerful need to project an aspirational image of affluence.

Table 15. Carl August Hartung's Finances in Cöthen and Braunschweig Compared

Cöthen (First Quarter of 1755)	Braunschweig (First Quarter of 1761)
Total Income = 590 Groschen	Total Income = 1641 Groschen
Baptisms: 62	New Years gifts: 435
Composing: 66	Travel Expenses from Cöthen: 120
Music Lessons: 72	Composing the Cöthen New Year's Cantata: 72
Salary: 132	Music teaching: 408
School: 254	Copying music: 96
Tuning: 4	Salary: 510
Total Expenses = 82 Groschen	Total Expenditures: 1289 Groschen
Clothing: 32	Textiles and clothing: 97
Gifts/tips: 14	Household expenses: 567
Manuscript music: 12	Food and drink: 565
Aderlaßen: 4	Meat: 159
Printed Music: 10	Eggs: 7
Food and Drink: 6	Starch: 103
Tobacco: 4	Fat: 73
	Grains: 24
	Seasonings: 27
	Vegetables: 10
	Fish: 13
	Fruit: 2
	Beverages: 147
	Gifts/tips: 29
	Servants: 17
	Tobacco: 14

Table 16. Carl August Hartung's Income in Cöthen and Braunschweig by Percentage

Sources of Income	Cöthen	Braunschweig
Salary	26%	29%
Private teaching:		
Music	30%	48%
Other subjects	31%	2%
Composing	7%	6%
Baptisms	3%	0%
Weddings	1%	0%
Music-related sales:		
Instruments	1%	4.5%
Music prints	0.5%	0.5%
Music manuscripts	0.5%	10%

੩&

Hartung retained his position at Braunschweig's Church of St. Bartholomew for the remaining forty years of his life. Little is known about his daily routine after 1765, when he stopped documenting his income and expenditures in the account book. In 1782 he issued a collection of "Odes and Songs with Melodies and with the Accompaniment of the Keyboard" (*Oden und Lieder mit Melodien und mit Begleitung des Claviers*).[173] An undated second volume followed some years later.[174] For the most part, his odes are love songs and sentimental pieces addressing loss and death: "playing my lyre and singing for my beloved is enough of a kingdom for me"; "the mourning song of a bride burying her beloved"; "God protect my poor heart"; "a young woman becomes a slave to love"; "the melancholy song of a nightingale." In 1790 he published "Six Modern Waltzes for the Pianoforte" (*Six valses modernes pour le pianoforte*).[175] The subscription list for the *Oden und Lieder* reveals the names of several former students: Johann Jonathan Rindfleisch and August Friedrich Vierthaler in Cöthen; "Herr Registrator Aldefeld," Georg Jonas, and "Madame Rettmeyer" in Braunschweig. These students kept in touch with their teacher long after their lessons had come to an end, and in some cases decades after he had moved away from their city.

Carl August Hartung was a tremendous aficionado for the music of Johann Sebastian Bach. It was probably his uncle, Johann Christoph Schmid, who first introduced him to this repertoire.[176] His interest likely grew during his time in Cöthen, where he befriended Bernhard Christian Kayser.[177] Hartung himself went on to systematically collect keyboard works by J. S. Bach. In Braunschweig, he made at least two catalogs of incipits, presumably in order to keep track of the materials he possessed, and to offer an overview for colleagues or acquaintances who might wish to commission copies. The works in Hartung's catalog include the *Well Tempered Clavier* (BWV 846–869), the *Goldberg Variations* (BWV 988), the *Keyboard Partitas* (BWV 825–830), and the *Art of the Fugue* (BWV 1080), as well as a host of more obscure compositions.[178] Perhaps he received some of these materials directly from Bach's eldest son, Wilhelm Friedemann, who played concerts and applied for an organist position in Braunschweig in the early 1770s.[179] By the end of the eighteenth century, Hartung was known well beyond the confines of Braunschweig as a Bach specialist. Bach's first biographer, Johann Nikolaus Forkel, was in contact with him at the end of the eighteenth century and owned one of his two surviving sales catalogs as well as several manuscripts in Hartung's hand. At some point in the early nineteenth century Forkel wrote to a colleague that the elderly organist in Braunschweig was "an excellent copyist and, beyond this, knew very well in such [Bach-related] matters, so that he was able to supply me with some items that without his help I would probably never have been able to find."[180]

Carl August and Johanna Sophie ("Hannichen") Hartung remained together for nearly forty years. On the occasion of their twenty-five-year ("silver") anniversary—October 14, 1785—friends in Braunschweig prepared a commemorative poem that highlighted the joy they felt in one another's company, the beauty of their daughter, Henriette Conradine, and their anticipation of soon being surrounded by a gaggle of grandchildren.[181] As Spohr noted, Hartung became too ill to teach toward the end of his life and died of a stroke (*Schlagfluß*) at age seventy-six, on August 31, 1800.[182] Hannichen survived him by fifteen years, dying at the age of eighty-four on November 13, 1815.[183]

☙

Carl August Hartung's career trajectory can be taken as typical of that of an eighteenth-century organist. It was not unusual for aspiring musicians to hold positions in orphanages while applying for more prestigious and better-compensated posts in churches and courts.[184] From cobbling together a living by playing baptisms and weddings, composing for school celebrations, playing in various churches, teaching Latin, math, the catechism, and private keyboard lessons, they moved on to occupy permanent organist positions that allowed them more freedom to pursue personal musical interests.

Hartung's account book offers insight into the ways that successful organists of the eighteenth century were connected with their communities. Other musicians, too, must have received beaver hats from their students whose fathers were hat-makers, fire grates from their students whose fathers were metal workers, and bread from their students whose fathers were bakers. The men who pumped the organ bellows every Sunday also chopped their firewood and borrowed a few groschen now and then. Those who kept watch over the city at night scoured their tin plates. Those who shaved them and bled their feet when they were feeling ill also brought them their daily newspapers. Other musicians, too, came to the aid of ailing colleagues and students, offering timely donations and loans and trusting that they would receive the same in their own moments of need. The bonds forged through music also must have made both joys and sorrows more acute. We can only imagine how Hartung must have felt when he heard the news that his former student Augusta Friederica Clæpius had died in childbirth at age twenty-five after "enduring brief but tremendous birth pains and mortal terror," just six months after her final lesson.[185]

Hartung was enmeshed with his contemporaries in networks of obligation held together by trust. When he suffered financial indignities—for
example, when students abandoned him mid-quarter because he became
ill, when grooms failed to pay him for wedding music, when he received
less than he had negotiated for a musical instrument, when he had to
lobby school officials in order to be paid for a cantata performance—he
never sought legal recourse. He vented his frustration on the pages of his
account book and no doubt also to his friends and colleagues. He trusted
or at least hoped that he would be somehow vindicated.

Hartung is typical of organists of his time in that he desired to be seen as
more than a physical laborer. He sought admiration not only for his music
but also for his learning. His yearly base salary of eighty-five and later 125
reichstaler was far lower than that of court employees in Braunschweig,
who generally earned salaries of around 250 reichstaler. In Cöthen he had
earned still less. Yet in both cities he aspired to be magnanimous. At the
baptism for which he served as godfather, he spent four reichstaler and nine
groschen, just short of the five reichstaler and fourteen groschen Christiane
Sibÿlla Bose spent when she herself served as godmother. Fräulein Bose had
vastly greater financial resources than did Herr Hartung, and yet he came
close to matching her in generosity. On March 19, 1761, he paid a tailor
one reichstaler and twenty groschen to make his wife a black Andrienne
dress, the same style purchased by Fräulein Bose. The pocket watch he
carried as a young man in Cöthen was worth twenty-seven reichstaler. In
Braunschweig he finally parted with this luxury item, but the fact that
he sold it to a horn player suggests that he was not the only professional
musician who sought to affect an image of affluence.

Hartung and many other musicians of his time regarded music as a
branch of learning. His collection of theoretical tracts included Johann
Carl Conrad Oelrichs's 1752 "Historical Report on Academic Degrees in
Music" (*Historische Nachricht von den akademischen Würden in der Musik*), the
first sentence of which reads: "That music belongs to learning would not be
easy for anyone to dispute."[186] Oelrichs went on to consider the different
fields that others argued music belonged to, asking rhetorically, "Is music
a type of philosophy, theology, grammar, poetry, math, or natural science?"
He devoted numerous pages to praising England for granting academic
degrees in music, a practice that had not yet spread to Germany. According to Oelrichs, doctors of music in England were held in "great esteem,"
accorded the rank of knight, and entitled to wear "silver chains around
their necks and silver spurs on their feet."[187] His book constituted a plea
for greater academic respect for music and armed like-minded individuals
with potent arguments for achieving this end.

Given Hartung's manifest interest in asserting music's respectability, he likely also read the extensive treatment of this subject in another book he owned: Johann Adolf Scheibe's *Critischer Musikus*. In a segment first published in 1739, Scheibe argued that music was at once a "science and an art" because it required both "learned insight" (*gelehrtes Nachdenken*) and "physical exercise" (*Leibesübung*): "This explains why a composer must be a learned person; because he must understand his science fundamentally, judging and substantiating all aspects of his work, because he must put all of this into practice by creating works of music, and finally because he must also instruct others in all aspects of music."[188] Scheibe shared with Oelrichs the goal of seeing music enshrined as a regular course of study within the German university:

> Observe, however, the constitution of our universities! [. . .] You will find plenty of musical ensembles but nowhere will you find that music is treated with the same respect as other arts and sciences, including some that are of far less use. [. . .] Who would deny that a teacher of music is far more necessary in the academy than is a teacher of foreign languages? The latter can be taught by one who simply understands his own language, without any requirement that he be a philosopher, a critic, an orator, or a poet. Does not a professor of music, by contrast, need to be a mathematician, a musician, and a philosopher? Must he not possess sharp insight into criticism, elocution, and poetry, though he may not need to practice directly in these diverse disciplines? To what degree philosophers, orators, poets, and mathematicians are superior to language instructors does not require an investigation. [. . .] When one finally recognizes how useful music is to young people, how it raises their spirits, how it is capable of having a notable influence on their entire lives, and how useful music scholars and performers are in ordinarily life, in the church as well as in the school and at court, one must certainly deplore the curiously damaging, unfair, and condemnable neglect of music in our universities.[189]

Writers like Oelrichs and Scheibe and readers like Hartung were uncomfortable with music's lack of legitimacy in the minds of their contemporaries. To them, it was more than a superfluous galanterie. It was a subject of endless fascination, an essential service for their communities, and a force for good in the world. It was also a primary source of income. They wished that more nonmusicians were able to see past the physical demands of their work and recognize the intellectual challenges that it imposed.

Carl August Hartung and other German professional musicians of his era idolized Johann Sebastian Bach. Hartung enjoyed collecting and studying Bach's works and also trading and discussing them with kindred spirits. His closest friends were fellow professional musicians such as Bernhard

Christian Kayser and Johann Marius Christoph Hartung, who shared his affinity for Bach.[190] Something about this repertoire, and perhaps about the man himself, inspired their deepest admiration. They were awed by Bach's unwillingness to compromise, his indefatigable creativity, technique, and drive to realize the highest intellectual aspirations of their art.

One might expect that Hartung would share Bach's music with his pupils; he apparently did not. Though he copied dozens of works for students over the course of the thirteen years covered by his account book, and had them buy prints of many more, he never once assigned any of them a work composed by Bach. Nor do Hartung's own compositions, aimed at a broad public, reveal any hint of his favorite composer's influence. This was repertoire for specialists like Hartung, Kayser, and others who traded manuscripts among themselves. Its difficulty was not a drawback but rather a source of its appeal. This particular composer affirmed their treasured view of music as more than a mere diversion, and the professional musician as more than a mere entertainer.

Conclusion

Music is not an object but rather a means by which human beings relate to one another. Its meaning can never be fixed because it is as complex and malleable as the personal relationships it helps to develop and define. J. S. Bach's contemporaries, like people of all times and places, interpreted music in social terms, listening for what a given musical experience revealed about the human beings involved.

When a young lady performed at the keyboard in eighteenth-century Germany, those gathered around her listened for clues to her character. Purely musical matters—the names of the composers whose works she performed, the tempi she chose, how elegantly she ornamented the melody lines—were of interest not so much in and of themselves but rather for what they revealed about her intelligence, her temperament, her taste. While she might have displayed the contents of her character in other ways—for example, by sewing a fancy dress, by cooking a delicious meal, or by building up an impressive library—few forms of social interaction offered guests such efficient and reliable insight into her cast of mind. Help with sewing, cooking, or selecting books could be bought. A musical performance was different. No matter how much money was at her disposal, no matter how inspiring her teacher, the musical sounds she created under the watchful eyes of a critical audience were undeniably her own.

As such, music offered her a way to tell her own story, her own way. Some sought to project an image of amiable discipline by brilliantly executing fast galanterien exactly as they appeared on the page. Others tested social boundaries by performing slow, melancholy, or contrapuntal repertoire, by choosing instruments not traditionally associated with women, by playing music they had written down themselves, by improving, or by composing. Every choice came with its own risks and rewards, and the range of freedom a woman enjoyed was closely correlated with her degree of financial and social independence.

For men too, music was a powerful tool for display, though the decisions they made were interpreted quite differently. Music making was a sign of domesticity and tractability for men, just as it was for women. But while galant-era women were encouraged to devote copious leisure hours to recreational music-making, men were regularly cautioned to avoid squandering precious time on such a frivolous activity. The male recreational musicians who persevered, however, were applauded more frequently than their female counterparts for approaching music creatively, and for cultivating skills in music theory, improvisation, and composition. Whereas women were expected to make music largely at home, men were explicitly encouraged to use music as a means of socializing with like-minded peers in semi-public spaces. Finally, while female musicians were expected to remain passive objects of admiration, maintaining the pretense that their performances were undertaken out of an innocent love of music rather than a desire to seduce, their male counterparts were free to directly deploy musical skills in the service of courtship.

Keyboard instruments were tools of discipline in Bach's world. It is no coincidence that clavichords, harpsichords, and organs were expensive luxury items owned most often by affluent persons—that is, those who had the most to lose through destabilization of existing hierarchies. Nor is it a coincidence that the primary means of expression on most keyboards were timing and ornamentation; rubato, trills, turns, and rolled chords undercut the regularity of music's pulse, making patterns less predictable and thereby discouraging physical responses. More effectively than any other instrument, keyboards abetted the galant project of channeling the effects of music away from the body and into the mind.

But while keyboards were regarded by Bach's contemporaries as having a civilizing effect upon those who played them, the innocence with which they were associated often acted as a veil that hid more controversial activities. A chaste love of melody served young men and women as an excuse to spend time in close proximity, with the keyboard acting as an incubator for illicit desires. The solidarity so engendered could cut across otherwise inviolable social boundaries. The dramatic proliferation of keyboard instruments and solo repertoire in eighteenth-century Germany was thus driven not only by its promotion of civilizing values but also by its ability to stealthily undercut those values.

The vast majority of solo keyboard repertoire published and performed in eighteenth-century Germany was galant in character. It was explicitly advertised as projecting an image of cosmopolitan grace and carefree affluence. The music was social, outward looking, welcoming of a wide range of listeners. Its commercial triumph caused a reorientation of the entire market for printed music in Germany over the course of J. S. Bach's lifetime. Bach's own music was intended to be performed with galant elegance and grace, but musicians faced extraordinary challenges in trying to bring it to a point at which this was possible. And even when executed with consummate skill, the relentless counterpoint and harmonic tension that characterized Bach's style often frustrated listeners. For many people, he was an extraordinarily gifted composer whose works projected an image they did not wish to embrace. The introverted, intellectual character of Bach's music did, however, impress a small but influential group of followers. For those who sought a challenge rather than an indulgence—chiefly professional musicians and connoisseurs—Bach was an idol. It was not until the nineteenth century, however, that their judgment came to dominate public discourse.

I hope that this book has served to make eighteenth-century music lovers more familiar to modern readers. The lives of these people were no less complicated than our own. Music offered a means of coming to terms with the world's overwhelming complexity, of clarifying social positions, of initiating, maintaining, and furthering interpersonal relationships. For J. S. Bach's contemporaries, every musical act—whether composing, performing, or listening—was an appeal for the affections of those who surrounded them. They were deeply interested in music, but they were even more interested in people.

Notes

For notes containing an asterisk, there is additional information on the book website at www.press.uillinois.edu/books/talle/beyond_bach.

A Note on Currency

1. Talle 2008, 111, 122.
2. Talle 2008, 112, 115, 123.
3. Talle 2008, 116.

Introduction

1. Thomas 1974, 45.
2. Hirschmann 2013.
3. Weber 1977.
4. Goehr 1994.
5. More comprehensive accounts of Bach's life have recently been published in Geck 2000, Wolff 2000, and Williams 2012.
6. Dok II, Nr. 16.
7. Dok II, Nr. 49, 53.
8. Dok II, Nr. 84.
9. Dok I, Nr. 23. See also Maul 2012.
10. Dok II, Nr. 53b, 58, 58a.
11. Dok II, Nr. 522.*
12. Dok II, Nr. 400.*

13. Dok II, Nr. 666.*

14. Dok II, Nr. 409.*

15. Dok II, Nr. 591.*

16. US-R: M11. B118 C6 1739.

17. For good examples see Dreyfus 1996, Dürr 1998, Schulenberg 2006, Williams 1980–1984, Yearsley 2002 and 2012, as well as many of the essays in Schulze 1984, Stauffer and May 1986, and Wolff 1994.

18. See Biba 2009; Fortino 2003; Head 1995; Head 1999; Head 2013; Klassen 2009; Libin 1976 and 2010; Müller 1989; Rampe 1995 and 2000.

19. See Edler 1982, Rampe 1999, 2000, 2003–2005, and 2007.

Chapter 1. Civilizing Instruments

1. Stadtarchiv Leipzig: Sektion 2, M. 659 Bd. 1 (1741) and 2 (1753). These *Galanterie-Waren* ranged in price from twelve groschen for the shirt buttons to twenty-eight reichstaler for the silver clock. In his *Frauenzimmer-Lexicon* of 1715 Gottlieb Siegmund Corvinus used the word *Galanterien* to describe embroidered pillows, chair coverings and handbags. See Corvinus 1715, 571.

2. Gottsched 1725, 73–74.

3. Florin 1702, 32.

4. Thomasius 1701, 14.*

5. Gottsched 1725, 74.*

6. For a valuable overview of the word *galant* in music and beyond see Sheldon 1975.

7. Simons 2001, 344.*

8. Wiedemann 1969, 72; Gottsched 1725, 74–75.

9. Pigs from Westphalia were known to be fatter and tastier than those from other regions of Germany. See Sieglerschmidt 1996, 22.

10. Parker 1987, plates 23a, 23b, 23c; Dietz 1923, 30–37.

11. Friedrichs 1987, 188.

12. Stier and von Hippel 1996, 253; Schirmer 2000, 311–23.

13. Denzel 1994, v.

14. Gerber 1717, 2:403.

15. Denzel 1999, 152.

16. Gerber 1717, 1:574; Czok 1999, 1:187.

17. Weitz 1728, 1.*

18. Kruedener 1973, 8.

19. Simons 2001, 282.

20. Hohberg 1687, appendix.

21. Gerber 1717, 2:1002.*

22. Vogel 1714, 918; Beachy 2005, 21–28.

23. Müller 2007, 238.*

24. Dülmen 1992, 2:23–27; Mörke 1996.

25. Treue 1999, 114.

26. Dülmen 1992, 2:23–27; Mörke 1996.

27. Schultz 1890, 31–32.

28. Hiller 1784, 184–86.

29. Scharffenberg 1713.

30. Lange 1704, 14, 73–74.

31. Simons 2001, 277–282.

32. Wustmann 1889–1995, 244, 355.

33. Gottsched 1751, 739; Kreutzer 2005, 93–95.

34. Kleeberger 1911.

35. Döring 2000a, 11–12.

36. Kempe 2003, 30–43.

37. Cohen 1985, 164.

38. Beyer 1999, 201.

39. D-LEsa: Riemer-Chronik, 546.

40. Israel 2001, 242–46, 552–55.

41. Mattheson 1713, 316.*

42. Zedler 1731–1754, 22:1388–1405 ("Musick").

43. Albrecht 1734, 55.*

44. Albrecht 1734, 67.*

45. Hunold 1708, 223–25.*

46. Mattheson 1739, 36.*

47. Cramer 1747–1748, 110–12.

48. Gerlach was organist and music director at Leipzig's Neukirche and director of Bach's Collegium Musicum in the 1740s. Landvoigt was a former pupil at the Thomasschule and librettist of a lost Bach cantata, "Thomana saß annoch betrübt" (BWV Anh. 19).

49. Cramer 1747–1748, 116–21.*

50. Hunold 1708, 221.*

51. Lange 1704, 73–74.*

52. Dietz 1915, 211.*

53. Reviewing the documentary literature on the origins of the keyboard in his *Syntagma Musica* of 1619, Michael Prætorius noted that Pope Vitalian sanctioned the use of organs in church already in the year 660, but hypothesized that keyboard instruments must have been in common use elsewhere before this time. See Prætorius 1619, 89–90; and Wolf 1899.

54. For a survey of keyboard instruments in Bach's time see Libin 1994.

55. "Pandalon" here refers to Pantaleon Hebenstreit, the inventor of a dulcimer with ninety strings called the *cymbal*. See Ficker 1731.*

56. Preußner 1949, 41–42.

57. LLL Universitätsbibliothek Göttingen, Cod. Ms. Achenw. 218 I, fol. 77v (Oct. 12, 1743).*

58. Adlung 1758, 139.

59. Bärwald 2008.

60. Heinz 2012, 26.

61. Roughly 555 German organs built during Bach's lifetime are known to survive today, while 116 more are known to have been destroyed. I would like to thank

Piet Bron for providing this information. See also Ahrens and Langrock 2003, 16. Gottfried Silbermann built forty-four new instruments over the course of his career, thirty-two of which survive today. Losses were undoubtedly much higher for instruments built by less famous makers.

62. Adlung 1768, 197, 206, 219, 221, 224, 226, 237, 250, 254, 263, 267, 272, 280, 285.

63. Lediard 1740, 241. "The Organs are, in general, very fine here, of a prodigious Size, and finely adorn'd: That in St. *Catherine*'s Church is said to consist of above 6000 Pipes, of which I, myself, observ'd two that were so large, that I could but just grasp them with the Extent of my arms." US-NHub: Osborn c295, 136. "Sunday the 17th [Sept. 1730] in the morning we went to St. Katherines & heard the fine organ there. It has a fine, clear, mellow tone."

64. Hildebrandt earned 858 reichstaler from domestic keyboard manufacturing in 1744–1745 and 885 reichstaler in 1747. Flade 1953, 200; Dähnert 1961, 106–7, 231.

65. Dähnert 1961, 106–7, 231.

66. Dok I, Nr. 23.

67. For more information see the discussion of Carl August Hartung's finances in chapter 11.

68. Adlung 1768, 2: xi; Heyde 1986, 49–54; Müller 2007, 119–20.

69. Friedrich 1989, 55, 96.

70. Henkel 1991 documents a chamber organ "in extreme disrepair" (*so sehr baufällig*) offered at auction for twenty-five reichstaler, a "small, spoiled" (*klein, verdorben*) harpsichord offered for two groschen, and clavichord that ranged in price from two groschen to two reichstaler. In one Leipzig coffeehouse, "Butterbrödte mit klatem Braten oder Servelat-Wurst" cost four groschen and "Die Portion Chocolate in Wasser gekocht" cost six groschen. See Jugler 1779, 106–7.

71. Adlung 1768, 2:158.

72. Holtkötter 1986, 95–113.

73. Wheatley 1952, 5:395.

74. Hafner 1996, 212–13.

75. Dok 2:352.

76. Hankins and Silverman 1999, 3.

77. Bach 1753, 1.*

78. Mattheson 1739, 106.*

79. Burkardt, Gantner-Schlee, and Knieriem 2006, 213; Edler 1982, 98.

80. Rose 2005; Gottsched 1725–1726, 2:346; Voigt 1742, 44–45, 75.

81. Preußner 1949, 41–42.

82. Klose 1849, 148.

83. These statistics represent a compilation of all works printed in German-speaking countries in RISM, publishers' catalogs including those of Balthasar Schmid (Heussner 1963), Johann Ulrich Haffner (Hoffmann-Erbrecht 1954, 1955), and Johann Jakob Lotter (Rheinfurth 1977) and book fair catalogs (Göhler 1902). A work is counted as a unique publication if it could be purchased individually. Bach's Keyboard Partitas (BWV 825–830), for example, were published separately between 1726 and

1730 and are thus counted as six separate works. The twenty-five installments of Telemann's *Der getreue Music-Meister,* by contrast, were purchased by subscription in 1728 and are thus counted as a single work.

84. The most important of these were Balthasar Schmid and Johann Ulrich Haffner in Nuremberg, and Johann Jakob Lotter in Augsburg.

85. Zohn 2005.

86. The term *Galanterien* referred initially to a broader range of repertoire but was refined over the first half of the eighteenth century to refer primarily to minuets, bourrées, gavottes, and other quick works in four-bar phrases.*

87. The preface to Georg Muffat's *Florilegium Primum* of 1695 is quoted from Strunck and Treitler 1998, 645–46 (translation by Oliver Strunck and Margaret Murata).*

88. Quantz 1752, 269. Distinctions between dance music for dancing and dance music for playing and singing appear in Mattheson 1713, 186–87, and Mattheson 1739, 224–32.

89. Leppert 1988, 149–54.

90. Krieger 1697, preface.*

91. The rather sudden proliferation of printed galanterien around 1730 has sometimes been interpreted as marking the dawn of a new musical era (Ahrens 1986; Radice 1999) or signaling a precipitous drop in the technical proficiency of amateur keyboardists (Rampe 1995; Rampe 2000). In fact, the minuets, bourrées, and gavottes published in the 1730s and 1740s are not fundamentally different in style or technical demands from the those found in prints and manuscripts of the late seventeenth century (See D-Ngm: Hs. 31781; Jung 1991, 92; Leisinger 2000; Maul 2008; Epstein 1940; and Haensel 1974.). The fact that this music was frequently marketed as "easy" and "light" after 1730 is a result of professional publishers entering the market on a large scale. Such terms are advertisements for these collections, not objective descriptions of their contents.

92. Mattheson 1713, title page.*

93. Mattheson 1713, 202; Mattheson 1721, 179.*

94. Scheibel 1721, 41–42.

95. Hellmund 1719, 18–19.*

96. Fuhrmann 1706, 87–88.*

97. Buttstedt 1716, 9.*

98. Mattheson 1717, 42–44.*

Chapter 2. The Mechanic and the Tax Collector

1. D-BS: C 1 8: Nr. 43, 538r–541v.*

2. Fleichsig 1962–1964, 48, no. 2: 47.*

3. The four standard types are: four octaves, fretted; five octaves, fretted; five octaves, unfretted; five octaves and a third, unfretted. In 1728, for a certain Herr Rademacher in Königslutter, Fritz built "ein doppeltes Clavier nebst Pedal." See Fritz 1757, 25.

4. Fritz 1757, preface.*

5. Victoria and Albert Museum, Inv.Nr. 339–1882. For a description see Schott 1998, 78–80. The clavichord was formerly in the collection of Carl Engel, a German musicologist residing in England, who acquired it on a visit to his native country in 1874. See Simmonds 2008. The evidence for the connection between this instrument and J. H. Heyne is as follows. The title that Fritz gave the list of clavichord customers he published as an appendix to Fritz 1757 suggests that the names are presented in chronological order. It reads: "The names of the persons who received clavichords from me as I completed them one after the next in the years listed below" (*Namen derjenigen Personen, welche in nachbenanten Jahren neue Claviere, so wie solche nach einander von mir verfertiget sind, erhalten habe*). They are listed not only by year but also chronologically within each year. Given that only four Fritz clavichords survive to the present (Musikinstrumenten-Museum Berlin, Inv.Nr.3594; Museum Bochum, Inv. Nr.1540; Victoria and Albert Museum, Inv.Nr.339–1882; and Städtisches Museum Braunschweig, Inv.Nr.0012–0111–00), it is remarkable that two of them were produced in very close proximity: the Bochum instrument is dated January 1751, while the London instrument is dated February 1751. It is all the more remarkable that both of these belong to the largest and rarest category of instruments Fritz made. According to his published sales list, he built just three with this range in 1751: they occupy positions one, two, and four of seventeen total. Number one was sold to "The Accountant, Mr. May" (*Hr. Buchhalter May*), presumably the same accountant May who earned seventy-two reichstaler and thirty-three groschen per quarter from the government administration of Braunschweig-Wolfenbüttel in 1750–1751 (Staatsarchiv Wolfenbüttel: Sig. 17 III Alt, 170, f. 78r). Number two was sold to "The Tax Collector, Mr. Heyne" (*Hr. Einnehmer Heyne*). Number four was sold to "The Theology Student, Mr. Drechsler" (*Hr. Cand. Theol. Drechsler*), presumably Augustus Brandanus Drechsler of Braunschweig, who enrolled at the University in Jena on April 19, 1747 (Köhler 1969, 3:498). The London instrument cannot have belonged to Mr. May; his clavichord was the first of the year in 1751 and the London instrument cannot have been earlier than second of the year (it is dated February, whereas the Bochum clavichord is dated January). Given Fritz's ordinary rate of production for the period, by far the most plausible scenario is that Mr. May's instrument was completed in January, Mr. Heyne's in February, a small clavichord for another client in early March, and Mr. Drechsler's in late March or early April. Aligning these names with the surviving instruments, May would have received the Bochum instrument (dated January), Heyne the London instrument (dated February), and Drechsler the last (now lost).

6. For biographical information on Barthold Fritz see Fleichsig 1962–1964, 48, no. 2: 46–49 and 50, no. 2: 53; and Gerber 1790–1792, 1:456.

7. Braunschweig had 15,600 residents in 1671 and 22,500 in 1758. Meibeyer 1966, 129.

8. Albrecht 1980, 382–95.

9. Fleichsig 1962–1964, 48, no. 2: 48.*

10. Fritz became a citizen on July 12, 1720. See Schröder 1928, 48. For information on Fritz's purchase of the house at Marstall 12 (Brandversicherungsnummer 2812) see D-BS: C 1 8: Nr. 43, 538r–541v.

11. Sack 1853; Albrecht 1980, 359–60.

12. Fleichsig 1962–1964, 48, no. 2: 47.*

13. Only 310 of the 322 clavichords Fritz sold can be connected with particular locations: Ammendorf (1); Amsterdam (Holland) (4); Arkhangelsk (Russia) (3); Berlin (1); Braunschweig (171); Bremen (1); Calvörde (1); Celle (4); Clausthal (23); Dessau (1); Dingelstedt (1); Dorstadt (1); Eisleben (1); Fallersleben (2); Frankfurt am Main (1); Gibraltar (England) (1); Glendorf (1); Göttingen (2); Haag (Holland) (1); Halberstadt (10); Hamburg (14); Hannover (1); Harpke (2); Harzburg (2); Helmstedt (1); Homburg (1); Hornburg (1); Kassel (1); Königslutter (2); Land Hadeln (1); Lauenburg (1); London (1); Lucklum (2); Magdeburg (1); Mecklenburg (1); Moordorf (1); Münden (1); Neuhaus (2); Norway (3); Ölper (1); Oschersleben (1); Quedlinburg (1); Quenstedt (3); Riddagshausen (1); Rinteln (1); Saldern (1); Schlesien (1); Schwarzburg (2); Sickte (1); Söllingen (1); Vorsfelde (1); Walbeck (1); Wallau in der Pfalz (2); Wendenzelle (1); Wernigerode (2); Westphalen (1); Wieda (1); Wiederstedt (1); Wiesbaden (1); Wolfenbüttel (11); Zellerfeld (1); Zerbst (1); Zilly (1).

14. In analyzing these materials, I have drawn a distinction between agents (those who bought Fritz's instruments "in commißion" on behalf of others) and owners (those who eventually owned the instruments, whether they bought them directly from Fritz or from an agent). This distinction is sometimes problematic because one suspects Fritz was not absolutely consistent in his designations; for example, a customer who purchased ten keyboards but is only listed five times as buying "in commißion" is considered here to be an agent in all ten cases, though he may have bought some instruments for his personal use. Conversely, a customer who ordered three instruments in quick succession but is never listed as buying "in commißion" is considered an owner in all three cases, though he may well have sold some of them.

15. Three pastors sold nine instruments; eight professional musicians sold twenty-five instruments; three merchants sold another twenty-five instruments.

16. Fritz sold instruments to 172 apparently unique individuals who did not have aristocratic names.

17. The "Hr. Hofgerichts-Assessor Lüdecke in Braunschweig" who bought a clavichord from Fritz in 1735 must be identical with the *Hofgerichts Assessor* Levin Christian Luedecke referenced in court employment records. See Staatsarchiv Wolfenbüttel, 17 III Alt, 154, f. 31r. Fritz's "Hr. Cammerconsulent Seyden in Braunschweig" is certainly identical with Friedrich Seiden, *Kammerkonsulent* referenced in court employment records. See Staatsarchiv Wolfenbüttel, 17 III Alt, 552. The "Hr. Cammerdiener Jenichen zu Braunschweig" who purchased a clavichord from Fritz in 1754 must be identical with the *Cammerdiener* Jänichen employed by the court. See Staatsarchiv Wolfenbüttel, Sig: 17 III Alt, 170, f. 51r.

18. Fritz lists among his customers, for example, "Hr. Buchhalter May zu Braunschweig" and "Hr. Buchhalter Gerlach zu Braunschweig," who must certainly be identical with the court employees *Buchhalter* May and *Buchhalter* Gerlach. See Staatsarchiv Wolfenbüttel 17 III Alt, 170, f. 78r, 79r. Fritz's "Hr. Postsecret. Emperius in Braunschweig" must be identical with the "Emperius, Sekr. d. Kayserl. Posten in Braunschweig" referenced in Staatsarchiv Wolfenbüttel Sig: 37 Alt Nr. 3272. The

"Hr. Leibchirurgus Ramdohr zu Braunschweig" who bought a clavichord from Fritz in 1741 must certainly be identical with the court *Leib Chirurgus* Ferdinand Benedikt Ramdohr. See Staatsarchiv Wolfenbüttel 17 III Alt, 170, f. 52v. The "Hr. Tanzmeister Grüneberg in Wolffenbüttel" who purchased a clavichord from Fritz in 1740 must be identical with the *Tantzmeister* Grünenberg employed by the court in 1751. See Staatsarchiv Wolfenbüttel, 17 III Alt, 170, f. 37v.

19. Fritz identified 196 male customers (87 percent) and thirty female customers (13 percent).

20. Customer designations such as "Frau Commißionsräthinn von Kalm" and the "Frau Commißionsräthinn von Flögen" suggest that their husbands held courtly appointments. The latter was presumably the wife of Julius Justus von Flögen, *Hof-Commissionsrat* in Wolfenbüttel. See Staatsarchiv Wolfenbüttel Alt III, 552, 34 (1765) and 569 (1744–1765).

21. Düsterdieck 1983, Nr. 2, 45, 51, 104, 105, 131, 151, 152, 158, 189, 190, and 256. The music instructor was Nikolaus Georg Weinholtz, the French instructor was Jean Randon, and the chamberlain was Johann Daniel Richter. See Albrecht 1986, 68–69, 96.

22. Chrysander 1863, 285.

23. Voigt 1742, 109–11.*

24. Fritz 1757, 22–24.

25. Fritz 1757, 8–9.*

26. Fritz 1757. The first edition appeared in 1756.

27. Fritz 1757, preface to the 1757 edition.*

28. Sorge 1749.

29. Sorge 1758, 7.*

30. Marpurg, 1760–1764, 280 (February 23, 1760).*

31. Fritz 1757, preface to the 1757 edition.*

32. The preface to the second edition is dated April 4, 1757.

33. Fleichsig 1962–1964, 48, no. 2: 49.

34. For the record of Heyne's birth see Evangelisch-Lutherischer Stadtkirchenver-band Hannover, Stadtkirchenkanzlei, Kirchenbuchamt. Clausthal Taufen 1681–1720, 242.

35. Eschebach 2005.

36. Stadtarchiv Braunschweig, Braunschweig Neubürgerbuch (Nbb. 1724–1757. S. 750–51. Signatur: C I 2 Bd. 3, S. 750–51.)

37. Hönn 1724, 3–4.

38. The average is calculated on the basis of known salaries for the *Tantzmeister* Grüneberg (150 reichstaler), the *Leib Chirurgus* Ramdohr (200 reichstaler), the *Buchhalter* Gerlach (266 reichstaler), and the *Zoll und Accise Einnehmer* Heyne (366 reichstaler). See Staatsarchiv Wolfenbüttel 17 III Alt, 170, f. 37v, 52v, 71r, and 78r (1750–1751).

39. Before 1778, Johann Christian Dietrich Heyne served as copyist (*Copist bey der Berglandlungs Casse*), from 1778 to 1783 he was a cashier (*Caßirer*), from 1783 to 1789 he was a registrar (*Registrator beÿm Fürstl. Finanz Collegio*) and after 1789 he

was senior finance agent (*Ober-Factor*). Staatsarchiv Wolfenbüttel Sig. 3 III Nr. 559, f. 45–47, and Nr. 552, f. 59, 70, 85.

Chapter 3. *A Silver Merchant's Daughter*

1. One "ell" corresponded to the distance between the elbow and the tip of the index finger. Stadtarchiv Leipzig, Vormundschaftsstube Nr. 442, Bd. 1, f. 95r–95v.*

2. Neumann 1970.

3. Neumann 1970, 21–22. For comparison see Lediard 1740, 260–62.

4. Jens Müller 1989, 54–58.

5. Fritz 2005, 17–19.

6. Talle 2008, 72–75.

7. Eger 1745, 27, 48–49, 145–46.

8. Lediard 1740, 258. "In their Housekeeping they are frugal to a Fault, or rather mean: A large Piece of smoaked or salted Beef, boil'd on *Sunday*, is served up the whole Week, with Vegetables, or a Dish of Fish, which is extreamly cheap and good here; while their Servants are chiefly fed with sundry Sorts of Spoon-Meat, made of the Soop of their Salt-Meat and Herbs, or of sundry Groots, boiled in Milk, Water or Beer. But as sparing as they are in their own Families, as extravagant are they when they treat Strangers." See also Dimpfel 1929, 85–86.

9. Blochberger 1749, 3:660 ("Wasser").

10. Rambach 1737, 288.

11. Marie-Thérèse Dancourt had popularized the dress while playing the title role in Terence's *Andria*.

12. Das kirchliche Archiv Leipzig. Taufbuch St. Nikolai 1728–1734, 499.

13. Wustmann 1889–1895, 222.

14. Schulze 1997, 152.*

15. Rambach 1732, 184.*

16. Rambach 1732, 1169.*

17. During the randomly selected years 1726–1731, one in twenty babies was miscarried or stillborn, and for every ten who survived childbirth six died as infants. One of every three who survived infancy died before reaching adulthood. See the printed summaries made by the *Leichenschreiber* in Leipzig during these years. See D-LEsa: Riemer-Chronik.

18. Dürr 1996, 189.

19. Gottsched 1725–1726, 2:284.*

20. Petersen 2003, 13.

21. Schultz 1890, 4–5.

22. Dürr 1996, 196.

23. Gräbner 1711, 64–65.

24. Recke 1795, 59–60.

25. Dürr 1996, 201.*

26. Dürr 1996, 192–193.*

27. Recke 1795, 29–30.*

28. Roloff 1984, 1:21.*

29. Curas 1723, 73–86.

30. Freilinghausen 1719, 118–30.

31. Hohberg 1687, 2:281.*

32. Leporin 1742, 102.*

33. Luther 1730, unpaginated.

34. Petersen 2003, 12.*

35. Seybold 1785, vol. 4/91.*

36. Petersen 2003, 16, 37–38.

37. Gräbner 1711, 70.*

38. Gräbner 1711, 68.*

39. Barth 1720, 76.*

40. Taubert 1717, 1003; Corvinus 1715, 1960–61.

41. Gräbner 1711, 66.

42. Hellmund 1719, 2.*

43. This description appears in J. F. W. Zachariä's poem "Der Renommiste" of 1744. See Zachariä 1761, 1:24.*

44. Petersen 2003, 23.*

45. Gräbner 1711, 66–67.*

46. Recke 1795, 59–60.

47. See Neumann 1970. Head 1999, 207–8 notes that the *Frauenzimmer Lexicon* (Corvinus 1715) contains no entries for musical instruments other than the zither, lute, and keyboard.

48. Georgi 1742, 2:368.*

49. Scholze 1743, Nr. 46.*

50. Gellert 1747, 123–24.*

51. Marpurg 1750a, 101–2 (May 27, 1749).*

52. A *Licentiat* was a recipient of an academic degree roughly equivalent to a doctorate.

53. Uffenbach 1753, 2:99–101. See also D-Gs: Cod.Ms.Uffenbach.25, IV: 958–59.

54. Schmoller, Krauske, and Loewe 1898, 496.

55. D-Gs: Cod.Ms.Uffenbach.29, II: 177–178.*

56. Brockes 1721–1748, 2:223.*

57. Recke 1795, 49, 53–54.

58. Lediard 1740, 5; Elsholtii 1682, 341; Dimpfel 1929, 83.

59. Petersen 2003, 11–23.

60. Möser 1871, 16–19. Blochberger 1749, 3:637–638 ("Wäsche").

61. Dimpfel 1929, 83–85.

62. Zedler 1731–1754, 2:526 ("Parfum für das Frauenzimmer zu den Händen"); 26:446 ("Aqua Cosmetica").

63. Zedler 1731–1754, 19:166 ("Magen-Balsam"); 29:683 ("Pulver [Zahn-] Rhunraths").

64. D-LEsa: Vormundschaftsstube Nr. 1055, fol. 5v–6r. See also Fritz 2005.

65. Zarncke 1909, 78, Müller 2007, 47–48.

66. Crell 1725, 57–58, 105.

67. Müller 2007, 203.

68. Schering 1926, 306.

69. Crell 1725, 61–62.

70. Dietz hearing Kurrende. Line is from "Durch Adams Fall ist ganz verderbt."

71. Cramer 1747; Henkel 1991.

72. Dietz 1923, 259.

73. Taubert 1717, 429–30.

74. Maul 2010, 163–64.

75. Hilgenfeldt 1850, 172.*

76. Taubert 1717, 454–57.

77. Marpurg 1765, 5–6.

78. Vetter 1713; Rose 2005.

79. Kretschmar 1909. A keyboard notebook that originally belonged to Charlotte Fredericke Zeumer was inherited by her son, Johann Friedrich Zeumer, who apparently continued the book while having keyboard lessons with J. G. Görner in Leipzig. Zeumer left Görner 400 reichstaler upon his death in 1774. See Schönfuß 2015, 126.

80. J. P. Kirnberger added "l" and "r" indications in a copy he prepared of J. S. Bach's "Giga" (BWV 825/7), presumably for a student. See D-B: Mus.ms.Bach.P1206.

81. That C. S. Bose's lessons were interrupted during this period is suggested by the dates of her payments to Görner. See Stadtarchiv Leipzig, Vormundschaftsstube Nr. 442, Bd. 1, f. 172v (January 1733: "Herr Görnern vor *Information* auf 2 Monate à 2 Rthl." [four reichstaler]); f. 173r (August 1733: "Herr Görnern vor *Information* auf 2 Monate à 2 Rthl." [four reichstaler]); f. 173r (November 1733: "Herr Görnern p. *Information* auf 1 Monat." [two reichstaler]).

82. Talle 2008, 69–70.

83. Faced with the 1727 ban that followed the death of Augustus's wife, Prince Electress Christiane Eberhardine von Sachsen, Görner appealed to the authorities in hopes that his Collegium Musicum ensemble would be granted an exception on the grounds that it was educational rather than entertaining. See Spitta 1873–1880, 2:789.

84. BPH Brandenburg-Preußisches Hausarchiv. Rep. 46 König Friedrich Wilhelm I. W Nr. 67. Vol. 1. Fasz. 2. fol. 102r–102v. Herzogin Philippine Charlotte of Braunschweig-Lüneburg-Bevern, geb. Prinzessin in Preußen writing to her brother, King Friederich "The Great" of Prussia on December 30, 1743. " . . . *il faut que je vous dise pour vous divertir, quapresent lorsque je suis seulle je fais venir L Opera d Artaxerce sur mon lit je remüe les doits comme si je joües du Claffsin et puis je mimagine entendre chanter la Gasparini et la Benedetta . . .*" I would like to thank R.-S. Pegah for calling my attention to this document.

85. A collection of drawings from the life of Elisabeth von Zinzendorf includes an ink drawing by Friedrich von Watteville of the young lady having a lesson at the clavichord in 1751 with a female teacher in the presence of two other women. See Libin 2010, 230.

86. Lediard 1740, 141–42, 122–23.

87. Gottsched 1771–1772, 2:37–39 (November 20, 1751).*

88. Gottsched 1722–1766, 6:215–216 (November 25, 1739).*

89. I would like to thank Rashid-Sascha Pegah for drawing my attention to this document.

90. Hauptstaatsarchiv Dresden: 10026 Geheimes Kabinet. Loc 383/05, f. 175r–v, 181r.*

91. Hauptstaatsarchiv Dresden: 10026 Geheimes Kabinet. Loc 383/05, f. 180r: "[. . .] aus eben die Weise, als andere dergl. außländischen in unseren Diensten stehenden Personen geschehet [. . .]."

92. D-Ua: Klunzin Nr. 1 (1711) and Klunzin Nr. 2 (1720). The 1717 book has been lost, though a portrait of Barbara Kluntz now in the Ulmer Museum reveals its title page.

93. Blessinger 1913, 24. The document Blessinger cites has been lost.

94. See Schultz 2005, 34.*

95. Koldau 2005, 934–43.

96. Neubacher 2009, 254–61. Female singers did sometimes participate in church subscription concerts—for example, those initiated in Lübeck by Johann Paul Kuntzen. See Hennings 1951, 125.

97. Ziegler 1731, 136.*

98. Berg 2009, 46–47.*

99. Rohr 1728, 502.

100. Wolff 2000, 204–5.

101. Ernst Ludwig Gerber probably learned this information from his father, Heinrich Nikolaus Gerber, who studied with J. S. Bach in the 1720s. Gerber 1790–1792, 1:76.*

102. Recke 1795, 70.*

Chapter 4. A Dark-Haired Dame and Her Scottish Admirer

1. Boswell 1928, 22.

2. Caroline Kircheisen went on to marry a war councillor and privy secretary named Friedrich August Ludwig Buchholtz.

3. Boswell 1928, 23.

4. Ibid., 27–28.

5. Ibid., 29–30.

6. Ibid., 30.

7. Crawford 1997, 106 (July 23, 1764).

8. Hunold 1708–1709, 1:417–18.*

9. Müller 2007, 218–19; Simons 2001, 50.

10. Recke 1795, 43–44.*

11. Recke 1795, 44.*

12. Pütter 1798, 1:240–41.

13. Petersen 2003, 17.*

14. Petersen 2003, 20–21.*

15. Petersen 2003, 10.*

16. In 1727, for example, a total of 877 children were baptized in Leipzig's St. Thomas and St. Nicholas Churches, 105 of whom had parents who were unmarried. See D-LEsa: Riemer-Chronik.

17. Anna Constantia von Cosel, spent forty-nine years in prison after a lengthy affair with Augustus the Strong went sour in 1716. See Hoffmann 1984.

18. D-LEsa: Riemer-Chronik, 196.

19. Gräbner 1711, 34–35.*

20. Spitta 1894, 221.*

21. The fictional letter is dated May 1, 1749, and allegedly sent from "Klangburg." Marpurg 1750a, 88.*

22. Printz 1691, 110–12.

23. The book belonged to Sophie Margaretha von Holleben (née von Normann) and was prepared mostly before her marriage at age nineteen in 1747. Spitta 1894, 240–41.*

24. These mottos were written by Elisabeth Dorothea Landgräfin zu Hessen-Darmstadt, who signed the book "E. D. L. Z. H. D. Ao 1692. d. 7 Julÿ" when she was sixteen years old. D-DSsa: D 11 Nr. 71/3.*

25. Elizabeth Dorothea's older brother, Philip Landgraf zu Hessen-Darmstadt, copied an aria into the book, signing it "Aria P. L. Z. D. H."

26. Gressel 1716, 370.*

27. For comparable examples, see the poems in Gressel 1716, 112–13, and in Corvinus 1710, 141.

28. König 1745, 318.*

29. Neukirch 1704, 49–50.*

30. Fassmann 1742, 5:148.

31. Pöllnitz 1735, 171–72.*

32. Boswell 1928, 39.

33. Ibid., 40.

34. Ibid., 41–42.

35. The translations from Boswell's diary and letters are adapted from Frederick Pottle's translations in Boswell 1928. US-NHub: GEN MSS 89, series 1, letters, box 5, folder 156, L 836–37 (August 10, 1764).*

36. US-NHub: GEN MSS 89, series 2, correspondence, box 25, folder 600, C 1669–1670 (August 18, 1764).*

37. US-NHub: GEN MSS 89, series 2, correspondence, box 25, folder 600, C 1669–1670 (August 18, 1764).*

38. US-NHub: GEN MSS 89, series 1, letters, box 5, folder 156, L 836–37 (August 10, 1764).*

39. Boswell 1928, 78.

40. Ibid., 87–88.

41. Ibid., 91–92.

42. Ibid., 82, 91–92, 95.

43. Ibid., 92.

44. Ibid., 98.

45. Ibid., 98–99.

46. See US-NHub: GEN MSS 89, series 1, letters, box 5, folder 156, L 836–37 (October 2, 1764). See also Boswell 1928, 123.

47. The translation is my own. US-NHub: GEN MSS 89, series 1, letters, box 5, folder 156, L 836–37 (October 2, 1764).*

48. Boswell 1928, 42–43. That Caroline Kircheisen was also a brunette is suggested by his earlier having likened her to an "Indian princess."

49. Boswell 1928, 123–24.

50. US-NHub: GEN MSS 89, series 2, correspondence, box 25, folder 600, C 1669–1670 (February 2, 1765).*

Chapter 5. Two Teenage Countesses

1. See Jaeneke 1973.

2. Speer 1687, 124–31.*

3. Speer 1687, 130–131.

4. Examples include Johan Joachim Agrell's *Sonates pour le Clavecin accomp. de quelques petites Aires, Polonaises & Menuettes, composés pour le Divertissement des Dames* (Nuremberg: Christoph Riegel's widow, ca. 1751–52); Johann Nikolaus Müller's *Des Musicalischen Frauenzimmers Musicalisches Divertissement* (Nuremberg: Balthasar Schmid, ca. 1739–1745); Christoph Nichelmann's *Sei brevi sonate da cembalo massime all'uso delle dame* (Nuremberg: Balthasar Schmid, ca. 1745), and *Brevi sonate da cembalo all'uso di chi ama il cembalo massime delle dame* (Nuremberg: Balthasar Schmid, ca. 1748); Michael Scheuenstuhl's *Gemüths- und Ohr-ergötzende Clavier-Übung, bestehend in VI. leichten und nach heutigen Gusto gesezten Galanterie-Partien, welche meistentheils vor Frauenzimmer componirt* (Nuremberg: Johann Ulrich Haffner, [≥1742]) and *Die beschäfftigte Muse Clio oder zum Vergnügen der Seele und Ohrs eingerichtete III. Galanterie-Suiten auf das Clavier, in welchen vornehmlich der heutige Geschmack beobachtet wird, Zum Dienst des Music-liebenden FrauenZimmers verfertiget* (Nuremberg: Johann Ulrich Haffner, [1745]); Johann Nikolaus Tischer's *Das vergnügte Ohr und der erquickte Geist in Sechs Galanterie-Parthien zur Clavier-Ubung für das Frauenzimmer in einer leichten und applicablen Composition dargestellet* (Nuremberg: Johann Ulrich Haffner, ca. 1742–1746).

5. Dok II, Nr. 492.

6. Johann Ludwig Krebs, *Andere Piece, Bestehend in einer leichten, und nach dem heutigen Gusto, Wohl-eingerichteten Suite Denen Liebhabern der edlen Music, Besonders des Claviers, Zur Gemüths-Ergötzung, Und Angenehmen Zeit-Vertreib* (Zwickau, 1741). An advertisement in the newspaper for the same collection emphasizes that it is "playable by women without much trouble." See Ahrens 1986, 71. Advertised on January 7, 1741, in the *Leipziger Post-Zeitung* as "im heutigen Gusto" and "auch von einem Frauenzimmer ohne große Mühe gespielet werden." A similar ad appeared in 1740 in the *Hamburger Relations-Courier* (see Becker 1956, 43). In his next publication, Krebs tried to have it both ways, offering an *Ouverture* aimed at those who seek what he called the "plus

ultra" in music, while the remaining movements (*Lentement, Vivement, Païsan, Menu-etts, Gavotte, Air, Passepieds, Rigadon*) were "to be understood simply as *Galanterien* for women."

7. Marpurg 1750a, 11 (March 7, 1749).*

8. The view would remain standard for much of the eighteenth century. As Charles Burney (1726–1814) noted in 1771: "Ladies [. . .] though frequently neat in execution, seldom aim at expression." See Head 2013, 27.

9. D-WRgs, Herzogin Anna Amalia Bibliothek: M 8:29b. See Maul 2008. The *Clavierbuch* of Princess Sophia Augusta of Anhalt-Zerbst (D-WRgs, Herzogin Anna Amalia Bibliothek: M 8:29b) was copied in the years around 1685 by the court organist in Zerbst, Bernhard Meyer, and the court organist in Weimar, Johann Effler. Its contents consist primarily of arias from Adam Krieger's *Das erste Zehen* (Dresden, 1657) and *Das Fünftes Zehen* (Dresden, 1667), and from Johann Caspar Horn's *Parergon musicum; oder, Musicalisches Neben-Werck* (Leipzig, 1663). The book also includes a popular street song (*Guten Morgen Garten Man*), as well as keyboard galanterien (for example, *Der Klap Tantz, Der Himmel Tantz, Die Sieben Sprünge, Brandle de Boische, Französischer Tantz, Sarabande, Gavotte, Gigue, Allemande, Ballo*), some of which have programmatic titles (for example, *Gringoletta, La Marionette, Der Ticktack*).

10. A-Wn: SM 19455. See Leisinger 2000. The *Clavierbuch* of Princess Wilhelmine Amalia von Braunschweig-Lüneburg was copied around 1693 and contains primarily excerpts from operas by J. B. Lully and anonymous dances (courante, minuet, bourée, passepied, sarabande, chaconne), some of which can be safely attributed to various French composers. There are also some exercises in note reading and two works attributed to "Madame la princesse" and "Madame la daufine," which she may well have composed herself. The heavy French influence in this notebook can be attributed to her having spent most of her early life in Paris, where at least some of this book was probably copied.

11. DK-Kk: Pos. Thott 292.80. See Epstein 1940, 92–94, and Haensel 1974. The *Clavierbuch* of Christiane Charlotte Amalie Trolle was prepared at the convent in Preetz around 1700, probably by Heinrich Scheele, who served as organist there from 1678 to 1718 and was charged with teaching the *Schul-Jungfrauen*. The book, dated 1699 and 1702, contains eighty-five works for keyboard solo (including forty-eight minuets, as well as various preludes, variations, arias, and other dances) and thirty-two chorales. Fräulein Trolle's exact relationship with the convent remains unclear, but it clearly did not hinder her from collecting secular galanterien.

12. D-WRsa: Hausarchiv, Abt. A XV Sophie Charlotte Albertine Nr. 1. See Jung 1991, 92. The keyboard book of Sophie Charlotte Albertine von Brandenburg-Culmbach was copied around 1724–1727 when she was twelve to fourteen years old. It was copied for the most part by her keyboard teacher, the court musician Johann August Bomhard, who was paid two Reichstaler per month for his trouble. The book begins with an introduction to reading music and continues with a variety of galanterien, some attributed to Georg Philipp Telemann. Unfortunately, most of the book is blank, suggesting that the princess was somewhat less inclined toward

music making than her teacher had expected. Its contents correspond closely to the published repertoire marketed to the women.

13. D-Ngm: Hs. 31781. See Epstein 1940, 90–94.

14. See the discussion of Johanna Catharina Burchardi in chapter 11.

15. Ziegler 1731, 406–9.*

16. Ibid., 392–93.*

17. Debuch 2001, 15–58.

18. The instrument now stands in the *Kirche zur Frohen Botschaft* in Berlin-Karlshorst.

19. Wutta 1989, 48–49. The translations from this source are adapted from Berg 1998, 481.*

20. Wutta 1989, 49.*

21. Princess Amalia signed one of the letters quoted here: "Amelie, Organiste."

22. In 1567 the territory of Hessen-Darmstadt had around twenty thousand residents living on perhaps thirteen hundred square kilometers. Darmstadt had only about twelve hundred residents and was still quite rural. The numbers given in the text have been adjusted for territorial acquisitions between 1567 and the period 1688 to 1739, when Ernst Ludwig was in power. See Franz and Wolf 1980, 13.

23. Hoferichter 1980, 69–74.

24. Two million gulden. See Franz and Wolf 1980, 17.

25. Hoferichter 1980, 77.

26. D-DSsa: D4 379/6 (August 24, 1741); D4 379/6 (November 12, 1746): "[. . .] das[s] auch die kaum aufgewachsene bubens, mich fast über den hauffen lauffen, und nicht einmahl mich zu honoriren an ihren huth greiffen, wenige dan[n] solchen vor mich abnehmen, und noch gar vor das schlos Herraus fordern wollen."

27. D-DSsa: D4 379/5 (February 7, 1744).*

28. D-DSsa: D4 378/5 (March 23, 1742).*

29. D-DSsa: D45 378/5; Huber 1980, 391.

30. D-DSsa: D4 379/6.

31. The *Tanzmeister de Moll* refers to Petrus Franciscus de Moll, who is documented as an employee of the Darmstadt court from 1739. See Maaß 2006, 94. The "Fräuleins von Meinigerode" presumably refers to daughters of Heinrich von Minnigerode, who served as head forester and hunter as well as home secretary to the court of Hessen-Darmstadt. D-DSsa: D4 379/6 (November 12, 1746).*

32. The advanced level of the music copied for them that year suggests that the countesses' music training predated 1742.

33. While most of the manuscripts are signed "Me," four are signed "Mre" (D-B: N.Mus.ms.BP10, N.Mus.ms.BP11, N.Mus.ms.BP203, N.Mus.ms.BP205) and one is signed "Mrle" (D-B: N.Mus.ms.BP202). An archival documented (D-DSsa: D4 379/7) dated February 18, 1743, reveals that Luise Charlotte passed her test for confirmation in the Lutheran church "vermittelst der treuen und sorgfältigen Unterweisung des *Informatoris* Mörle." A comparison of the birth, death, and marriage records Johannes Merle kept during these years with the handwriting of the movement titles in the countesses' manuscripts reveals beyond a shadow of a doubt that they are the work of the same person. See D-DSk: Best. 244, KB Ginsheim Nr. 2, Film Nr. 1797

("Ginßheimer Kirchen buch angefangen von Johann: Merle zeitige Pfarrer Rauschenberga Hasso. den 24. Jun. 1759."). Johannes Merle's parents were Johann Stephan Merle and Eva Elisabeth Milchsack. He had a younger brother named Augustus who was also a musician. For biographical information about the Merle family I would like to thank Ulrich Kison and Käthe Vaupel (née Merle) of Rauschenberg and especially Günter Merle of Darmstadt.

34. Johannes Merle matriculated at the University of Marburg on October 20, 1735, and at the University of Jena on April 16, 1731. See Habicht 1927, 214, and Köhler 1969, 3:160.

35. It is clear from the foliation of these manuscripts that the pieces within could have followed no order other than that in which they are bound. The organization by key and splitting up of larger works was clearly not an accident but rather intended from the beginning.

36. D-B: N.Mus.ms.BP712; N.Mus.ms.BP719.

37. There is a particularly large collection of works with pedal-tone in D-B: N.Mus. ms.BP 711.

38. As noted in Jaeneke 1973, the composer attributions in these manuscripts are not always correct. Of the thirty-three works entirely without attribution, three were composed by François Couperin. One piece credited to Johan Joachim Agrell is actually by Jean Philippe Rameau, and three are probably by Gottfried August Homilius. Six movements composed by the Trier organist Joseph Torner were credited to his publisher, Ernst Kolborn.

39. Noack 1967, 167–72, 215, 220, 233.

40. Apparently, Rasbach had previously served as cantor in Landau, where some of his children were baptized between 1714 and 1717. His death was on July 13, 1760. My thanks to Helmut Klingelhöfer of the Hessisches Staatsarchiv Marburg for providing this information. Engel 1957, 29.*

41. D-DSsa: D 4 Nr. 378/5 ("Übergabe der Töchter des Gräfin Luise Sophie v. Seiboldsdorf in die Erziehung bei Frau v. Löwenstern.").

42. This practice is well known for early-eighteenth-century composers such as Telemann, who liked to style himself *Melante*, and François Couperin, who published some works under the pseudonym *Pernucio*.

43. D-B: N.Mus.ms.BP701.

44. D-B: N.Mus.ms.BP27.

45. D-B: N.Mus.ms.BP670.

46. D-B: N.Mus.ms.BP83/2; N.Mus.ms.BP 83/3.

47. D-B: N.Mus.ms.BP397; N.Mus.ms.BP692.

48. D-B: N.Mus.ms.BP670.

49. D-B: N.Mus.ms.BP692/3: "NB. Hier muß die 2. Violin und Alto besonders ausgeschrieben werden."

50. D-B: N.Mus.ms.BP95: "SONATA à Cembalo Solo | ex C dur | del Madam. Illustr: F. S. C. Z. E. || Dst. 1744. 8br."

51. D-B: N.Mus.ms.BP558; N.Mus.ms.BP559.

52. D-B: N.Mus.ms.BP670.

53. Jakob Adlung likened a musician copying brilliant passages from printed works to a student copying pithy quotes from Latin authors. See Adlung 1758, 726.

54. D-DSsa: D 4 379/4.

55. Corneilson 1992, 85 reveals that the opera in question is Hasse's *Demofoontey.* D-DSsa: D4 400/3.*

56. Darmstadt *Kabinets-Archivar* Adam Budde wrote the text of this story on February 21, 1876, and reports that it stems from Count Ludwig III von Hessen und bei Rhein, who himself had it indirectly from Friederica Sophie and her husband, Ludwig Freiherr von Pretlack. D-DSsa: D4 379/5.*

57. Anna Magdalena Elisabeth Merle died on September 16, 1762, at age thirty-six, after being bedridden for six months with gout and two hours after giving birth to their last child, a boy, who was buried with her on her arm. Johannes Merle himself died on December 30, 1783, at age seventy-four. See Ginsheim Kirchenbuch Nr. 2, 230 (Nr. 14) and 264 (Nr. 17). My thanks to Günter Merle for providing this information.

58. Noack 1908, 15–16.*

59. D-DSsa: D4 524/6 (July 4, 1768).*

Chapter 6. A Marriage Rooted in Reason

1. Both J. C. and Luise Gottsched's letters are currently being edited and published by the Sächsische Akademie der Wissenschaften in Leipzig. See Gottsched 1722–1766. Although Luise Gottsched's letters were edited by her friend Dorothea von Runckel before publication in 1782, I believe that they nonetheless constitute a valuable source of insight into the private sentiments of their original author. See Heuser 1998 and Kord 2000, 23–40.

2. Gottsched 1968–1987, 10:509–11.

3. Döring 2000b, 157–58.*

4. Gottsched 1968–1987, 1:27.*

5. Gottsched 1738, 1:4.*

6. Gottsched 1968–1987, 1:27.*

7. Gottsched 1968–1987, 1:26–30.*

8. I am not persuaded by Susanne Kord's theory that Luise Kulmus wished to accept J. C. Gottsched as a mentor but was hostile to the prospect of a romantic relationship with him. To cite one of many instances in which our interpretations of the letters she wrote differ fundamentally, Johann Christoph once likened himself and Luise to Orpheus and Euridice. She responded "No, I do not wish to be Euridice and you shall not be my Orpheus" (*Nein ich mag keine Euridice und Sie sollen nicht mein Orpheus seyn*). Kord interprets this as evidence that Luise "firmly refused to enter into any kind of emotional dialogue" with Johann Christoph (Kord 2000, 54). She neglects to mention that Luise's very next line is "Let the bond between us never be broken" (*Lassen Sie uns unsern Bund nie brechen*). In my view, Kord does not adequately take into account the role of the Kulmus family in hindering the couple's courtship and

marriage negotiations. See, for example, Gottsched 1722–1766, 3:213–14 (October 1, 1734).

9. Hennig 1790, 324.

10. Gottsched 1722–1766, 1:228 (July 12, 1729).*

11. Gottsched 1722–1766, 1:431–32 (September 20, 1730).*

12. Gottsched 1722–1766, 2:7–8 (January 7, 1731).*

13. Gottsched 1722–1766, 2:146 (November/December 1731).*

14. Gottsched 1722–1766, 2:146–47 (December 15, 1731).*

15. The work, *Laß, Fürstin, laß noch einen Strahl* (BWV 198), was first performed in Leipzig's university church on October 17, 1727.

16. Dok II, Nr. 249: "[. . .] der Herr Capellmeister Bach ist in Sachsen das Haupt unter seines gleichen."

17. Gottsched 1722–1766, 1:167 (January 9, 1732).*

18. Gottsched 1722–1766, 2:233.*

19. See the discussions of "Capricen" in Fuhrmann 1706, 86 ("Fantasia"); Mattheson 1713, 176; Mattheson 1739, 232; Walther 1732, 141. It is possible, though by no means certain, that the Bach work Gottsched sent Luise was the second Keyboard Partita (BWV 826), the final movement of which is entitled "Capriccio."

20. See Gottsched 1742, foreword.*

21. Gottsched 1722–1766, 2:233 (May 30, 1732).*

22. Peters 2008.

23. The translation here is from Kord 2000, 50–51. Gottsched 1722–1766, 2:268–69 (July 19, 1732).*

24. Gottsched 1722–1766, 2:268–69 (July 19, 1732).*

25. Gottsched 1722–1766, 2:312 (October 15, 1732).*

26. Gottsched 1722–1766, 2:369–70 (January 16, 1733).*

27. Gottsched 1722–1766, 2:387–88 (February 15, 1733).*

28. Gottsched 1722–1766, 2:392 (March 7, 1733).*

29. Gottsched 1722–1766, 3:213–14 (October 1, 1734).

30. Döring 2006, 43–44.

31. Gottsched 1767, 222–23, 232–35.

32. Gottsched 1722–1766, 3:386 (July 25, 1735).*

33. Gottsched 1722–1766, 3:390 (August 15, 1735).*

34. Gottsched 1738, dedication.*

35. Gottsched 1733–1734.

36. Döring 2000b, 157–58.

37. Gottsched 1738, 253–54.*

38. Gottsched 1739.

39. Brown 2012.

40. Gottsched 1722–1766, 6:605 (1740).*

41. Mertens 1968, 17.*

42. For this insight, I am indebted to Kord 2000, 74–75.

43. Plachta 1994, 89; Mertens 1968, 144–145.

44. Mertens 1968, 155. The victim was an orthodox preacher in Hamburg named Erdmann Neumeister.

45. Gottsched 1722–1766,4:217–18 (November 14, 1736).*

46. Gottsched 1968–1987, 10:518–19.*

47. Johann Ludwig Krebs, dedication to *Erste Piece, bestehend in sechs leichten, und nach dem heutigen gusto, wohl-eingerichteten Praeambulis* (Nuremberg: Schmid, 1740).*

48. Gottsched 1968–1987, 10:519.

49. Gottsched 1763, 178–92.*

50. Ball 2006, 250–51.

51. Ibid. In 1739, Johann Adolph Scheibe sent Luise Gottsched "Arien" at her husband's request. See Gottsched 1722–1766, 6:97–98 (September 28, 1739).

52. Lorenz Mizler, *Zweyte Sammlung auserlesener moralischer Oden zum Nutzen und Vergnügen der Liebhaber des Claviers* (Leipzig: Author, [1740] [Not in RISM]); Johann Friedrich Gräfe, *Sammlung verschiedener und auserlesener Oden [. . .] II. Theil* (Halle: Author, 1739 [RISM G 3267]).

53. See Gottsched 1722–1766, 5:237 (October 25, 1738); 5:358–59 (March 22, 1739). Schlobach and Eichhorn-Jung 1998, 70–72. Much or all of Luise Gottsched's collection of lute music came into the possession of the Breitkopf publishing firm after her death and was sold at auction in 1836. A substantial portion was acquired by François-Joseph Fétis and is preserved today in the *Koninklijke Bibliotheek* in Brussels, Belgium. See B-Br: Ms. II. 4086, 4087, and 4089.

54. Gottsched 1968–1987, 10:509.

55. Schulze 1968, 203.*

56. Gronau was Luise Kulmus's music teacher in Danzig, as confirmed by a 1738 letter from Adam Falckenhagen, who asked her to send him a trio by "von Ihren Meister aus Danzig." One copy of this letter has a contemporaneous note in the margin that makes explicit that the composer in question is Gronau. See Gottsched 1722–1766, 5:237 (October 25, 1738).

57. The only keyboard works she certainly acquired in Leipzig are Johan Joachim Agrell, *Sei Sonate per il Cembalo solo accompagnate da alcune Ariette, Polonesi e Menuetti composta da Giov. Agrell. Opera seconda* (Nuremberg: Haffner, [1748] [RISM A 422]) and Friedrich Wilhelm Marpurg, *Raccolta della più nuove composizioni di clavicembalo di differenti maestri ed autori per l'anno 1756 (=1757) fatta stampare dal sig. Feder. Guiglielmo Marpurg* (Leipzig: Breitkopf, 1756 [RISM M 722]). See Gottsched 1767, 235.

58. Bach's name appears only once in her estate catalog: "1 dergl. [Buch] von Seb. Bach und Gronau." See Ball 2006, 250–51. The fact that Bach's music is bound with that of her teacher in Danzig, Gronau, is a sure sign that this collection dates from before her marriage.

59. The excerpt is drawn from the second movement of J. S. Bach's "Ach Gott vom Himmel sieh darein" (BWV 2).*

60. Gottsched 1730.

61. Döring 2010, 79–80.

62. Gottsched 1737, 340 (quoting his own translation of Seneca's *Hercules Oetaeus*).*

63. For associations of Seneca and Lohenstein see Gottsched 1737, 341, 346, 623, 682.

64. Gottsched 1737, 341 (quoting Lohenstein's *Ibrahim Sultan*).*

65. Gottsched 1737, 97 (quoting book 2 of Opitz's *Trostgedichte in Widerwertigkeit deß Kriegs*).*

66. Gottsched 1730, 358–64.

67. Ibid., 604.*

68. My assertion that Luise Gottsched reworked the discussion of music in the 1737 edition of Gottsched's *Critische Dichtkunst* is based on the fact that nearly all of the music discussed came from her personal library. See Ball 2006, 250–51. It seems clear, too, from Johann Adolph Scheibe's letter of September 28, 1739, that Gottsched routinely turned music-related matters over to his wife. See Gottsched 1722–1766, 6:97–98.

69. Gottsched 1737, 413–15; Gottsched 1742, 470–72.

70. Gottsched 1737, 414–15: "Er hat sich darinn aller der Fehler enthalten, die bey andern Componisten so gemein sind. Die Wiederholungen sind sparsam, nemlich nicht über dreymal; die Recitative sind voller Melodie, und es ist kein einziges Wort darinn gezerret; sondern alles wird hintereinander verständlich weggesungen."

71. Writing as *Misogynis*, Scheibe produced works with titles such as "Well Founded Reasons to Hate Women, Particularly Those Filled with Deceitfulness, Evil, Jealousy, Duplicity . . . and Other Countless Vices; Published as a Warning to Men by One Who Suffered for Seventeen Years in the Clutches of One Such Female Beast." See Scheibe 1750; 1753; 1762.

72. Maul 2010, 169–70.

73. Dok II, No. 400.

74. The English text presented here comes, with slight adjustments, from Wolff, Mendel, and David 1999, 337–38.*

75. Dok II, Nr. 409.*

76. The most comprehensive account of the conflict is offered in Maul 2010.

77. Gottsched 1722–1766, 5:447–451 (June 10, 1739).*

78. Luise Gottsched's authorship of the review of *Der Critische Musikus* is acknowledged in Johann Adolph Scheibe's letter of September 28, 1739. See Gottsched 1722–1766, 6:97–98. Gottsched 1737, 413–15.

79. Dok II, Nr. 483: "In die Streitigkeiten welche der Herr Verfasser mit Herrn M. Birnbaum gehabt, wollen wir uns hier gar nicht einlassen." See Maul 2010, 176.

80. Birnbaum was, like Gottsched, a member of a debating club known as the *Deutsche Redner-Gesellschaft*. Bach had set texts by Gottsched to music, not only in 1727 but most recently on the occasion of a visit to Leipzig by the Saxon elector's family in 1738. The resulting work, "Willkommen, ihr herrschenden Götter der Erden" (BWV Anh. 113), does not survive.

81. The original text appears in *Beyträge zur critischen Historie der Deutschen Sprache, Poesie und Beredsamkeit, herausgegeben von einigen Liebhabern der deutschen Litteratur. Drey und zwanzigstes Stück* (Leipzig 1740), 464–65. It is quoted here from Maul 2010, 176.*

82. The pairing with Silvius Leopold Weiss has sometimes been taken as a sign of

support for Bach because at the end of her life, Frau Gottsched owned a great deal of Weiss's music. See Maul 2010, 176. At the time she wrote this review, however, she had never met Weiss, and her experience with his music may well have been quite limited. See Gottsched 1722–1766, 6:97–98 (September 28, 1739) and 6:215–16 (November 25, 1739); and Gottsched 1968–1987, 10:509 (1763).

83. Gottsched 1771–1772, 2:158–59.*

84. GB-Lbl: Ms.Add. 15768, 67.

85. Addison 1735.

86. "Chambers's perspective" here refers to Chambers 1726, which is a translation of Dubreuil 1642.

87. GB-Lbl: Ms.Add. 15768, 65–66.

88. GB-Lbl: Ms.Add. 19939 (November 20 / December 1, 1736).

89. Gottsched AW 10:579 (1763).*

90. I would like to thank Rüdiger Otto for providing this annotated source. Elisabeth Dorothee von Mosheim was the wife of the Lutheran theologian Johann Lorenz von Mosheim (1693–1755). Mademoiselles Lambalet and Ritter are unidentified Swiss acquaintances. Otto 2010, 123–24.*

91. The quote is from Friedrich Melchior Grimm. Gottsched 1722–1766, 7:424 (April 19, 1741).*

92. Döring 2009b.

93. Gottsched 1771–1772, 3;165 (February 15, 1762).*

94. Gottsched 1968–1987, 10:540–41.

95. The letter is dated October 3, 1754. Döring 2003, 225.*

96. Döring 2003, 238; Goodman 2009, 78–80. The letter is dated April 19, 1755.

97. Döring 2003, 241.

98. For this reference I am indebted to Döring 2003, 237. Gottsched 1771–1772, 2:167 (December 19, 1753).*

99. Seybold 1784, 115–17.*

100. Döring 2000, 108–11.

101. Gottsched 1771–1772, 3:104 (February 4, 1758)*

102. Gottsched 1771–1776, 3;169 (March 4, 1762).*

103. Gottsched 1968–1987, 10:573.*

104. Gottsched 1771–1776, 3:169 (March 4, 1762).*

105. Gottsched 1968–1987, 10:576.*

Chapter 7. Male Amateur Keyboardists

1. The advice is drawn from Rambach 1739, 314 and 318; and Erasmus of Rotterdam 1731, 15 and 39.

2. Bahrdt 1790, 1:59–61.

3. According to a chronicle of the time, a mother may begin a boy's education but then the father must take over "weil nur ein Mann den künftigen Mann bilden kann." See Lampe 1963, 1:20.

4. This quote from Johann Ludwig Huber's *Etwas von meinem Lebenslauf und etwas*

von meiner Muse auf der Vestung (Stuttgart: Steinkopf, 1798) appears in Hardach-Pinke and Hardach 1981, 153–54.*

5. Bahrdt 1790, 1:55–56.

6. Ibid., 1;37.*

7. Bahrdt 1790, 1:38–40.*

8. Bahrdt 1790, 1;70–72.*

9. Jan Minelli was a Dutch schoolteacher whose style of marginal translations and annotations in the works of classical authors was well known to early-eighteenth-century German schoolboys. Bahrdt 1790, 1:70–72.*

10. Bahrdt 1790, 1;87–88, 102.

11. Ibid., 1:82–83.

12. Ibid., 1:84–85.*

13. Ibid., 1:86–87.*

14. Ibid., 1:88–89.

15. *Leipziger Post-Zeitungen* 1731 (August 6).*

16. Bahrdt 1790, 1;95–96, 100–101, 106, 127.

17. Ibid., 1:97–98.*

18. Ibid., 1:106–9.*

19. Ibid., 1:111.

20. Wagenseil 1705, 70–71.*

21. Zimmermann 1906, 135.*

22. Gräbner 1711, 45.*

23. Esias Reussner, preface to *Neue Lauten-Früchte* (Leipzig, 1676).*

24. Johann Kuhnau, preface to *Neuer Clavier-Übung* (Leipzig, 1689).*

25. Voigt 1742, 106–7.*

26. D-GOl: Chart. B 1251.

27. Friedrich III signed the title page of the book and seems to have copied much of the musical material within. Comparative samples of the young duke's handwriting are lacking, but the scribe of much of this music notebook was young and relatively inexperienced, and one struggles to imagine a situation in which this could have been anyone but Friedrich III himself. The obvious youth of the scribe undercuts claims in Fett 1951, 228, and Gaensler 1938 that the book belonged to Duke Friedrich II.

28. Folia 26v to 135v are blank.

29. One presumes that the professional scribe represented here was his teacher, perhaps the organist at the court in Gotha, Christian Friedrich Witt, who is known to have taught Friedrich. See Fett 1951, 228.

30. Lediard 1740, 86.

31. PL-GD: Ms. 854, 116–17.

32. PL-GD: Ms. 854, 5–6.

33. Gerber 1790–1792, 1:493.

34. Burkardt, Gantner-Schlee, Knieriem 2006, 209.*

35. Talle 2008, 110–30.

36. Students had to be careful, as servants were known to steal expensive clothing. See PL-GN: Ms. 854, 7.*

37. Talle 2008, 111.*
38. Pütter 1798, 1:61.*
39. Elwert 1799, 386–87.*
40. Pütter 1798, 1:48–49.*
41. The price comes from Heinrich Zernecke's description of the courses he took at the University of Wittenberg. See PL-GN: Ms. 854, 28.*
42. Bahrdt 1790, 1:205–13.
43. PL-GN: Ms. 854, 7, 28.
44. Pütter 1798, 1:51.*
45. Ibid., I: 24–31.
46. Ibid., I: 48–51.
47. Elwert 1799, 386–87.
48. Talle 2008, 88–89.
49. PL-GN: Ms. 854, 113.*
50. Wustmann 1889–1895, 1:296.
51. Bahrdt 1790, 1:125.*
52. Quistorp 1743, 521.*
53. Pütter 1798, 1:25.*
54. Quistorp 1743, 543.*
55. Simons 2001, 316.*
56. Klose 1849, 100–101.
57. Müller 2007, 116.
58. Bahrdt 1790, 1:67–69. *
59. Wustmann 1889–1895, 1:440.
60. Müller 2007, 214.*
61. Salmen 1969, 23.*
62. Weiße 1807, 123–124.*
63. My thanks to Michael Maul for calling this source to my attention. Staatsarchiv Altenburg, Familienarchiv Seckendorf, Nr. 1113, f. 220–21 (January 6, 1753).*
64. Talle 2008, 115–20.
65. Toerring-Jettenbach-Archiv, Nr. C 112 [Notes on expenses made by Count "August de Terring" in 1746–48 as a university student in Strasbourg]: "Maitre de Musique. Il est venu la premiere fois le 1re Novemb. 1746. On lui donne 12. [livres] par mois. le 1re juin il ne vient que 2. fois par semaine a cause du droit public moyenant quoi on lui donne des billet."
66. Schuchardt wanted to take four hours per week (apparently the norm) but his teacher told him "daß er nicht wohl mehr als 2 Stunden nützen könnte." See D-LEu: Rep. VI 25d, 45.
67. D-LEu: Rep. VI 25d, 316, 351.
68. D-LEu: Rep. VI 25d, 34, 99, 311, 416.
69. Gottsched 1725–1726, 26 (January 4, 1725).*
70. Hintzsche 1971, 24.*
71. Frank 1715a, 220.*
72. Selamintes 1713, 150–52.*

73. Klose 1849, 41.*
74. Jung 2007, 122–23.
75. Dok III, Nr. 902. See also Fedorowskaja 1990, 27.
76. Dok II, Nr. 387.
77. Voigt 1742, 110.*
78. Hunold 1717–1722, 331–32.*
79. Voigt 1742, 42–44 and 75.
80. Frank 1715b, 56.*
81. D-Gs: Cod.Uffenbach.25, I: 68–70 (November 17, 1712).*
82. Pütter 1798, 1:14–18.
83. Ibid., 1:24–31.
84. Ibid. 1798, 1:19–20.*
85. Ibid., 1:88–89.*
86. Ibid., 1:190–91.*
87. Joseph Martin Kraus, a law student and composer in Göttingen, recorded these observations in 1777. See Loos 1987, 81–82.*
88. Hessisches Staatsarchiv Marburg: 90a Nr. 226, f. 16.*
89. Hessisches Staatsarchiv Marburg: 90a Nr. 226, f. 62–63.*
90. "[. . .] *ein Original und Muster eines thätigen Geschäftsmannes.*" See Gerber 1812–1814, 4:796.
91. For the birth and death dates of Fischer and also Fructuosus Röder, I would like to thank Edgar Kutzner, archivist at the Bischöfliches Generalvikariat Fulda.
92. Peter 2005, 45–55.
93. Henkel 1882, 11: "Bezüglich der Musik war Fischer namentlich auch in der Theorie sehr praktisch erfahren und machte sich ein Vergnügen daraus, Andere zu unterweisen. Er besass eine für damalige Zeit belangreiche und ausgesuchte musikalische Bibliothek, welche er in 109 Bänden noch bei Lebzeiten der Fuldaer Bibliothek schenkte." E. L. Gerber suggested that Fischer's library consisted of 80 volumes of musical, theoretical, and practical content: "Seine ausgezeichnete Bibliothek, welche er noch bey Lebzeiten der allgemeinen dasigen Bibliothek schenkte, enthielt nur allein im musikalisch- theoretisch- und praktischen Fache 80 Bände." See Gerber 1812–1814, 4:796.
94. "Nachrichten von der ordentlichen Bibliothek zu Fulda, welche ich, Peter Böhm, derselben erster Bibliothekar, aus meinen Tagebüchern zusammengetragen habe. 1811." The text appears in Theele 1928.
95. Fischer's books on music are identifiable by his signature on title pages and by identical, light brown bindings.
96. Gerber 1812–1814, 4:796.*
97. K.W.F. 21/63.*
98. K.W.F. 21/79.*
99. K.W.F. 21/71.*
100. K.W.F. 14/85.*
101. The *Clavier-Übung I* print bears an early call number ("N. 3"), which accords with two more in Fulda: the Musical Offering ("N. 5") and the first volume of Nichel-

mann Sonatas ("Nro. 25"). If the music was organized alphabetically by composer, as is implied by the fact that Fischer underlined the "N" in Nichelmann's name, he presumably owned about fifty music prints, given that "N" (for Nichelmann) is only halfway through the alphabet.

102. Nothing is known of Hazarinus Greser's biography.

103. Fischer's print of Bach's *Clavier-Übung I* was described in the auction catalog of the estate of Werner Wolffheim in 1928 but subsequently disappeared. It reappeared and was sold by Sotheby's to the Pierpont Morgan Library in New York City on May 25, 2000, where it is now in the Mary Flagler Cary Music Collection (call number 1360). Sotheby's 2001, 12–13 (item 6). Fischer's print of Bach's *Clavier-Übung II* was formerly in Fulda's *Hochschul- und Landesbibliothek.* There was apparently a reference to Fischer and/or Fructuosus Röder on the title page of Fischer's print of the Italian Concerto and French Ouverture as well. See Emery and Wolff 1977, 29–30.

104. Theophilo Röder attended the *Infirma* in Fulda in 1757–1758, the *Secunda* in 1758–1759, and the *Syntaxklasse* in 1759–1760, distinguishing himself in formal examinations in philosophy, mathematics, physics, and theology. See Leinweber 1991, 324 and Henkel 1882, 8.

105. See Henkel 1882, 7–8, and Gerber 1812–1814, 4:820.

106. Dok II, 546. Pauli received eighty Gulden (= fifty-three reichstaler, eight groschen) in 1756 and 4,800 Gulden (= 200 reichstaler per year) from 1757 to 1766. See Hessisches Staatsarchiv Marburg. 90a Nr. 226 (Bl. 5v–10v). For more on his biography see Henkel 1882, 16, and Rehm 1997, 11.

107. The beginning of Pauli's journey is undocumented but he returned to Fulda shortly before June 25, 1748, as revealed by a letter Pauli wrote to Padre Martini on that date, advising Martini of his safe return. See I-Bc: H. 86–94.

108. Dok II, Nr. 597a and Nr. 597b.

109. The two works in question are presumably the *Sonate d'intavolatura per l'organo e 'l cembalo* published in Amsterdam in 1742 and the *Sonate per l'organo e il cembalo* published in Bologna in 1747. The identification of these two collections is made possible by Pauli's next letter, dated August 20, 1748, in which he informs Martini that he need not send the Sonatas because he can get them directly from Amsterdam. See I-Bc: H. 86–95.

110. He referred specifically to the views of Andrea Basili.

111. Serauky 1935–1943, 2.2:30, 85–86.

112. Thereafter the paper was cut down, presumably for rebinding, and the words *Laus Deo* are slightly cut off in two of three cases. At some point the date on the title page (1731) was erased, and a number of mostly illegible annotations on the publication history of Opus 1 were added in pencil, probably in the early twentieth century.

Chapter 8. A Blacksmith's Son

1. Stralsund, Ratsarchiv: Hs. 367–369. The first two volumes have been edited and published as Müller 2007 and Müller 2013 by Katrin Löffler, with the help of Nadine Sobirai.

2. Müller 2007, 41–42.*

3. Ibid., 48.*

4. Ibid., 49. See Dok II, Nr. 457.

5. Müller 2007, 51–52, 341.

6. Ibid., 52–53.

7. Ibid., 63–65.

8. Pütter 1798, 1:52–53.

9. Müller 2007, 54.*

10. Ibid., 65–66.*

11. Ibid., 167.*

12. Pütter 1798, 1:26.

13. Müller 2007, 72–73.*

14. Ibid., 72.*

15. Ibid., 56.*

16. Ibid., 17.

17. Ibid., 206–7.

18. On clavichords with lute stops see Adlung 1758, 568.*

19. Müller 2007, 82.*

20. On other boys misbehaving see Müller 2007, 86–87, 109, 114.

21. Ibid., 69, 75, 84–86.

22. Ibid., 93 and 97.*

23. Ibid., 98.*

24. Ibid., 116.

25. Ibid., 98 and 190.

26. Ibid., 172–73.*

27. Müller 2007, 103.*

28. Ibid., 119–20.*

29. Ibid., 187–88.*

30. Ibid., 201–2. Müller writes that he spent eight to twenty *Schillinge* (Lübisch) per meal, which is the equivalent of four to ten groschen.

31. Ibid., 214.*

32. Ibid., 201 and 244.

33. Ibid., 242.

34. Quistorp and Fischer matriculated at Leipzig University on October 25, 1742, and February 26, 1741, respectively. Erler 1909, 3:88, 314.

35. Müller 2007, 205.*

36. Ibid., 216.*

37. The play is *Der Eilfte Junius, ein Lustspiel in fünf Handlungen.* See Holberg 1750–1752, 4:43.

38. *Sperontes Singende Muse an der Pleiße* (Leipzig, 1736), Nr. 89.*

39. Müller 2007, 205–6.*

40. Ibid., 206–7.

41. Ibid., 310–11.*

42. Ibid., 315 and 329.

43. Ibid., 330.*

44. Müller 2013, 21–25, 48.

45. Ibid., 82–83.

46. Ibid., 116–17.

47. Ibid., 128.*

48. Ibid., 348.*

49. Von Lilleström's eldest daughter, Sophie Catharina Augusta, was already married to a neighbor. One of his sons, Friedrich Ludwig, was serving as a page at the court of Sachsen-Weissenfels.

50. Müller 2013, 256.*

51. Ibid., 256–59.

52. Ibid., 270, 294, 304, 320.

53. Ibid., 263.*

54. Ibid., 260–61, 267, 286, 305.

55. Ibid., 293–94.*

56. Ibid., 305.*

57. Ibid., 330.*

58. Ibid., 299–300.*

59. Ibid., 336–37.*

60. Ibid., 342–46.

61. Ibid., 344.*

62. Ibid., 347.

63. Ibid., 363.*

64. Ibid., 311.*

65. Ibid., 341. The term of address Lotchen used is "Euer Hoch Edelgeboren."

66. Ibid., 376.*

67. Lotchen's eventual husband, Carl Fredrik Hök, was a major in the Swedish Cavalry Regiment.

68. Müller 2013, 329. As Müller put it in his autobiography, "Diese Leute hätten ein allgemeines Lob, und ich würde Wol thun wenn ich auch an der Versorgung der Priester Kinder dächte." See Stralsund Ratsarchiv, Hs. 368, S. 734.

69. Stralsund Ratsarchiv, Hs. 368, 745.*

Chapter 9. May God Protect This Beautiful Organ

1. The clothing listed here can be found in the estate of Christian Friedrich Abesser, who served as cantor in Rötha from 1731–1751, and his wife. See D-LEsta: 20532 ("Rittergut Rötha mit Trachenau"), Nr. 3100, f. 12r, 14v. For pigs on living room floors in winter, honeybee cultivation, and the importance of sheep see Stadt- und Heimatverein Rötha 2000.

2. The city had 367 residents in 1779. See Schumann 1822, 9:370.

3. Stadt- und Heimatverein Rötha 2000, 8.

4. Brause and Hentschel 1992, 8–9.

5. Schumann 1822, 370.

6. Pasch 2001, 9–12.

7. Ibid., 10.

8. Ahrens and Langrock 2003, 27.*

9. Werner 1899–1900, 424.

10. Johann Christian Langbein described Ibach's organ as "ein alter Bley-Klumpen." See Ahrens and Langrock 2003, 26.

11. Mathe 1905–1906, 1051.

12. The contract for the new organ admits that the old one in 1718 was "dermaßen eingegangen, daß selbigen durch keine Reparatur geholffen werden mögen." See Pasch 2001, 15.

13. Brause and Hentschel 1992, 7–8.

14. Friesen 1941, 28.

15. D-LEsta: 20532 ("Rittergut Rötha mit Trachenau"), Nr. 5448, f. 13r–13v.

16. Pfarrarchiv Rötha. Sign. Loc. XIII, 1 ("Die Erbauung neuer Orgeln in der St. Georgen- und St. Marien-Kirche zu Rötha"), unpaginated first page of a letter from C. A. von Friesen to Solomon Deyling dated July 19, 1721.

17. Friesen 1899, 1:195–208.

18. Ahrens and Langrock 2003, 19 and 21.

19. Pasch 2001, 25.*

20. Rubardt 1953, 9–10.

21. Pfarrarchiv Rötha. Sign. Loc. XIII, 1, unpaginated 6–7.

22. See Pasch 2001, 16, and Rubardt 1953, 10–11.

23. In 1717 Kuhnau, in a more critical mood, had described Silbermann's tuning system as deeply flawed. See Pasch 2001, 16.

24. See Adlung 1758, 347. See also Trommer 1742, 584–86.*

25. Ahrens and Langrock 2003, 23.

26. Ibid., 135.*

27. Holberg 1749, 115–16.*

28. Ahrens and Langrock 2003, 17.*

29. Ibid., 27.*

30. Ibid., 28.*

31. Ibid., 24.*

32. Ibid., 25.

33. For enabling me to play this instrument, and for providing details from an organist's perspective, I would like to thank Elizabeth Höpfner.

34. Ahrens and Langrock 2003, 28.

35. Brause and Hentschel 1992, 8–9; Stadt- und Heimatverein Rötha 1996, 2–3.

36. The construction of a Silbermann organ in Glauchau in 1730 was a sign that the town had recovered from a 1712 fire. See Ahrens and Langrock 2003, 48–49.

37. Pfarrarchiv Rötha. Sign. Loc. XIII, 1 ("Die Erbauung neuer Orgeln in der St. Georgen- und St. Marien-Kirche zu Rötha").*

38. Ahrens and Langrock 2003, 29.*

39. Rubardt 1953, 11.*

Chapter 10. How Professional Musicians Were Compensated

1. Dok III, Nr. 820.*

2. Mattheson 1740, 343–44.*

3. Mattheson 1740, 356.*

4. Merian 1920, 141–42.

5. D-LEsa (Leipzig, Stadtarchiv): Richterstube Strafakten Nr. 630.

6. D-Gs: Cod. Uffenbach 25, 1:56 (November 8, 1712).*

7. Edler 1982, 95.*

8. Ibid., 93–95.

9. The duke to whom Hurlebusch referred is Ferdinand Albrecht II of Braunschweig-Wolfenbüttel. Gurlitt 1913, 22–23.*

10. Johann Georg Hoffmann.

11. Johann Paul Kuntzen.

12. Johann Peter Kellner.

13. Johann Conrad Dreyer and Michael Kirsten.

14. Mattheson 1740, 110.*

15. Ibid., 111.*

16. Ibid., 138–39.*

17. Ibid., 139.*

18. Reichardt 1795, 167.*

19. Mattheson 1740, 139.*

20. The "Herr Quiel" mentioned here is Johann Heinrich Quiel. Mattheson 1740, 111–12.*

21. Kaemmel 1909; Maul 2012.

22. Mattheson 1740, 160; Döring 2009, 606.

23. Bernd 1973, 111.*

24. Mattheson 1740, 160.*

25. Adlung 1768, 12.*

26. Zohn 2011, 416.

27. Henze-Döhring 2003, 23–32.

28. Riepe 2003, 44–47.

29. Rampe 2004, 174.

30. To cite one prominent example, Johann Gottfried Walther, organist at the Church of St. Peter and Paul in Weimar, was hired initially to give keyboard lessons to the duke of Saxe-Weimar and was eventually awarded the formal title of *Hof-Musicus* (court musician). See Beckmann and Schulze 1987, 71–72. See also Edler 1982, 83.

31. Klose 1849, 148.

32. Burrows 1985, 39.

33. Gerber 1790–1792, 1:493.*

34. Klose 1849, 6–7. Telemann and Stölzel attained the same title. See Zohn 2011, 417, and Mattheson 1740, 346.

35. In Mecklenburg, court organists served simultaneously as "Kellermeister" or served in some other capacity "welches mit weitläuftigen Rechnungen verbunden war." See Kemmler 1970, 18. Gerber 1790–1792, 495.*

36. Zohn 2011, 418.

37. The text is taken and the translation adapted from Zohn 2011, 420.*

38. Rampe 2004, 171.

39. Glöckner 1988, 137–44.

40. Mattheson 1740, 124.

41. Greve 1985, 21–22.

42. Mattheson 1740, 94; Stahl 1952, 69.

43. Edler 1982, 105–6.

44. Dok II, Nr. 253.

45. Edler 1982, 199.

46. Mattheson 1740, 164.

47. Edler 1982, 115.

48. Maul 2009, 232–35.*

49. Wollny 1995, 185–90.

50. Maul 2009, 226–27.

51. Ziller 1935, 126.*

52. Ibid., 126–27.*

53. Mattheson 1739, 473.

54. Edler 1982, 191.*

55. Burkardt, Gantner-Schlee, and Knieriem 2006, 213.*

56. Mattheson 1739, 473.*

57. Mizler 1740, 62.*

58. Edler 1982, 191.

59. Ibid.*

60. Voigt 1742, 44.*

61. Ibid., 9.*

62. J. Gottfried Donati, *Einige Discourse zweyer Orgel-Freunde, Welche bey Gelegenheit des von Tit. HERRN Gottfried Silbermann[. . .] Am 1. Advent dieses 1742sten Jahres zu Fraureuth im Voigtlande verfertigten schönen Orgelwercks geführet worden* (Greiz: Abraham Gottlieb Ludewig, 1742) quoted in Jung 2007, 115.*

63. Mattheson 1740, xxxii–xxxiii.*

64. In some cases the cantorship was a strictly administrative post. The Brothers von Uffenbach described a situation in the town of Mölln in which the cantor was merely a position for those with ambitions to become rectors; most could not even read music. See Uffenbach 1753–1754, 2:7–8.

65. Edler 1982, 98.

66. Ibid., 108–9.

67. Ibid., 110, and Michaelsen 1958, 200.

68. Bach's predecessor in Leipzig, Johann Kuhnau, served for many years as organist at St. Thomas Church, during which time he worked as a professional lawyer and also authored several novels.

69. Edler 1982, 114–15.

70. Beckmann and Schulze 1987, 133; Rampe 2003–2005, 4/5:96.

71. Walther 1732, 657.

72. I would like to thank Jürgen Neubacher for drawing my attention to this source. Kreising 1742, 146r.*

73. Schnizzer 1938, 182–83.*

Chapter 11. *The Daily Life of an Organist*

1. Spohr 1968, 4–5.*

2. D-BS: H III 3:99. The book is titled *Kleine Wirthschafft Rechnung über Einnahme und Ausgabe, angefangen Cöthen den 2. Januarii 1752. C. A. Hart.* The only known reference prior to Talle 2011 appeared in Hartung 1972, 17. A few biographical details about Hartung appeared in Buchmann 1987, 170–71.

3. Hartung's birth record reads as follows: "342. Carl August Hartung Ein Ehelicher Sohn Johann Christoph Hartungs, Fürstl. Leibschneiders und Bürgers und Albertina Charlotta Schmidin gebohren den 13 8br. getauft von mir den 17. dit." I would like to thank Manuel Bärwald for consulting the 1723 *Taufbuch* of the Reformed Church in Harzgerode on my behalf. C. A. Hartung's father, Johann Christoph Hartung, was apparently still alive in 1769 in the midst of a legal battle over Johann Christoph Schmidt's estate. See D-DElsa: DE, Z 38 Amt und Justizamt Harzgerode, Nr. 43, as well as Hartung 1972, 40. Hartung's siblings were named Johann Christian Marcus Laurentius, Johann Wilhelm, Sophie Marie, Elisabeth, and Victoria. See D-DElsa: DE, Z 38 Amt und Justizamt Harzgerode, Nr. 43, f. 26r–v.

4. C. A. Hartung, his younger brother, Johann Christoph Marcus Laurentius Hartung, and Johann Christoph Marius Hartung were all students of cantor Johann Nikolaus Schröter in 1734. D-DElsa: DE, Z 18, C 18 Nr. 6, f. 11r–12r.

5. C. A. Hartung referred to Schmid as "Hr. Vetter Land-Richter." See D-BS: H III 3:99, 225. Close family ties are evident in any case from documents relating to Schmid's estate, some of which went to Hartung and his siblings. See D-DElsa: DE, Z 38 Amt und Justizamt Harzgerode, Nr. 43. Schmidt copied a Bach prelude (BWV 921) already in 1713. The manuscript in which it appears (D-B: Mus.ms.Bach.P222) was at some point acquired by Hartung. See Wollny 2011, 85 and 90–91.

6. One of the manuscripts in the Berlin State Library—a copy of a *Præludium* attributed to G. F. Händel—was begun by Schmidt and completed by Hartung. See D-B: Mus.ms.30382. Schmidt copied the first twenty-eight measures of the piece (48v–49r) and Hartung the final forty-four (49r–50r). The handwriting of both is also found in D-B: Mus.ms.Bach.P222.

7. These numbers represent estimates. According to a document entitled "Größe und Einwohnerzahl Köthens" prepared by museum employees in the the 1950s and kindly provided by Ingeborg Streuber of the *Historisches Museum und Bachgedenkstätte Köthen*, Cöthen had 3,300 residents in 1730 and 567 houses in 1747.

8. Hartung 1900, 254.

9. Crell 1725, 57.

10. A letter dated October 12, 1764, describes Johann Christian Marcus Hartung as the "erster" to *Oberkoch* Schlegel. In the same letter he applied for the position of the deceased *Mund Koch* Schöne. See D-DElsa: DE, C 5h Nr. 2 Bd. X, f. 109r. It is not known exactly when J. C. M. Hartung began living in Cöthen, but he married Maria Dorothea Pönert there on October 17, 1752, suggesting that he had established residency some years earlier. See Buchmann 1987, 170.

11. The bylaws of the orphanage signed by Prince Leopold in 1723 required that

"jedes mahl auff 20. Kinder im *Præceptor* gehalten wird, damit selbige die *Informa-tion* umb so viel beßer abwarten können; und damit auch andere arme außer dem Waÿsenhause lebende Kinder, sie seÿn *Reformin*ter so wohl als Lutherischer *Religion*, einen Nutzen vom solchem Waÿsenhause haben" Dessau, Archiv der Evangelischen Landeskirche Anhalts: "Acten der Herzogl. Superintendentur zu Cöthen betr. das Waisen-Institut zu Coethen und die damit verbundene Freischule. Allgemeine Acten." Litt. W. No.1. Vol. I. Jahr 1706, f. 13r.

12. The estimate of around forty comes from the payments in 1758–1759 to a tailor to patch thirty-three vests and to a shoemaker to make forty-two pairs of shoes (D-DEIsa: DE, Z 73 [Cöthen Cammer-Rechnungen] 1757–1758, 153–54). The by-laws of the orphanage signed by Prince Leopold in 1723 require that "jedes mahl auff 20. Kinder im *Præceptor* gehalten wird, damit selbige die *Information* umb so viel beßer abwarten können; und damit auch andere arme außer dem Waÿsenhause lebende Kinder, sie seÿn *Reformin*ter so wohl als Lutherischer *Religion*, einen Nutzen von solchem Waÿsenhause haben" Dessau, Archiv der Evangelischen Landeskirche Anhalts: "Acten der Herzogl. Superintendentur zu Cöthen betr. das Waisen-Institut zu Coethen und die damit verbundene Freischule. Allgemeine Acten." Litt. W. No.1. Vol. I. Jahr 1706, f. 13r.

13. Dessau, Archiv der Evangelischen Landeskirche Anhalts: Waisenhaus Proto-kolbuch 1723, f. 16r–16v.

14. Hensel 1736, 8: "Lieben Menschen, unterwinde sich nicht jederman Lehrer zu seyn, und wisset, daß wir destomehr Urtheil empfahen werden."

15. Jablonski 1693; Laurentius 1731; Lobethan 1729; Mosheim 1757; Saurin 1755; Teller 1736.

16. Pescheck 1735.

17. Pescheck 1738.

18. Freyer 1752.

19. Richter 1731.

20. Gellert 1758.

21. Holberg 1750–1752.

22. D-DEIsa: DE, C 5h Nr. 2 Bd. VII, f. 449r–450r.

23. St. Jakob Köthen, Geborene, 1749–1763, 327: "[. . .] ein Catholischer Ital-iäner, welcher mit Kleiner wahre handelt."

24. The bookbinders Hartung used were Johann Christoph Hohmann and Chris-tian Ehricke. Their names are both listed in the baptism record for Hohmann's daughter, Maria Elisabeth, who was born on April 10, 1758. See St. Jakob Köthen, Geborene, 1749–1763, 386.

25. *Neu-eröffnetes Welt- und Staats-Theatrum: Welches die in allen Theilen der Welt, sonderlich aber in Europa vorfallende Staats-, Kriegs- und Friedensaffairen[. . .] vorstellet* (Erfurt: Jungnikol, 1725–1739; or Erfurt: Nonne, 1740–1750). Hartung possessed at least *Eröffnungen* 1–16. The latest issue he is known to have had appeared in 1753. Some he had bound in calf's leather.

26. In the fourth quarter of 1760 he spent four Reichstaler and twelve Groschen to have a local woodworker named Creutzer make him a bed (D-BS: H III 3:99, 294:

"demselben vors Bette"). He must certainly have had a bed before 1760, which he paid an orphan girl to make earlier in 1760 (D-BS: H III 3:99, 288: "dem Waÿsen Mädgen Kirchhofin vor das Bette zu machen"). The secretary cabinet was commissioned from Creutzer for eight Reichstaler and sixteen Groschen (D-BS: H III 3:99, 277: "Mstr. Creutzern auf Abschlag eines Treßur Schranks behandelt vor 8 Rthl. 16 gl.").

27. D-BS: H III 3:99, 344–45.

28. D-BS: H III 3:99, 289: "[4 Gr.] der Nachtwächtern vors Zinn zu scheuren [scheuern] p. T. Ostern."

29. D-BS: H III 3:99, 215: "[14 Groschen] vor 1/2 [Unze] Knaster."

30. Wilhelm Gottfried Scheibe married Eleonora Amalia Jäger on July 12, 1750. See St. Jakob Köthen, Getraute 1721–1769, 353.

31. D-BS: H III 3:99, 227: "Mstr. Kleen vor die ledernen Hosen, zu schwärtzen."

32. Ibid., 213.

33. Ibid., 213.

34. Hartung omits from his *Rechenbuch* but they are listed in the *Cammer Rechnungen*. See D-DElsa: DE, Z 73, 1755–1756 for two payments of five Reichstaler, twelve made on January 22, 1756, and June 23, 1756, which Hartung omits from his account book.

35. See D-DElsa: DE, Z 73 (Cöthen Cammer-Rechnungen) 1755–1756, 142; 1756–1757, 143; 1757–1758, 144; 1757–1758, 152–55.

36. Hartung also purchased the following theological tomes during his time in Cöthen: Jablonski 1693; Laurentius 1731; Lobethan 1729; Mosheim 1757; Saurin 1755; Teller 1736.

37. D-BS: H III 3:99, 262: "[4 Groschen] vor Pulv: Vital. 4 Dosis." 266: "der Waÿsen Magd Magdalenen vors Aufwarten in meiner Kranckheit."

38. D-BS: H III 3:99, 47–48: "In diesem Viertel Jahre habe nur 6 Wochen Schule gehalten, weilen die übrige Zeit an einer harten Kranckheit darniedergelegen [. . .]"

39. Hartung noted in his account book that Voigt's first lesson payment should have been two Reichstaler but that he was twelve Groschen short. Hartung also loaned Voigt two Reichstaler and twenty Groschen in May 1759, which Voigt eventually paid back. See D-BS: H III 3:99, 351. The book Hartung purchased, *Holfelds Comœdien*, was probably Holberg 1750–1752.

40. Hartung lists collection payments only once for March 1752 and twice for the *Erndte Dankfest* (1752 and 1759) for a total of twenty-four, but in all likelihood he received such payments twice per year, for a total of sixteen per year (though not in 1760, because he left Cöthen before the *Erndte Dankfest* that year); this amounts to 136. These payments came from collection plates from all around Sachsen-Anhalt. As noted above, Hartung himself was responsible for keeping the records of these payments.

41. Hartung's account book documents payments of just sixteen Groschen per year in donations: eight in the spring and eight in the fall. The figure of eight Groschen is corroborated by an account of income for donations for 1757, which, coincidentally, was prepared by C. A. Hartung himself, apparently on behalf of the administration of the *Schloßkirche*. Dessau, Archiv der Evangelischen Landeskirche Anhalts: Superintendenturarchiv Köthen D: "Kirchen Collecten-Buch de. a. 1757" (f. 1 from the back).

42. D-BS: H III 3:99, 345: "1 dutzend Geld Körbichen."

43. Dessau, Archiv der Evangelischen Landeskirche Anhalts: "Acten der Herzogl. Superintendentur zu Cöthen betr. die Herzogl. Schlosskirche in Cöthen." Litt: C²a, no. 1, vol. 1, Jahr 1724: "Ein jeder wolle den Tag vorher seine Ankunft mir wißen laßen, damit der Schloß-Cantor die Gesänge möge abholen können."

44. D-BS: H III 3:99, 209, 215.

45. Ibid., 246.

46. Ibid., 252.

47. Ibid., 282.

48. Ibid., 175: "Vors Violoncello, war behandelt vor 2 Rthl. habe aber nur [1 Rthl 18 gr.] erhalten."

49. For example, in 1755: "Bettziechen, dem Schloß Calcanten zum Neuen Jahr." See D-BS: H III 3:99, 240. The average tip was one groschen and four pfennige.

50. In 1758 Martin Bettzieche borrowed three Groschen from Hartung on June 21 and paid him back on September 12. He then borrowed four Groschen on September 27 and paid him back on October 3. See D-BS: H III 3:99, 351.

51. "Von einem fremden Manne, welcher die Schloß Orgel weisen müßen, Tranck-Geld." Ibid., 173.

52. Ibid., 7: "12 [*Groschen*] von dem Laquay Eisenbergen, so beÿ dem Stallmeister de Wietersheim in diensten vor die Taufe. Weilen er sich mit seiner fr. zwar in unehren zusammen gefunden u. selbige nur 14. Tage zur Ehe gehabt, hat er müßen doppelt bezahlen." Three years later, in 1755, Hartung made a similar annotation. Ibid., 27: "12 [Groschen] von der Elisabeth Jänickin vor die Taufe: NB. war ein unehliches, u. wurde im Hause getaufft."

53. For a 1754 wedding described as "von dem Musquet Werner vor die Traue, weilen er in das Superintentur getrauet word[en]" Hartung was paid twleve Groschen, presumably because of the unusual location. Ibid., 3:99, 22.

54. Ibid., 17: "[2 Rthl. 16 Gr.] von dem Hrn. Cammer *Consulent* Behr vor die Traue"; 43: "[24 Gr.] von dem Koch Schreiber vor die Traue."

55. Ibid., 15: "[4 Groschen] von dem Gren: Sergeanten Pillgram vor die Traue. Es wären mir von Rechtswegen 8 gl. zu gekommen, weilen er sich aber geweigert ein solches zu geben, u. das Geld in meiner abwesenheit an Mons: Finger zahlet, so habe es freÿl. Gut heißen müßen, bin also um 4 gr. zu kurtz gekommen."

56. Ibid., 254: "vor Pappier zum Act: Cantaten."

57. Ibid., 174: "Von denen reform: Schülers p: Compositione der neuen Jahrs Cantata, war behandelt vor 4 Rthl: habe aber nur [3 Reichstaler] erhalten."

58. Ibid., 177: "10 [Reichstaler] Vor die Actus Music von der reform: Schule, habe noch um dis Geld Aerger und Verdruß gehabt."

59. See Talle 2011, 71.

60. For information on Kayser see Talle 2003, Jung 2005, and Talle 2011.

61. Evangelisches Pfarramt St. Jakob in Köthen. "Getraute," Jahrgang 1733, p. 129, Nr. 14.

62. Potsdam Landeshauptarchiv: Rep 37 Lübbenau Nr. 5068, f. 2v.*

63. Kayser's difficult financial situation during this period is documented in a let-

ter he wrote on November 2, 1756, to Fürst Karl Georg Lebrecht of Anhalt-Cöthen in which he describes his "bisherigen schlechen Umstände." Three years earlier—in 1753—Kayser began receiving fifty Reichstaler per year "vor die Orgel," but requests more money now "[w]eil ich aber nun mehro den Flügel wieder mit *tractir*e, [. . .]." He also notes that "das wenige so ich bishero von der Orgel bekommen, habe nur erst dreÿ Jahr genoßen, da ich doch solche schon vorhero 24 Jahr [since 1729] bespielet habe und mir niemahls etwas dafür sonst ausgemacht worden ist; als was ich die letzten dreÿ Jahre genoßen habe. Wie ich nun bishero immer das Unglück gehabt, daß ich zweÿ gangbahre Proceße, wegen meiner Kinder so wohl erster als ander Ehe gehabt und dadurch in Schulden kommen bin; Als nehme meine unterthänigste Zuflucht zu Eu. Hoch fürstl. durchl. geheiligten Füßen, bittende mich unwürdigen, beÿ jetziger schlechten Zeit in Gnaden anzusehen, daß ich doch ebenfals wie die andern Herrn Cammer *Musici* mein *Tractement* erhalte." See LHASA, DE, Z70, Abteilung Köthen, C5 h, Nr. 2 Bd. 9. The "gangbahre Proceße" alluded to here may refer to the deaths of Kayser's wives (in 1742 and 1754).

64. Mizler 1736–1754; Niedt 1706; Mattheson 1713, 1717, or 1721; Mattheson 1739; Scheibe 1745.

65. Wollny 2011, 92–93.

66. D-BS: H III 3:99, 254 ("dem *Comiss*: Kayser vor die Bachischen Cantaten."). The manuscripts may have been Kayser's scores of "Mein liebster Jesus ist verloren" (BWV 154) and "Ärgre dich, O Seele, nicht" (BWV 186). See D-B: Mus.ms.Bach. P130 and Mus.ms.Bach.P53.

67. D-BS: H III 3:99, 271 ("Käÿsern vor Halsbänder von Schmeltz u. kleinen *Coralli*"); 272 ("dem W. Knaben Käÿser vor 2 Paar Ohr Pommeln"); 274 ("dem W. K. Kaÿser vor 1 P. Halß Bänder zu machen").

68. Ibid., 2 ("Cammer Diener Kuntzschen"); 5 ("Gutscher Zabel"); 5 ("Hr. Bothenmeisters Ritters Kinder"); 7 ("Laquay Knauff"); 27 ("Musquetier Richter"); 33 ("Keller Knecht Siebert"); 33 ("Reit Knecht Trümper"); 33 ("Heÿducken Klauß"); 50 ("Tagelöhner Friedrichs Kinder").

69. Ibid., 22 and 246 ("Mstr. Großmann vor einen Huth" [Heinrich Gottfried Großmann was a hat maker—See St. Jakob Köthen, Geborene 1733–1749, 431, 492, 640]); 19 and 240 ("Wendt" [by whom Hartung regularly had his shoes repaired]); 15 and 236 ("Streuber" [described by Hartung as a tailor]), ("Assessor Herrmann"); 2 and 226 ("Paldamußin" [probably one of the youngest daughters of the "Darmann in mittelsten Braun" or "Malß-Därrer" Ernst David Paldamus—see St. Jakob Köthen, Geborene 1733–1749, 655, 790]); and 48 ("4 Kerstens Kinder, dem Becker seine").

70. Ibid., 18: August Friedrich Vierthaler paid twenty-four Groschen per quarter, three times as much as the ordinary students. Ibid., 11: Businessmen also sent their apprentices to Hartung, probably for private tutoring ("12 Gr. von Dörffling, so bey Hr. Branigk die Handlung lernet"). Ludwig Bramigk was a *Rathmann* and *Kauff und Händels-Mann* in Köthen who married Henrietta Christiana Behr, daughter of L. A. Behr, in 1745, and was still active in 1759. (St. Jakob Köthen, Getraute 1721–1787, 108, 315–16, 359); "16 Gr. vom Krebs, welcher beÿ Hr. Behr u. Vierthaler die Handl[ung] lernet." Ibid., 36: The daughter of Andreas Gottfried Holtzmann,

Hochfürstl. Accis-Commissarius, Charlotte Friederica Holtzmann (baptized September 8, 1746—Schlosskirche Köthen, Geborene 1608–1814, 476) paid Hartung sixteen groschen per quarter, somewhat more than his ordinary students paid.

71. Ibid., 50: "Siegmann, ein feuer Stahl vors Geld."

72. At least twenty-two of the twenty-four students associated with communion in Hartung's account book were female.

73. Laurentius 1731, 254–55.

74. D-BS: H III 3:99, 262: "Als die Abendmahls Kinder das *Præsent* brachten, ist aufgegangen, vor Caffee [4 Gr.] vor Milch u. Eÿ [1 Gr. 3 Pf.] vor Zwieback darzu [2 Gr.]."

75. Ibid., 27 ("Von der Nitschin habe ein schön Gold Täschgen mit silbern Spitzen besetzt, erhalten; Von der Nebelin habe einen zinnern Teller bekommen; Von der Frau Pönertin habe eine schöne große zinnern Rand Schüßel zum Geschenck bekommen"); 51 ("Brandtin, Friedrichen, Schönerleinin und Langin, 4 Abendm: M, haben zum Präsent eine zinnerne Schüßel u. 2 zinnerne Teller gegeben").

76. Ibid., 48: "In diesem Viertel Jahre habe nur 6 Wochen Schule gehalten, weilen die übrige Zeit an einer harten Kranckheit darniedergelegen[. . .] Nachstehende sind in eine andere Schule gegangen, u. haben mir um ein halb Viertl. Jahr betrogen. Grundmann [8 Gr.], 4 Kerstens Kinder, dem Becker seine [16 gr.]."

77. Monsieur Böttcher's payments were entered on March 19, 1753, September 11, 1753, December 24, 1753, April 2, 1754, and September 23, 1754.

78. G. F. Gerlach's payments were entered in 1753 on June 27, August 29, September 26, October 25, November 26, and December 20; in 1754 on January 31, February 27, March 28, May 2, June 27, July 22, August 19, September 30, November 18, and December 14; in 1755 on January 29, February 20, March 20, April 21, May 28, June 25, September 3, October 27, and December 8; in 1756 on February 17, April 7, July 10, September 11, and November 1 (D-BS: H III 3:99, 173: "Not: Es hat nunmehro selbige völlig aufgehört").

79. The only male students who could conceivably have been married were those about whom we have little information: Böttger, Kreßler, and Voigt.

80. In 1766 Johann Heinrich Allihn became cantor in Raguhn. See Dessau, Archiv der Evangelischen Landeskirche Anhalts: Vierthaler Kartei (Edderitz). Johann Gottlieb Heinrich Proft assisted his father as schoolmaster and organist in Wolfen beginning in 1754. See also Vierthaler Kartei (Wulfen) and "Acten der herzogl. Superintendentur zu Cöthen betr. die Schule in Wulfen. Litt. W 5, No. 5, Vol. I, Jahr 1706."

81. D-BS: H III 3:99, 184: "[16 Gr.] von Gebhardten noch vor etl. Stunden Inform. auf dem Clav: u. hat derselbe nunmehro aufgehört weil er ein Knopfmacher wird den 2. April [1760]."

82. Ibid., 167: "NB: hat aufgehört weilen sie nach Dessau gezogen."

83. Hartung was frequently paid to tune keyboard instruments, but never those of his own students, suggesting that tuning services were included in the price of lessons. Hartung is documented in one case as having tuned the instrument of a former student, Augusta Friederica Clæpius, but only after she had ceased to pay

him for lessons. The price ranged between four and eight Groschen, depending on the state of the instrument. Maria Catharina Frießleben, the daughter of a deceased brewer and leather tanner, paid Hartung to tune her harpsichord, both before and after her marriage to the brewer and businessman David Lebrecht Friedrich. Students occasionally paid him extra to undertake more serious repairs on their instruments. See D-BS: H III 3:99, 178: "Von Mons: Vierthaler vor den Flügel zu rechte zu machen."

84. RISM A422. D-BS: H III 3:99, 160: "[1 Reichstaler, 4 Groschen] von dem Hr. Registrator Bieler vor VI. Sonaten aufs Clav. die Agrell in Kupffer"]. The work is Johan Joachim Agrell's *Sei sonate per il cembalo solo, accompagnate da alcune Ariette, Polonesi e Menuetti, Etc., opera seconda* (Nuremberg: Haffner, 1748).

85. Not in RISM. D-BS: H III 3:99, 167: ("Fr. Kretschmarin geb: Leziussin vor die Psalmen Davids zu schreiben"). The work is Daniel Wolleb's published psalm settings. *Die Psalmen Davids, mit Beybehaltung der übligen Melodien übersetzt* (Halberstadt: Delius, 1751).

86. D-BS: H III 3:99, 173–74: "Von dem Herrn Justiz Rath Paessler in Hartzgerode, zum Geschenck vor Musical." Paessler offered counsel to the Hartung family in a legal dispute in Harzgerode. See D-DElsa: DE, Z 38 Amt und Justizamt Harzgerode, Nr. 43, f. 32r.

87. D-BS: H III 3:99, 223 ("Hr: Rosen vor die neuen Dreßdner Pol: u. Menuets de ao. 1753"). Perhaps this was a publication similar to J. Adam, *Recueil d'airs à Danser executés sur le Théâtre du Roi à Dresde accommodés pour le clavecin* (Leipzig, 1756) (RISM A/I: A 223).

88. D-BS: H III 3:99, 167 ("von dem Hr. Assessor Herrmann vor Dreßdner Polonoisen de ao. 1753 zu schreiben").

89. Ibid., 253: "desgl. [Post-Geld] nach Berlin an den Music: Meyer" and "demselben vor einen Catalogum."

90. Ibid., 209 ("Herr Cörnern, vor die Psalmen Davids von dem Königl. Hoff Prediger Wolleb: in Halberstadt verferttiget"). Cörner was described around this time as "*Lieutenant* und *Adjutanten* beÿ unserer *Guarde*." See D-DElsa: D, C 5h Nr. 2 Bd. VII, f. 449r–450r.

91. D-BS: H III 3:99, 211 ("vor Wolleb. Psalmen Davids in Frantz Band").

92. Carl Heinrich Christian Geißler (baptized July 10, 1740) as well as his older brother, Johann Friederich Gottfried (baptized February 2, 1738), and his two sisters, Johanna Dorothea (baptized November 12, 1736) and Friederika Henrietta Christiana (baptized October 29, 1742), studied in Hartung's *Waisenhaus* school between 1752 and 1758. (See Schlosskirche Köthen, Geborene 1608–1814, 259, 313, 364, 385, 425, 448).

93. D-BS: H III 3:99, 158: "[. . .] weilen sein Hr. Vater ein guter Freund von mir ist."

94. Dessau, Archiv der Evangelischen Landeskirche Anhalts: Vierthaler Kartei (Groß Paschleben).

95. D-BS: H III 3:99, 168: "NB: er hätte müßen noch einmahl so viel zahlen, allein so habe ihn die noch zu zahlende 4 Rthl. erlaßen, weilen seine Eltern mit dem Vieh Sterben heimges: worden."

96. Ibid., 230: "Schrötern in Groß Poschleben vor 3 Gänse, welche meinem Bruder geschencket, ich habe aber mit gegeßen 1 - â 9 gl."

97. Milton 1742.

98. D-BS: H III 3:99, 235: "[4 Reichstaler] ist auf der Hartzgeröder Reise überhaupt aufgegangen."

99. Ibid., 225 and 252.

100. Ibid., 222 and 225.

101. Johann Marius Christoph Hartung was born on September 22, 1725, in Harzgerode. See Hartung 1972, Nr. 101: XII, 12.

102. Though C. A. Hartung typically emphasizes family relationships in his account book (for example, "Mein Bruder der Koch," "Vetter Walter von Bernburg," and the like), he consistently refers to J. M. C. Hartung simply as "Herr Cantor Hartung" (see, for example, D-BS: H III 3:99, 264). See also Hartung 1972, Nrs. 101:XII,12, 101:XIII,12, 101:XII,70 and 101:XIII,70.

103. That he attended school together with C. A. Hartung in 1734 is documented in D-DElsa: DE, Z 18, C 18 Nr. 6, f. 11r–12r. C. A. Hartung's account book reveals that J. M. C. Hartung was alive until at least 1759.

104. Brandt 2000, 12.

105. D-BS: H III 3:99, 264: "[. . .] weil der Herr Cantor Hartung mit seiner fr: liebsten u. Tochter von Bernburg ist hier gewesen, ist aufgegangen." In 1759, he recorded the expenditure of one Reichstaler and eight Groschen "as the Cantor Herr Hartung was here with Bernhard," as well as four Groschen "as a tip for the Cantor Herr Hartung's maid." See Ibid., 278–79.

106. Ibid., 264 and 268: "Bothen Lohn vor Sechte von den Herrn Cantor Hartung in Bernburg."

107. Ibid., 281: "der Fr. so den Gevatter Brief von Bernburg gebracht [8 gr.]," "In Bernburg auf der Gevatterschafft ist aufgegangen beÿ dem Hr. *Cantor* Hartung in die Waÿsen Hauß Büchse [8 gr.]," "in die *Hospital* Büchse [5 gr.]," "vor Wein und *Confect* [1 Rthl. 16 gr.]," "der Kind Mutter Magdalenen [8 gr.]," "der Magd [8 gr.]," "der Warte Frau [8 gr.]," "Reise Kosten [4 gr.]," "in Cöthen vor *Marcepan* Rübgen [6 gr.] vor 1 [Pfund] Aepffel [8 gr.], vor 1 [Pfund] Welsche Nüße [1 gr. 8 pf]."

108. Christian August Jokel was baptized on July 19, 1694 (St. Jakob Köthen, Geborene 1688–1722, 149). He married Catharina Elisabeth Brand on February 1, 1725 (St. Jakob Köthen, Getraute 1721–1769, 42). The couple had eight children, of which August Ludwig Jokel was seventh, born January 14, 1738 (St. Jakob Köthen, Geborene 1732–1747, 436).

109. Born on November 4, 1740, Maria Christina Jokel was the youngest sibling of the family (St. Jakob Köthen, Geborene 1732–1747, 644).

110. Johanna Sophie Jokel was born on August 23, 1731 (St. Jakob Köthen, Geborene 1721–1732, 467).

111. D-BS: H III 3:99, 265: "[1 Groschen, 4 Pfennige] vor 1 Stücke blau band zum Schürtzen vor Hannichen"; 269: "[6 Pfennige] dem Korbmacher vor einen Hanck an Hannichen ihre Thee Kanne"; 276: "[1 Groschen, 6 Pfennige] der fr. Siedeln vor 1 El: roth Taff. Band vor Hannichen"; 277: "[5 Groschen] vor 1 Paar weiße baum wollene Klop Händschken vor Hannichen zum Jahr marckt"; 281: "[14 Groschen]

vor eine Sammt binde Hannichen"; 282: "[22 Groschen] der Fr: Siedeln vor 5 2/4 El: band zu Leib bänder a 4 gl. vor Hannichen"; 284: "[6 Groschen] vor 1 Glaß Essentia dulcis Hannichen."

112. Population statistics for Braunschweig are thin on the ground but it is known that in 1671 there were 15,570 residents; in 1783, 27,063. See *Braunschweig in der Statistik: Entwicklung der Einwohnerzahl seit 1551*, produced in 2008 by the city's *Referat Stadtentwicklung und Statistik* and available at www.braunschweig.de/statistik (accessed March 7, 2013).

113. Fuhrich-Grubert 2004, 150–51. A university student who wrote quite a lot about other Braunschweig churches in 1733 but mentioned Hartung's church only in passing: "In *transitu* besahen wir die *Reformi*rte Kirche, welche kleine und schlecht erbauet." See PL-GD: Ms. 854, 110.

114. Pape 1966, 46, lists the registration in 1900 as follows: "Prinzipal 8' (Baß und Diskant), Subbaß 16' (Baß und Diskant), Gedackt 8,' Octave 4,' Rohrflöte 4,' Quinte 3,' Octave 2,' Mixtur 3f, Cymbel 2f, Trompete 8' (Baß und Diskant). Angehängtes Pedal." Hartung's Braunschweig organ and its clock survived into the twentieth century but was destroyed in a bombing raid on the night of October 14–15, 1944.

115. Fuhrich-Grubert 2004, 150; Pfeiffer 1929, 130–31.

116. A "Musician" (*Musikus*) in Braunschweig named Hartung purchased clavichords from Barthold Fritz in 1753 and 1755, the latter on commission. This cannot refer to Carl August Hartung, who arrived in Braunschweig in 1760. Nor can it refer to his his nephew, Johann August Ludwig Hartung, son of the cook in Cöthen, who later served as violinist in Braunschweig's princely chapel.

117. Aside from some correspondence with residents of Braunschweig—a letter sent in 1756, two sinfonias received in 1757, and a letter delivered personally to him in 1759—the account book contains no hint of an application for the organist position or an impending move.

118. Hartung would eventually earn sixty reichstaler (one hundred reichstaler after 1764) from the German congregation and twenty-five reichstaler from the French congregation.

119. Braunschweig, Archiv der Evangelisch-Reformierten Kirche, A 44 (Akte "Kopien zu Bediensteten der Gemeinde").*

120. D-BS: H III 3:99, 344: "Von Meubles habe meinen Hannichen in Cöthen aufzuheben gegeben u. zurückgelaßen [. . .]"

121. St. Jakob Köthen: Getraute 1721–1787, 448.

122. D-BS: H III 3:99, 292–94.

123. Ibid., 296, 302: "[1 Groschen] vor Sand" and 295: "[4 Groschen, 8 Pfennige] vor einen Besen von Pürstbinder."

124. D-BS: H III 3:99, 296: "[4 Rthl. 18 Gr.] vor 1 Fuder Holz den 11 Nov: [1760]"; "[8 Gr.] Schäfern dem Bälgentreter vors Klein Machen"; "[2 Gr.] einen Becker, der es hat helffen handeln."

125. Ibid., 357: "[5 Rthl] vor ein Decke Bette"; "[5 Rthl, 12 Gr.] vor ein Unter Bette."

126. Ibid., 322–26; 186–89.

127. Ibid., 310: "[8 Gr.] der Frau vors Bier zu bringen."

128. Coffee and tea were commonly listed on the same line as sugar and milk, with a single price for the combined purchase. See Ibid., 301.

129. Ibid., 291: "[4 Rthl.] vor 1 Paar wieße seidene Strümpffe."

130. Ibid., 291: "[8 Gr.] dem Peruquenmacher Gesellen Tranckgeld"; "[2 Rthl.] dem Peruquenmacher Herrn Bauer p. Term: Mich:"; 299: "[4 Gr.] dem Peruquen-macher Jungen vor die neue Peruque Tranck Geld"; 307: "[2 Rthl. 12 Gr.] Herr Böh-men dem Peruquenmacher vor eine neue Peruque," "[2 Gr.] dem Peruquenmacher jungen."

131. Ibid., 303. We lack the writing samples to definitively identify the handwriting as Hannichen's, but it is clearly not Hartung's, and one struggles to imagine anyone else adding expenditures to his account book.

132. Ibid., 300–319 (generally), and 165: "[14 *Groschen*] vor 3 Halßbänden, welche nach Cöthen gekommen."

133. Ibid., 141: "NB. Im Monath Septembr habe kein Inform: Geld verdienet, weilen den gantzen Monath in Cöthen zugebracht."

134. Johanna Rahel Henriette Hartung was baptized on August 1, 1762. See D-BS: G III 1: E251d (T. 2), 801.

135. D-BS: H III 3:99, 354: "[4 *Pfennige*] Nelcken."

136. Ibid., 356: "der Fr. Meÿern, so die Brüste ausgesogen."

137. The payments are varied. See Ibid., 301: (4 Gr. for "Dorotheen Utschen vor Woche aufzuwarten"); 312: (8 Gr. for "dem Mädgen Mieth Pfennig"); 316: (1 Gr. "vor 1 Quartier Mumme"). By way of comparison, the servant of a Leipzig university student in 1733 received one Reichstaler per week. See Talle 2008, 110–30.

138. Henriette Conradine Hartung was baptized on June 28, 1765. See D-BS: G III 1: E251d (T. 2), 813.

139. Johanna Sophia Carolina Hartung was baptized on September 13, 1767. See Ibid., 822.

140. Johanna Rahel Henriette Hartung died on February 27, 1766 (Braunschwei-gische Anzeigen 1766, Spalte 104), and Johanna Sophie Caroline Hartung died on December 4, 1767 (Braunschweigische Anzeigen 1767, Spalte 1064). I would like to thank Hartmut Nickel of the Stadtarchiv Braunschweig for providing this informa-tion.

141. D-BS: H III 3:99, 295: "vor eine Kohl Pfanne dreÿfuß u. Schüppe." Organists commonly used coal to warm their fingers during the winter. See Stahl 1952, 69.

142. For a complete list of the works purchased see Talle 2011.

143. For a complete list of all the music associated with C. A. Hartung see Talle 2011, 61–78.

144. D-BS: H III 3:99, 208: "einen *Ducat*en in Gold [. . .] von des Engl. Abge-sandten an dem Landgräfl: Hofe Bedienten, *Mons: Andreæ*, für 6. *Partit*en auf die Harfe."

145. Ibid., 99, 208.

146. Ibid., 99: "[1 Rthl.] Von Herrn Lambelet, als ein Geschenck wegen der Frie-dens Music den 18. April [1763]."

147. Ibid., 135: "Von dem Kaufmann Herrn Favreau aus Magdeburg zum Prasent für den Hochzeit Carmen, das Geld in 2 doppelten Braunschweig. Louis d'or in Golde, â 1 Louis dor zu 9 Rthl: C. Geld gerechnet, erhalten den 21. Junii."

148. The painter (*Schönfärber*), Herr Rittmeÿer, was charged one Reichstaler and eight Groschen each month for sixteen hours of instruction for his children. The wife of the riding master (*Rittmeister*), Herr von Embst, was charged two Reichstaler for sixteen hours, probably because of the greater number of subjects Hartung taught her daughters. See D-BS: H III 3:99, 64 and 65.

149. Ibid., 62: "[6 Reichsthaler] von Hr. Ahlefeld Informations Geld für seine Söhne, welche seit dem 17. Novembr. 1760 bis zum April 1761 täglich 2 Stunden im Schreiben und Lesen unterrichtet habe den 10. April."

150. If they paid the same rate as the painter's children—two Groschen per hour— the six Reichstaler they paid would have bought them just two hours per week for eighteen weeks (allowing for the Christmas and New Year holidays), which is impossible to reconcile with Hartung's remark that he taught the boys "two hours daily."

151. D-BS: H III 3:99, 309: "[2 Gr.] Tranckgeld H. Ahlefelds [sic] Holzhacker"; 326: "[8 Gr.] Hr. Ahldefelds Clav. auszubeßern."

152. Ibid., 123: "9 Rthl. oder einen Louis d'or in Golde, von dem Kaufmann Herrn Sack in Lübeck vor das Meß Logis. ist aber diesmahl nicht gekommen. den 31. Januarii [1764]."

153. Walther 1987, 133.

154. In 1762, for example, Hartung earned just over 232 Reichstaler from keyboard teaching, making his average income from this source over nineteen Reichstaler per month.

155. D-BS: H III 3:99, 124: "Von Mons: Jonas für die Opera Adriano von Graun aufs Clav: 30 Bogen â 3 ggl. in C. Geld den 20. Febr: an statt des Geldes habe einen Schlafrock von baumwollen Zeuge, u. 1. Schüßel voll Butter erhalten."; 200: "[2 Rthl.] von der Madem: Bausen für einen Monath Clavier Inform: ist abgerechnet gegen ein Paar Manchetten."

156. See for example Ibid., 120 and 122.

157. As in Cöthen, most of Hartung's Braunschweig students were unmarried. The only male students whose marital status cannot be determined are Chenel and Jordan.

158. D-BS: H III 3:99, 108. "[2 Reichstaler] Von der *Madem: Burchardi* für einen *Monath Clav. Infor:* den 2. *Augusti* hat aufgehört, weilen sie den Hr. *Pastor Gericke* heÿrathet." Christian Caspar Jacob Gercke, pastor in Dedeleben, married Johanna Catharina Burchardi, the daughter of a deceased Braunschweig merchant, on October 2, 1763 (D-BS: G III 2: E72, II: 356, and III: 565–66).

159. See also the earlier discussion of a *Clavierbuch* in Nuremberg's *Germanisches Museum* (D-Ngm: Hs. 31781), which once belonged to Anna Margaretha Bassi (née Stromer).

160. D-BS: H III 3:99, 155: "[1 Rthl.] von Mons: Engelbert Bausen für einen halben Monath auf dem Violoncell zu informiren."

161. Ibid., 122: "Von der Madame Bausen auf der breiten Straße ein fein gedruckt blau bunt Frauenzimmer Halstuch, 1/2 [Unze] schönen Thee, und 1 [Unze] Coffee Bohnen, zum neuen Jahr den 4. Jan. [1764]."

162. Ibid., 198: "[16 Gr.] Von eben derselben [Mademoiselle Daniels] für einen Monath für die Mittwohs u. Sonnabends Information an Roß Geld den 30. Sept. [1761]."

163. Ibid., 76: "Besoldung p. Termino Mich: den 28. Julii von der Frau Diekmeiern erhalten in C. Gelde."

164. Ibid., 302: "[2 Groschen, 8 Pfennige] dem Glaser vor Liebauens Laterne welche ich entzweÿ geschmißen." At night it was important to walk with a tin lantern held on a pole to light the cobblestone streets, as anyone out after ten o'clock without a light was assumed to be a thief and could be arrested by the Braunschweig police. See Boswell 1928, 67.*

165. D-BS: G III 2: E321, 180. J. L. Lambelet married Magdalena Elisabeth Lambelet (née Pielat) in 1753, not long after the death of his first wife. For the first nine months of keyboard lessons for "Kleine Mademoiselle Lambelet," Hartung recorded payments for *kl. Madem: Lambelet & Madame*, suggesting that Magdalena Elisabeth herself studied the keyboard alongside her step-daughter. See D-BS: H III 3:99, 74–75.

166. D-BS: H III 3:99, 70: "[2 Rthl.] Profit auf ein Clav: von dem seel: Leidenroth, welches Herr Lambelet bekommen. den 29ten April [1762]."

167. Ibid., 206: "[2 Rthl.] Von Mons: Mühlrath, diener bey Hr: Lambelet, vor Clavier Sachen, als vor 2 Theile von Kobrich und 2 Theile von Tischers galanter: Parthien den 26. April [1762]." The works were Johann Anton Kobrich's *Sechs Leichte und dabey angenehme Clavier-Partien* (Nuremberg: Haffner, ca. 1750) and all three volumes of Johann Nikolaus Tischer's *Das vergnügte Ohr und der erquickte Geist in Sechs Galanterie-Parthien zur Clavier-Ubung für das Frauenzimmer in einer leichten und applicablen Composition dargestellet* (Nuremberg: Haffner, ca. 1742–46).

168. D-BS: H III 3:99, 193–94: "[1 Reichstaler 21 Groschen] Von dem Fürstl. Cammer Musici Herrn Großen, für 2 Flügel Concerts," "[21 Groschen] Vor Herrn Großen für einen Fl: Trav: Conc: von Riedt," and "[1 Reichstaler 12 Groschen] Von Herrn Großen für 2 Flöten Concerts."

169. Ibid., 119: "An Ihro durchl. dem Erb-Printz von Anhalt Bernburg habe 6 Stück Schwanenbergische Sinfonien übersendet." The crown prince referenced here was presumably Franz Adolf von Anhalt-Bernburg-Schaumburg-Hoym.

170. Ibid., 119: "Von dem Mohr Pauli für etl: Stück Sinfonien den 4. Jan. [1763]."

171. Ibid., 311, 319, 329. Hartung's lottery expenditures totaled more than two Reichstaler.

172. Ibid., 64: "[27 Rthl. 12 Gr.] vor eine silberne Minuten Uhr, von dem Fürstl. Waldhornisten Herrn Falke den 12 Juli. [1761]."

173. *Oden und Lieder mit Melodien und mit Begleitung des Claviers* (Braunschweig: self-published, 1782) [RISM H 2207].

174. This second volume, and probably also the first, was printed in Kassel at the orphanage printing house.

175. Carl August Hartung, *Six valses modernes pour le pianoforte* (Braunschweig: Spehr, 1790).

176. Schmidt copied a Bach prelude (BWV 921) already in 1713. The manuscript in which it appears (D-B: Mus.ms.Bach.P222) was at some point acquired by Hartung. See Wollny 2011, 85, 90–91.

177. Wollny 2011, 92–93.

178. Ibid., 82–87.

179. Ibid., 93–94.

180. Dok VI, Nr. B 105: "Er war ein vortrefflicher Notenschreiber und er wußte außerdem gar guten Bescheid in solchen Dingen, so daß er mir gar manches verschafft hat, was ich ohne seine Hülfe vielleicht nicht hätte finden können." See also Wollny 2011, 94.

181. The poem reveals that only one of their daughters was still alive in 1785. D-Wa: P 2600 g–k: "Er gab Euch eine Tochter—Eurem Bilde | Wie Blumenknospen schon Entkeimten gleich, | Es zeigt von ihr im lachenden Gefilde | Die schönste Aussicht neue Freuden Euch."

182. D-BS: G III 2: E251d, I: 1284.

183. "[D]es verstorbenen Organisten bei der reformierten Gemeine Hr. Carl August Hartung Witwe Frau Johanne Sophie, geb. Jockeln" died of "Entkräftung" on November 13, 1815, at age eighty-four. See D-BS: G III 2: 266b, 2.

184. Johann Christian Troldenier served as teacher at the orphanage in Magdeburg before being appointed cantor at the reformed church in Cöthen in 1749. His successor in 1769 was Emanuel Rudolph Heiden, who had previously served as teacher at the orphanage in Zerbst. See D-DElsa: Rep. 15 B Konsistorium Köthen. IXa Nr. 23. My thanks to Michael Maul for kindly providing these references.

185. She died in childbirth "nach ausgestandenen zwar kurtzen aber desto grosseren Geburths-Schmertzen und Todes-Angst ohne erfolgter Entbindung" on March 21, 1755 at age twenty-five years and four months. See St. Jakob Köthen, Geborene 1748–1762, 343 and 413; Dessau, Archiv der Evangelischen Landeskirche Anhalts: St. Marien in Dessau, Defuncti 1710–1759, 1755 Nr. 9, p. 624–25.

186. Oelrichs 1752, 1: "Daß die Musik ein Theil der Gelehrsamkeit sey, wird wohl nicht leicht iemand in Zweifel ziehen."

187. Ibid., 10.*

188. Scheibe 1745, 570.*

189. Scheibe 1745, 572–73.*

190. Wollny 2011, 91.

Bibliography

Abbreviations

BWV = (Bach-Werke-Verzeichnis) Wolfgang Schmieder, ed. 1990. *Thematisch-system-atisches Verzeichnis der musikalischen Werke von Johann Sebastian Bach.* Wiesbaden: Breitkopf and Härtel.

Dok = (Bach-Dokumente) Werner Neumann, Hans-Joachim Schulze, et al., eds. 1963–2008. *Bach-Dokumente.* 7 vols. Kassel: Bärenreiter.

GWV = (Graupner-Werke-Verzeichnis) Oswald Bill, et al., eds. 2005–. *Christoph Graupner: Thematisches Verzeichnis der musikalischen Werke.* Stuttgart: Carus.

HWV = (Händel-Werke-Verzeichnis) Bernd Baselt, ed. 1978–86. *Händel-Handbuch: Thematisch-systematisches Verzeichnis der musikalischen Werke von Georg Friedrich Händel,* 4 vols. Kassel: Bärenreiter.

NBA = (Neue-Bach-Ausgabe) *Johann Sebastian Bach: Neue Ausgabe sämtlicher Werke.* 1954–. Edited by the Johann-Sebastian-Bach-Institut, Göttingen, and the Bach-Archiv, Leipzig. Kassel: Bärenreiter; Leipzig: Deutscher Verlag für Musik.

NBA/KB = Kritischer Bericht ("Critical Report") of the NBA.

RISM = Répertoire International des Sources Musicales.

Printed Literature

Addison, Joseph. 1735. *Cato: Ein Trauerspiel; Aus dem Englischen des Herrn Addisons übersetzt von Luise Adelg. Victoria Gottsched.* Leipzig: Breitkopf.

Adlung, Jacob. 1758. *Anleitung zu der musikalischen Gelahrtheit.* Erfurt: Jungnicol.

———. 1768. *Musica Mechanica Organoedi; das ist, Gründlicher Unterricht von der Struk-*

tur, Gebrauch und Erhaltung, etc. der Orgeln, Clavicymbel, Clavichordien, und andere Instrumente [. . .]. Berlin: Birnstiel.

Ahrens, Christian. 1986. "Johann Sebastian Bach und der 'neue Gusto' in der Musik um 1740." *Bach-Jahrbuch* 72:69–80.

Ahrens, Christian, and Klaus Langrock, eds. 2003. *Geprießner Silbermann! Gereimtes und Ungereimtes zur Einweihung von Orgeln Gottfried Silbermanns*. Köstritzer Schriften 1. Altenburg: Kamprad.

Albrecht, Helmuth. 1986. *Catalogus Professorum der Technischen Universität Carolo-Wilhelmina zu Braunschweig. Teil 1: Lehrkräfte am Collegium Carolinum 1745–1877*. Braunschweig: Universitätsbibliothek der Technischen Universität Carolo-Wilhelmina Braunschweig.

Albrecht, Johann Wilhelm. 1734. *Tractatus physicus de effectibus musices in corpus animatum*. Leipzig: Martini.

Albrecht, Peter. 1980. *Die Förderung des Landesausbaues im Herzogtum Braunschweig-Wolfenbüttel im Spiegel der Verwaltungsakten des 18. Jahrhunderts (1671–1806)*. Braunschweig: Waisenhaus.

Anonymous. 1757. *Sammlung einiger Nachrichten von berühmten Orgel-Wercken in Teutschland mit vieler Mühe aufgesetzt von einem Liebhaber der Musik*. Breslau: Meyer.

Auerbach, Cornelia. 1930. *Die deutsche Clavichordkunst des 18. Jahrhunderts*. Kassel: Bärenreiter.

Bach, Carl Philipp Emanuel. 1753. *Versuch über die wahre Art das Clavier zu spielen*. Berlin: Author.

Bahrdt, Carl Friedrich. 1790. *Geschichte seines Lebens, seiner Meinungen und Schicksale: Von ihm selbst geschrieben*. 4 vols. Berlin: Vieweg.

Ball, Gabriele. 2006. "Die Büchersammlungen der beiden Gottscheds: Annäherungen mit Blick auf die *livres philosophiques* L. A. V. Gottscheds, geb. Kulmus." In *Diskurse der Aufklärung: Luise Adelgunde Victorie und Johann Christoph Gottsched*, edited by Gabriele Ball, Helga Brandes, and Katherine R. Goodman, 213–60. Wiesbaden: Harrassowitz.

Baron, Ernst Gottlieb. 1727. *Historisch-theoretische und practische Untersuchung des Instruments der Lauten*. Nuremberg: Rüdiger.

Barth, Johann Christian. 1720. *Die galante Ethica, in welcher gezeiget wird, wie sich ein junger Mensch bey der galanten Welt, [. . .] recommandiren soll*. Dresden: Lesch.

Bärwald, Manuel. 2008. "'[. . .] ein Clavier von besonderer Erfindung'-Der Bogenflügel von Johann Hohlfeld und seine Bedeutung für das Schaffen Carl Philipp Emanuel Bachs." *Bach-Jahrbuch* 94:271–300.

Beachy, Robert. 2005. *The Soul of Commerce: Credit, Property, and Politics in Leipzig, 1750–1840*. Leiden: Brill.

Becker, Heinz. 1956. "Die frühe Hamburgische Tagespresse als musikgeschichtliche Quelle." In *Beiträge zur Hamburgischen Musikgeschichte*, edited by Heinrich Husmann, 22–45. Hamburg: Musikwissenschaftlichen Instituts der Universität Hamburg.

Beckmann, Klaus, and Hans-Joachim Schulze, eds. 1987. *Johann Gottfried Walther: Briefe*. Leipzig: Deutscher Verlag für Musik.

Berg, Darrell. 1998. "C. P. E. Bach's Organ Sonatas: A Musical Offering for Princess Amalia?" *Journal of the American Musicological Association* 51 (3): 477–519.

———. 2009. *The Correspondence of Christian Gottfried Krause: A Music Lover in the Age of Sensibility.* Burlington: Ashgate.

Bernd, Adam. 1973 [1738]. *Eigene Lebens-Beschreibung: Samt einer Aufrichtigen Entdeck-ung, und deutlichen Beschreibung einer der grösten, obwol großen Theils noch unbekannten Leibes- und Gemüths-Plage [. . .].* Edited by Volker Hoffmann. Munich: Winkler.

Beyer, Peter. 1999. "Leipzigs Auseinandersetzung mit Frankfurt am Main (1706–1726): Symptom des Aufstiegs zur führenden deutschen Messestadt." In *Leipzigs Messen 1497–1914,* edited by Hartmut Zwahr, Thomas Topfstedt, and Günter Bentele, 1:193–204. Cologne: Böhlau.

Biba, Otto. 2009. "Die Wiener Klavierszene um 1800. Klavierunterricht, Klavierspiel, Klaviermusik, Klavierbau." In *La cultura del fortepiano [Die Kultur des Hammerklaviers] 1770–1830,* edited by Richard Bösel, 213–59. Bologna: Ut Orpheus.

Blechschmidt, Eva Renata. 1965. *Die Amalien-Bibliothek: Musikbibliothek der Prinzessin Anna Amalia von Preußen (1723–1787); Historische Einordnung und Katalog mit Hin-weisen auf die Schreiber der Handschriften.* Berlin: Merseburger.

Blessinger, Karl. 1913. "Studien zur Ulmer Musikgeschichte im 17. Jahrhundert, insbe-sondere über Leben und Werke Sebastian Anton Scherers." In *Ulm und Oberschwa-ben: Mitteilungen des Vereins für Kunst und Altertum in Ulm und Oberschwaben* 19: 1–79.

Blochberger, Michael, ed. 1749. *Allgemeines Haushaltungs-Lexicon.* 3 vols. Leipzig: Blochberger.

Bohse, August. 1706. *Der getreue Hoffmeister adelicher und bürgerlicher Jugend.* Leipzig: Gleditsch.

Boswell, James. 1928. *Boswell on the Grand Tour: Germany and Switzerland, 1764.* Edited by Frederick A. Pottle. New York: McGraw Hill.

Brandt, Thomas. 2000. *Johann Christoph Oley. Erschließung biographischer Dokumente aus dem Archiv der Reformierten Gemeinde in Aschersleben.* Schriftliche Diplomarbeit zur B-Prüfung für Kirchenmusik: Evangelische Hochschule für Kirchenmusik Halle/Saale.

Brause, Horst, and Helmut Hentschel. 1992. *700 Jahre Stadt Rötha.* Rötha: Author.

Brockes, Barthold Heinrich. 1721–1748. *Irdisches Vergnügen in Gott: Bestehend in Physi-calisch- und Moralischen Gedichten nebst einem Anhange verschiedener dahin gehörigen Uebersetzungen.* 9 Vols. Hamburg: Kißner.

Brown, Hilary. 2012. *Luise Gottsched the Translator.* Rochester: Camden House.

Buchmann, Lutz. 1987. "Friedrich Wilhelm Rust (1739–1796). Untersuchungen zu seinem Liedschaffen und seinem Beitrag zur Überlieferung der Werke Johann Sebastian Bachs." Dissertation, Martin-Luther-Universität Halle-Wittenberg.

Burkardt, Johannes, Hildegard Gantner-Schlee, and Michael Knieriem, eds. 2006. *Dem rechten Glauben auf der Spur: Eine Bildungsreise durch das Elsaß, die Niederlande, Böhmen und Deutschland; Das Reisetagebuch des Hieronymus Annoni von 1736.* Zürich: Theologischer Verlag.

Burney, Charles. 1771. *The Present State of Music in France and Italy; or, The Journal of a Tour through those Countries, Undertaken to Collect Materials for a General History of Music.* London: Becket.

———. 1773. *Carl Burney's der Musik Doctors Tagebuch einer Musikalischen Reise. Durch Böhmen, Sachsen, Brandenburg, Hamburg und Holland.* Hamburg: Ebeling.

Burrows, Donald. 1985. "Handel and Hanover." In *Bach, Handel, Scarlatti: Tercentenary Essays*, edited by Peter Williams, 35–59. Cambridge: Cambridge University Press.

Butler, Gregory. 1986. "The Engraving of J. S. Bach's Six Partitas." *Journal of Musicological Research* 7 (1): 3–27.

Buttstedt, Johann. 1716. *Ut, mi, sol, re, fa, la: Tota Musica et Harmonia Æterna*. Erfurt: Werther.

Chambers, Ephraim. 1726. *The Practice of Perspective*. London: Bowles and Bowles.

Chrysander, Friedrich. 1863. "Geschichte der Braunschweig-Wolfenbüttelschen Capelle und Oper vom 16. bis zum 18. Jahrhundert." *Jahrbücher für musikalische Wissenschaft* 1:146–286.

Cohen, Bernard. 1985. *Revolution in Science*. Cambridge: Harvard University Press.

Corneilson, Paul. 1992. "Opera at Mannheim, 1770–1778." PhD diss., University of North Carolina at Chapel Hill.

Corvinus, Gottlieb Siegmund. 1710. *Proben der Poesie in galanten-, verliebten-, Schertz-, und satyrischen Gedichten*. Frankfurt: Stocken.

———. 1715. *Nutzbares, galantes, und curiöses Frauenzimmer-Lexicon [. . .] von Amaranthes*. Leipzig: Gleditsch.

Courtin, Antoine. 1671. *Nouveau traité de la civilité*. Amsterdam: Le Jeune.

Cramer, Johann Andreas, ed. 1747–1748. *Der Jüngling*. Vol. 1/8, 108–23. Königsberg: Kanter.

Crawford, Thomas, ed. 1997. *The Correspondence of James Boswell and William Johnson Temple 1756–1795*. Edinburgh: Edinburgh University Press.

Crell, Johann Christian. 1725. *Das in gantz Europa berühmte, galante und sehens-würdige königliche Leipzig in Sachsen*. Leipzig: Martini.

Curas, Hilmar. 1723. *Einleitung zur Universal-Historie worinnen die merckwürdigste Begebenheiten von Anfang der Welt bis auf diese Zeit in Frag und Antwort kurz vorgetragen werden*. Berlin: Nicolai.

Czok, Karl. 1999. "Leipzig und seine Messen im Augusteischen Zeitalter." In *Leipzigs Messen 1497–1997: Gestaltwandel, Umbrüche, Neubeginn*, edited by Hartmut Zwahr, Thomas Topfstedt, and Günter Bentele, 1:183–92. Cologne: Böhlau.

Dadelsen, Georg von. 1957. *Das Klavierbüchlein für Anna Magdalena Bach*. NBA/KB V/4.

Dähnert, Ulrich. 1961. *Der Orgel- und Instrumentenbauer Zacharias Hildebrandt: Sein Verhältnis zu Gottfried Silbermann und Johann Sebastian Bach*. Leipzig: Breitkopf and Härtel.

Debuch, Tobias. 2001. *Anna Amalia von Preußen (1723–1787): Prinzessin und Musikerin*. Berlin: Lagos.

Denzel, Markus A. 1994. *Währungen der Welt X: Geld- und Wechselkurse der deutschen Messeplätze Leipzig und Braunschweig*. Stuttgart: Steiner.

Dietz, Johann. 1915. *Meister Johann Dietz, des Großen Kurfürsten Feldscher und Königlicher Hofbarbier*. Ebenhausen bei München [Schäftlarn]: Langewiesche-Brandt.

———. 1923. *Master Johann Dietz, Surgeon in the Army of the Great Elector and Barber to the Royal Court, from the Old Manuscript in the Royal Library of Berlin*. Translated by Bernard Miall. New York: Dutton.

Dimpfel, Rudolf. 1929. "Ein Leipziger Haushalt vor 200 Jahren." *Schriften des Vereins für die Geschichte Leipzigs* 14:78–105.

Döring, Detlef. 2000a. *Johann Christoph Gottsched in Leipzig.* Leipzig: Sächsische Akademie der Wissenschaften.

———. 2000b. "Johann Christoph Gottscheds Bedeutung für die deutsche Aufklärung." In *Lessing: Kleine Welt—Große Welt,* edited by Dieter Fratzke and Wolfgang Albrecht, 143–64. Kamenz: Lessing-Museum.

———. 2003. "Luise Viktorie Adelgunde Gottsched (1713–1762)." In *Sächsische Lebensbilder* 5, edited by Gerald Wiemers, 213–46. Leipzig: Sächsische Akademie der Wissenschaften.

———. 2006. "Die Leipziger Lebenswelt der Luise Adelgunde Victorie Gottsched." In *Diskurse der Aufklärung—Luise Adelgunde Victorie und Johann Christoph Gottsched,* edited by Gabriele Ball, Helga Brandes, and Katherine R. Goodman, 39–63. Wiesbaden: Harrassowitz.

———. 2009a. "Anfänge der modernen Wissenschaften: Die Universität Leipzig vom Zeitalter der Aufklärung bis zur Universitätsreform, 1650–1830/31." In *Geschichte der Universität Leipzig 1409–2009,* edited by Enno Bünz, Manfred Rudersdorf, and Detlef Döring, 1:517–771. 5 vols. Leipzig: Leipziger Universitätsverlag.

———. 2009b. "Der Literaturstreit zwischen Leipzig und Zürich in der Mitte des 18. Jahrhunderts: Neue Untersuchungen zu einem alten Thema." In *Johann Jakob Bodmer und Johann Jakob Breitinger im Netzwerk der europäischen Aufklärung,* edited by Anett Lütteken and Barbara Mahlmann-Bauer, 60–104. Göttingen: Wallstein.

Dreyfus, Laurence. 2004. *Bach and the Patterns of Invention.* Cambridge, Mass.: Harvard University Press.

Dubreuil, Jean. 1642. *La perspective practique.* Paris: Tavernier.

Dülmen, Richard van. 1992. *Kultur und Alltag in der Frühen Neuzeit.* 3 vols. Munich: Beck.

Dürr, Alfred. 1998. *Johann Sebastian Bach—Das Wohltemperierte Klavier.* Kassel: Bärenreiter.

Dürr, Renate. 1996. "Von der Ausbildung zur Bildung: Erziehung zur Ehefrau und Hausmutter in der Frühen Neuzeit." In *Geschichte der Mädchen und Frauenbildung,* edited by Elke Kleinau and Claudia Opitz, 1:189–206. 2 vols. Frankfurt: Campus.

Düsterdieck, Peter. 1983. *Die Matrikel des Collegium Carolinum und der technischen Hochschule Carolo-Wilhelmina zu Braunschweig 1745–1900.* Hildesheim: Lax.

Edler, Arnfried. 1982. *Der nordelbische Organist: Studien zu Sozialstatus, Funktion und kompositorischer Produktion eines Musikberufes von der Reformation bis zum 20. Jahrhundert.* Kassel: Bärenreiter.

Eger, Susanna. 1745. *Leipziger Kochbuch.* Leipzig: Schuster.

Elsholtii, Johann Sig. 1682. *Diaeteticon: Das ist Newes Tisch-Buch, oder Unterricht von Erhaltung guter Gesundheit durch eine ordentliche Diät und insonderheit durch rechtmäßigen Gebrauch der Speise und des Geträncks.* Cologne: Author.

Elwert, Johann Kaspar Philipp. 1799. *Nachrichten von dem Leben und den Schriften jetztlebender Ärzte.* Hildesheim: Gerstenberg.

Emery, Walter, and Christoph Wolff. 1977. *Zweiter Teil der Klavierübung, Vierter Teil der Klavierübung, Vierzehn Kanons.* NBA/KB V/2.

Engel, Hans. 1957. *Die Musikpflege der Philipps-Universitaet zu Marburg seit 1527.* Marburg: Elwert.

Epstein, Ernesto. 1940. *Der französische Einfluß auf die deutsche Klaviersuite im 17. Jahrhundert.* Würzburg-Aumühle: Triltsch.

Erasmus of Rotterdam. 1731. *Civilitas Morum Puerilium Latinis [et] Germanicis Quæstionidus in nevum teneræ ætatis usum eleganter disposita; das ist, Galante Höflichkeit, wodurch fürnemlich die grünende Jugend für den politischen Augen der heutigen Welt sich also aufführen kan, daß sie allenthalben beliebt und angenehm werde.* Leipzig: Schuster.

Erler, Georg. 1909. *Die jüngere Matrikel der Universität Leipzig, 1559–1809.* 3 vols. Leipzig: Giesecke and Devrient.

Eschebach, Erika. 2005. "Braunschweig wird wieder Residenzstadt—Landesherrliche Maßnahmen und gesellschaftliche Entwicklungen zur Zeit Herzog Carls I von Braunschweig-Lüneburg." *Braunschweiger Rokoko.* Braunschweig: Städtisches Museum.

Fassmann, David. 1742. *Des angenehmen Passe-Tems, durch welches, zwey Freunde, den Leser mit sinnreichen und lustigen Discursen vergnügen.* Frankfurt: Anonymous.

Fedorowskaja, Ludmilla. 1990. "Bachiana in russischen Bibliotheken und Sammlungen: Autographe, Abschriften, Frühdrucke, Bearbeitungen." *Bach-Jahrbuch* 76: 27–36.

Fett, Armin. 1951. *Musikgeschichte der Stadt Gotha von den Anfängen bis zum Tode Gottfried Heinrich Stölzels.* Diss., Universität Freiburg.

Ficker, Wallfriedrich. 1731. Advertisement for a New Keyboard Instrument. *Leipziger Post-Zeitungen,* October 22.

Flade, Ernst. 1953. *Gottfried Silbermann—Ein Beitrag zur Geschichte des deutschen Orgel- und Klavierbaus im Zeitalter Bachs.* Leipzig: Breitkopf and Härtel.

Fleichsig, Werner. 1962–1964. "Ostfälische Musikinstrumentenmacher des 18. und frühen 19. Jahrhunderts." *Braunschweigische Heimat* 48, no. 2 (July 1962): 46–49; 48, no. 3 (October 1962): 89–96; 48, no. 4 (December 1962): 110–15; 49, no. 1 (April 1963): 9–16; 49, no. 2 (July 1963): 42–48; 49, no. 3 (October 1963): 83–89; 49, no. 4 (December 1963): 109–13; 50, no. 1 (April 1964): 9–14; 50, no. 2 (July 1964): 53–59.

Florin, Franz Philipp. 1702. *Oeconomus Prudens Et Legalis. Oder allgemeiner Klug- und Rechts-verständiger Haus-Vatter bestehend in Neun Büchern.* Nuremberg: Riegel.

Forkel, Johann Nikolaus. 1802. *Über Johann Sebastian Bachs Leben, Kunst, und Kunstwerke.* Leipzig: Hoffmeister and Kühnel.

Fortino, Sally. 2003. "'Gefährtin meiner Einsamkeit'—Sehnsucht nach dem Clavichord." In *Fundament aller clavirten Instrumente: Das Clavichord Symposium im Rahmen der 26. Tage Alter Musik in Herne 2001,* 31–44. Munich: Katzbichler.

Frank, Michael Erich. 1715a. *Die rachgierige Fleurie.* Frankfurt5.

———. 1715b. *Des glückseeligen Ritters Adelphico Lebens- und Glücksfälle, in einem Liebes-Roman der Galanten Welt vorgestellet.* Christian-Erlang: Lorberischer Buchladen.

Franz, Eckhart, and Jürgen Rainer Wolf. 1980. "Hessen-Darmstadt und seine Fürsten im Zeitalter des Barock und Rokoko (1678–1780)." In *Darmstadt in der Zeit des Barock und Rokoko,* edited by Eva Huber, 13–19. Mathildenhöhe: Magistrat der Stadt Darmstadt.

Freilinghausen, Johann Anastasius. 1719. *Compendium oder kurtzer Begriff der gantzen Christlichen Lehre in XXXIV. Articuln.* 5th ed. Halle: Waisenhaus.

Freyer, Hieronymus. 1752. *Nähere Einleitung zur Universal-Historie*. Halle: Waisenhaus.

Friedrich, Felix. 1989. *Der Orgelbauer Heinrich Gottfried Trost: Leben, Werk, Leistung*. Wiesbaden: Breitkopf and Härtel.

Friedrichs, Christopher. 1987. "The War and German Society." In *The Thirty Years' War*, edited by Geoffrey Parker, 186–92. London: Routledge.

Friesen, Ernst Freiherr von. 1899. *Geschichte der reichsfreiherrlichen Familie von Friesen*. 2 vols. Dresden: Heinrich.

Friesen, Heinrich Freiherr von. 1941. "Schloß Rötha und die Freiherren von Friesen." In *Rötha in Sachsen: Geburtsort und Heimat unserer Ahnen Kohlmann-Schönberg*, edited by Manfred Joachim Kryzeminski, 20–50. Süssen: Author.

Fritz, Anja. 2005. "Die Gold- und Silberwaren-Manufaktur." In *Bachs Nachbarn. die Familie Bose. Kabinettausstellung im Bach-Museum Leipzig*, edited by Bach-Museum Leipzig, 17–19. Leipzig: Bach-Archiv Leipzig.

Fritz, Balthasar. 1757. *Anweisung, wie man Claviere, Clavecins, und Orgeln, nach einer mechanischen Art, in allen zwölf Tönen gleich rein stimmen könne, daß aus solchen allen sowohl dur als moll wohlklingend zu spielen sey*. Leipzig: Breitkopf.

Fuhrich-Grubert, Ursula. 2004. *"Öffentlich und ungehindert": 300 Jahre Evangelisch-reformierte Gemeinde Braunschweig*. Wuppertal: Foedus.

Fuhrmann, Martin Heinrich. 1706. *Musicalischer-Trichter, dadurch ein geschickter Informator seinen Informandis die edle Singe-Kunst nach heutiger Manier bald und leicht einbringen kan, darinn Vitiosa ausgemustert [. . .]*. Frankfurt an der Spree: Author.

———. 1729. *Die an der Kirchen Gottes gebauete Satans-Capelle [. . .]*. Cologne: Heilige drey Könige Erben.

Fux, Johann Joseph. 1725. *Gradus ad Parnassum*. Vienna: Ghelen.

Gaensler, Heinrich. 1938. "Das Notenbuch Herzogs Friedrich II. von Gotha-Altenburg." *Rund um den Friedenstein: Blätter für Thüringische Geschichte und Heimatgeschehen* 15, no. 22.

Geck, Martin. 2000. *Bach: Leben und Werk*. Reinbek: Rowohlt.

Gellert, Christian Fürchtegott. 1747. *Lustspiele: Faksimiledruck nach der Ausgabe von 1747*. Stuttgart: Metzlersche.

———. 1758. *Leben der schwedischen Gräfinn von G*. 2 vols. Leipzig: Wendler.

Georgi, Theofilo. 1742. *Allgemeines Europäisches Bücher-Lexicon*. 4 vols. Leipzig: Georgi.

Gerber, Christian. 1717. *Die unerkannten Wohlthaten Gottes, in dem Chur-Fürstenthum Sachsen, und desselben vornehmsten Städten, darinnen zugleich der Schul- und Kirchen-Staat enthalten [. . .]*. 2 vols. Dresden: Winckler.

Gerber, Ernst Ludwig. 1790–1792. *Historisch-Biographisches Lexicon der Tonkünstler*. 2 vols. Leipzig: Breitkopf.

———. 1812–1814. *Neues historisch-Biographisches Lexicon der Tonkünstler*. 4 vols. Leipzig: Kühnel.

Glöckner, Andreas. 1988. "Gründe für Johann Sebastian Bachs Weggang von Weimar." In *Bericht über die Wissenschaftliche Konferenz zum V. Internationalen Bachfest der DDR in Verbindung mit dem 60. Bachfest der Neuen Bachgesellschaft. Leipzig, 25. bis 27. März 1985*, edited by Winfried Hoffmann and Armin Schneiderheinze, 137–44. Leipzig: Deutscher Verlag für Musik.

————. 1990. *Die Musikpflege an der Leipziger Neukirche zur Zeit Johann Sebastian Bachs* (Beiträge zur Bach-Forschung 8). Leipzig: Nationale Forschungs- und Gedenkstätten Johann Sebastian Bach.

————. 2013. "'Zu besser Bequemligkeit der Music': Über einige neue Quellen zur Leipziger Kirchenmusik." *Bach-Jahrbuch* 99:335–48.

Goehr, Lydia. 1994. *The Imaginary Museum of Musical Works: An Essay in the Philosophy of Music.* Oxford: Oxford University Press.

Göhler, Albert. 1902. *Verzeichnis der in den Frankfurter und Leipziger Messkatalogen der Jahre 1564 bis 1759 angezeigten Musikalien.* Leipzig: Kahnt, 1902.

Goodman, Katherine, ed. 2009. *Adieu divine Comtesse: Luise Gottsched, Charlotte Sophie Gräfin Bentinck und Johann Christoph Gottsched in ihren Briefen.* Würzburg: Königshausen and Neumann.

Gottsched, Johann Christoph. 1722–1766. *Briefwechsel unter Einschluß des Briefwechsels von Luise Adelgunde Victorie Gottsched.* Edited by Detlef Döring, Franziska Menzel, Rüdiger Otto, and Michael Schlott. 8 vols. (25 planned). Berlin: De Gruyter, 2007–2014.

————. 1725–1726. *Die vernünftigen Tadlerinnen.* 2 vols. Leipzig: König. Reprint: Helga Brandes, ed., Hildesheim: Olms, 1993.

————. 1730. *Versuch einer critischen Dichtkunst.* Leipzig: Breitkopf.

————. 1737. *Versuch einer critischen Dichtkunst: Zweyte und verbesserte Auflage.* Leipzig: Breitkopf.

————. 1738. *Die vernünftigen Tadlerinnen.* 2 vols. Leipzig: König. Reprint: Helge Brandes, ed., Hildesheim: Olms, 1993.

————. 1742. *Versuch einer critischen Dichtkunst: Dritte und vermehrte Auflage.* Leipzig: Breitkopf.

————. 1751. *Versuch einer critischen Dichtkunst: Vierte sehr vermehrte Auflage.* Leipzig: Breitkopf.

————. 1763. "Leben der weil. hochedelgebohrnen, nunmehr sel. Frau, Luise Adelgunde Victoria Gottschedinn, geb. Kulmus, aus Danzig." In *Sämmtliche kleinere Gedichte, nebst dem, von vielen vornehmen Standespersonen, Gönnern und Freunden beyderley Geschlechtes, Ihr gestifteten Ehrenmaale, und Ihrem Leben, herausgegeben von Ihrem hinterbliebenen Ehegatten,* by Luise Adelgunde Viktorie Gottsched. Leipzig: Breitkopf.

————. 1767. *Catalogus Bibliothecæ, qvam Jo. Ch. Gottschedivs, Philosophiæ Primæ in Acad. Lipsiensi [. . .].* Leipzig: Breitkopf.

————. 1968–1987. *Ausgewählte Werke.* 12 vols. Edited by Joachim Birke (vols. 1–5) and Philip Marshall Mitchell (vols. 6–12). Berlin: De Gruyter.

Gottsched, Luise Viktorie Adelgunde. 1736. *Die Pietisterey im Fischbein-Rocke, oder die Doctormäßige Frau.* Rostock: Anonymous [Leipzig: Breitkopf]. Reprint: Wolfgang Mertens, ed., Stuttgart: Reclam, 1968.

————. 1739. *Triumph der Weltweisheit: Nach Art des französischen Sieges der Beredsamkeit der Frau von Gomez, nebst einem Anhang dreyer Reden.* Leipzig: Breitkopf.

————. 1744. *Die Hausfranzösin oder die Mammsell: Ein deutsches Lustspiel in fünf Aufzügen.* In *Die Deutsche Schaubühne nach den Regeln und Exempeln der Alten,* edited by J. C. Gottsched, vol. 5. In 6 vols. Leipzig: Breitkopf, 1741–1745.

———. 1771–1772. *Briefe der Frau Louise Adelgunde Victorie Gottsched gebohrne Kulmus.* Edited by Dorothee Henriette von Runckel. 3 vols. Dresden: Harpeter.

Gräbner, Christian. 1711. *Unmaßgebliche Gedancken von Erziehung eines Honetten Menschen Männlichen und Weiblichen Geschlechts/ Was bey solchen vom Anfang seiner Geburt Biß ins männliche Alter in acht zu nehmen nöthig/ Nebst einem Anhang/ Worinnen von der MUSIC und Tantzen Unvorgreifflich sentiret wird.* Leipzig: Tietz.

Gressel, Johann Georg [*Celander*]. 1709. *Der verliebte Student oder Poussieren geht über Studieren.* Cologne: Marteau. Reprint edition, Helmut Fleskamp, ed., Munich: Heyne, 1969.

———. 1716. *Verliebte, galante, Sinn-, vermischte und Grab-Gedichte.* Hamburg and Leipzig: Liebezeit.

Greve, Werner. 1985. *"Musicam habe ich allezeit lieb gehabt": Leben und Wirken Braunschweiger Organisten, Spielleute und Kantoren an der Altstadt-Kirche St. Martini in Braunschweig 1500–1800; Ein Beitrag zur Musikgeschichte Braunschweigs.* Braunschweig: Gesellschaft zur Förderung der Musik an St. Martini.

Gurlitt, Wilibald. 1913. "Ein Brief des Braunschweiger Organisten Heinrich Lorenz Hurlebusch aus dem Jahre 1725." *Braunschweigisches Magazin* 2:22–23.

Habicht, M. E. 1927. *Suchbuch für die Marburger Universitätsmatrikel von 1653–1830.* Darmstadt: Hessische Chronik.

Haensel, Uwe. 1974. *Das Klavierbuch der Christiana Charlotte Amalia Trölle (1702): Einleitung und Ausgabe* (Quellen und Studien zur Musikgeschichte Schleswig-Holsteins Bd. 3). Neumünster: Wachholtz.

Hafner, Klaus. 1996. *Der badische Hofkapellmeister Johann Melchior Molter (1696–1765) in seiner Zeit.* Karlsruhe: Badische Landesbibliothek.

Hankins, Thomas, and Robert Silverman. 1999. *Instruments and the Imagination.* Princeton, N.J.: Princeton University Press.

Hardach-Pinke, Irene, and Gerd Hardach, eds. 1981. *Kinderalltag: Deutsche Kindheiten in Selbstzeugnissen 1700–1900.* Reinbek: Rowohlt.

Hartung, Günther. 1972. *Genealogie Hartung VII: Die Hartungs im Gebiet des Harzes; Stammtafel und Stammliste 101; Nach arbeiten von Bernhard Hartung um 1908.* Munich: Author.

Hartung, Oskar. 1900. *Geschichte der Stadt Cöthen bis zum Beginn des 19. Jahrhunderts.* Cöthen: Schulz.

Hartung, Philipp Christoph. 1749. *Musicus theoretico practicus.* Nuremberg: Felßecker.

Head, Matthew. 1995. "'Like Beauty Spots on the Face of a Man': Gender in 18th-Century North-German Discourse on Genre." *Journal of Musicology* 12 (3): 143–67.

———. 1999. "'If the Pretty Little Hand Won't Stretch': Music for the Fair Sex in Eighteenth-Century Germany." *Journal of the American Musicological Society* 52 (2): 203–54.

———. 2013. *Sovereign Feminine: Music and Gender in Eighteenth-Century Germany.* Oakland: University of California Press.

Heinz, Otmar. 2012. *Frühbarocke Orgeln in der Steiermark: Zur Genese eines süddeutsch-österreichischen Instrumententyps des 17. Jahrhunderts.* Vienna: Lit.

Hellmund, Egidius Günther. 1719. *Thelogische Antwort auf die Frage: Ob das heutige weltliche Tantzen Sünde sey?* Halberstadt: Schultz.

Henkel, Heinrich. 1882. *Mittheilungen aus der musikalischen Vergangenheit Fuldas.* Fulda: Maier.

Henkel, Hubert. 1991. "Musikinstrumente im Nachlass Leipziger Bürger." In *Johann Sebastian Bachs historischer Ort* (*Bach-Studien* 10), edited by Reinhard Szeskus, 56–67. Wiesbaden: Breitkopf and Härtel.

Hennig, Ernst. 1790. "Leben des Professor Fischer in Königsberg." *Preußisches Archiv,* April, 312–33. Königsberg: Königliche Deutsche Gesellschaft.

Hennings, Johann. 1951. *Musikgeschichte Lübecks.* Vol. 1: *Weltliche Musik.* Kassel: Bärenreiter.

Hensel, Martin. 1736. *Evangelischer Herztens-Wecker, für Gott suchende Küster und Dorfschulmeister, Ihr wichtiges Amt an Kirche und Schule redlich auszurichten.* Züllichau [Sulechów]: Frommann.

Hentschel, Helmut. 1997. "275 Jahre Silbermannorgel in der Georgenkirche zu Rötha (1721–1996)." In *Heimatblätter des Bornaer Landes* 6:53–56.

Henze-Döhring, Sabine. 2003. "Der Stellenwert der Musik im höfischen Zeremoniell." In *Musik der Macht—Macht der Musik: Die Musik an den sächsisch-albertinischen Herzogshöfen Weißenfels, Zeitz und Merseburg,* edited by Jiliane Riepe, 23–32. Schneverdingen: Wagner.

Herbst, Kurt. 1961. *Der Student in der Geschichte der Universität Leipzig.* Leipzig: Koehler and Amelang.

Hertel, Johann Wilhelm. 1757. *Sammlung musikalischer Schriften, größtentheils aus den Werken der Italiäner und Franzosen übersetzt, und mit Anmerkungen versehen.* 2 vols. Leipzig: Breitkopf.

Heuser, Magdalene. 1998. "Neuedition der Briefe von Luise Adelgunde Victorie Gottsched." In *Chloe: Beiheft zum Daphnis. Editionsdesiderate zur Frühen Neuzeit,* edited by Hans-Gert Rolff and Renate Meincke, 319–39. Amsterdam: Rodopi.

Heussner, Horst. 1963. "Der Musikdrucker Balthasar Schmid in Nürnberg." *Die Musikforschung* 16:348–62.

Heyde, Herbert. 1986. *Musikinstrumentenbau: 15.–19. Jahrhundert Kunst-Handwerk Entwurf.* Wiesbaden: Breitkopf and Härtel.

Hilgenfeldt, Carl Ludwig. 1850. *Johann Sebastian Bach's Leben, Wirken, und Werke.* Leipzig: Hofmeister.

Hiller, Johann Adam. 1784. *Lebensbeschreibungen berühmter Musikgelehrten und Tonkünstler neuerer Zeit.* Leipzig: Dyk.

Hintzsche, Erich. 1971. *Albrecht Hallers Tagebücher seiner Reisen nach Deutschland, Holland und England 1723–1727: Neue verbesserte und vermehrte Auflage mit Anmerkungen.* Bern: Huber.

Hirschmann, Wolfgang. 2013. "'He Liked to Hear the Music of Others': Individuality and Variety in the Works of Bach and His German Contemporaries." In *Bach and His German Contemporaries* [= *Bach Perspectives* 9], edited by Andrew Talle, 1–23. Urbana: University of Illinois Press, 2013.

Hoferichter, Carl Horst. 1980. "Der Hofstaat Ernst Ludwigs." In Huber, *Darmstadt,* 69–79.

Hoffmann, Gabriele. 1984. *Constantia von Cosel und August der Starke: Die Geschichte einer Mätresse.* Bergisch Gladbach: Bastei.

Hoffmann, Winfried. 1982. "Leipzigs Wirkungen auf den Delitzscher Kantor Christoph Gottlieb Fröber." *Beiträge zur Bachforschung* 1:54–73.

Hoffmann-Erbrecht, Lothar. 1954. "Der Nürnberger Musikverleger Johann Ulrich Haffner [Part 1]." *Acta Musicologica* 26:114–26.

———. 1955. "Der Nürnberger Musikverleger Johann Ulrich Haffner [Part 2]." *Acta Musicologica* 27:141–42.

Hohberg, Wolf Helmhard von. 1687. *Georgica Curiosa Aucta; das ist, Umständlicher Bericht und klarer Unterricht von dem Adelichen Land- und Feld-Leben.* 2 vols. Nuremberg: Endter.

Holberg, Ludwig von. 1749. *Briefe von verschiedenen historischen, politischen, metaphysischen, moralischen, philosophischen, auch scherzhaften Materien, in zween Theile getheilet: Erster Theil—Aus dem Dänischen übersetzt.* Copenhagen: Wentzel.

———. 1752. *Die dänische Schaubühne.* 4 vols. Copenhagen: Rothe.

Holtkötter, Michael. 1986. "Die Ausstattung des Leipziger Bürgerhauses in der ersten Hälfte des 18. Jahrhunderts." In *Leipzig: Aus Vergangenheit und Gegenwart. Beiträge zur Stadtgeschichte* 4:95–113. Leipzig: Fachbuchverlag.

Hönn, Georg Paul. 1724. *Betrugs-Lexikon, worinnen die meisten Betrügereyen in allen Staenden nebst denen darwieder guten Theils dienenden Mitteln entdecket.* Coburg: Pfotenhauer.

Huber, Eva, ed. 1980. *Darmstadt in der Zeit des Barock und Rokoko.* Mathildenhöhe: Magistrat der Stadt Darmstadt.

Huber, Marie. 1731. *Le monde fou préféré au monde sage, en vingt-quatre promenades de trois amis, Criton, Philon, Eraste.* Amsterdam: Les Wetsteins et Smith.

Hunold, Johann Christian [*Menantes*]. 1708. *La Civilité Moderne; oder, Die Höflichkeit der heutigen Welt.* German translation of Courtin, 1671. Hamburg: Schiller.

———. 1708–1709. *Die allerneueste Art höflich und galant zu schreiben; oder, Auserlesene Briefe, in allen vorfallenden auch curieusen Angelegenheiten, nützlich zu gebrauchen nebst einem zulänglichen Titular- und Wörter-Buch von Menantes.* 2 vols. Hamburg: Liebernickel.

———. 1717–1722. *Auserlesene neue Briefe: Nebst einer Anleitung, wie in den allermeisten Begebenheiten die Feder nach dem Wohl stand und der Klugheit zu führen an das Licht gestellet von Menantes.* Halle: Waysenhause.

Israel, Jonathan I. 2001. *Radical Enlightenment: Philosophy and the Making of Modernity.* Oxford: Oxford University Press.

Jablonski, Daniel Ernst. 1693. *Christliche Predigten über verschiedene auserlesene Sprüche, Heil, Schrifft, zu verschiedenen Zeiten gehalten.* Zehend IV. Berlin: Haude.

Jacobi, Erwin. 1965. "Johann Christoph Ritter (1715 bis 1767), ein unbekannter Schüler J. S. Bachs und seine Abschrift (etwa 1740) der 'Clavier-Übung' I/II." *Bach-Jahrbuch* 51:43–62.

Jaeneke, Joachim. 1973. *Die Musikbibliothek des Ludwig Freiherrn von Pretlack 1716–1781.* Wiesbaden: Breitkopf and Härtel.

Jugler, Johann Heinrich. 1779. *Leipzig und seine Universität vor hundert Jahren: Aus den gleichzeitigen aufzeichnungen eines Leipziger Studenten.* Leipzig: Breitkopf and Härtel.

Jung, Hans-Rudolf. 1991. "Ein unbekanntes 'Clavier-Buch' mit Klavierstücken und Arien von Georg Philipp Telemann in Weimar." In *Georg Philipp Telemann—Werküber-*

lieferung, Editions- und Interpretationsfragen, edited by Wolf Hobohm and Carsten Lange, 75–94. *Cologne:* Tank.

———. 2005. "Der Bach-Schüler Bernhard Christian Kayser als Bewerber um die Hof- und Stadtorganistenstelle in Schleiz," *Bach-Jahrbuch* 91:281–85.

———. 2007. *Musik und Musiker im Reußenland.* Weimar and Jena: Hain.

Kaemmel, Otto. 1909. *Geschichte des Leipziger Schulwesens vom Anfange des 13. bis gegen die Mitte des 19. Jahrhunderts (1214–1846).* Leipzig: Teubner.

Kemmler, Erwin. 1970. *Johann Gottfried Müthel und das nordostdeutsche Musikleben seiner Zeit.* Marburg: Herder-Institut.

Kempe, Michael. 2003. *Wissenschaft, Theologie, Aufklärung: Johann Jakob Scheuchzer (1672–1733) und die Sintfluttheorie.* Epfendorf: Biblioteca Academica.

Klassen, Janina. 2009. "Musikalische Repräsentation, Gender- und soziokulturelle Aspekte der Klavierkultur zwischen 1770 und 1830." In *La cultura del fortepiano [Die Kultur des Hammerklaviers] 1770–1830,* edited by Richard Bösel, 167–178. Bologna: Ut Orpheus.

Kleeberger, Karl. 1911. "Zwei Streitgedichte über die Oberpfalz aus dem Jahre 1750." *Die Oberpfalz. Monatsschrift für Geschichte, Volks- und Heimatkunde* 5:149–52.

Klose, Carl Rudolph Wilhelm, ed. 1849. *Joh. Chr. Edelmann's Selbstbiographie: Geschrieben 1752.* Berlin: Wiegandt.

Kobuch, Agatha. 1988. *Zensur und Aufklärung in Kursachsen: Ideologische Strömungen und politische Meinungen zur Zeit der sächsisch-polnischen Union (1697–1763).* Weimar: Böhlau.

Köhler, Otto. 1969. *Die Matrikel der Universität Jena.* 3 vols. Halle: Niemeyer.

Koldau, Linda Maria. 2005. *Frauen—Musik—Kultur: Ein Handbuch zum deutschen Sprachgebiet der Frühen Neuzeit.* Cologne: Böhlau.

König, Johann Ulrich. 1745. *Des Herrn von Königs Gedichte aus seinen von ihm selbst verbesserten Manuscripten gesammlet und herausgegeben.* Dresden: Walther.

Kord, Susanna. 2000. *Little Detours: The Letters and Plays of Luise Gottsched, 1813–1762.* Rochester: Camden House.

Kording, Inka, ed. 1999. *Luise Gottsched—"Mit der Feder in der Hand": Briefe aus den Jahren 1730–1762.* Darmstadt: Wissenschaftliche Buchgesellschaft.

Kreising, Hinrich Conrad. 1742. *Dem verdienten allgemeinen Nachruhme Der am 6ten November 1742 dem Hochedlen und Hochgelehrten HERRN Johann Samuel Müller, der Hamburgischen Johannis-Schule hochverdientem Rectori, etc. durch einen frühzeitigen und plötzlichen Tod entrissenen Höchstgeliebten, tugendhafftesten Ehegattin FRAU Catharinen Louisen Hartmannin, konte noch mit wenigem beyzustimmen, auch dem Hochbetrübten Herrn Witwer und insbesondere dem Hochgeschützten Paare der einer unvergleichlichen Mutter beraubten Waysen sein hertzliches Mitleid zu bezeugen nicht umhin Dero geehrtesten Hauses ergebenster Diener H. C. Kreysing.* Hamburg: König.

Kretschmar, Gottfried. 1704. *Einweihungs-Predigt, welche bei Einweihung der neuen Orgel in der Hauptkirche SS: Petri und Pauli zu Görlitz [. . .] gehalten.* Görlitz: Laurentius.

Kretschmar, Hermann. 1909. "Das Notenbuch der Zeumerin." *Jahrbuch der Musikbibliothek Peters* 16:57–72.

Kreutzer, Hans Joachim. 2005. "Weltalldichtung und Vollendung der Natur—Aspekte der Literaturtheorie der Bach-Zeit." In *Musik, Kunst und Wissenschaft im Zeitalter J. S. Bachs*, Leipziger Beiträge zur Bach-Forschung 7, edited by Ulrich Leisinger and Christoph Wolff, 67–98. Hildesheim: Olms.

Krieger, Johann. 1697. *Sechs Musicalische Partien*. Nuremberg: Endter.

Kruedener, Jürgen. 1973. *Die Rolle des Hofes im Absolutismus*. Stuttgart: Fischer.

Lambert, Anne-Thérèse de. 1727. *Réflexions nouvelles sur les femmes par une dame de la Cour de France*. Paris: le Breton.

———. 1731. *Neue Betrachtungen über das Frauenzimmer*. Translated by Luise Adelgunde Viktorie Kulmus. Leipzig: Breitkopf.

Lampe, Joachim. 1963. *Aristokratie, Hofadel und Staatspatriziat in Kurhannover: Die Lebenskreise der höheren Beamten an den kurhannoverschen Zentral- und Hofbehörden 1714–1760*. 2 vols. Göttingen: Vandenhoeck and Ruprecht.

Lange, Johann Christian. 1704. *Vernunfft-mässiges, bescheidenes und unparteyisches Bedencken über die durch mancherley öfftern angeregte Streitigkeit vom Tantzen*. Frankfurt: Schall.

Laurentius, Gotthilf August. 1731. *Anweisung zu Christl: Erziehung der Jugend*. Leipzig: Frommann.

Lediard, Thomas. 1740. *The German Spy; or, Familiar Letters from a Gentleman on His Travels through Germany, to His Friend in England*. Second edition. London: Cooper.

Leinweber, Josef. 1991. *Verzeichnis der Studierenden in Fulda von 1574 bis 1805*. Frankfurt: Knecht.

Leisinger, Ulrich. 2000. "Das Klavierbüchlein der Prinzessin Amalia von Braunschweig-Lüneburg." In *Ständige Konferenz Mitteldeutsche Barockmusik, Jahrbuch* 1999, 169–78. Eisenach: Wagner.

Leporin, Dorothea Christiane. 1742. *Gründliche Untersuchung der Ursachen, die das weibliche Geschlecht vom Studiren abhalten*. Berlin: Rüdiger.

Leppert, Richard. 1988. *Music and Image: Domesticity, Ideology and Socio-Cultural Formation in Eighteenth-Century England*. Cambridge: Cambridge University Press.

———. 1995. *The Sight of Sound: Music, Representation, and the History of the Body*. Oakland: University of California Press.

Libin, Laurence. 1976. "An Eighteenth-Century View of the Harpsichord," *Early Music* 4, no. 1 (January): 16–18.

———. 1994. "The Instruments." In *Eighteenth-Century Keyboard Music*, edited by Robert Marshall, 1–32. New York: Schirmer.

———. 2010. "Keys to the Heart: The Clavichord in Moravian Life." In *Self, Community, World: Moravian Education in a Transatlantic World*, edited by Heikki Lempa and Paul Peucker, 228–46. Bethlehem, Penn.: Lehigh University Press.

Lingke, Georg Friedrich. 1766. *Die Sitze der Musikalischen Haupt-Sätze in einer harten und weichen Tonart*. Leipzig: Breitkopf.

Litzmann, Berthold. 1885–1886. "Briefe von Anna Maria von Hagedorn an ihren jüngeren Sohn Christian Ludwig 1731–32." In *Aus Hamburgs Vergangenheit: Kulturhistorische Bilder aus verschiedenen Jahrhunderten*, edited by Kai Koppmann, 1:79–180. 2 vols. Hamburg: Voss.

Lobethan, Johann Conrad. 1729. *Die Enge Pforte zur Seeligkeit*. Leipzig: Gleditsch.

Loesser, Arthur. 1954. *Men, Women, and Pianos: A Social History.* New York: Simon and Schuster.

Loos, Fritz. 1987. *Rechtswissenschaft in Göttingen: Göttinger Juristen aus 250 Jahren.* Göttingen: Vandenhoeck and Ruprecht.

Luther, Martin. 1730. *Kleiner Katechismus, samt dessen zwantzig Frag-Stücken, für diejenigen, welche Unterricht zum H. Abendmahl vonnöthen haben.* Augsburg: Henchel.

Maaß, Rainer. 2006. "Pagen und ihre Lehrer am Darmstädter Hof des 18. Jahrhunderts." *Hessisches Jahrbuch für Landesgeschichte* 56:73–114.

Manecke, Lorenz. 1866. "Tagebuch der Reise eines Rügenschen Predigers nach Hamburg im Jahre 1745." In *Zeitschrift des Vereines für hamburgische Geschichte,* 5:135–48. Hamburg: Meißner.

Marpurg, Friedrich Wilhelm. 1750a. *Des critischen Musicus an der Spree.* Berlin: Haude and Spener.

———. 1750b. *Die Kunst das Clavier zu spielen.* Berlin: Henning.

———. 1755–1758. *Handbuch bey dem Generalbasse und der Composition mit zwey- drey- vier- fünf- sechs- sieben- acht- und mehrern Stimmen.* Berlin: Lange, 1755–1758. 3 vols.

———. 1756. *Abhandlung von der Fuge.* Berlin: Haude and Spener.

———. 1757. *Anfangsgründe der Theoretischen Music.* Leipzig: Breitkopf.

———. 1759. *Kritische Einleitung in die Geschichte der Music.* Berlin: Lange.

———. 1760–1764. *Kritische Briefe über die Tonkunst.* 3 vols. Berlin: Birnstiel.

———. 1765. *Anleitung zum Clavierspielen, der schönern Ausübung der heutigen Zeit gemäß.* Berlin: Haude and Spener.

Mathe, Moritz Hugo. 1905–1906. "Die Parochie Rötha." In *Neue Sächsische Kirchengalerie. Die Ephorie Borna,* edited by Die Geistlichen der Ephorie Borna. Leipzig: Strauch.

Mattheson, Johann. 1713. *Das neu-eroffnete Orchestre [. . .].* Hamburg: Author.

———. 1717. *Das beschützte Orchestre [. . .].* Hamburg: Schiller.

———. 1719. *Exemplarische Organisten-Probe.* Hamburg: Schiller and Kißner.

———. 1721. *Das forschende Orchestre [. . .].* Hamburg: Wittwe and Kißner.

———. 1731. *Grosse General-Baß-Schule [. . .].* Hamburg: Kißner.

———. 1735. *Kleine General-Baß-Schule [. . .].* Hamburg: Kißner.

———. 1737. *Kern melodischer Wissenschaft [. . .].* Hamburg: Herold.

———. 1739. *Der vollkommene Capellmeister [. . .].* Hamburg: Herold.

———. 1740. *Grundlage einer Ehren-Pforte [. . .].* Hamburg: Author.

———. 1747. *Behauptung der Himmlischen Musik aus den Gründen der Vernuft, Kirchen-Lehre und heiligen Schrift.* Hamburg: Herold.

———. 1749. *Mithridat: Wider den Gift einer welschen Satyre; "La Musica."* Hamburg: Author.

———. 1750. *Matthesons bewährte Panacea, als eine Zugabe zu seinem musikalischen Mithridat.* Hamburg: Author.

———. 1754–1755. *Plus Ultra, ein Stückwerk von neuer und mancherley Art.* 3 vols. Hamburg: Martini.

Matthews, Lora. 1989. "Johann Kuhnau's Hermeneutics: Rhetorical Theory and Musical Exegesis in His Works." PhD diss., University of Western Ontario.

Maul, Michael. 2008. "Zwei Clavierbücher aus der Herzogin Anna Amalia Bibliothek

Weimar als Quellen zur Zerbster Musikpflege um 1680." In *Musik an der Zerbster Residenz. Bericht über die Internationale Wissenschaftliche Konferenz vom 10. bis 12. April 2008 im Rahmen der 10. Internationalen Fasch-Festtage in Zerbst*, edited by Stadt Zerbst in Zusammenarbeit mit der Internationalen Fasch-Gesellschaft (Fasch-Studien 10), 41–68. Beeskow: Ortus Musikverlag.

———. 2009. "'Alte' und 'Neue' Materialien zu barocken Organistenproben in Mittel- und Norddeutschland." *Basler Jahrbuch für historische Musikpraxis* 31:217–44.

———. 2010. "Johann Adolph Scheibes Bachkritik: Hintergründe und Schauplätze einer musikalischen Kontroverse." *Bach-Jahrbuch* 96:153–98.

———. 2012. *"Dero berühmter Chor": Die Leipziger Thomasschule und ihre Kantoren 1212–1804.* Leipzig: Lehmstedt.

Meibeyer, Wolfgang. 1966. "Bevölkerungs- und sozialgeographische Differenzierung der Stadt Braunschweig um die Mitte des 18. Jahrhunderts." *Braunschweigisches Jahrbuch* 47:125–57.

Merian, Wilhelm. 1919–1920. "Aus einem Reisetagebuch des 18. Jahrhunderts." In *Neue Folge der Berner Taschenbücher*, 215–38 (Part 1, 1919) and 139–63 (Part 2, 1920).

Mertens, Wolfgang. 1968. "Literaturverzeichnis" and "Nachwort." In *Die Pietisterey im Fischbein-Rocke, oder die Doktormäßige Frau*, edited by Luise Adelgunde Viktorie Gottsched, 144–48 and 151–67. Stuttgart: Reclam.

Michaelsen, Franz. 1958. "Glückstädter Organisten vor und nach 1700." *Die Heimat* 65:199–201.

Milton, John. 1742. *Johann Miltons Episches Gedichte von dem verlohrnen Paradiese.* Translated by Johann Jakob Bodmer. Zürich: Orell and Leipzig: Gleditsch.

Mizler, Lorenz. 1736–1754. *Musikalische Bibliothek oder Gründliche Nachricht nebst unpartheyischem Urtheil von alten und neuen musikalischen Schrifften und Büchern, worinn alles, was aus der Mathematik, Philosophie und den schönen Wissenschafften zur Erläuterung und Verbesserung sowol der theoretischen als practischen Musik gehöret, nach und nach beygebracht wird.* 4 vols. Leipzig: Mizler.

———. 1740. *Musikalischer Staarstecher.* Leipzig: Graff.

Mörke, Olaf. 1996. "Social Structure." In *Germany: A New Social and Economic History—Volume 2: 1630–1800*, edited by Sheilagh Ogilvie, 134–63. London: Arnold.

Möser, Justus. 1871. *Patriotische Phantasien.* Edited by Reinhard Zöllner. 2 vols. Leipzig: Brockhaus.

Mosheim, Johann Lorenz. 1757. *Heilige reden über wichtige wahrheiten der lehre Jesu Christi.* Hamburg: Bohn.

Muffat, Georg. 1695. "Deß Authoris Vorred an den günstigen Liebhaber." In *Florilegium Primum*, vol. 1, edited by Heinrich Riepsch. Augsburg: Koppmeyer. Reprint, Denkmäler der Tonkunst in Österreich. Vienna: Artaria, 1894.

Müller, Jens. 1989. "Zur Baugeschichte und denkmahlpflegerischen Erneuerung des Boseschen Hauses am Thomaskirchhof." In *Das Bosehaus am Thomaskirchhof: Eine Leipziger Kulturgeschichte*, edited by Armin Schneiderheinze, 31–138. Leipzig: Peters.

Müller, Johann Christian. 2007. *Meines Lebens Vorfälle und Nebenumstände, Teil 1: Kindheit und Studienjahre (1720–1746).* Edited by Katrin Löffler and Nadine Sobirai. Leipzig: Lehmstedt.

———. 2013. *Meines Lebens Vorfälle und Nebenumstände, Teil 2: Hofmeister in Pommern (1746–1755).* Edited by Katrin Löffler and Nadine Sobirai. Leipzig: Lehmstedt.

Müller, Ruth. E. 1989. *Erzählte Töne: Studien zur Musikästhetik im späten 18. Jahrhundert.* Stuttgart: Steiner.

Murschhauser, Franz Xaver Anton. 1721. *Academia musico-poetica bipartita; oder, Hohe Schul der musicalischen Composition in zwey Theil eingetheilt.* Nuremberg: Endters.

Neidhardt, Johann Georg. 1734. *Gäntzlich erschöpfte, mathematische Abtheilungen des diatonisch-Chromatischen, temperirten Canonis monochordi.* Königsberg: Eckart.

Neubacher, Jürgen. 2009. *Georg Philipp Telemanns Hamburger Kirchenmusik und ihre Aufführungsbedingungen (1721–1767).* Hildesheim: Olms.

Neukirch, Benjamin. 1704. *Herrn von Hoffmannswaldau und andrer Deutschen auserlesener und bißher noch nie zusammen-gedruckter Gedichte . . .* [vol. 4]. Glückstadt: Lehmann.

Neumann, Werner. 1960. "Das 'Bachische Collegium Musicum.'" *Bach-Jahrbuch* 47:5–27.

———. 1970. "Eine Leipziger Bach-Gedenkstätte: Über die Beziehungen der Familien Bach und Bose." *Bach-Jahrbuch* 56:19–31.

Niedt, Friedrich Erhardt. 1706. *Musicalische Handleitung.* Hamburg: Schiller.

Noack, Elisabeth. 1967. *Musikgeschichte Darmstadts vom Mittelalter bis zur Goethezeit.* Mainz: Schott.

Noack, Friedrich. 1908. "Eine Reise durch das Großherzogtum Hessen im Frühling 1760." In *Mitteilungen des Oberhessischen Geschichtsvereins: Neue Folge,* 16:1–22. Giessen: Töpelmann.

Oelrichs, Johann Carl Conrad. 1752. *Historische Nachricht von den akademischen Würden in der Musik.* Berlin: Voß.

Otto, Rüdiger. 2010. "Gesprächsprotokolle: Die Tagebuchaufzeichnungen des Schweizer Theologen Gabriel Hürner während seines Aufenthaltes in Leipzig im Mai 1738." *Stadtgeschichte—Mitteilungen des Leipziger Geschichtsvereins e. V,* 75–188. Leipzig: Sax.

Pape, Uwe. 1966. *Die Orgeln der Stadt Braunschweig.* Berlin: Pape.

Pape, Uwe, and Alfred Schirge. 2005. *Die Orgelbauerfamilie Papenius und ihre Schüler* (*Norddeutsche Orgelbauer und ihre Werke* 3). Berlin: Pape.

Parker, Geoffrey, ed. 1987. *The Thirty Years' War.* London: Routledge.

Pasch, Gerhart. 2001. "St. Georgenkirche." In *Rötha und die Orgeln Gottfried Silbermanns,* edited by Brigitte Steinbach and Frank-Harald Greß, *Südraum Journal* 13:8–25. Leipzig: Passage-Verlag.

Pepys, Samuel. 1952. *The Diary of Samuel Pepys.* Edited by Henry Wheatley. 8 vols. London: Bell.

Peretz, Isabelle, and José Morais. 1993. "Specificity for Music." In *Handbook of Neuropsychology* 8, edited by Francois Boller and Jordan Grafman, 373–90. New York: Elsevier.

Pescheck, Christian. 1735. *Geographischer Haupt Schlüssel, welcher die Thüre zu dieser galanten und unentbehrlichen Wissenschafft [. . .] aufschliesset.* Budissin: Richter.

———. 1738. *Allen dreyen haupt-ständen nöthige Rechen-Stunden.* Zittau: Schöpss.

Peter, Christian. 2005. "'Dass das Decorum Unseres Hoffstaats bey inheimisch- und auswärtigen nicht verächtlich gemacht werdten möge'—Der Hof der Fürstäbte und Fürstbischöfe von Fulda im 18. Jahrhundert." *Fuldaer Geschichtsblätter* 81:35–84.

Peters, Mark. 2008. *A Woman's Voice in Baroque Music: Mariane von Ziegler and J. S. Bach.* Burlington, Vt.: Ashgate.

Petersen, Johanna Eleonora. 2003. *Johanna Eleonora Petersen, geb. von und zu Merlau's Leben, von ihr selbst mit eigener Hand aufgesetzt.* Edited by Prisca Guglielmetti. Leipzig: Evangelische Verlagsanstalt.

Pfeiffer, Hilde. 1929. "Unsere Orgel und vom Bau und Geschichte der Orgel im allgemeinen." *Gemeindeblatt der Evangelisch-Reformierten Gemeinde zu Braunschweig* 15 (9): 127–32.

Plachta, Bodo. 1994. *Damnatur, Toleratur, Admittur: Studien und Dokumente zur literarischen Zensur im 18. Jahrhundert.* Studien und Texte zur Sozialgeschichte der Literatur, vol. 43. Tübingen: Niemeyer.

Pöllnitz, Karl Ludwig Wilhelm von. 1735. *Das galante Sachsen: Aus dem Franzoesischen übersetzt von einem Deutschen.* Amsterdam: [unknown].

Prætorius, Michael. 1619. *Syntagmatis musici (Tomus Secundus): De Organographia.* Wolfenbüttel: Holwein, 1619.

Preußner, Eberhard. 1949. *Die musikalischen Reisen des Herrn von Uffenbach.* Kassel: Bärenreiter.

Printz, Wolfgang Caspar. 1691. *Musicus Curiosus; oder, Battalus, der vorwitzige Musicant, in einer sehr lustigen, anmuthigen, unertichteten und mit schönen Moralien durchspickte Geschichte vorgestellet von Mimnermo, des Battali guten Freunde.* Freiburg: Mieth.

Pütter, Johann Stephan. 1798. *Johann Stephan Pütters Selbstbiographie zur dankbaren Jubelfeier seiner 50jährigen Professorstelle zu Göttingen.* 2 vols. Göttingen: Vandenhoeck and Ruprecht.

Quantz, Johann Joachim. 1752. *Versuch einer Anweisung die Flöte traversiere zu spielen.* Berlin: Voß.

Quistorp, Theodor Johann. 1743. "Abschiedsrede aus der Vormittäglichen deutschen Rednergesellschaft in Leipzig, worinnen erwiesen wird: Das dis Caffeehäuser die wahren Schulen der schönen Wissenschaften sind, gehalten von Theodor Johann Quistorp, aus Rostock, derselben Mitgliede," In *Sammlung der Uebungsreden, welche unter der Aufsicht Sr. Hochedelgeb. des Herrn Profess. Gottscheds, in der vormittäglichen Rednergesellschaft sind gehalten worden*, edited by Johann Christoph Löschenkohl, 515–52. Leipzig: Breitkopf.

Radice, Mark. 1999. "The Nature of the Style Galant: Evidence from the Repertoire." *Musical Quarterly* 83 (4): 607–47.

Rambach, Johann Jacob. 1732. *Betrachtungen über das gantze Leiden Christi [. . .] Andere Auflage.* Jena: Hartung.

———. 1737. *Wohlunterwiesener Informator; oder, Deutlicher Unterricht von der Information und Erziehung der Kinder.* Züllichau: Frommen.

Rampe, Siegbert. 1995. "Zur Sozialgeschichte des Claviers und Clavierspiels in Mozarts Zeit." *Concerto* 104:24–27 (Part 1); 105:28–30 (Part 2).

———. 1999. "Allgemeines zur Klaviermusik." In *Bach Handbuch*, edited by Konrad Küster, 715–46. Kassel: Bärenreiter; Stuttgart: Metzler.

———. 2000. "Zur Sozialgeschichte der Saitenclaviere im deutschen Sprachraum zwischen 1600 und 1750." In *Das deutsche Cembalo. Symposium im Rahmen der 24. Tage Alter Musik in Herne*, edited by Christian Ahrens and Gregor Klinke, 68–93. Munich: Katzbichler.

———. 2003–2005. "Abendmusik oder Gottesdienst? Zur Funktion norddeutscher Orgelkompositionen des 17. und frühen 18. Jahrhunderts." *Schütz-Jahrbuch* 25:7–70 (Part 1); 26:155–204 (Parts 2 and 3); 27:53–127 (Parts 4 and 5).

———. 2004. "Sozialstatus und Wirkungsbereich mitteldeutscher Hoforganisten des 17. und 18. Jahrhunderts." In *Mitteldeutschland im musikalischen Glanz seiner Residenzen: Sachsen, Böhmen und Schlesien als Musiklandschaften im 16. und 17. Jahrhundert*, edited by Peter Wollny, 171–82. Beeskow: Ortus.

———. 2007. "Klavier- oder Orgelwerke? Zur Sozialgeschichte der Tastenmusik 1685–1750." In *Bachs Klavier- und Orgelwerke. Das Handbuch*, edited by Siegbert Rampe, 33–65. Regensburg: Laaber.

———. 2014. *Orgel- und Clavierspielen 1400–1800: Eine deutsche Sozialgeschichte im europäischen Kontext*. Munich: Katzbichler.

Recke, Elisa von der. 1787. *Nachricht von des berüchtigten Cagliostro Aufenthalt in Mitau im Jahre 1779 und dessen magischen Operationen*. Berlin: Nikolai.

———. 1795. *Elisa von der Recke: Aufzeichnungen und Briefe aus ihren Jugendtagen*. Edited by Paul Rachel. Leipzig: Dieterich.

Rehm, Gottfried. 1997. *Musikantenleben: Beiträge zur Musikgeschichte Fuldas und der Rhön im 18. und 19. Jahrhundert*. Fulda: Parzeller.

Reichardt, Johann Friedrich. 1795. "Ernst Wilhelm Wolf." In *Berlinisches Archiv der Zeit und ihres Geschmacks*, 162–67, 273–83. Berlin: F. Maurer.

Reiske, Johann Jacob. 1783. *Johann Jakob Reiskens von ihm selbst aufgesetzte Lebensbeschreibung*. Leipzig: Buchhandlung der Gelehrten.

Rembold, Johann Christoph. 1710. *Perspectiva Practica oder vollständige Anleitung zu der Perspectiv-Reißkunst*. Augsburg: Wollf.

Rheinfurth, Hans. 1977. *Der Musikverlag Lotter in Augsburg*. Tutzing: Schneider.

Richter, Ernst Eusebius. 1731. *Seu Decisiones Medico-Forenses; das ist, Juristische und Medicinische Aussprüche und Responsa über allerhand schwere, zweiffelhaffte und seltene, in Praxi vorgefallene, in die Medicin und Chirurgie lauffende und causam vulnerationem betreffende Fragen und Fälle*. Leipzig: Richter.

Richter, Maik. 2008. "Die Köthener Hofmusik zur Zeit des Fürsten August Ludwig." In *Musik an der Zerbster Residenz: Bericht über die Internationale wissenschaftliche Konferenz vom 10. bis 12. April 2008 im Rahmen der 10. Internationalen Fasch-Festtage in Zerbst*, edited by Internationale Fasch-Gesellschaft, 167–82. Beeskow: Ortus.

Riedel, Friedrich Wilhelm. 1960. *Quellenkundliche Beiträge zur Geschichte der Musik für Tasteninstrumente in der 2. Hälfte des 17. Jahrhunderts (vornehmlich in Deutschland)*. Kassel: Bärenreiter.

Riepe, Juliane. 2003. "Hofmusik in der Zeremonialwissenschaft des 18. Jahrhunderts." *Händel Jahrbuch* 49:27–52.

Riepel, Joseph. 1754. *Anfangsgründe zur musicalischen Setzkunst*. 5 vols. Regensburg: Montag.

———. 1755. *Grundregeln zur Tonordnung.* Frankfurt: Wagner.

———. 1757. *Gründliche Erklärung der Tonordnung insbesondere, zugleich aber für mehresten Organisten insgemein.* Frankfurt: Author.

Rohr, Julius Bernhard von. 1728. *Einleitung zur Ceremoniel-Wissenschafft der Privat-Personen.* Berlin: Rüdiger.

Roloff, Hans-Gert, ed. 1984. *Der Patriot.* 4 vols. Berlin: De Gruyter.

Rose, Stephen. 2005. "Daniel Vetter and the Domestic Keyboard Chorale in Bach's Leipzig." *Early Music* 33 (1): 39–53.

Rost, Johann Leonhard. 1713. *Das neu-eröffnete teutsche Briefe Cabinet.* Nuremberg: Lochner.

Rubardt, Paul. 1953. *Die Silbermannorgeln in Rötha.* Leipzig: Breitkopf and Härtel.

Sack, Carl Wilhelm. 1853. "Künste und Gewerke in der Stadt Braunschweig." *Braunschweigisches Magazin* 66:1–6, 9–13, 17–22.

Salmen, Walter. 1969. *Haus- und Kammermusik: Privates Musizieren im gesellschaftlichen Wandel zwischen 1600–1900.* Edited by Heinrich Besseler and Werner Bachmann for *Musikgeschichte in Bildern* 4 (3). Leipzig: Deutscher Verlag für Musik.

Samber, Johann Baptist. 1704. *Manuductio ad Organum.* Salzburg: Mayr.

———. 1710. *Elucidatio Musicæ choralis.* Salzburg: Mayr.

Saurin, Jacques. 1755. *Jacob Saurins, ehmaligen Predigers im Haag, Predigten über die Leidenschaften Jesu.* 2 vols. Leipzig: Teubner.

Scharffenberg, Friedrich Wilhelm. 1713. *Die Kunst complaisant und galant zu conversiren, oder in kurtzen sich zu einen Menschen von guter Conduite zu machen.* Chemnitz: Stössel.

Scheibe, Johann Adolf. 1738. *Gültige Zeugnisse über die jüngste Matthesonisch-musicalische Kern-Schrift.* Hamburg: Author.

———. 1745. *Der Critische Musikus: Neue, vermehrte und verbesserte Auflage.* Leipzig: Breitkopf.

———. 1750. *Misogynis wohlgegründete Ursachen, das weibliche Geschlecht zu verachten, besonders aber die, von Arglist, Boßheit, Eyfersucht, Falschheit, [. . .] und anderen unzähligen Lastern angefüllte Böse Weiber; dem männlichen Geschlecht zur Warnung ans Licht gestellt von einem, der in Allem schon ganzer siebenzehen Jahre in den Banden eines solchen weiblichen Unthiers seuffzet.* Published by the author.

———. 1753. *Die Allerneueste erfundene Art, nach Morgenländischer Weise, mit guter Manier ein Böses Weib los zu werden, wodurch zugleich theils Weiber Bosheit entdecket, und deren ungewissenhafte Kunstgriffe, welche ihnen ihre Eigenschaft, Temperament und Müßiggang eingeben, mit natürlichen Farben abgeschildert werden: Zum Trost dererjenigen, so unter diesem unerträglichen Joche seuffzen.* Published by the author.

———. 1762. *Misogynis abgeschilderte böse Weiber: Dem männlichen Geschlecht zur Warnung ans Licht gestellt von einem, der in Allem schon ganzer siebenzehn Jahre in den grausamen Banden eines solchen weiblichen Unthiers seufzet, und durch derselben Bosheit, Verschwendung und Rachgier zum Verderben gebracht worden.* Published by the author.

Scheibel, Gottfried Ephraim. 1721. *Zufällige Gedancken von der Kirchen-Music, wie sie heutiges Tages beschaffen ist: Allen rechtschaffnen Liebhabern der Music zur Nachlese und zum Ergötzen wohlmeinende ans Licht gestellet von Gottfried Ephraim Scheibel.* Frankfurt: Author.

Schering, Arnold. 1926. *Musikgeschichte Leipzigs von 1650 bis 1723*. Leipzig: Kistner and Siegel.

———. 1941. *Johann Sebastian Bach und das Musikleben Leipzigs im 18. Jahrhundert*. Leipzig: Kistner and Siegel.

Schirmer, Uwe. 2000. "Die wirtschaftlichen Wechsellagen im mitteldeutschen Raum (1480–1806)." In *Leipzig, Mitteldeutschland und Europa. Festgabe für Manfred Straube und Manfred Unger zum 70. Geburtstag*, edited by Hartmut Zwahr, Uwe Schirmer, and Henning Steinführer, 293–330. Beucha: Sax.

Schlobach, Jochen, and Silvia Eichhorn-Jung, eds. 1998. *Friedrich Melchior Grimm: Briefe an Johann Christoph Gottsched; Im Anhang: Vier Briefe an Luise Gottsched*. St. Ingbert: Röhrig Universitätsverlag.

Schmoller, Gustav, Otto Krauske, and Viktor Loewe. 1898. *Die Behördenorganisation und die allgemeine Staatsverwaltung Preußens im 18. Jahrhundert*. Vol. 2 (July 1714 to the end of 1717). Berlin: Parey.

Schnizzer, Matthias Solomon. 1938. *Chronica der Statt Neüstatt an der Aÿsch*. Neustadt an der Aisch: Schmidt.

Scholze, Johann Sigismund. 1743. *Sperontes Singende Muse an der Pleiße . . . Zweyte Fortsetzung*. Leipzig: Breitkopf.

Schönfuß, Renate. 2015. "Das Erbe des Churfürstlich Sächsischen Hof- und Justizraten Johann Friedrich Zeumer (1717–1774)." In *Altenburger Geschichts- und Hauskalender 2015*. Altenburg: Reinhold.

Schott, Howard. 1998. *Catalogue of Musical Instruments in the Victoria and Albert Museum. Part I: Keyboard Instrument*. London: V and A.

Schröder, Hans. 1928. *Verzeichnis der Sammlung alter Musikinstrumente im Städtischen Museum Braunschweig* und *Instrumente, Instrumentenmacher und Instrumentisten in Braunschweig* (Werke aus Museum, Archiv und Bibliothek der Stadt Braunschweig, vol. 3). Braunschweig: Appelhans.

Schulenberg, David. 2006. *The Keyboard Music of J. S. Bach*. Second edition. New York: Routledge.

Schultz, Alwin. 1890. *Alltagsleben einer deutschen Frau zu Anfang des achtzehnten Jahrhunderts*. Leipzig: Hirzel.

Schultz, Ilse. 2005. *Verwehte Spuren: Frauen in der Stadtgeschichte*. Ulm: Süddeutsche Verlagsgesellschaft.

Schulze, Hans-Joachim. 1966. "Wer intavolierte Johann Sebastian Bachs Lautenkompositionen?" *Die Musikforschung* 19:32–39.

———. 1968. "Ein unbekannter Brief von Silvius Leopold Weiß." *Musikforschung* 21:203–4.

———. 1983. "'Monsieur Schouster': Ein vergessener Zeitgenosse Johann Sebastian Bachs." In *Bachiana et alia musicologica, Festschrift Alfred Dürr zum 65. Geburtstag*, edited by Wolfgang Rehm, 243–50. Kassel: Bärenreiter.

———. 1984. *Studien zur Bach-Überlieferung im 18. Jahrhundert*. Leipzig: Peters.

———. 1997. "Anna Magdalena Bachs 'Herzens Freündin': Neues über die Beziehungen zwischen den Familien Bach und Bose." *Bach-Jahrbuch* 83:151–53.

Schumann, August. 1822. "Rötha." In *Vollständiges Staats- Post- und Zeitungs-Lexikon von Sachsen*, 9:369–76. 18 vols. Zwickau: Schumann.

Selamintes. 1713. *Der närrische und doch beliebte Cupido; oder, Ein Schertzhaffter Roman, welcher in verschiedenen neuen und raren Geschichten die Aufführung der jungen Welt vorstellet: Nebst einer Vorrede, die zu einer Recommendation des neulich heraußgekommenen lieblichen und doch kriegerischen Cupido dienen kan; außgefertiget von Selamintes.* Leipzig.

Serauky, Walter. 1935–1943. *Musikgeschichte der Stadt Halle.* Vol. 2, book 2: "Von Wilhelm Friedemann Bach bis Robert Franz" (1940). Halle: Max Niemeyer.

Seybold, David Christoph, ed. 1784. *Magazin für Frauenzimmer auf 1784.* Strassburg: Kehl.

———, ed. 1785. *Magazin für Frauenzimmer auf 1785.* Strassburg: Kehl.

Sheldon, David A. 1975. "The Galant Style Revisited and Re-evaluated." *Acta Musicologica* 47:240–70.

Sicul, Christoph Ernst. 1715–1719. *Neo-Annalium Lipsiensium PRODROMUS.* 4 vols. Leipzig: Author.

Sieglerschmidt, Jörn. 1969. "Social and Economic Landscapes." In *Germany: A New Social and Economic History,* edited by Sheilagh Ogilvie, 2:1–38. London: Arnold.

Simmonds, Paul. 2008. "Carl Engel and the Clavichord." *Galpin Society Journal* 61 (April): 105–13.

Simons, Olaf. 2001. *Marteaus Europa oder der Roman, bevor er Literatur wurde: Eine Untersuchung des deutschen und englischen Buchangebots der Jahre 1710 bis 1720.* Amsterdam: Rodopi.

Sorge, Georg Andreas. 1749. *Ausführliche und deutliche Anweisung zur Rational-Rechnung, und der damit verkünpfften Ausmessung und Abtheilung des Monochords.* Lobenstein: Author.

———. 1758. *Zuverlässige Anweisung, Claviere und Orgeln behörig zu temperiren und zu stimmen.* Leipzig: Author.

———. 1760a. *Compendium harmonicum.* Lobenstein: Author.

———. 1760b. *Anleitung zum Generalbass und zur Composition.* Berlin: Lange.

Sotheby's. 2001. *Sotheby's Printed and Manuscript Music.* London.

Speer, Daniel. 1687. *Grundrichtiger, kurtz, leicht und nöthiger Unterricht der musikalischen Kunst.* Ulm: Kühn.

Spiess, Meinrad. 1746. *Tractatus Musicus Compositorio-Practicus.* Augsburg: Lotter.

Spitta, Philipp. 1873–1880. *Johann Sebastian Bach.* 2 vols. Leipzig: Breitkopf and Härtel.

———. 1894. "Sperontes' 'Singende Muse an der Pleiße': Zur Geschichte des deutschen Hausgesanges im achtzehnten Jahrhundert." In *Musikgeschichtliche Aufsätze,* 175–295. Berlin: Paetel.

Spohr, Louis. 1968. *Lebenserinnerungen.* Tutzing: Schneider.

Stadt- und Heimatverein Rötha. 1996. *Die Feuerwehr von Rötha* [Röthaer Heimatblätter 6]. Rötha: Author.

———. 2000. *Die Landwirtschaft in Rötha* [Röthaer Heimatblätter 10]. Rötha: Author.

Stahl, Wilhelm. 1952. *Musikgeschichte Lübecks* [vol. 2] *Geistliche Musik.* Kassel: Bärenreiter.

Starke, Christoph. 1748. *Synopsis Bibliothecae exegeticae in novum testamentum.* Vol. 3. Biel: Heilmann.

Stauffer, George, and Ernest May, eds. 1986. *J. S. Bach as Organist: His Instruments, Music, and Performance Practices.* Bloomington: Indiana University Press.

Stier, Bernhard, and Wolfgang von Hippel. 1996. "War, Economy, and Society." In *Germany: A New Social and Economic History. Volume 2: 1630–1800*, edited by Sheilagh Ogilvie, 233–62. London: Arnold.

Strunck, Oliver, and Leo Treitler, eds. 1998. *Strunck's Source Readings in Music History*. New York: Norton.

Stüven, Wilfried. 1964. *Orgel und Orgelbauer im halleschen Land vor 1800*. Wiesbaden: Breitkopf and Härtel.

Talle, Andrew. 2003. "Nürnberg, Darmstadt, Köthen—Neuerkenntnisse zur Bach-Überlieferung in der ersten Hälfte des 18. Jahrhunderts." *Bach-Jahrbuch* 89:143–72.

———. 2008. "'Ein Ort zu studiren, der seines gleichen nicht hat': Leipzig um 1730 in den Tagebüchern des Königsberger Professors Christian Gabriel Fischer." In *Stadtgeschichte: Mitteilungen des Leipziger Geschichtsvereins*, 55–138. Leipzig: Sax.

———. 2011. "Die 'kleine Wirthschafft *Rechnung*' von Carl August Hartung." *Bach-Jahrbuch* 97: 57–80.

Taubert, Gottfried. 1717. *Rechtschaffener Tanzmeister; oder, Gründliche Erklärung der frantzösischen Tantz-Kunst*. Leipzig: Lanckischens Erben.

Teller, Romanus. 1736. *Sammlung moralischer Reden, so an heiliger Stätte gehalten worden*. Eisleben: May.

Theele, Joseph, ed. 1928. *Aus Fuldas Geistesleben: Festschrift zum 150-jährigen Jubiläum der Landesbibliothek Fulda*. Fulda: Verlag der Fuldaer Actiendruckerei.

Thomas, Lewis. 1974. *The Life of a Cell: Notes of a Biology Watcher*. New York: Viking.

Thomasius, Christian. 1701. "Welcher Gestalt man denen Frantzosen in gemeinem Leben und Wandel nachahmen solle?" In *Allerhand bißher publicirte kleine teutsche Schrifften*, edited by Christian Thomasius, 1–70. Halle: Salfeld.

Treue, Wilhelm. 1999. *Wirtschaft, Gesellschaft und Technik in Deutschland vom 16. bis zum 18. Jahrhundert*. Gebhardt Handbuch der deutschen Geschichte 12. Munich: Deutscher Taschenbuch.

Trommer, David. 1742. *Seelige Land- und Bauer-Weißheit; oder, Land und Haus Bostill, bestehend in allerhand Ehren und Lehren der Land-Leute*. Culmbach: Becker.

Uffenbach, Zacharias Conrad von. 1753–1754. *Herrn Zacharias Conrad von Uffenbach Merkwürdige Reisen durch Niedersachsen, Holland und Engelland*. 3 vols. Ulm: Gaum.

Vetter, Daniel. 1713. *Musicalische Kirch- und Hauß-Ergötzlichkeit*. Leipzig: Author.

Vogel, Johann Jakob. 1714. *Leipzigisches Geschicht-Buch Oder Annales; das ist, Jahr- und Tage-Bücher Der Weltberühmten Königl. und Churfürstlichen Sächsischen Kauff- und Handels-Stadt Leipzig*. Leipzig: Friedrich Lanckinschens Erben.

Voigt, Johann Christian. 1742. *Gespräch von der Musik, zwischen einem Organisten und Adjuvanten*. Erfurt: Jungnicol.

Vollhardt, Reinhard. 1899. *Geschichte der Cantoren und Organisten von den Städten im Königreich Sachsen*. Berlin: Issleib. Reprint, Leipzig: Peters, 1978.

Wagenseil, Johann Christoph. 1705. *Von Erziehung einse jungen Printzen, der vor allen Studiren einen Abscheu hat, daß er dennoch gelehrt und geschickt werde*. Leipzig: Heinrich.

Walther, Johann Gottfried. 1732. *Musikalisches Lexicon oder musikalische Bibliothek*. Leipzig: Deer.

Weber, William. 1977. "Mass Culture and the Reshaping of European Musical Taste, 1770–1870." *International Review of the Aesthetics and Sociology of Music* 8 (1): 5–22.

Weiße, Felix Christian. 1807. *Lieder und Fabeln für Kinder und junge Leute.* Edited by Samuel Gottlob Frisch. Leipzig: Crusius.

Weitz, Anton. 1728. *Verbessertes Leipzig, oder die vornehmsten Dinge, so von Anno 1698. an biß hieher bey der Stadt Leipzig verbessert worden, mit Inscriptionibus erleutert.* Leipzig: Lanckisch.

Werckmeister, Andreas. 1700. *Cribrum Musicum oder musicalisches Sieb.* Quedlinburg: Calvisius.

———. 1702. *Harmonologia Musica oder kurtze Anleitung.* Frankfurt: Calvisius.

———. 1707. *Musicalische Paradoxal-Discourse.* Quedlinburg: Calvisius.

Werner, Arno. 1899–1900. "Samuel und Gottfried Scheidt—Neue Beiträge zu ihrer Biographie." In *Sammelbände der Internationalen Musikgesellschaft,* edited by Oskar Fleischer and Johannes Wolf, 1:401–45.

Wiedemann, Conrad, ed. 1969. *Der galante Stil, 1680–1730.* Tübingen: Niemeyer.

Williams, Peter. 1980–1984. *The Organ Music of J. S. Bach.* 3 vols. Cambridge: Cambridge University Press.

———. 2012. *J. S. Bach: A Life in Music.* Cambridge: Cambridge University Press.

Witt, Ursula. 1996. "Wahres Christentum und weibliche Erfahrung: Bildung und Frömmigkeit im Pietismus des 17. und beginnenden 18. Jahrhunderts." In *Geschichte der Mädchen und Frauenbildung,* edited by Elke Kleinau and Claudia Opitz, 263–74. 2 vols. Frankfurt: Campus.

Wolf, Johannes. 1899. "Zur Geschichte der Orgelmusik im vierzehnten Jahrhundert." *Kirchenmusikalisches Jahrbuch* 14:14–31.

Wolff, Christoph. 1974. *Kanons, Musikalisches Opfer.* NBA/KB VIII/1.

———. 1994. *Bach: Essays on His Life and Music.* Cambridge, Mass.: Harvard University Press.

———. 2000. *Johann Sebastian Bach: The Learned Musician.* New York: Norton.

———. 2005. "Die historischen Orgeln der Thomaskirche." In *Die Orgeln der Thomaskirche zu Leipzig,* edited by Christoph Wolff, 9–18. Leipzig: Evangelische Verlagsanstalt.

Wolff, Christoph, Arthur Mendel, and Hans T. David. 1999. *The New Bach Reader. A Life of Johann Sebastian Bach in Letters and Documents.* New York: Norton.

Wolff, Christoph, and Markus Zepf. 2008. *Die Orgeln Johann Sebastian Bachs: Ein Handbuch.* Second edition. Leipzig: Evangelische Verlagsanstalt.

Wollny, Peter. 1995. "Ein frühes Schriftzeugnis aus Carl Philipp Emanuel Bachs Berliner Zeit." *Bach-Jahrbuch* 81:185–90.

———. 2011. "Carl August Hartung als Kopist und Sammler Bachscher Werke." *Bach-Jahrbuch* 97:81–102.

Wustmann, Gustav. 1889–1895. *Quellen zur Geschichte Leipzigs.* 2 vols. Leipzig: Duncker and Humblot.

Wutta, Eva Renata. 1989. *Quellen zur Bach-Tradition in der Berliner Amalien-Bibliothek.* Tutzing: Schneider.

Yearsley, David. 2002. *Bach and the Meanings of Counterpoint.* Cambridge: Cambridge University Press.

———. 2012. *Bach's Feet: The Organ Pedals in European Culture.* Cambridge: Cambridge University Press.

Zachariä, Justus Friedrich Wilhelm. 1761. *Scherzhafte Epische und Lyrische Gedichte von Friedrich Wilhelm Zachariä.* 2 vols. Braunschweig: Schröders Erben.

Zarncke, Friedrich. 1909. *Leipzig und seine Universität im 18. Jahrhundert—Aufzeichnungen des Leipziger Studenten Johann Heinrich Jugler aus dem Jahre 1779.* Leipzig: Breitkopf and Härtel.

Zedler, Johann Heinrich, ed. 1731–1754. *Grosses vollständiges Universal-Lexicon aller Wissenschafften und Künste [. . .].* 68 vols. Leipzig: Zedler.

Ziegler, Christiane Mariane von. 1731. *Moralische und vermischte Send-Schreiben, an einige Ihrer vertrauten und guten Freunde gestellet.* Leipzig: Braun.

Ziller, Ernst. 1935. *Der Erfurter Organist Johann Heinrich Buttstedt (1666–1727).* Halle: Buchhandlung des Waisenhauses.

Zimmermann, Paul. 1906. "Abt Jerusalems Berichte über die Erziehung der Kinder Herzog Karls I., insbesondere des Erbprinzen Karl Wilhelm Ferdinand." In *Jahrbuch des Geschichtsvereins für das Herzogtum Braunschweig,* 5:129–64.

Zohn, Steven. 2005. "Telemann in the Marketplace: The Composer as Self-Publisher." *Journal of the American Musicological Society* 58 (2): 275–56.

———. 2011. "'Die vornehmste Hof-Tugend': German Musicians' Reflections on Eighteenth-Century Court Life." In *Music at German Courts, 1715–1760: Changing Artistic Priorities,* edited by Samantha Owens, Barbara Reul, and Janice B. Stockigt, 413–27. Woodbridge: Boydell and Brewer.

Manuscript Sources and Other Materials

Manuscripts, images, and objects held in the following institutions are referenced in this book. Where available, RISM Sigla have been used in the citations and are given in parentheses below.

Austria
Vienna, Österreichischen Nationalbibliothek (A-Wn)

Belgium
Brussels, Bibliothèque royale de Belgique (B-Br)

Denmark
Copenhagen, Det Kongelige Bibliotek (DK-Kk)

England
London, The British Library (GB-Lbl)

Germany
Altenburg, Thüringisches Staatsarchiv (D-ALa)
Berlin, Gemäldegalerie
Berlin, Musikinstrumenten-Museum
Berlin, Staatsbibliothek (D-B)
Bochum, Museum
Braunschweig, Archiv der evangelisch-reformierten Kirche
Braunschweig, Stadtarchiv und Stadtbibliothek (D-BS)

Darmstadt, Hessisches Staatsarchiv (D-DSsa)
Darmstadt, Zentralarchiv der evangelischen Kirche in Hessen und Nassau (D-DSk)
Dessau, Archiv der evangelischen Landeskirche Anhalts
Dessau, Landeshauptarchiv Sachsen-Anhalt (D-DElsa)
Dresden, Sächsische Landesbibliothek - Staats- und Universitätsbibliothek (D-Dl)
Gotha, Forschungsbibliothek (D-GOl)
Göttingen, Niedersächsische Staats- und Universitätsbibliothek (D-Gs)
Hannover, Evangelisch-Lutherischer Stadtkirchenverband, Stadtkirchenkanzlei, Kirchenbuchamt.
Köthen, Jakobskirche
Köthen, Schlosskirche
Leipzig, Custodie und Kunstsammlungen der Universität Leipzig
Leipzig, Das kirchliche Archiv Leipzig
Leipzig, Sächsisches Staatsarchiv, Staatsarchiv Leipzig (D-LEsta)
Leipzig, Stadtarchiv (D-LEsa)
Leipzig, Universitätsarchiv
Leipzig, Universitätsbibliothek (D-LEu)
Marburg, Hessisches Staatsarchiv (D-MGs)
Nuremberg, Germanisches Museum (D-Ngm)
Potsdam, Brandenburgisches Landeshauptarchiv
Stralsund, Ratsarchiv
Ulm, Haus der Stadtgeschichte/Stadtarchiv (D-Ua)
Weimar, Stadtarchiv (D-WRsa)
Weimar, Stiftung Weimarer Klassik, Goethe- und Schiller-Archiv (D-WRgs)
Wolfenbüttel, Herzog August Bibliothek (D-W)
Wolfenbüttel, Niedersächsisches Staatsarchiv (D-Wa)

Italy
Bologna, Museo Internazionale e Biblioteca della Musica (I-Bc)

Poland
Gdańsk, Biblioteka Główna Politechniki Gdańskiej
Gdańsk, Biblioteka Gdańska Polskiej Akademii Nauk (PL-GD)

United States of America
New Haven, Beinecke Rare Book and Manuscript Library (US-NHub)
New York, Morgan Library and Museum (US-NYpm)
Rochester, Eastman School of Music Sibley Library (US-R)

Index

ANDREW TALLE teaches musicology at the Peabody Conservatory and is a Gilman Scholar of the Johns Hopkins University. He is the editor of *Bach Perspectives, Volume Nine: Bach and His German Contemporaries.*

The University of Illinois Press
is a founding member of the
Association of American University Presses.

———————————————————————

Composed in 10.25/13 ITC New Baskerville
with Historical Fell Type display
by Jim Proefrock
at the University of Illinois Press
Jacket designed by Jim Proefrock
Jacket illustration: Barthold Fritz: Clavichord
for Johann Heinrich Heyne (1751).
Copyright Victoria and Albert Museum
Manufactured by Sheridan Books, Inc.

University of Illinois Press
1325 South Oak Street
Champaign, IL 61820-6903
www.press.uillinois.edu